The Community of the College of Justice

Edinburgh and the Court of Session, 1687–1808

John Finlay

EDINBURGH
University Press

First published in hardback in 2012
This paperback edition 2014

Edinburgh University Press Ltd
The Tun – Holyrood Road
12 (2f) Jackson's Entry
Edinburgh EH8 8PJ
www.euppublishing.com

Typeset in Sabon by
3btype.com, and
printed and bound in Great Britain by
CPI Group (UK) Ltd, Croydon CR0 4YY

A CIP record for this book is available from
the British Library

ISBN 978 0 7486 4577 0 (hardback)
ISBN 978 0 7486 9467 9 (paperback)
ISBN 978 0 7486 4578 7 (webready PDF)
ISBN 978 0 7486 6442 9 (epub)

Contents

Acknowledgements

Acknowledgements should probably be kept short, even if the list of intellectual debts is long.

I would first of all like to thank a number of people who have assisted in the completion of this book or have given me very useful feedback. Athol Murray was kind enough to comment on three chapters and has saved me from a number of errors for which I owe a great debt of gratitude. Olivia Robinson and Alex Murdoch kindly looked at chapters and I very much appreciate the feedback they provided. My thanks go to Ms Fiona Macdonald for research assistance. I am also grateful to David J. Brown, in the National Archives and, for their encouragement, to David Sellar, Hector MacQueen and John Cairns. To Sharon Adams, now of Freiburg, I owe a debt for discussing the book on a number of occasions. Any failings which remain in this work are, of course, my own responsibility.

One of the pleasures (perhaps not always) of preparing a book based so heavily on primary research is the use of specialist archives and libraries. An undoubted pleasure was reading the Session Papers. I am delighted to acknowledge my thanks to successive Keepers and the staff of the Advocates Library for having granted me access to these papers and for giving me permission to quote from them. In particular, I am grateful to Rosemary Paterson and Lindsay Levy for facilitating my use of this valuable resource over the last ten years. I also wish to mention with thanks the efficiency and kindness of the staff at the National Records of Scotland (formerly the National Archives of Scotland and, such has been the gestation of the book, before that, the Scottish Record Office). I should like to thank the staff at the National Library of Scotland and, in particular, those in the local archives mentioned in the text, every one of which I very much enjoyed visiting. Glasgow University staff members, in the Special Collections department of the Library and in the university archives, have also been most helpful; as has Mrs Ellen Gallagher in the School of Law workshop. Having read through more than a century's worth of manuscript town council records, I spent a considerable amount of time in Edinburgh City Archive and owe my thanks to the archivist, Richard Hunter, and his staff, for their kind assistance and encouragement. I gratefully acknowledge the permission of the Keeper of the Records of Scotland and the Trustees of the National Library of Scotland for permission to quote from sources in their care and to Sir Robert Clerk of Penicuik, Bt, for his kind permission, as copyright holder, to quote from family papers.

I would like also to thank the School of Law at the University of Glasgow for providing me with periods of research leave without which this volume could not have been written. In particular, the assistance of successive heads of School, Tom Mullen and Rosa Greaves, has been much appreciated. I am grateful to the staff at Edinburgh University Press, particularly John Watson, for their encouragement and efficiency.

I ought to confess that one of the sources I have used, my own edition of the *Admission Register of Notaries Public in Scotland 1700–1799*, is still in preparation and has not yet been published. Although this is unusual, I felt it would be more useful to refer to this text than directly to the manuscript registers, and I apologise if readers, pending publication of the text by the Scottish Record Society, should find this inconvenient.

Finally I would like to dedicate this book to my parents and also to my dear friend, Ilenia Ruggiu.

John Finlay
Stair Building, Glasgow
1 December 2011

Abbreviations and References

DEPOSITORIES

AL	Advocates Library
BL	British Library
DAC	Dumfries Archive Centre
ECA	Edinburgh City Archives
EUL	Edinburgh University Library
GCA	Glasgow City Archives
GUA	Glasgow University Archives
GUL	Glasgow University Library
NLS	National Library of Scotland
NRS	National Records of Scotland (formerly National Archives of Scotland)
PKCA	Perth and Kinross Council Archive
SCA	Stirling Council Archives
Spec. Coll.	Special Collections Department (EUL, GUL)
TCM	Edinburgh town council minutes (held in ECA)

SECONDARY SOURCES

ARNP	Finlay, ed., *Admission Register of Notaries Public in Scotland, 1700–1799*
JR	*Juridical Review*
SHR	*Scottish Historical Review*
TDGNHA	*Transactions of the Dumfriesshire and Galloway Natural History & Antiquarian Society*

MANUSCRIPT COLLECTIONS AND OTHER RECORDS

ALSP	Advocates Library, Session Papers
CS1	Court of Session, books of sederunt
FR	Faculty Records, Faculty of Advocates
GD220	Montrose papers

GD495	Papers of the WS Society
HMC	*Historical Manuscripts Commission*
Min. Bk	Minute Books of the Faculty of Advocates (Stair Society)
RPS	Records of the Parliament of Scotland to 1707
SLSP	Signet Library, Session Papers

OFFICE HOLDERS

Adv.	Advocate
AFC	Advocate's first clerk
BEx(S)	Baron of Exchequer in Scotland
CBEx(S)	Chief Baron of Exchequer in Scotland
DCS	Depute clerk of session
HMA	Lord Advocate
JP	Justice of the peace
LJC	Lord Justice Clerk
LP	Lord President
NP	Notary public
PCS	Principal Clerk of Session
SCJ	Senator of the College of Justice (Lord of Council and Session)
SG	Solicitor general
WS	Writer to the signet

1

Introduction

> The union of any number of persons occupied in one employment constitutes a *College*. Such are the College of Cardinals, or sacred college,—*Le College des Avocats,*— *Le College de Secretaires du Roi* in France,—The College of Heralds, &c in England,—Colleges of Literature everywhere.—The selection of Judges and Lawyers, made at this period in Scotland for the constant determination of the civil affairs of the kingdom, was with much propriety termed *The College of Justice.*[1]

The following study aims to identify and examine the lives and activities of those who made up the community of the College of Justice in Edinburgh between 1687 and 1808. Since the College was founded in 1532 as Scotland's central civil court, and can trace its institutional structure back to the early fifteenth century, it may be asked why those particular start and end dates were selected.[2] The answer is that they reflect two important events. The first was an act of sederunt in 1687 by which the judges (properly known as lords of council and session or senators of the College of Justice) provided an authoritative definition of its membership, one which expanded significantly on the situation in May 1532.[3] The second was legislation in 1808 which saw the restructuring of the court into two divisions, a form still recognisable today.[4] Between these events the surviving historical sources are relatively plentiful, at least compared to the period prior to the Restoration, and allow us to gain a good appreciation of the day-to-day environment of the College.

This book is concerned with the idea of 'community', but this word also needs explanation and this chapter will investigate its meanings. The community of the College was quite separate from the community of Edinburgh in which the College, a *national* institution, was situated. Yet, in another sense, it formed an important part of that community. In modern terms, the European institutions in Brussels and Strasbourg, or the United Nations in New York, share this same quality of particular communities with special privileges temporarily living within a wider community with whom they share the same social space. At the same time, the College itself contained more than one community and more than one type of community. It consisted of lawyers, judges, clerks and ancillary office-holders. Some of these were joined together in their own professional societies and some developed less formal bonds of self-interest linking them to fellow office-holders or, simply, to those who shared the same writing chamber. At all levels within the College there were also family, financial, and political networks that created relationships and communities of different kinds.

THE COMPOSITION OF THE COLLEGE

The business of the College of Justice was the delivery of justice to the king's subjects. The judicial function was paramount and all the members of the College, and many of those they employed, were subservient to it. It might be said, therefore, that the community itself existed only to meet the needs of the lords of session. Some members did this in a way that is immediately obvious, such as the advocates who presented detailed arguments on points of law for the judges to consider, or the house-keepers who ensured that order was kept in precincts of the court. Others had roles that were less immediate and their work is less obvious. That being the case, it is helpful to give a short formal statement of the membership of the College. The following, which dates from 1761 but is based on the act of sederunt of 23 February 1687, is one of the shortest complete definitions:

> The College of Justice was instituted in the reign of James the 5th Anno 1532. The Members of this College are very Numerous, such as – 1st The Judges, who are called <u>Lords of Session</u> or <u>Senators of the College of Justice</u>, 2dly The Advocates 3dly The Clerks of Session, 4thly The Writers to the Signet, 5thly The Director of the Chancery, his Deputy & two clerks 6thly The Writer to the Privy Seal & his Deputy 7thly The Clerks to the General Register of Hornings, Sasing &c 8th The Macers 9thly The Keeper of the Minute Book 10thly The Keepers of the Rolls 11thly The Extracters of Decrees 12th One Clerk belonging to each of the Judges 13th One Clerk belonging to each of the Lawyers 14th Two Clerks appointed by the Lord Clerk Register for Keeping the Public Records 15th The Keepers of the Session House, & Lastly The Keeper of the Advocates Library.[5]

There had not always been sixteen categories of office-holder. Hannay, in his classic study of the early College, refers to the 'inclusive tendencies' of those who held privileges which caused them to extend those privileges to others.[6] The judges, who had acknowledged to Queen Anne in 1708 that the privileges of the College had been 'confirmed & often augmented' by the crown in every reign since 1532, were themselves willing to innovate.[7] In

1687, for the first time, they as College members had one servant each for themselves, one for each advocate, and also the keeper of the Advocates Library, an institution not yet imagined in 1532 and still not yet formally opened.[8] Similar privileges, albeit not actual membership of the College, were granted to members of the justiciary court in 1692 and then to members of the Court of Exchequer when it was created in 1708.[9]

The growth of the College sparked tension with the local town council. It is true that being the seat of justice attracted many litigants to Edinburgh and boosted the local economy, as did the spending power of College members and, increasingly, the incidental benefits which the law brought to the printing and other trades.[10] Among their privileges, however, College members claimed freedom from local taxation and, as the number of members increased, this represented a growing loss of revenue for the town. As the dean and Faculty of Advocates liked to point out, when parliament taxed the 'inhabitants' or 'burgesses' of Edinburgh, the judges never construed this to mean College members, since they were 'looked upon to be only temporary residenters for the Service of the ledges during the sittings of the Courts'.[11] For generations, the council had tried to have this tax exemption removed. In 1637, for example, the advocates had responded to one such threat by seeking to defend their 'ancient priviledges and immunities' with a supplication to parliament.[12] Stressing the high status of advocates in Rome, particularly in the time of the Emperors Theodosius and Valentinian, they based their claims upon the recognition of similar privileges which were agreeable to the customs 'of all peoples and kingdoms in all ages' and, not least, in contemporary France where the noble status of the *avocat* had been recognised by the king. The Scottish parliament, they claimed, would have no wish to discourage those 'free and lairned spirits', the next generation of advocates, from following their vocation and, indeed, had defended their privileges on several occasions.[13]

THE SETTLEMENT OF 1687

In 1686 parliament passed an act for cleansing the streets of Edinburgh.[14] This imposed liability on the magistrates collectively, for a fine of £1,000 payable to the lords of session, should they fail, through negligence, to clean the streets and purge them of beggars. They were to report any proposals they had for doing so to the lords of session who were empowered to impose, with the consent of the magistrates, 'such taxes upon all the inhabitants, burgesses and others within the said town ... as they shall find just and necessary for purging and cleansing the said town'.

College members, disturbed to find that the legislation neglected to mention their traditional privileges, set out to defend them. In terms of realpolitik, they were in a reasonably strong position to do so. The dean of the Faculty of Advocates, Sir George Mackenzie of Rosehaugh, removed as lord advocate in May 1686, was perfectly free to lend his weight to their arguments.[15] He was also a recent creditor to the town council.[16] In fact, many College members, including the lords of session, regularly lent money to the council which, only in June 1686, had borrowed 12,000 merks from Roderick Mackenzie PCS.[17]

The result of this dispute has the appearance of a compromise. College members, including the lords of session, the advocates, clerks and writers to the signet, voluntarily agreed to contribute 'their respective proportions' of an annual £500 tax (or 'stent') which the lords ordered to be imposed for three years on the inhabitants of Edinburgh and its suburbs.[18] This was not to prejudice their 'priviledge of being free from all stents and impositions within the towne of Edinburgh'. In fact, this was a victory for College members in two respects. First, they had brought an action of declarator inviting the judges to define their privileges in detail, and this they proceeded to do in a decreet on 23 February. To ensure fairness, the judges in their decision also made arrangements for an advocate and a writer to the signet from each quarter of the town to oversee the collection of any tax imposed by parliamentary authority on College members. Secondly, the decreet provided the new, more extensive, definition of College membership that was described earlier, and the legal action had clearly been an opportunity to appeal to the 'inclusive tendencies' of the judges. It prompted advocates' servants to persuade the dean and Faculty of Advocates to raise an argument for College privileges to be extended to them so that they may be 'the more incouraged and capacitat to wait upon their employment'.[19]

The 1687 compromise did not completely bring an end to complaints. In 1718, for instance, there is reference to the 'great abuses' of advocates who were accused of unwarrantably extended the privilege by, among other things, falsely granting certificates naming men as their principal servants when they were not.[20] Though sporadic and continuing, however, complaints did not mask the inherent pride of the town council in playing host to the College, nor the usefulness to the town of being Scotland's legal centre. As the lord provost wrote to the town's MP in 1784, Edinburgh's greatest claim upon the British public was the building and maintenance of Parliament House, because it was unique 'in Brittain that a Corporation should build & uphold a house for the reception of the supreme Courts of a Kingdom'.[21]

THE PRIVILEGES OF COLLEGE MEMBERS

By the time of the foundation of the College of Justice, the idea of a college of judges or lawyers had a long medieval pedigree across Europe. These ranged from institutions such as the College of Capitoline Notaries in late medieval Rome or the *Collegio dei Guidici* that were instituted in Italian city states, to the College of Advocates, better known as Doctors' Commons, in London.[22] A university college had its own privileges and statutes, and the wider concept of a legal privilege, also familiar within the *jus commune*, would have been well recognised in sixteenth-century Scotland. In canon law, the twelfth-century *Decretum* of Gratian notably recognised privileges as ordinances made for the benefit of private individuals; in effect, exempting them in some particular ways from the general law.[23] Ultimately, however, they were made for the wider benefit of the res publica.[24]

For members of Scotland's College of Justice, two types of privilege existed: those unique to a particular group and those general to all groups. The general privileges were four in number. First, College members had the right to have any legal action concerning them removed from an inferior court and heard by the lords of council and session. An example of this is a prosecution brought before the sheriff of Sterling in 1738 against James Graeme of Buchlivie, advocate, for beating one of his tenants over the head with his gun.[25] Graeme's defence was that he was exempt from the sheriff's inferior jurisdiction and that the case could be heard only by the College of Justice, the rationale being that if they had to answer cases before inferior local judges it would interfere with their ability to attend in Edinburgh.[26]

In the second place, College members were exempt from common duties within the burgh, such as the traditional obligation of watching and warding (or any financial payment made in lieu thereof). Third, they were free from customs dues and shore dues (charged at ports for importing foreign produce) on the production of a certificate that any such goods brought into Edinburgh were for their personal use. In November 1688 the council put in place arrangements with the tacksman (leaseholder) of the impost on wines to scrutinise and try to stem the growth of orders of imported wine for the private use of lords of session and others but, in reality, there was little they could effectively do.[27] In 1783 the then tacksman, John Begrie, brought a complaint narrating that many persons who were importing wine free of duty claimed to be advocates' clerks who could not possibly be so because they worked in lines of business that were incompatible with the office of lawyer's clerk, or were clerks to men who had become advocates but were now in the army or had never resided in Edinburgh.[28] A list of such transgressors was made up and passed to the dean of Faculty. It included Kenneth Mackenzie WS who had received free impost warrants but had allegedly used them to import hogsheads of porter (a dark beer) that were delivered not to him but to a local baker and a vintner, both surnamed Mackenzie.[29] The tacksmen of the fruit market customs were in an equally challenging position because College members were exempt from the tax that was imposed on the importation of all 'fruit and garden stuff' provided this was for their private use only.[30] The limits of the exemption were explored in one case where it was acknowledged that any College member who converted his house into a fruit shop would be as liable to the tax as any other retailer, as would any who sold it from a stand in the street.[31]

College members did, in fact, own or lease shops and, though they may not have directly engaged in trade themselves, their wives may have done. The advocate James Cochrane and his wife Cecilia Oliphant, for instance, became infeft in shops and vaults in the Lawnmarket in 1744.[32] Ann Strachan, wife of the advocate John Polson, was a well-known milliner.[33] The daughters and heirs of George Chalmers WS took title in 1763 to a shop on the south side of Parliament Close, and David Murray DCS leased a shop in the same area in 1796.[34] Many lawyers had interests in shops but these probably represented investments, and it is not always clear whether title was taken personally or in a professional capacity as a trustee. John Davidson WS, for example, is recorded as selling two shops in Parliament Close to a merchant in 1770; why he came to have title to them is unknown.[35] It was, however, a clear rule that any member of the College who actually exercised a trade, or kept a shop or tavern, lost all the privileges and exemptions which they would otherwise have enjoyed. In 1565 the advocate John Moscrop was alleged to have fallen into this category. In general, however, few College members had what, in the case of eighteenth-century writer-turned-merchant, James Scott, was described as an 'enterprising disposition'.[36]

The fourth, and most important, general privilege related to exemption from any local tax imposed for the benefit of the town. This included, but was wider than, the stent, that is, the assessment of the value of property within the burgh which formed the basis of a tax payable by those who lived there. College members were exempt from the stent but they were not exempt from the national land tax known as the cess.[37] They elected their own annual stent-masters to meet those appointed by the council and to ensure that the cess was fairly imposed on College members on the basis of a proper valuation of the land they held within the town.[38] The balance of taxation between the landed interest and trade was kept 'a profound secret in all burghs' but the College's stent-masters tried hard, to the point of litigation, to obtain their own copy of entries made in the town's cess-books.[39] The judges, as the town council noted, conceded them no more than the right, at set times, to inspect the master copy in the presence of the town's own collectors.[40]

There were pressing circumstances, not least in the compromise of 1687, when the stent might be extended to College members but only with their agreement. A voluntary contribution which they made in 1798, for the benefit of the wives of men fighting abroad, provides an interesting example.

When proposed by the council, the contribution was agreed to by a committee of College members which included judges, the dean of the Faculty of Advocates and the deputy keeper of the signet.[41] It took the form of an assessment of 2 per cent on the rents of houses, to be applied for two years to all inhabitants including members of the College. Anyone who failed to pay was to be reported to the judges who would authorise legal procedures to be used to recover the debt.[42] To ensure fairness, and indicative of mistrust, it was again provided that representatives from the College were to be present when the stent was determined, to ensure it was imposed fairly.

The privileges specific to each group within the College will be discussed in later chapters dealing with those groups. By far the most important professional privileges were the advocates' right of audience and the monopoly which writers to the signet had in dealing with papers relating to legal actions. In the controversial case of Patrick Haldane, whose admission to the bench was blocked for political reasons in 1721–2, it was pleaded that service as an advocate in the College meant

> attending on that station in which an advocate as such is by his admission privileged to act … [he] has the sole privilege of appearing at your Lordships Bar as procurator for the Leidges, of arguing causes of presenting petitions and answers and giving out and returning processes &c.[43]

These privileges had no less an economic value than the right to import wine free of customs.

IN DEFENCE OF CONTINUING PRIVILEGE

In the 1780s the question of College privileges arose again amid a concerted campaign by the council and Edinburgh's Merchants' Company. In 1780 the latter had demanded that every city inhabitant should be made to contribute to a tax in support of a police force.[44] With the charity workhouse operating at a deficit, the council wanted to increase its revenues, and pressure fell again on College members to be compelled to contribute. A bill was drafted for this purpose (the so-called 'Poor's Bill' of 1784) which would have imposed a property tax, for the benefit of the poor, on all those in Edinburgh occupying property over a specified rental value.[45]

College members responded vigorously and collectively, with the advocates and writers to the signet taking the lead. At least three members of the Faculty of Advocates, including George Wallace and (probably) Matthew Ross, made separate remarks and suggestions with regard to a memorial produced for the Faculty.[46] In the course of this dispute, the legal authorities were reviewed, going all the way back to the original papal bull by which the College was founded and the earliest case, in 1565, in which the advocates and writers to the signet are known to have defended their freedom from 'all stents, taxations and contributions quatsumever [whatsoever]'.[47] The council made much of a 1579 statute that had authorised town councils to raise funds from the inhabitants of burghs, without exception, for poor relief.[48] This argument was countered by the consideration that College members had gone almost two centuries free from any compulsory assessment and, in that time, there had been only eight years during which voluntary contributions had been made (1687–90; 1712–14; 1731–4).[49] The defenders were not above mentioning the profligacy of the magistrates, particularly their excessive tavern expenses. In 1786 a joint meeting of the advocates and the writers to the signet took place as both prepared to petition the House of Commons against the council's proposed bill. In the event, the clause seeking to remove the College's exemption did not survive the committee stage. The council withdrew it when members of the Commons committee, influenced by the arguments of the Faculty and the Society of Writers to the Signet (henceforth the WS Society), expressed doubts about proceeding until the matter 'should be tried in a court of law'.[50] It soon was, with the Court of Session in January 1788 unanimously finding in favour of the College. An appeal to the House of Lords was heard but dismissed in 1790 with the costs of their London agent, James Chalmers, being borne equally by the Faculty of Advocates and the WS Society.[51]

THE SIZE OF THE COLLEGE

The distinct groups within the College generally operated in complementary spheres of business. Some regulation was necessary, however, because, since their interests were not identical, there was always the potential for competition between them. Therefore, within a century-and-a-half of 1532, the two largest groups, the advocates and the writers to the signet, had for their members' mutual self-interest created the WS Society and the Faculty of Advocates. By the eighteenth century smaller groupings, such as the clerks of session, the macers and the extractors, were also active in promoting their own interests. These groups developed their own internal rules, governing everything from the distribution of the fees and profits of office to the question of who was entitled to attend informal end-of-session dinners.

The town council in the seventeenth century had been right to be concerned that were no effective constraints on the growth in size of the College. At its foundation in 1532, the number of members had not been precisely fixed. The lords of session did make provision for the admission of up to ten general procurators (that is, advocates) but this *numerus clausus* disappeared by the 1550s.[52] Later attempts to limit the numbers of writers to the signet came to an end during the seventeenth century. In 1687 no limits were reimposed and the number of advocates continued to expand rapidly until the 1710s. Some offices, however, were fixed and remained relatively static. For instance, there were never more than four ordinary macers, the number of ordinary lords of session remained fixed, and the six principal clerks of session continued to oversee three separate offices, in each of which remained two depute clerks and four extractors.

To assess the extent to which membership of the College fluctuated, Tables 1(a) and 1(b) look at the admission rate of key groups across the same period, 1700–99 (inclusive). Of these, only the ordinary lords of session were subject to a limit. The notaries public were not by right members of the College but they were drawn from across the country and, though most of them worked in the provinces, many trained as writers in Edinburgh.[53] Indeed, this training is one of the major points of contact which the College community had with local practitioners. It is, therefore, fair to assume that the demand for the services of writers to the signet and notaries is indicative of the general demand for legal services across the country. Equally, it is reasonable to assume that the popularity of the bar bears some relation to the prospects of employment and thereby to the amount of litigation in the Court of Session. The only way to test these assumptions is to consider the rate of admissions across the century and to relate this to what is known about the level of business in the court.

The remarkable thing about the rates of admission is the uniformity of the picture they present. Immediately following the Union of 1707, the number of lawyers within the College began to contract. The intake of advocates and writers to the signet decreased significantly and it did not begin to recover until 1750. Likewise, the number of notaries public also declined from a high point in the first decade of the century, suggesting a decline in the demand for legal services. There is evidence of a similar decline in litigation rates elsewhere in Europe, in places as diverse as Paris, London and Bremen.[54] Between 1726 and 1780, the municipal courts in Bremen saw a particularly dramatic downturn in business in terms of civil cases brought per head of population. In the College of Justice, analysis of the Outer House rolls suggests a very similar pattern of development. There is a clear relationship between the business in the court and admission to the bar and the WS Society. The pattern is broadly mirrored by that of the admission rate of notaries public, with contraction [Table 1(a)] followed by an accelerating rate of expansion [Table 1(b)].

The tables reflect patterns of office-holding within the College and permit comparison with two groups of non-College members; locally, procurators in the bailie court of Edinburgh, and, nationally, notaries public. The figures do not necessarily represent discrete individuals because the same man might

Table 1(a) *Admissions per decade, 1700–49*[55]

Category	1700–09	1710–19	1720–29	1730–39	1740–49	Total
Ordinary lords	10	7	5	7	3	32
Advocates	99	85	83	64	33	364
Writers to the signet	57	31	39	36	30	193
Edinb. procurators	8	8	7	8	2	33
Notaries public	314	229	293	295	205	1,336

Table 1(b) *Admissions per decade, 1750–99*

Category	1750–59	1760–69	1770–79	1780–89	1790–99	Total
Ordinary lords	12	10	4	7	11	44
Advocates	57	71	64	73	98	363
Writers to the signet	26	45	60	99	133	363
Edinb. procurators	2	8	8	7	22	47
Notaries public	228	299	349	381	440	1,697
College agents	53	6	55	35	44	193

feature in more than one category. David Armstrong, for example, is unique in having been both an agent in the College of Justice and then an advocate although many writers to the signet were notaries public and, after 1707, virtually all ordinary lords of session were former advocates. Of all these categories, only the number of ordinary lords remained fixed, never rising above fifteen (including, for this purpose, the lord president).

The number of bailie court procurators may have been fixed on a de facto basis, because admission depended on the concurrence of existing procurators (formed into a local society) who might wish to limit competition by maintaining a steady number. This was certainly a practice prevalent in other local courts with societies of procurators.[56] There is, however, no absolute evidence to confirm this. Bailie court regulations, produced in 1789 in response to a petition from the 'Praeses and Society of Solicitors before the Town Court of Edinburgh', say nothing explicitly of any cap on admissions. The only clue as to why so many new solicitors should have been admitted in 1790s lies in the justification for collecting and revising the regulations, namely:

'the many alterations of circumstances arising from the Extention of the

Royalty, the great increase of Inhabitants within the City & Libertys and the various questions and suits which fall under the cognizance of the court'.[57]

The extension of the royalty (the area of land which the town held of the crown by royal charter) and the development of the New Town were pressures that would also have augmented Court of Session business. If, as seems likely, this helps explain the jump in the number of writers to the signet, wider economic factors must explain the rise in the number of notaries public.

The failure of the College to continue its exponential increase in size at the beginning of the eighteenth century relieved some of the pressure on its relationship with the town council. This was also a period of entrenchment for the College, allowing a number of legal families to consolidate a power base, among them emerging dynasties, such as the family of Dundas of Arniston, the Pringles, Fergussons and Boswells of Auchinleck.

THE COURT AND THE COLLEGE

The community of the College existed solely to serve the court. Although the focus here is not on legal procedure, it is useful to say something about how the court conducted its business.[58] The Court of Session had fourteen lords ordinary and a president.[59] Important decisions were taken by 'the hail fifteen', sitting in the Inner House, while a lord ordinary of the week was appointed to sit in the Outer House, dealing with ordinary and extra-ordinary actions. In the case of ordinary actions, which were the vast majority, the lord ordinary would generally make interlocutors on matters of procedure, at various points in the process, and then finally decide the case. In extraordinary actions, dealing with important points such as the reduction of heritable titles, he would prepare the cause for a hearing in the Inner House which exercised an exclusive jurisdiction in such matters. In an ordinary action, if a point of importance emerged, the lord ordinary might report that to his brethren for 'advising' or deliberation.

Delegated tasks were also given to the lord ordinary on concluded causes, the lord ordinary on oaths and the lord ordinary on witnesses, all of whom had roles in preparing and ranking evidence in readiness for cases to be reported to the judges in the Inner House. Any judge, except the president, might sit as a lord ordinary, and this was done by rotation. Judges were also delegated to perform other tasks, such as examining the qualification of prospective notaries public. Since Scots procedure favoured fairness over speed, it was possible to reclaim against interlocutors and to do so repeatedly. Lords ordinary were regularly called upon to review their own decisions, as were the judges in the Inner House, and cases could continue for several years without a final resolution.

The Bill Chamber, as well as functioning as a vacation court, dealt with various business, including actions of lawburrows and the granting of authority for certain forms of diligence.[60] It was here that litigants brought bills of advocation and bills of suspension. Through a bill of advocation they sought to have proceedings in Scotland's inferior courts moved to the Court of Session where it became an ordinary action; by the latter bill, litigants attempted to have an inferior judgment suspended and to have the matter heard before the lords of session. The lord ordinary on the bills (normally the lord ordinary of the week) presided in this chamber which had a separate clerk to those in the Outer House.

Business was conducted in a bustling, often over-crowded, atmosphere. The physical surroundings of the court were described in some detail by Professor William Forbes whose description reinforces the sense of community.[61] The Inner House, a large square room within Parliament House, was entered by the judges from a waiting room in which they, the clerks and the advocates, donned their gowns. It was also here that boxes were placed in which, 'according to the example of the most famous Judicatories abroad', the lords and clerks of session received petitions, informations and other papers between set hours every day.[62]

The judges, wearing purple robes faced with scarlet satin, sat around a semicircular bench. In front of them, dressed in black gowns, the six principal clerks sat at a table where, if he were present, the lord clerk register would sit. Opposite the bench was the bar where the advocates attended when they were required to debate before the judges.

To the east of the chamber, in the corner, the lord ordinary on the bills had his own table attended either by the clerk on the bills or his deputy. On the west side of the chamber were two doors leading to the Outer House where the lord ordinary for the week sat on a high bench, set close to the wall. Before him was a long table, at which the depute clerks of session would sit (without gowns, unlike the principal clerks). At a desk, on the left-hand side of this table, sat the keeper of the minute book. Opposite the bench, at a bar known as the fore-bar, the advocates made their pleadings. The passage between the bench and fore-bar was kept free, to be entered only by the lord advocate, solicitor general or their servants, unless a party or witness was required to step forward to take an oath. On either side of the fore-bar were benches where advocates' clerks could sit, and behind it, enclosed with rails, was a square containing seats where the advocates might sit until called to speak. To gain entry to this area, it was necessary to pass one of the doorkeepers, whose batons marked them out. These black-gowned figures, employed by the Faculty of Advocates, kept out everyone except advocates, writers to the signet or 'persons of note'.

A staircase on the east of the Outer House led to a loft inside the Inner

House from where the proceedings might be followed. High up, on the west side of the Outer House, there was a window through which the Outer House clerks made announcements, intimating, for example, deliverances made on bills or reading out the minute book.

A COMMUNITY FROM COMMUNITIES

Although the College was thus centred in Parliament House, where the period of its sittings dominated Edinburgh's social calendar, its members remained rooted in local communities from the Borders to Shetland. These local links they continued to foster; as well as being places of repose during the vacation, local estates brought clients, tenants, income and political influence. Many College members were local justices of the peace. Some, the lords of session, the lord advocate, the solicitor general and (after 1748) the local sheriff-depute were, *ex officio*, JPs in every county, but others gained appointment in a personal capacity through their landed interests. In Aberdeenshire, for example, eleven advocates, two lords of session and at least one writer to the signet were among the JPs appointed in 1761; the equivalent list for Dumbartonshire contains the names of seven advocates and three writers to the signet.[63] One of them, Ilay Campbell, was also proposed as a JP in Renfrewshire. Charles Areskine, as lord justice clerk (who himself had been appointed a JP in Dumfries in 1750), took advice from local men when nominating new justices of the peace to the lord chancellor. In Dumbarton, he sought the view of the advocate James Smollet, the local sheriff-depute; in Orkney, he asked Patrick Honyman of Graemsay, father of the future advocate and judge, William.

The number of days upon which the court sat decreased markedly, from a norm of about 125 days per year in the 1690s to about 118 days by the 1740s, with a further reduction by the end of the century, with only 112 sederunt days in 1801. This change brought with it a slight adjustment to the timing of the traditional spring and harvest vacations but they broadly continued to cover the months March until May (or, after 1752, mid-June), and August to November, respectively.

The vacations of the court were preceded by 'the hurry of the session', as writers and advocates scrambled to present petitions and bills that might secure interlocutors that would delay or discomfit their adversaries, or permit diligence to take place, before the court resumed sitting. This 'hurry in the heat of a session', according to Samuel Mitchelson WS, was the only thing that could 'ever prevent any Client of mine from receiving a return [that is, an instant reply to correspondence] in due course'.[64] The closing days of the session were hectic for judges, advocates and writers alike. So busy was James Graham of Airth in March 1712 that he lacked time to write to his client, the Duke of Montrose, detailing the outcome of a conference with his fellow advocate Sir Walter Pringle. Instead, as he put it, 'the hurry of the session' had obliged him to remit the matter to George Robertson, Montrose's law agent.[65] According to Robert Dundas, the hurry of the last days of the session 'cuts off' all social interaction.[66] At such times, the judges were so busy that often they could do little more than postpone cases until the start of the next session.

These busy periods were the prelude to a mass exodus from Edinburgh. In August 1726 the young advocate Kenneth Mackenzie complained that the town so lacked people 'that I scarse know any body in it; I never saw it so thin, & [it] affords so little to divert one that is heartily weary of it'.[67] The vacation was the time for judges and advocates to go to their country estates, to catch up on correspondence, to indulge themselves in gardening and estate management or the pursuits of literature and local politics. The first words sent from Edinburgh by Robert Craigie, on being promoted to the important government office of lord advocate, were that he would have to 'surrender my projects of toiling here eight months and four months at my farm'.[68] It was in the vacations that first-hand accounts of events in Edinburgh made their way into the localities.

Arrival back home was not always an occasion for leisure, as a letter of George Robertson to the Duke of Montrose in 1719 makes clear. Montrose wanted James Graham of Airth to give him his opinion upon two memorials but Graham, one of the busiest advocates at the bar, could not find the time to do so amid the rush at the end of the session. As Robertson put it:

> ... the throng of business then upon his hand could not allow him to get time to consider & ansyr [answer] them. The Lords did ryse on Fryday and on Saturday Mr Graham went for Airth, and I went with him, and carried the memorials with me. But the throng of visitors & countrie affairs of his own did so take him up whyll I was there, that I could get not time to have his serious thoughts on these memorials, all I could doe was to leave the memorials with him, and he promised to consider them with first conveniencie, and then wryt to yow ...'[69]

Robertson's excursion to Airth (near Falkirk) was not unusual. Writers and writers to the signet often took the opportunity in the vacation to visit clients, particularly when there was some legal task to be carried out locally or accounts to be settled. For those leaving Edinburgh to return home, the journey was an opportunity to visit friends. On the way to his estate in Buchan, the advocate and local justice of the peace John Gordon used to spend a day with the Douglas family at Fechil in Aberdeenshire. Sylvester Douglas, who later made his name at the English bar, vividly remembered that as a boy he was inspired to learn French by a gift of Voltaire's *Candide* made to him by Gordon on one such trip.[70]

THE SENSES OF COMMUNITY

There were many kinds of community within the College, and its members may variously be subdivided into networks linked by family ties, professional relationships and political allegiances. These include: scribal communities, whose members lent and borrowed books and manuscripts and commented on printed legal pleadings; communities of political patronage, within which some eagerly participated in wider electoral manoeuvring; and communities of friendship and support that bound individuals together at all levels of the College, in ways that sometimes cut across their narrow professional functions. The professional associates of the advocate David Armstrong, for example, tended to be drawn, like many of his clients, from his native Dumfriesshire.[71] This was also where Armstrong's major patrons, the dukes of Queensberry, had their own power base, and it was thanks to them that he and his son successively held the office of sheriff-depute of Dumfries. Local knowledge counted not only for the writers who brought clients to advocates – in Armstrong's case men from the south-west such as Robert Irving WS and John Syme WS – but for the advocates themselves. The network of Dumfries connections in Armstrong's career was replicated in similar networks surrounding advocates from Fife, Aberdeenshire and elsewhere, and their neighbourhood connections often also provided links to a judge or two, because the lords of session were also drawn from across the country.

In terms of the strongest bond, family, it is no surprise that sons often followed their fathers into the legal profession. A young man could be trained by his father in the practical arts and styles of the law, with access to his library and office, or he might be farmed out to the writing chamber of a fellow practitioner. Successful law agents (known generically as writers) with an eye to upward social mobility, had the wherewithal to send their most promising sons abroad for education in civil law with a view to sending them to the bar.[72] The legal profession was seen as a family investment and, in this, Scotland is no different from many other early modern jurisdictions.[73] In Naples, for example, according to the German writer, Johannes Brunneman, not only was the son of an existing advocate naturally to be preferred to any outside candidate, he was often admitted to the court free of charge.[74] On the other hand, this can be pushed too far. Barristers in Toulouse in the period 1750–89 were more than twice as likely as a contemporary Scottish advocate to have followed his father to the bar.[75]

Two scholars, Nicholas Phillipson and John Shaw, have both

investigated the social status of Scottish advocates in the eighteenth century.[76] These studies are helpful although, to some degree, they reflect inherent difficulties in accurately comparing the parental backgrounds of intrants to the Faculty, particularly in terms of wealth and social prominence. Many were the sons of 'lairds' yet, as a matter of economic reality, this might include the sons of men in a variety of circumstances, from substantial landholders to men of more limited means. Shaw, in particular, uses a narrower categorisation in comparing members of the bar from 1707 with members of parliament. His general conclusion is that the social status of the bar remained fairly high throughout the eighteenth century, and the legal profession, without attracting members of the nobility of the first rank, did appeal to a significant proportion of men within the higher social groups.[77] This is a fair and useful generalisation. The bar certainly did lose some of its appeal because of the attraction of London after 1707. This was particularly true for potential members of parliament but it applies also to a significant number of Scots attracted south to train, in the words used of Alexander Hume-Campbell, 'as an English lawyer'.[78]

(a) *Marital relationships*

Beyond the sometimes hereditary nature of the legal profession, there is much to interest genealogists in the history of the College of Justice. The links between members extended far beyond marriage to include apprentice-ship, business relationships – particularly in respect of ad hoc trading ventures – and friendships or relationships based on shared interests, including music and horticulture. As we shall see, the College was a hierarchical body. Even so, links of various kinds, whether or not intended to be the basis of permanent relationships, managed to cut across boundaries of status within the College, at least among its more learned members.

Published sources provide only an incomplete picture of the marital relationships of leading College members, with data on writers to the signet particularly disappointing. It is nonetheless worth reviewing (see Table 2). Of the 556 writers to the signet admitted between 1 January 1700 and 31 December 1799, the vast majority are known to have married, although the identity of the first married partner is known in only 22.4 per cent of cases. Of those, more than a quarter were the daughters of College members, the slight majority of whom (nineteen in number) were fellow writers to the signet.[79] Another twenty-two marital partners can safely be identified as women with a strong Edinburgh connection, the daughters of writers, merchants, magistrates, ministers, one baron of exchequer (Mathilda Cockburn, married to Sir Robert Dundas WS) and four Edinburgh-based 'civil servants', for want of a better term.[80] Generally, writers to the signet seem to have married women whose fathers were professional men, merchants, and craftsmen although sixteen of them married the daughters of baronets.

Table 2. *Marital partners*

	Total	Married	Spouse known	College-related spouse
WS	556	526	119 (22.6%)	35 (29.4%)
Adv.	727	644	476 (73.9%)	54 (11.3%)
SCJ	84	82	70 (85.4%)	16 (22.9%)

In the same period, which saw 727 advocates admitted, eighty-three are known not to have married. Information about spouses is available with regard to 73.9 per cent of them, of whom only about one in nine married the daughter of a College member. The rest married daughters falling broadly into the same profile as was the case with writers to the signet although two features stand out. First, a few advocates married above the social level of baronet's daughter (evidently the glass ceiling for members of the WS society); twenty-three were married to earls' daughters and three married the daughters of dukes.[81] Secondly, no less than 231 advocates (41.3 per cent) married lairds' daughters (some of whom would have had strong links to the town of Edinburgh). More than four out of every five advocates, of whose wives we are informed, do, however, appear to have married outside the College and the burgh.

With regard to the smallest group, the eighty-four advocates who were elevated to the bench as ordinary lords of session during this period, the marital status of eighty-two is known. Conclusions can be drawn about the marriages of seventy of them, because ten never married and nothing is known about the wives of the other two. Of these, sixteen married within the College. This is more than double the proportion for advocates in general. A lord of session was also more than twice as likely to be the son-in-law of a lord of session as was true either of the bar as a whole or of members of the WS Society. The particularly limited knowledge concerning the wives of writers to the signet is problematic here. Five of them are known to have married judges' daughters and this represents 4.2 per cent of the total number of spouses whose origins are known. It seems likely that this percentage figure is inflated, because these marriages were more likely than most to be recorded.

Finally, the close working relationship of advocates with writers to the signet might suggest a basis for intermarriage between these two branches of the profession but barely one in a hundred advocates had a WS as a father-in-law.[82] The traffic was in the opposite direction, with writers marrying advocates' daughters although the small sample makes it difficult to extrapolate how common this was. The known figures suggest that about one WS in every twenty married an advocate's daughter but that, as a group, they were about three times more likely to marry the daughter of another WS.

Only a small minority of College members, therefore, had a father-in-law within the College. There is no necessary link between success at the bar and any family relationship (despite sons often following their fathers into that profession). Men practising there who had an advocate as a father-in-law, like Robert Dalziell or the more successful Andrew Macdouall or Ilay Campbell, might still reasonably expect to benefit from his experience and advice and might even take over some of his clients when he died or retired from the bar. Marrying a judge's daughter was likewise no guarantee of success but judicial favouritism could be a great advantage and may have assisted the careers of men like Alexander Lockhart, George Brown, David Dalrymple of Westhall, George Carre and Alexander Maconochie, all of whom reached the bench themselves.

(b) Fiduciary relationships

A family or professional link often featured when College members were called upon to act as tutors or curators. Their legal skills, and contacts within the court, were much in demand by those who wanted to ensure the smooth administration of their children's inheritance in the event of their death. Care, however, had to be taken before agreeing to enter into such fiduciary relationships because they might prove both onerous and risky. Lord Grange was hesitant to become one of the curators of the young Francis Wemyss because the young man had inherited English estates and Grange insisted that advice be taken from English lawyers as to what his potential liability might be should he make negligent acts or omissions.[83] Lord Dun, also approached, had declined to act because of the pressure of his private affairs but having two lords of session among a group of curators or trustees was not particularly unusual.

The tutors of Agnes Murray-Kynnynmond, who were involved in lengthy and complex litigation concerning her estate, included Lord Grange, Lord Drummore and Alexander Cunningham WS.[84] Agnes, the only daughter of the advocate Hugh Murray-Kynnynmond, was through her mother granddaughter of Hugh Somerville WS, and there were many family legal connections. The same might be said of the daughter of the late James Elphinstone, a writer, who was the subject of dispute in 1726 between her tutors, Charles, Lord Elphinstone, and the judge Lord Coupar (James Elphinstone, later Lord Balmerino), because they had each identified a different potential husband for her. The matter almost became academic when she was carried off by force from the custody of Couper's servant, at his estate in Bo'ness, by a local man attracted by her £3,000 estate. Matters of this kind lay open the range of family and professional networks at play within the College. Lord Alva and Alexander Cunningham WS, for example, were two of the curators who, in 1780, sought to interdict the thirteen-year-old Elizabeth Gartmore from leaving Scotland with her mother to live in Lisbon.[85]

Mortifications (*mortis causa* public trusts) were another, more public, context in which men drawn from across the College might co-operate together.[86] An example is the fund of 5,000 merks which Adam Christie DCS left in trust, the income from half of which was to support a bursar at the University of Edinburgh with the remainder to be spent in support of the widows and orphans of advocates and writers.[87] The trustees were, *ex officio*, the lord president and the dean of the Faculty of Advocates together with the heirs of Sir Alexander Gibson PCS. The lords of session audited the accounts annually. This fund was regularly reinvested and funds were lent out with the approval of the judges. The trust set up by John Strachan of Craigrook WS (d.1719) was administered by two advocates, two writers to the signet and two lords of session, although this seems to have been done in co-operation with the presbytery of Edinburgh.[88] As the trust continued to be administered, new trustees were occasionally assumed although they seem to have served for life; Lord Elliock, for one, continued in this office for over twenty years.[89]

In the private sphere, there were many opportunities for co-operation and conflict between College members. In many debt actions and sequestrations, the creditors included an array of judges, advocates and writers to the signet. In fact, they often took a lead in sequestration matters, being appointed to represent their fellow creditors. Lords Milton and Murkle, and the advocate John Campbell of Succoth, for instance, were among the trustees for the creditors of the Earl of Roseberry in 1736.[90] Lord Drummore had to decline hearing a case in 1751, a dispute over annual rents between the advocates John Stuart of Allanbank and Archibald Inglis, because his nephew, James Stewart, had an interest in the matter.[91]

Although they were rarely directly involved in trade, they did invest in commerce, sometimes on a regional basis. Many of them, sometimes at the urging of clients and patrons, invested in the Ayr Bank and suffered significantly from its collapse in 1772.[92] They also provided financial backing to joint ventures. Thus, the advocate Robert Fraser, for instance, went into a venture in the tobacco trade in 1708 on the basis of a verbal agreement with the Edinburgh merchant, John Watson, who was to manage the business.[93] Twenty years later, Alexander Mackenzie of Delvine PCS invested in the riskier venture of attempting to salvage treasure from wrecked ships.[94] The most remarkable example of such a venture must be that of another advocate, Robert Gordon of Cluny.[95] Because he was personally acquainted with John Law, Cluny was sent to France in 1719 by his relative Sir William Gordon in order to invest some of the latter's money in French stocks. Cluny managed Gordon's Mississippi stocks and spent time playing chess among the foreign ministers resident in Paris. The investments, like Law's schemes, ended in disaster.

(c) *Patronage relationships*

As a working environment, patronage was as rife in the College of Justice as it was anywhere else in eighteenth-century Scotland.[96] The College contained an abundance of men seeking patronage, at almost every level, and it also contained a range of office-holders who might grant lesser offices or intercede with others to do so. This institution itself contained offices of variable value and status for which there was often strong competition involving the highest to the lowest about the court. At the same time, a number of offices elsewhere, such as in the universities or in public bodies and corporations, were filled by College members *ex officio*, often through the influence or election of other members of the College. Legal disputes generated by the disposal of patronage, for instance whether an office-holder enjoyed the right to appoint a depute for life, often fell to be resolved judicially by the lords of session. Election disputes, which arose even more frequently, were linked strongly to the system of patronage and placed the College as an institution at the heart of Scottish civil and political life.

Aside from the brokering of patronage at the exalted level of political agents and managers, such as Lord Milton and Henry Dundas, men used professional links in a very informal way to gain favours.[97] The lawyers in the College, in particular, often had strong connections to commercial life in Scotland, dealing as they did with clients' monies, uplifting rents and borrowing and lending. They might be persuaded by a client directly either to take on an apprentice writer themselves or to seek a place for a young man in another legal office in Edinburgh. The Glasgow merchant James Dunlop sent his son, George, to David Balfour WS to train as a writer, armed with a letter of introduction from Balfour's client, and Dunlop's correspondent, Sir William Forbes.[98] Dunlop went on to become a WS himself. Equally, a lawyer might use his influence with a client, as James Dundas WS did, to place a young man in a large Glasgow trading office.[99] In this way, lawyers could use their contacts as a currency in a world dominated by personal associations in which men might advance themselves by the exchange of favours, professional or political. The advocate James Graeme of Buchlyvie, for instance, was rewarded with the office of Surveyor General of Tobacco in Greenock for help in ensuring the election to parliament of James Campbell of Ardkinglass in 1754. This office, worth £150 per annum, was below his station but it was seen as a stopgap while something better, such as the office of commissary of Glasgow, might be arranged.[100]

If offices were not available, lawyers wanted patronage to provide them with clients. Sometimes it did so as a by-product. The young Alexander Lockhart, an advocate from a Jacobite family, was unsuccessful when he approached Lord Milton for the vacant office of commissary of Edinburgh in 1732. His father, Sir George Lockhart of Carnwath, had had links both to the Duke of Argyll and to Andrew Fletcher of Saltoun, Milton's uncle, and it was likely on Milton's advice that a few months later, John Marnees in Williamswood wrote to Lockhart. Marnees asked Lockhart to help a prisoner languishing in the Tolbooth prison. Although the prisoner was from a poor family, and had little from which to pay a lawyer, two comments are of interest in Marnees's letter. First, he expressed the wish that Lockhart was better known in his country so that he might 'have more trouble from our people' (that is, gain more business) and second, he added a telling postscript, 'when better clients comes in my way if I can yow shall have them'.[101] In short, if Lockhart took the case, for whatever meagre sum it was worth, then he would benefit in future from potentially more lucrative clients. This must have been typical of the kind of calculation made by any advocate at the bar whose reputation was still to be made.

Patronage was certainly a factor in how men lived their lives. For an advocate, the hope of gaining or pleasing a patron or judge might determine to whom he chose to dedicate his printed theses, or it might encourage him to go further, even to the point of publishing a legal treatise. At a less exalted level, it might encourage a writer or an extractor to seek a lectern in a particular writing office in the hope of future advancement, because the College, like the town council, normally promoted from within. In short, the system of patronage provided an incentive for individuals to identify a strategy for their own promotion and, in doing so, to inform themselves about how the College worked, who influenced its internal organisation, what functions its offices served and what the relative values of those offices were. Part of the strategy involved making use of any local connections, particularly among the nobility, which might prove influential to men in Edinburgh or London. Even if a vacant office was in the gift of the clerks of session or the judges, that did not mean they might not be influenced by a word from outside the College. The writer Samuel Shaw, for instance, had a tenuous link with the Chief Baron of Exchequer in Scotland (James Montgomery) and played it for all it was worth. He bid first to replace an extractor in one of the offices of the principal clerks of session in 1785, then to have Montgomery intercede with Lord Ankerville to appoint him as his clerk, and finally in 1789 to help him replace the late John Flockhart as keeper of the general register of hornings.[102] Shaw was one of those men, and there were many, who took a great interest in the health of those about him, particularly anyone whose office, should it fall vacant, might be within the reach of him, his friends or relations.

When the level of litigation was low, as it was particularly in the 1740s, and fee income within the College was hard won, the demand for minor offices was particularly keen. Not everyone played fairly. The death of the Edinburgh commissary Andrew Marjoribanks, in April 1742, led to the emergence of no less than six candidates for his office, all but one of whom were at the bar. The sixth, William Baillie WS, literally sought to gain a march on his competitors by heading off to London, bearing a demission by Marjoribanks in his favour, for which he had paid the ailing man £500.[103] The following year, when John Dalrymple PCS died, there were said to be twenty-two candidates for the vacant office.[104] This was an unsalaried office although its fees were variously estimated to be worth £370 to £400 sterling per annum. This level of demand was as nothing to the clamour at the bar to gain a sheriff-deputeship in 1748 following the abolition of heritable jurisdictions, a cause more easily won with influential backing from noble patrons; or, indeed, to the manoeuvrings sometimes undertaken to gain appointment to the bench or, once on the bench, to the criminal circuit.

(d) *Support relationships*

A final feature of the College community, and the mark of any community, is its concern for its weakest members. In Edinburgh, the town council provided subsistence to its pensioners, generally the heirs and dependants of impoverished merchants and craftsmen. These included local writers in distressed circumstances, and their widows, who received modest quarterly payments for life at least until the city treasurer, in July 1744, was ordered to cease direct payments.[105] In future, subsistence was to be provided from funds appropriated to the new charity workhouse.[106] Exempted from this provision was Magdalene Fleming, widow of Andrew Keay, who had been one of the keepers of Parliament House until he demitted office in 1736.[107] Keay had ostensibly resigned office in order to provide a place for a burgess who would otherwise require financial assistance from the council and, as a quid pro quo, the council had agreed to pay £10 annually to support his wife, daughter of Sir James Fleming, a former lord provost.[108] This payment continued beyond 1744 yet this is one instance where the pensioner, at least in theory, might have enjoyed a parallel claim on the College of Justice.

In fact, support of its poor was not a College responsibility and, given the privileges claimed by its members as part of a national institution, it was certainly not a town council one. Looking after their own poor was one of the reasons for the creation of the Faculty of Advocates and the WS Society and it is evident that other groupings within the College organised their own widows and dependants' funds. In 1733 the WS Society, seeking an increase in fees, complained that the cost of looking after the widows and dependants was increasing, acknowledging that as its 'numbers increase so must the poor'.[109]

In its earliest known constitution, the Faculty required advocates to make regular contributions to its charity box 'for the releife of decayed Advocatts there wyfes children and known servants'.[110] As we shall see, supporting their poor was one reason why the advocates insisted on raising their entry dues in the eighteenth century. This was an obligation not limited simply to the next generation. To focus on the Faculty of Advocates, its minute books are full of references to requests for charitable funds. Many petitions survive in the Faculty's records from advocates like Alexander Bruce who, in 1728, was suffering a 'present straitning condition', or from advocates' widows, like that of the late Alexander Campbell in 1725 who recounted the ill health which had plagued him for the last nine years of his life, leaving her and their children in difficult circumstances.[111] Family links to lawyers in these petitions are often stressed. Thus, that of Elizabeth Hamilton (née Grant), in a petition in 1788, mentioned her father-in-law, James Hamilton of Olivestob (Adm. 1703), who had been sheriff-depute of Haddington, had a 'considerable practice at the Bar, and will be remembered by many of the members as a very worthy man' (he died in 1757).[112] Unfortunately, he lost a large estate as a result of the South Sea Bubble in 1720. As a widow, Elizabeth had little more to fall back on except a list of her late husband's Hamilton relations. Olivestob had married a grand-daughter of Sir Thomas Nicolson (former lord advocate) whose other daughter married into a number of noble families. Olivestob's aunt had married the then lord president, Hew Dalrymple, and the only child of that marriage, Marion, married another advocate, Lewis Colquhoun of Luss (Adm. 1728).[113] This detailed ancestry was mentioned to establish the links between the petitioner's husband's family and the Faculty. Although Elizabeth had been supported by her relations, this had ceased when, following the death of her first husband, she had twice remarried beneath her rank. What she ultimately wanted was to get her children into the charity workhouse in Edinburgh.

College bodies did not stop at assisting their own poor. Apart from an assertion of the economic benefit Edinburgh enjoyed from having litigants attracted to the College, one of the arguments put forward by College members in defence of their privileges, against the threat of the 'Poor's Bill' in 1784, was the fact that 'we serve the publick & the poor & are compellable to do so'.[114] A small number of advocates, writers to the signet and (from

1755) agents in the College, were all nominated annually, by the Faculty, WS Society and the Society of Agents, to act gratis for litigants on the poor roll. This maintained a tradition of free representation for the poor that went back continuously to the sixteenth century and was linked to the fact that advocates in the College could be compelled to act for any litigant, rich or poor, by the judges.[115] An undated paper, attributed to the vice dean of the Faculty of Advocates, Andrew Crosbie (d.1785), and written to defend the exemption of College members from jury service, referred to the rule on compellability as authority for the view that the 'office of an advocate in the Service of his Client is in the use of Law not a voluntary but a necessary Service'.[116] This idea of a national public service reinforced the credentials of all College members as a community established to serve for the good of the wider community.

CONCLUSION

There was a sense among practising lawyers of the importance of attendance in Parliament House, the home of the Court of Session. Lord Cockburn thought it madness that any advocate promoted sheriff would possibly choose to reside in his sheriffdom all year, because any man who cut himself off from breathing 'the legal atmosphere of the Supreme Court', he thought, 'to a certainty loses his law'.[117] That legal atmosphere was shared not simply by advocates and judges but also by law agents, clerks, macers and keepers. Their sense of community was a palpable one, shaped not only by their shared privileges and common purpose but also by a myriad of social and family links that gave almost everyone a degree of relationship with someone else.

The atmosphere of the College was ripe for gossip and, in private correspondence, there are illusions to prospective marriages, elopements, idle table talk, and salacious stories often culled from litigation involving well-known figures or scions of well-known families. In the proof of an action in 1749 is one such letter in which the writer recounts the disappointment of her newly wed cousin who had, on their second night together, grabbed her unfortunate husband 'by the privy Members [sic]' and chastised him for his lack of stamina, drawing comparison with what she had heard of 'one Bogle, a Writer in Hamilton, who is married to a Sister of Sir William Fleming's, who never performed under ten Times a-night'.[118] It was indeed a small world and it was one in which professional men had to defend their reputations. When Alexander Cunningham WS, crediting false reports of his wife having committed adultery, accused various men of involvement (including William Graham, advocate), he was immediately subject to an action of defamation.[119]

Quite apart from personal and political rivalries and petty jealousies, the community of the College, as we have seen, was not one community. It was a series of interlinked communities combined together to compose a distinctive institution, set apart from other institutions within the town of Edinburgh. The next chapter will investigate more closely some of the points of contact between the members of the College and the town.

NOTES

1. W. Ross, *An Historical Account of the Privileges of the College of Justice* (Edinburgh, 1785), p. 5.
2. A College of 'cunning and wise men' was referred to in the legislation of 1532; the phrase College of Justice appeared in a later ratifying statute in 1540: K. M. Brown et al., eds, *The Records of the Parliaments of Scotland to 1707* (St Andrews, 2007–10), 1532/6, 1540/12/64.
3. R. K. Hannay, *Acts of the Lords of Council in Public Affairs, 1501–1554* (Edinburgh, 1932), pp. 374–8; *Acts of Sederunt of the Lords of Council and Session from 15th of January 1553, to the 11th of July 1790* (Edinburgh, 1790), pp. 176–7.
4. 48 Geo. III, c. 151.
5. National Library of Scotland [NLS], Saltoun, MS 17538, fo. 109r. Although the words 'such as' are used, this list of members is, in fact, complete.
6. R. K. Hannay, *The College of Justice* (repr. Edinburgh, 1990), xiii.
7. National Records of Scotland [NRS], Books of sederunt, CS1/10, fo. 70v.
8. J. M. Pinkerton, ed., *The Minute Book of the Faculty of Advocates, 1661–1712* (Stair Society, 1976), p. 77. The inaugural speech of Sir George Mackenzie, marking the completion of the Advocates Library, is dated 15 March 1689: T. I. Rae, 'The origins of the Advocates Library' in P. Cadell and A. Matheson, *For the Encouragement of Learning, Scotland's National Library 1689–1989* (Edinburgh, 1989), p. 1; J. St Clair and R. Craik, *The Advocates Library* (Edinburgh, 1989); J. W. Cairns, 'Sir George Mackenzie, the Faculty of Advocates, and the Advocates Library' in G. Mackenzie, *Oratio Inauguralis* (Edinburgh, 1989), 18–35. For the keepership, see D. Duncan, *Thomas Ruddiman* (Edinburgh, 1965), esp. pp. 24–40.
9. On 14 November 1692 similar privileges to those held by College members were extended to the lord justice clerk's servant and a macer in the justiciary court but strictly they were not members of the College: Glasgow University Library [GUL], W. Forbes, 'Great Body of the Law of Scotland', MS Gen 1245, fo. 1809. The lords of justiciary were, of course, also senators of the College. The barons in the Court of Exchequer were, by statute in 1707, given 'the same privileges and immunities of the

members of the College of Justice', except that they may have actions brought against them before the lords of session that were not competent in the exchequer: The Exchequer Court (Scotland) Act 1707 (6 Anne, c. 53), s. 18. The barons, ushers etc., were part of the social community of lawyers but not regarded as part of the College. On the significance of these courts, see A. Murdoch, *The People Above: Politics and Administration in mid Eighteenth-century Scotland* (Edinburgh, 1980), esp. pp. 14–17. On the exchequer specifically, see A. L. Murray, 'The post-Union Court of Exchequer' in H. L. MacQueen, ed., *Miscellany Five* (Stair Society, 2006), pp. 103–31.

10. For example, multiple copies of voluminous legal papers, running sometimes into hundreds of pages, had to be printed. The financial relationship between one lawyer and the printer Walter Ruddiman is set out in Advocates Library Session Papers [ALSP], *The Petition of William Taylor*, 22 Dec. 1767, Arniston collection, vol. 84, no. 23.

11. NRS, CS1/11, fo. 226r.

12. Advocates Library [AL], FR 339r/2/2, 'Reasons against the passing of the towne of Ed[inbu]r[gh]'s ratificatiune anno 1637'.

13. For example, *RPS*, 1587/7/30; 1633/6/38; 1661/1/325; 1685/4/46. The focus of some of this legislation (particularly the 1633 and 1685 acts) lies on the privileges granted to the lords, rather than to College members in general.

14. Ibid., 1686/4/38.

15. A. Lang, *Sir George Mackenzie, His Life and Times* (London, 1909), p. 291.

16. A bond in Mackenzie's name for 9,000 merks, lent by him to the council in Dec. 1685, was retired in May 1686; he lent a further 6,000 merks in Aug. 1688 (after he was restored as lord advocate) which the council sought to apply 'for payment of such urgent creditors as are pressing for their debts': Edinburgh City Archives, town council minutes [TCM], SL1/1/31, fos 241r, 361r; SL1/1/32, fos 1v, 225r. It is noticeable that Mackenzie's rival, John Dalrymple (then HMA), was appointed one of the council's assessors in March 1687: ibid., SL1/1/32, fo. 92r.

17. Ibid., SL1/1/32, fo. 1v.

18. NRS, CS1/8, fo. 118r; *Acts of Sederunt*, pp. 174–5. The proportion was to be worked out in accordance with the rents of their houses.

19. Pinkerton, *Min. Bk, 1661–1712*, p. 77.

20. TCM, SL1/1/46, fos 23–4.

21. Ibid., SL1/1/105, fo. 161.

22. L. Nussdorfer, *Brokers of Public Trust: Notaries in Early Modern Europe* (Baltimore, 2009), p. 43; Hannay, *College of Justice*, p. 49; G. D. Squibb, *Doctors' Commons: A History of the College of Advocates and Doctors of Law* (Oxford, 1977), pp. 5–7.

23. D.3.c.3. A. Freidberg, ed., *Corpus Iuris Canonici* (2 vols, Leipzig, 1878–81), I, p.5.

24. See the discussion in S. Di Noto Marrella, *'Doctores' Contributo alla storia degli intellettuali nella dottrina del diritto commune* (2 vols, Padua, 1994), ii, p.170.

25. ALSP, *The Petition of Mr James Graeme of Bucclivie, Advocate*, 27 July 1738, Kilkerran Collection, vol. 2, no. 59.

26. J. Finlay, 'Pettyfoggers, regulation and local courts in early modern Scotland' 87 (2008) *SHR*, 42–67.

27. ECA, SL1/1/32, fo. 260r. A tack is a lease.

28. Ibid., SL1/1/104, fos 320–7.

29. Ibid., SL1/1/104, fo. 322–3.

30. Ibid., SL1/1/66, fos 175–7.

31. ALSP, *The Petition of Daniel Stewart*, 6 Feb. 1789, Arniston collection vol. 180, no. 27, p. 6. Stewart was not a member of the College and, had he been, even this point might not have been conceded. His argument was drafted and presented by a College member, however.

32. TCM, SL1/1/64, fo. 215; SL1/1/72, fos 235–6.

33. E. C. Sanderson, *Women and Work in Eighteenth-century Scotland* (London, 1996), p. 210.

34. TCM, SL1/1/78, fo. 318; SL1/1/126, fo. 306. The daughters of Samuel Gray WS were shopkeepers: Sanderson, *Women and Work*, p. 206.

35. TCM, SL1/1/87, fo. 163.

36. ALSP, *The Petition of Mess. Gibson and Balfour*, 5 March 1772, Pitfour collection, vol. 51, no. 16.

37. J. M. Pinkerton, ed., *The Minute Book of the Faculty of Advocates, 1713–1750* (Edinburgh, 1980), p. 243; A. Stewart, ed., *The Minute Book of the Faculty of Advocates, 1751–1783* (Edinburgh, 1999), p. xliv.

38. The council's stent-masters were merchants and tradesmen; they were not selected from within the membership of the College nor from writers in Edinburgh.

39. ALSP, *Information for the Magistrates of Glasgow, Defenders Against John Wilson, senior, Merchant in Glasgow*, 12 Jan. 1759, Craigie collection, vol. 53, no. 24, p.1.

40. TCM, SL1/1/53, fos 51–2.

41. TCM, SL1/1/129, fos 397–403.

42. Except in regard to writers to the signet, who would be reported to the keeper, and commissioners of the WS Society who had 'full power over their members in the first instance'.

43. NRS, CS1/11, fos 69r–v. On the Haldane case, see J. Finlay, 'Advocacy, patronage and character at the eighteenth-century Scots bar' 74 (2006) *Tijdschrift voor Rechtsgeschiedenis*, 108–10.

44. The material on which this section is based may largely be found in the Faculty of Advocates Records: AL, FR339r/12. This is discussed in detail in A. Stewart and D. Parratt, eds, *The Minute Book of the Faculty of Advocates, 1783–1798* (Edinburgh, 2008), pp. 107–10.

45. Stewart and Parratt, *Min. Bk, 1783–1798*, pp. xxvi–xxix. The tax exemption for College members survived until removed by the Poor Law (Scotland) Act 1845 (ibid., xxix). Another Bill at this time, ostensibly to raise 'lamp money' (a tax for lighting Edinburgh), was opposed by the Faculty in 1786.

46. These are separate documents in FR339r/12.

47. This case is cited as *The Burgh of Edinburgh* v. *John Moscrop*, Nov.–Dec. 1765, in Balfour's *Practicks*, i, 270. It can be found at NRS, CS7/35, fos 104r–105r, 141r–142vr, where the lords of session are referred to as 'conservators of the privilege'. On the bull, see J. W. Cairns, 'Revisiting the Foundation of the College of Justice' in MacQueen, ed., *Miscellany Five*, pp. 27–50. An earlier case, involving the scribe, James Scott, in 1546, is mentioned in the pleadings: Stewart and Parratt, *Min. Bk, 1783–1798*, p. 108, n.173.

48. *RPS*, 1579/10/27; APS, ii, 139, c.12.

49. AL, FR339r/12.

50. TCM, SL1/1/107, fos 318–20.

51. Adv. Lib., FR339r/12. Stewart and Parratt, *Min. Bk, 1783–1798*, p. 110.

52. J. Finlay, 'Advocates unlimited: the *numerus clausus* and the college of justice in Scotland' 87 (2008) *Historical Research*, pp. 206–28.

53. See J. Finlay, *Notaries Admission Registers, 1700–1799* (Scottish Record Society, forthcoming).

54. C. W. Brooks, *Lawyers, Litigation and English Society since 1450* (London, 1998), chapter 3; H. Horwitz and P. Polden, 'Continuity or change in the court of Chancery in the seventeenth and eighteenth centuries?' 35 (1996) *Journal of British Studies*, pp. 24–57; R. L. Kagan, *Lawyers and Litigants in Castile, 1500–1700* (Chapel Hill, 1981), esp. pp. 137–40; C. Kaiser; 'The deflation in the volume of litigation at Paris in the eighteenth century and the waning of the old judicial order', *European Studies Review* (1980), pp. 309–36. Detailed analysis of Bremen's municipal courts reinforces the pattern of which there is anecdotal evidence elsewhere; C. Wollschläger, 'Civil litigation and modernization: the work of the municipal courts of Bremen, Germany, in five centuries, 1549–1984', 24 (1990) *Law and Society Review*, pp. 261–82.

55. The category of Ordinary lords includes those who were appointed lord president direct from the bar but excludes four extraordinary lords and two lord chancellors.

56. Finlay, 'Pettyfoggers, regulation and local courts in early modern Scotland', pp. 45–54.

57. TCM, SL1/1/113, fo. 158.

58. N. T. Phillipson, *The Scottish Whigs and the Reform of the Court of Session* (Edinburgh, 1990), chapter 2; J. Finlay, 'The History of delay in Civil Procedure: Scotland 1600–1808' in C. H. van Rhee, ed., *The History of Delay in Civil Procedure* (Berlin, 2010), pp. 121–52.

59. The College of Justice, from its definition, includes the Court of Session but is a wider institution, including figures, such as the keeper of the Advocates Library, who were strictly not part of the court. The High Court of Justiciary, on the other hand, is not part of the College, although some privileges were extended in 1692 to those of its members who were not College members (*supra*, n. 9).

60. *Guide to the National Archives of Scotland* (Edinburgh, 1996), pp. 113–14; *The Book of Scotland* (Edinburgh, 1830), p. 111.

61. This account follows closely that of Forbes, Great Body, MS Gen. 1248, fos 1741–3. See also H. L. MacQueen, 'Two visitors in the Session, 1629 and 1636' in ibid., ed., *Miscellany Four* (Stair Society, 2002), p. 155; Pinkerton, *Min. Bk, 1661–1712*, pp. vii–ix; *Introduction to Scottish Legal History*, pp. 454–7.

62. NRS, CS1/9, fo. 30r. The set hours varied over time.

63. NLS, Erskine Murray papers, MS 5130, fos 1r–2v, 50r–53v, 60r. Some men listed are described as advocates (those known to be in practice), some are not. For Honyman, see MS 5082, fo. 18r.

64. NRS, Sinclair of Freswick papers, GD136/417/10. The writer was the younger Samuel Mitchelson.

65. NRS, GD220/5/1707/7.

66. NSS, Sir Andrew Mitchell of Thainstoun papers, RH4/70/10/2.

67. NLS, Mackenzie of Delvine, MS 1209, fo. 146.

68. NLS, Yester, MS 7045.

69. NRS, GD220/5/1724/15.

70. F. Bickley, ed., *The Diaries of Sylvester Douglas, Lord Glenbervie,* 2 vols (London, 1928), ii, p. 357.

71. Armstrong's career is investigated in J. Finlay, 'Corruption, regionalism and legal practice in Eighteenth-century Scotland: the rise and fall of David Armstrong, advocate' (2012), *TDGNHA* (forthcoming).

72. The word 'agent' was used generally of a lawyer in the inferior courts where the word procurator was more typically used; in non-court business, such as estate management, the word 'writer' was the common term in use. Agent, however, could simply be a synonym for writer. The lords of session used the phrase 'solicitor or agent' to indicate those who managed actions before them, as opposed to the advocates who argued cases before them. Solicitor and solicitor-at-law, terms derived from English practice, grew in popularity towards the end of the eighteenth century.

73. P. Lucas, 'A collective biography of students and barristers at Lincoln's Inn, 1680–1804: a study in the "aristocratic resurgence" of the eighteenth century (1974), *Journal of Modern History*, 227–61 ; R. L. Kagan, 'Law students in Eighteenth-century France' (1975), *Past and Present,* 38–72; C. Vael, 'Avocats et procureurs au conseil provincial de Namur du XVᵉ au XVIIIᵉ siècle', 64 (1997), *Recueils de la Société Jean Bodin*, pp. 211–28.

74. J. Brunneman, *Commentarius in duodecim libros Codicis Justinianei* (Leipzig, 1688), 2.8.
75. In Toulouse during this period, 31.6 per cent of barristers (50 out of 158) were the sons of barristers: L. R. Berlanstein, *The Barristers of Toulouse in the Eighteenth Century* (Baltimore, 1975), p. 35. In Scotland, the comparative figure is only 13.6 per cent (36 out of 265). For the wider period 1700–99, the Scottish proportion is 16.5 per cent (120 out of 727). This does not include the sons of *greffiers*, *notaires*, *procureurs* or, in Scotland, writers and writers to the signet. If it did, 55 per cent of *avocats* came from this legal professional background in the period 1750–89, compared to 21.9 per cent of Scottish advocates. There are many societal differences, however, that make the comparison imperfect.
76. J. S. Shaw, *The Management of Scottish Society 1707–1764* (Edinburgh, 1983); N. Phillipson, *The Scottish Whigs and the Reform of the Court of Session, 1785–1830* (Edinburgh, 1990).
77. Shaw, *Management of Scottish Society*, p. 21.
78. NLS, Saltoun, MS16545, fo. 109; on Boswell's attraction to England, see J. J. Caudle, 'James Boswell (*H. Scoticus Londoniensis*)' in S. Nenadic, ed. *Scots in London in the Eighteenth Century* (Lewisburg, 2010), pp. 112–13, 123–8.
79. Although forty-two of these 556 writers to the signet were married more than once, this analysis ignores second and subsequent marriages unless the second marriage is the first or only one of which family details exist. In twenty-eight cases of multiple marriage, no details at all are recorded except the names of the spouses. Where the father-in-law is a baron of exchequer who had been an advocate, he is not treated as a member of the College but lords of session are.
80. These officers were (with sons-in-law in brackets): solicitor to the board of customs (Thomas Strachan WS); receiver-general of excise duties for Scotland (James Pringle WS); comptroller-general of customs (Richard Hotchkis WS); comptroller of stamps and taxes (Charles Bremner WS).
81. The sons-in-law of dukes were: Alexander Fraser of Strichen (1st Duke of Argyll); Alexander Fraser of Powis (1st Duke of Argyll) and Adam Drummond, younger, of Megginch (Duke of Bolton).
82. This figure is boosted slightly by the fact that two advocates, James Geddes and Hugh Murray-Kynnynmond, shared the same father-in-law, Hugh Somerville WS: *Information for Mrs Isabella Somervel*, 25 June 1744, Elchies collection, vol. 14 (F–Y), no. 18.
83. NLS, Saltoun, MS 16549, fo. 1r.
84. For the litigation, see NLS, Minto, MS 13281; ALSP, *Information for John Maxwell of Nether Pollock against Alexander Macmillan WS and others*, 9 Dec. 1740, Kilkerran collection, vol. 7, no. 171; Hamilton-Gordon collection, 1st ser., vol. 41, no. 61.
85. ALSP, *The Petition of James earl of Glencairn and others*, 5 July 1780, Arniston collection vol. 142, no. 20.

86. The lords sometimes declined appointments under deeds of mortification, e.g. NRS, CS1/17, fo. 32r.
87. Ibid., CS1/9, fo. 163r; CS1/14, fos 72r–v. It was still being paid by the Faculty treasurer in 1819: AL, FR339r/1.
88. NRS, CS1/11, fo. 193v; 1/14, fo. 56r; NLS, Mackenzie of Delvine, MS 1209, fo. 146.
89. E.g. NRS, CS1/14, fo. 56v; CS1/18, fo. 10v.
90. ALSP, *Information for Andrew Fletcher of Milton, Esq* [etc.], 7 July 1736, Kilkerran collection, vol. 2, no. 42 (see also vol. 3, no. 60).
91. ALSP, *The Petition of Sir John Stewart of Allanbank, and Mr Archibald Inglis Advocate*, 21 June 1751, Falconer collection, vol. 7, no. 8.
92. The list of partners in the Ayr Bank can be found in NRS, Papers of the Maule family, earls of Dalhousie, GD45/24/183; *The Scots Magazine* xxxiv (1772), 304–5.
93. ALSP, *The Petition of Thomas Watson WS*, 12 Jan. 1750, Miscellaneous collection, ser. xvi, box 2, no. 88. Fraser was wealthy and had lent 10,000 merks to Lord Prestonhall and his son some time before 1713: ibid., *The Petition of George Cuthbert*, 19 Dec. 1732, Elchies collection, vol. 5, no. 34.
94. ALSP, *The Petition of Alexander Mackenzie of Delvine, one of the principal clerks of session,* 24 Feb., 1732, Hamilton-Gordon collection, 1st ser. vol. 38, no. 58.
95. ALSP, *The Petition of Kenneth Gordon of Cluny, Advocate*, 25 July 1732, Craigie collection, vol. 6, no. 7.
96. R. M. Sunter, *Patronage and Politics in Scotland, 1707–1832* (Edinburgh, 1986); Murdoch, *The People Above, passim*.
97. On Milton, see Shaw, *The Management of Scottish Society*, esp. chap. 7.
98. NLS Acc. 4796/1. George Dunlop became NP on 11 July 1799 and WS on 23 June 1807.
99. Glasgow City Archive [GCA], Stirling of Keir papers, T–SK 18/9/28.
100. NLS, Saltoun, MS 16720, fos 28r, 36r.
101. Ibid., MS 16550, fo. 211.
102. NRS, Papers of Samuel Shaw, writer in Edinburgh, RH15/134. Flockhart, appointed 12 Nov. 1778 (ibid., CS 1/16, fo. 52r), died on 18 Oct. 1789.
103. NLS, Yester, MS 7046, fos 37r, 61r, 63r.
104. Ibid., MS 7055, f. 117r.
105. For example, the council paid £8 to Robert Montieth, writer, in 1710 (TCM, SL1/1/39, fo. 1005); £5 to Agnes Glen, widow of John Lowrie, writer, in 1718 (SL1/1/45, fo. 72). The pension of Mary Stewart, widow of Thomas Buchanan, writer, was rescinded in 1735 (SL1/1/56, fo. 67). Margaret Chiesly, widow of Samuel Gray, late procurator fiscal of Edinburgh, and his son, received 15s quarterly: SL1/1/59, fo. 23; SL1/1/64, fos. 4, 186; SL1/1/65, fo. 18. David Denham, writer, was employed to make the quarterly payments in 1737 and write the receipts: SL1/1/58, fo. 248.

106. Ibid., SL1/1/64, fo. 347.
107. Keay was appointed by the lords on 5 June 1729 (NRS, CS1/11, fo. 190v), selected from the town council's leet; he demitted on 26 Feb. 1736 (CS1/13, fo. 52r).
108. TCM, SL1/1/56, fos 254–6.
109. NLS, Minto, MS 11033, fo. 21v.
110. AL, FR339r/2.
111. Ibid., FR339r/9; Pinkerton, ed., *Min. Bk, 1713–1750*, p. 110. Campbell (d.1725) had spent seventeen years at the bar prior to his illness.
112. Hamilton of Olivestob's relation, the Edinburgh burgess John Hamilton, petitioned Edinburgh town council for a pension in 1690: TCM, SL1/1/33, fo. 133r.
113. Colquhoun took the surname Grant.
114. AL, FR339r/12.
115. J. Finlay, *Men of Law in Pre-Reformation Scotland* (East Linton, 2000), 82–6.
116. AL, FR339r/24/4.
117. H. Cockburn, *Letters Chiefly Connected with the Affairs of Scotland* (London, 1874), 48–9.
118. ALSP, *Replies for George Montgomerie-Moir of Leckie, Defender*, 10 July 1749, Miscellaneous series, vol. 5, Proof, p. ix.
119. ALSP, *The Petition of Alexander Cunnyngham*, 22 Feb. 1765, Arniston collection, vol. 76, no. 25.

2

The College and the Urban Community

> And its certain the Town of Edinburgh would make a very small Figure,
> if the *Colledge of Justice* were removed to other Cities, who would
> Court and Caress the *Colledge of Justice*, and never envy or grudge their
> priviledges ...[1]

In the eighteenth century it was the custom for judges and advocates to
dress at home and then proceed, bearing gowns, cravats and wigs, to
Parliament House. Robert Chambers sketches a picture of advocates, their
heads through open windows, taking the morning air and discussing with
neighbours the legal news of the day.[2] The presence in Edinburgh of College
members, for the half of the year when most of them resided there, was
obvious to any casual visitor. Court sittings influenced the capital's social
calendar, so much so that the time taken up with legal business seems to
have been inversely proportionate to the time devoted to social activities in
Edinburgh. This was highlighted in a letter written by the young Alexander
Tait (a future PCS) to his friend James Erskine of Alva in 1748, a stagnant
period for litigation:

> Never was there more diversion, never was there less money. In short – what
> with Plays, Assemblys, Consorts [Concerts], Balls & Marriages, the *beau
> monde* here have been in a continuall motion.[3]

To what extent, however, did the College form a community apart? What
status did its members have, or want to have, in society generally? Would
Edinburgh have been a very different place had the College been located in
Perth or Stirling?

This chapter and the next will investigate some of the ways in which
College members influenced all aspects of life, and the built environment,
in Edinburgh. This they achieved despite many of them, especially if they
were new to the law, having no natural link to Scotland's capital. Edinburgh's
burgess roll indicates that most men of the College who became burgesses
did so only by right of their wives, or for good service done to the town, and
not because their fathers held that status before them.[4] Yet, even if for local

purposes they were 'only temporary residenters for the Service of the liedges', the effects of their presence can be measured in many ways. They and their families filled prominent pews in Edinburgh's churches and impressive burial plots in Greyfriars' kirkyard; they participated in formal social gatherings and supported some of the most important societies and civic institutions in the capital. When not providing direct loans to the town, the College's lawyers often invested clients' funds in purchasing annuities from the council, boosting its capacity to pay for municipal expansion. They also organised public meetings and applied pressure for the creation of improvements, particularly during the construction of the New Town. A good example occurred in 1782 when David Dalrymple (Lord Westhall) had the idea of creating a paved road from the foot of the Advocates' Close in the High Street to the New Town.[5] He claimed public support, also petitioning on behalf of those who lived between the mercat cross and the Castlehill for the building of a large 'necessary house' between the Advocates' Close and Warriston's Close, in two apartments, one for the exclusive use of 'burgesses and inhabitants of rank' and the other 'for the use of the populace'. The need to combat 'the intolerable grievance from filth and nastiness for want of a privy' is a reminder of the unhealthy conditions everyone shared in the Old Town.

Yet things were changing in the eighteenth century. A practical means of tracing the integration of College members into Edinburgh's community, while helping locate them and measure their status, is to follow developments in plumbing. The council minutes reveal that the residences of judges and lawyers were conspicuously among the first to benefit from being linked to the city's various water supplies.[6] To obtain water for a private household, it was necessary to seek the privilege of having a small water pipe (a 'by-pipe') installed, creating a link, via a major pipe, to one of the town's wells.[7] Once pipes had been connected to a number of public buildings, including the hospitals, the Tolbooth, the charity workhouse and the surgeons' hall, College members counted heavily among the private petitioners who obtained pipes branching off them.[8] From the 1740s the council minutes not only allow private residences to be identified by recording such petitions but also demonstrate the extent to which properties were being bought for rental purposes rather than private use. One wonders how much, if at all, the coach house and stable in which John Davidson WS purchased a lease from the council in 1760 differed from that in which the Earl of Leven, one of the lords of session, had a similar investment interest in 1703.[9] Charters of confirmation, also recorded in the council minutes, demonstrate the size and quality of property being purchased as the New Town developed, while showing that conveyancers in the College were every bit as important in Edinburgh's expansion as the lawyers who framed legislation for the development of local roads, bridges and the docks in Leith. Such sources clearly indicate how lawyers helped to fund the New Town's development, purchasing property from builders which they then managed and let to others either personally or on behalf of clients.

LAWYERS AND EDINBURGH IN 1694

Helen Dingwall's research into Edinburgh using the 1694 poll tax records and the hearth tax revealed much about the importance of lawyers to the fabric of the city. The upper echelons of the legal profession tended to live in the heart of the burgh, with a concentration of advocates and writers to the signet in the New Kirk parish (located broadly in the vicinity of the modern City Chambers, on the north-west of the High Street, opposite the College of Justice).[10] If professional men tended to live centrally, they did not always own property there. Advocates, such as William Brodie, are found lodging with the likes of the merchant's widow, Elizabeth Tod.[11] Writers, a large group which tended to be more widely disseminated (most were in the New Kirk, Old Kirk, Tron and Tolbooth parishes but there was also a group in Greyfriars parish), likewise quite often lodged, sometimes in the house of a WS or, like William Leggat, in property owned by an advocate (in his case, Thomas Rigg).[12] As a social group, the legal profession was active in investing in the new Bank of Scotland and in the ill-fated Darien scheme; the 1694 poll tax rates applied to them provide evidence of their high economic value.[13] Above all, they formed a critical part of the professional milieu within the town; the 179 writers (not College members) formed one of the largest single occupational groups subjected to the 1694 tax.[14] The Edinburgh evidence conforms to a discernable pattern in the early modern urban landscape. Parallels may be drawn with contemporary London where, though attorneys were spread out, there were still concentrations of them in the vicinities of the northern Inns of Court and the Guildhall.[15] Again, many of them rented lodgings because of the relatively short sittings of the courts.[16] Similarly, in Toulouse, residential patterns saw functionaries of the court, at all social and administrative levels, living as neighbours and fellow parishioners in the environs of the *Palais de Justice*.[17]

In looking at how College members integrated into Edinburgh, both formal and informal links to the rest of the community should be considered. Since there are differences within the bodies that composed the College, the early part of this chapter will look at general issues and the second will investigate links between the city and the judiciary, the bar and the writers and clerks.

STATUS AND CIVIC CONNECTIONS

An obvious indicator of College members' civic standing can be seen in formal social occasions, such as public celebrations of the monarch's birthday or other notable events. It is manifest in the list of subscribers, those 'noblemen, and other principal gentlemen of quality and citizens of Edinburgh' who on 29 October 1760 added their names to the proclamation recognising the successor to George II.[18] After a procession from Parliament House to the new Exchange, where the new king had been formally proclaimed, the subscriptions were made in the city's 'Great Assembly Room'. The 165 names included judges, such as William Grant and Robert Pringle, leading advocates such as James Ferguson of Pitfour, Robert Dundas, Thomas Miller, Michael Menzies, David Rae and David Dalrymple of Westhall, and senior writers to the signet like William Forbes, John Russell and Samuel Mitchelson (both senior and junior).[19] At least twenty-two advocates and six writers to the signet were present, as were a number of ordinary writers. This is impressive considering this occurred during the vacation of the Court of Session, and only the day after news of the king's death had reached Edinburgh, although such information would have spread quickly in legal circles.[20]

Although recognised as 'gentlemen of quality', College members were usually not natural citizens of Edinburgh. As Figure 1 (in Appendix 1) demonstrates, only 121 advocates gained the status of burgess and gild brother in the period 1700–99. Of those who did, most were honorary burgesses, recognised for good service to the community, with only a minority entitled to burgess status through family or marital background. Looked at from the perspective of College membership as a whole, more than three out of five ordinary lords of session were burgesses, with only about one in seven advocates and one in twelve writers to the signet.[21] Behind these figures lies a number of marital and family links. Archibald Campbell WS, for instance, became a burgess because his father had been made one for his services as agent for the town; so did his brothers-in-law, Ronald Dunbar WS and John Buchanan WS, by right of their wives. Dunbar also gained election as Edinburgh's law agent.

More meaningful statistics may be drawn from the dataset of those who gained their offices in the College in the period 1700–99 (see Figure 2 in Appendix 1, which excludes anyone who became a College member prior to 1700). Of the ninety-six advocates in this sample admitted as burgesses, only three were admitted by right of their wives and thirty by right of their fathers. The main conclusion to be drawn from these data is that intermarriage to gain burgess status was not a priority for College members, because it added no particular advantage to their existing privileges. It was not simply advocates and judges who joined the burgess roll; a number of their servants did so, at least prior to 1750. In the seventeenth century such men themselves often went on to become advocates, although this died out once intrant fees increased and examination in Roman law became the norm.[22] The practice of rewarding the servants of advocates with the status of burgess also gradually disappeared. John Malice, servant of James Graham of Airth (one of the town's assessors), gained that status in December 1742. The next servant so honoured (the forty-eighth, and last, of the century) was John Whittet, clerk to Lord President Ilay Campbell. Whittet, who became a burgess in 1792, was clearly a favourite of the council which elected him keeper of Parliament House in 1794.[23]

In itself the election of the keepers of Parliament House illustrates one of the many formal links between the council and the College, either imposed by statute or created through mutual agreement. Because the town owned Parliament House, the keepers of the building were, under a contract signed in June 1694, appointed jointly by the lords of session and the council.[24] The professors of Scots law and the professors of universal civil history and Greek and Roman antiquities at the university were similarly appointed by the council on the basis of a leet (a shortlist) of two names provided to them by the Faculty of Advocates.[25] The right to appoint the professors of humanity in the university belonged jointly to the town of Edinburgh, lords of session, the Faculty of Advocates and the WS Society. Elections to this office were carried out by delegation, with the town and the judges collectively having two votes and the advocates and writers as a group each holding one vote.[26] The lords of session also appointed delegates, along with one from the advocates and one from the writers, to name a bursar under a mortification made by Laurence Dundas which took effect in 1735.[27] Dundas, former professor of humanities, had named them patrons in respect of three bursaries.[28] Under a similar mortification by William III, the barons of exchequer selected a bursar in divinity from a list of three candidates supplied by the council.[29] Adam Christie DCS had also set up a trust in part to maintain a bursar at the university and, in part, to help support the 'indigent poor widows and orphans of advocates and writers'.[30] These formal links also extended to organisations based in Edinburgh that were of national significance, the appointment of which was subject to patronage controlled from London.

Examples of less formal links are many but two will serve as illustrations of their diversity: civil defence and sport. In the seventeenth century there was a troop of horse made up of College members. In 1794, with the creation of the Edinburgh Volunteers, College members were again involved. A Whig commentator described Lord President Granton, referring to his service as a young man in the Volunteers, as a man who would have been 'more in his element at the head of a regiment than of a Court'.[31] Walter Scott was also a member, as was Robert Dundas WS who, like Scott, later became a PCS.[32] As for sport, apart from a keenness to support the annual king's plate horse race at Leith Links, College members were often devotees of fishing, hunting and golf (Lord Cowper was even struck on the jaw by a golf ball in 1732).[33] This was apparent in 1800 when the Honourable Edinburgh Company of Golfers received its seal of cause (long after the council minutes first make reference to golf in Edinburgh).[34] The captain was John Gray WS and the treasurer was David Murray DCS.[35] Gray, who had been Edinburgh's law agent, served as one of the town clerks from 1786 to 1811 and was probably involved in writing a memorial to the council in 1805 to remove trespassers from the course the Company of Golfers leased at Leith Links.[36]

LAWYERS AND EDINBURGH'S BUILT ENVIRONMENT

Generations of College members influenced Edinburgh's built environment, and this created permanent associations. Elevated to the bench in 1730 as Lord Strichen, Alexander Fraser gave this name to Strichen's Close (a close previously associated with Sir George Mackenzie of Rosehaugh).[37] In 1795 the managers of the Society for the Relief of the Industrious Blind, because they were not a body corporate, requested that the lord provost and the lord advocate, and their successors in office, act as trustees to take a disposition on their behalf of 'Lord Coalston's house' in Castlehill.[38] Coalston had died nearly twenty years before but the building remained strongly associated with him. Likewise Advocates' Close, Writer's Court (where the WS Society found its first permanent home in 1696), President's Close (and President's Stairs) and Foulis Close, among other places, all bore names indicative of Edinburgh's legal past.[39] Equally permanent memorials can be found in Greyfriars' churchyard. Burial was an important aspect of status, particularly for those whose descendants were likely to maintain some link to the College.

Eighteenth-century evidence of the place of residence of College members can be found in a wide variety of sources, including personal and business correspondence. The council minutes record petitions, such as that in 1705 from the advocate James Hamilton of Olivestob requesting permission to erect a staircase from the High Street to a tenement belonging to him at the head of Warriston's Close.[40] Private letters demonstrate, for instance, that Charles Areskine of Tinwald lived in Milne's Square as early as 1718.[41] He was still there in 1752. Legal disputes can also tell us a significant amount about where and how lawyers and clerks lived. An example is a petition by Robert Reid WS in August 1761.[42] Reid lived in Geddes Close. A neighbouring house, owned by the saddler Patrick Crichton, became empty when the tenant removed at Whit Sunday 1758 and Reid was left the key so that he might show round prospective tenants. The property remained empty and, in the late summer, Crichton offered to sell it to Reid who decided to purchase it, intending to 'throw two Rooms of it into his own house' and let the remainder to a tenant. The dispute related to the price and whether a valuation given by third parties was binding. Another case from 1767, involving a complaint to the dean of gild, concerned damage to cellars in the Cowgate fronting the foot of Marlin's Wynd owned by William Wemyss WS.[43] Wemyss alleged that the damage was caused by David Campbell WS, and the architect John Adam, engaging in the typical Edinburgh practice of throwing dirty water and filth from the windows of their houses on to the roof of the cellar.

Legal papers sometimes reveal transient circumstances. In one case, for instance, we learn that Mrs Jean Shaw, an elderly widow, took in as lodgers members of the Faculty of Advocates. Indeed, the advocate George Clerk lived and died in her house.[44] Other types of record also shed light, such as the account submitted by the painter Nicol Somerville for whitewashing the lodgings of Hugh Forbes PCS in the Lawnmarket.[45] Hugh evidently favoured white: between 1756 and 1758 he had the pantry, the 'Big Dineing room' and both bedrooms given the same treatment. The personal accounts of Thomas Tod WS provide some insight into his standard of living. In July 1755, for instance, he records how much he had spent on carpets as well as on everyday items such as a kettle, sugar tongs and a clock.[46] The quality of housing in Edinburgh was improving, and the fact that advocates could afford to live in better accommodation has been suggested as a possible reason why, as a group, they lived longer in the eighteenth century than they had done during the seventeenth.[47]

By the latter half of the eighteenth century early postal directories begin to permit systematic analysis of where lawyers lived. Peter Williamson's *Directory for the City of Edinburgh* (1773) contains the names of 182 men under the designation 'advocate' of whom 144 have an address listed. The most popular addresses were James' Court (eleven advocates), St Andrew's Square (seven), Brown's Square (seven), George Square (six) and Carruber's Close (six).[48] The Canongate also remained popular, with eight advocates living there, and the majority of the legal profession had not yet been enticed to the New Town. Some advocates had addresses only in the country, including the clerk to the bills, Robert Anstruther, who lived as far away as Rothiemay in Morayshire (the work of his office being carried on by a depute). Alexander Leith lodged with George Buchan-Hepburn, his fellow advocate, in James' Court, while a number of College members still lived in their fathers' houses. Thomas Baillie WS lived in James' Court, as did his son, the advocate William; Alexander Murray lived there, too, probably along with his aged father Archibald (both were at the bar); while

William Law of Elvington and his son Alexander, also both advocates, lived at the head of Chalmer's Close.

It is not always safe to assume that people at a similar address lived together or were necessarily related. George and Adam Ogilvy, for instance, contemporaries at the bar, both lived in Carrubber's Close but one was from Aberdeen while the other was from Selkirkshire and there is no obvious family relationship. Judges' sons who practised at the bar may have gained a particular advantage by living with their fathers. After eight years at the bar, Charles Brown still lived with his father Lord Coalston on Castlehill; James Ferguson, who had been an advocate for twice as long as Brown, lived with his father, Lord Pitfour, at the Luckenbooths.

Addresses are given for forty-four of the sixty-one advocates' first clerks listed in the directory. Six clerks were listed whose masters were not in the directory at all: presumably the latter were to be contacted through their clerks. In general, clerks and their masters had different addresses, although James Boswell and his clerk, Matthew Dickie, were both to be found in James' Court, James Grant and his clerk, Charles McIntosh, were both in the Post-house Stairs, and David Dalrymple and his clerk, Alexander Mason, were both in Advocates' Close (which, in total, housed five advocates and two advocates' clerks).

The *Directory of Edinburgh in 1752*, compiled by James Gilhooley, is an admirable piece of detective work based largely on annuity and window tax records. The data which he has compiled record the addresses of only nineteen members of the Faculty of Advocates (not including Alexander Lockhart of Craighouse, whose address is included but whose occupation is not given). A further twenty-three men are named who might possibly be identified with advocates; in some cases, this is certain or virtually so, such as Robert Dundas of Arniston, George Brown of Coalston, Andrew McDouall, William Wallace and Archibald Murray. Brown, McDouall, and Wallace, if indeed they were the advocates of the same name, lived in James' Court in the Lawnmarket near to the solicitor general, Patrick Haldane. Brown lived in Byre's Close opposite the Tolbooth and near to the advocate and town clerk Joseph Williamson. Archibald Murray of Cringeltie certainly lived in James' Court in 1773 and is likely to be the same man recorded as doing so in 1752; like Alexander Boswell, who was resident in Parliament Close, he saw no need to move in the intervening twenty years. Robert McQueen, on the other hand, lived (perhaps lodged) in Covenent Close in 1752 but, by 1773, he had moved to his own house in George Square. Likewise, James Burnett, while an advocate, had lived in Writer's Court in 1752 but had then moved to a house he purchased in St John's Street in the Canongate.

Comparison of the lists from 1752 and 1773 suggests that it was not unusual for lawyers to change address. Only two writers to the signet, for instance, remained at the same address for their entire careers. Antony Barclay and John Buchan both lived and worked in James' Court, the former for forty-two years and the latter for over half a century.[49] Moving address in itself was a serious undertaking for lawyers, and even the best of them were prone to mislaying documents on such occasions.[50] In late April 1725, George Robertson, in the process of moving from Gavinlock's Land in Forrester Wynd west along the High Street to Bank Close, admitted to Mungo Graeme that it would be 'some few days befor I can get my papers and things in order'.[51] Three days later, he acknowledged that he was still 'busied in flitting and not yet fully setled'.[52]

The bulk of lawyers in the 1750s still resided in the vicinity of the court, particularly in the Lawnmarket, Writers' Court and Parliament Close. As time went by, College members began to disperse to the south where Edinburgh had expanded into more spacious developments, such as Alison Square and Argyle Square (both created in the 1730s), Nicolson Street and Potterow, before later penetrating into the New Town. The more expensive, healthier and less densely packed accommodation to the south of the High Street, even if this was at some distance from the vicinity of the court, proved attractive.

The New Town offered the possibility of larger and more opulent houses than the cramped conditions of the Old Town and, in his classic study of Edinburgh, Youngson noted a considerable migration there between the early 1770s and the late 1780s.[53] That College members were at the forefront of this is clear from charters narrated in the council minutes. For instance, the advocate Edward McCormick and his wife acquired a house in Hanover Street in 1790 which consisted of two storeys, the 'uppermost and attick storys', containing eight rooms and a kitchen.[54] Robert Ross WS had six rooms, a closet and kitchen in his George Street house.[55] Grander still were the house, stables and coach house acquired by Professor David Hume in St Andrew's Square in 1787.[56] In 1793 the president's new house in Park Place had four storeys and a garden, stables, coach house and offices.[57] George Fergusson's house, acquired on the north side of Princes Street in 1782, contained two storeys; Kenneth Mackenzie WS bought a dwelling house with two storeys above it on North Castle Street in 1797.[58] Chief Baron Ord, though not a member of the College, owned a house in Queen Street and entered a fifteen-year lease of land in Bearford's Parks in 1771 in order to pasture his horses and cows.[59] The mason Robert Burn seems to have done particularly good business with College members. This included selling a house on Princes Street to the dean of Faculty, Henry Erskine, in 1791 and one on Queen Street to Alexander Ross DCS two years later.[60]

COLLEGE MEMBERS AT PARISH LEVEL

It is impossible to discuss at length the important subject of the prominence of College members in the pews of Edinburgh's churches. Yet the subject merits attention because where one sat in church reflected one's prosperity and social status.[61] Many College members regarded themselves as among the elite of Edinburgh society, a status that brought with it both social attention and a degree of responsibility. After all, Lord Dun had advised his fellow judge to 'shew himself a pattern to all, by living in a strict observance of his duty to God, in the constant practice of all acts of worship'.[62]

The picture of advocates and writers to the signet living cheek by jowl in the precincts of the court where they worked is confirmed by the fact that, for much of the century, they can be found renting seats in churches in the Edinburgh's central parishes. The migration to the modern districts to the south of the High Street, such as George Square, and then north to the New Town, can be traced through corresponding changes in pew rentals. According to Robert Chambers, the advocate Alexander Wight, who lived in St Andrew's Square, could afford to buy land on Princes Street, and construct a building there with a low roof, merely to prevent any higher building being constructed. Thus, did he preserve his view to the clock on St Giles, by which he timed his journey to the court.[63] In 1780 he also got himself a seat in the College Kirk, the most convenient available church for the New Town.[64]

Charles Melville, a young man from Perth making his first visit to Edinburgh in 1781, identifies why lawyers were migrating south from the central parishes. The houses in George Square, where the lodgings of the Duke of Argyll, the Countess of Gordon and the lord advocate were to be found (and, he might have added, the homes of Lords Braxfield and Stonefield, and Walter Scott WS), were the 'quintessence of finery', with the square built upon a plan 'so grand that I have not words to express it'.[65] In the same year the council had allowed a new church to be built in the extended royalty because the nine established churches could not accommodate Edinburgh's growing population. Since the extension of the royalty, 'a great number of Familys of distinction' had resided in the New Town and had difficulty being accommodated in the existing churches.[66]

Access to Edinburgh's churches had originally been free. Once seats were put in, access was circumscribed and, as Norrie put it, even the right of admission became 'a branch of Magisterial patronage'.[67] A council committee distributed the seats, approved the level of rents and employed a collector of seat rents. The distribution was subject to a limiting principle to ensure that all social ranks, including the poor, enjoyed access to churches for Sunday worship.[68] Seating plans, in the council minutes, indicate the different rental values attached to the seats and sometimes name the current possessors.[69] The value of a pew rental reflected the position and dimensions of the pew; this was the basis upon which the seats in the Tron kirk were revalued in 1744 to bring them more into line with seats of a comparable size in other churches.[70] There was a difference between obtaining a half share in a seat, or a quarter share of one as Donald Stewart WS did in the Tron kirk in 1775, and a more spacious loft or gallery.[71] Even something described as a 'seat' might have room for nine or ten persons.[72] A loft in the New Kirk, possessed by the recently deceased Lord Alemoor (Andrew Pringle), was sought in 1776 by his fellow judge, Lord Alva, whose petition for it narrated that he had been 'called by duty of office to attend divine service in St Giles'.[73] It was large enough to seat him, his family and Miss Pringle (presumably Alemoor's daughter) until she could be otherwise provided for.

Despite the council's obligation to provide private seats to representatives of all sections of the community, money and status helped in securing the best seats for members of Edinburgh's congregations. In 1726, for instance, a pecking order of sorts can be seen in the report of a council committee that had visited newly repaired seats in the Tron kirk.[74] At the highest rates of rental were Lord Minto (£22 Scots) and the solicitor general, Charles Areskine (£18 Scots). As well as being lawyers, both were from leading families and both had positions next to what is called 'the elder's seat', an honoured position free from rent, suggesting they had been placed in terms of social precedence. Below them in value were seats rented by the advocates Alexander Belsches (£14 Scots) and James Craig (£13 Scots) and the writer Robert Wallace (£12 Scots). A revised rental in the same church was made in November 1744 because some seats were thought undervalued compared to 'other Seats of the like Dimensions in the other churches of this City'.[75] This provides a list of the values of 126 seats and shows that the seat next to the elder's seat remained, at £22, the most expensive while the Marquis of Tweeddale's seat cost £20; the least expensive rental was £3 and the average rental value was just over £10 (all values still being in Scots money).[76]

Many College members rented seats privately for their families, and the same seat was often held successively by different members. In 1736, for instance, Lord Haining held a seat in the new North Church (Haddo's Hold), one of the three churches, each with its own parish, in St Giles.[77] This had formerly been possessed by Archibald Murray, advocate. In 1730, soon after his elevation to the bench, Haining had held another seat in the same church and he was still in that church at his death when his widow, and his son Andrew, were allowed to take over his seat rental.[78] There are many similar examples. The advocate James Baillie, for instance, took over the seat of David Home DCS in the Tron kirk in 1720.[79] In 1745, William Grant took a seat from a fellow advocate in the same church while, a year earlier, the advocate James Graham and Thomas Baillie WS had jointly taken possession of a seat in the New Kirk.[80] In contrast, some seats remained in the same family for a considerable period. The advocate Robert Pringle successfully petitioned, following his mother's death in 1754, to have a seat in the Tron kirk put into his name because Pringles had held it for years and 'his sister with his wife & family always sitt there'.[81] After his elevation to the bench, he moved to the College church which he attended until his death, with his colleague, Lord Stonefield, taking over his seat in 1764.[82]

The impression from the petitions preserved in the council's minute books is that College members long continued to prefer the central parishes of the city in the environs of the court. Individuals did move from one church to another. Lord Elchies, for instance, normally worshipped in Lady Yester's church in 1736 but, by 1749, had moved to the Tron kirk where he remained until he died; his friend Lord Milton, on the other hand, can be found in the Tron kirk both in 1727 and 1736, while the advocate Joseph Williamson attended the Tolbooth kirk throughout the 1740s.[83] Andrew Macdouall was perhaps typical. As an advocate, he is found in the Tron kirk in 1723; in 1749, he gained the whole of a seat having possessed half of one and, when he died in 1760 with the judicial title Lord Bankton, his widow, Helen Grant, kept his seat in the same church.[84] Judges, writers and advocates can be found in most of the churches although particular concentrations appear in the Tron kirk and, especially later in the century, Lady Yester's church. Seven petitions by two principal and five depute clerks of session, spanning the years from 1720 to 1775, involve six different churches.[85] When they were not taking over the seats of other College members, they were swapping places with lairds, merchants, the lesser nobility, councillors and former magistrates. If the council was agreeable, private arrangements for seating might be rubber stamped (despite an attempt to restrain this in 1749).[86] The Marchioness Dowager of Lothian, for instance, resigned her seat in the High church (in the Choir of St Giles) in favour of the advocate James Boswell in 1784.[87] He had, typically, identified that it was no disadvantage for a lawyer to be rubbing shoulders with the aristocracy in church. Boswell's journals reveal him to have attended a variety of churches in Edinburgh, some Sundays remaining there for two sermons, taking dinner in between.[88]

Parts of churches might be set aside for the use of civic bodies to project 'the image of a socially united town at worship'.[89] The council minutes refer in 1736 to Treasurer Young being ordered to purchase a carpet for the 'Lords of Sessions seat' in the New Kirk, which, at that time, housed the burgh elite.[90] A loft had been maintained there for the use of the lords of session since at least 1662 and it appears in a rental in 1723 with no rent assigned to it.[91] That rent-free status did not last. On 11 January 1758 the council, owing to the annual maintenance costs of Edinburgh's churches, resolved that in future no one should be excused the payment of seat rent except the ministers.[92] Two days later the judges set up a committee, consisting of themselves, the lord advocate and the solicitors-general, to inquire into the privilege of having seats rent free.[93] Their arguments did not impress the council which confirmed its decision in March, although this may not have ended the matter.[94] A month later, the city's solicitor borrowed records from the city's charter house to help him 'ascertain the points in issue betwixt the City and the Lords of Session in relation to the seats & pews possest by them in the several churches'.[95] Unfortunately, there seems to be no further discussion of the matter.

During his visit in 1781, Charles Melville was informed that the New Kirk was where 'all the Magistrates Lords of Session nobility gentry & people of distinction go to'.[96] He described this white-ceilinged church, its pulpit covered in crimson velvet fringed with gold, as the venue for ceremonial occasions. Formal events often involved collective acts of worship and remembrance, notably the ceremony on 5 November when the lords went to 'church in thir gownes to thare sermon in commemoration of the delyverance from the Gunpowder treasone'.[97] As well as housing the judges' communal loft, pews in that church were rented privately for family use. In 1737 Lord Kilkerran was allocated the private seat in that church which had been possessed, until his death, by Hew Dalrymple, lord president.[98] Both Baron Dalrymple and Lord Kennet are known to have had seats there in 1744 and 1769 respectively.[99] The council minutes record payment for a cushion for the new president's seat in the kirk in 1761.[100] Since this church was used by the luminaries of the legal profession, it was only a matter of time before advocates sought places in a church where they could be noticed. It is notable that no advocates appear in the 1723 New church rental, although it is known that the former solicitor general, Sir Patrick Home, had rented a seat there in 1722.[101] That may explain why up-and-coming advocates, such as Alexander Garden of Troup in 1729 and James Veitch and Alexander Boswell in the 1740s, obtained seats there; so did the influential WS, Alexander McMillan.[102] It would likewise have drawn attention when Archibald Stewart WS obtained the seat there formerly possessed by the late provost, James Coutts.[103]

CHURCH DISCIPLINE AND PRACTICE

Since the sixteenth century, advocates, including notable figures such as Thomas Craig and Edward Henryson, had acted as procurators for the

Church. They had their counterparts in William Grant in the 1730s, Joseph Williamson in the 1740s and David Dalrymple of Westhall in the 1750s and 1760s.[104] Principal William Robertson's son, a relatively young advocate also called William, held the same office in 1791.[105] The procurator acted in conjunction with a private prosecutor (normally an individual minister, a presbytery or a factor acting for several presbyteries). It was a useful office to have. One of the later procurators, John Connell, perhaps on account of it, enjoyed a substantial practice in the Teind Court giving him, as the senior judges put it in 1813, an 'insight into the Law of Tythes, which with us is a very intricate business'.[106] Litigation, however, did not always relate to financial matters, such as ministers' stipends and parish revenues. In 1766, for instance, David Dalrymple was involved in prosecuting a case against an Orkney minister accused of fornication, the issue being whether witnesses might be compellable on a warrant to give evidence to commissioners named by the General Assembly.[107] Advocates also derived benefit from holding less prominent legal offices, such as that of the king's solicitor for the late bishops' tithes (granted to George Douglas, advocate, in 1723 and later held by John Swinton).[108]

College members were also active within the Church as elders, although the extent of these activities is less obvious. According to a legal argument put forward by the advocate George Wallace, the elders in Edinburgh's churches comprised:

> ... Gentlemen of the best Education, Substance and Characters in the city; Judges of the Court of Session, Members of the Faculty of Advocates, Clerks to his Majesty's Signet; Physicians of great Name, Professors in the University, Merchants of the most extensive Trade, and the most distinguished Tradesmen in the Place.[109]

These he contrasted to the members of the town council (themselves largely merchants and tradesmen) who followed professions 'such as seldom are found to agree with Learning', arguing that the burgh constitution properly required the ministers and elders to be involved as a counterbalance to the town council in selecting ministers to vacant church livings within Edinburgh. This had been the customary position since 1689: new ministers were selected by the council, together with elders drawn from the kirk sessions plus the fifteen remaining ministers (collectively known as the 'General Sessions' of Edinburgh). The context of Wallace's argument was the attempt by Moderates within the Church to 'manage' the town council politically into sidelining the General Sessions when filling a vacancy in Lady Yester's church in 1762.[110]

Wallace's description of the elders did not reflect reality. He mentioned College members first but, in the list of those comprising the General

Sessions published in 1763, only two of the fifty-four elders, the advocate 'good honest plain Joseph' Williamson and James Graham WS, held that status.[111] An examination of the general kirk session lists for the period 1701–20 also presents a slightly different picture (see Figure 3 in Appendix 1). Each year six elders and six deacons were elected for each parish (and throughout this sample period Edinburgh had eight parishes). No lords of session were elders but other categories of College member were well represented in certain parishes (principally the New church, the Tron church, the Old church and Haddo's Hold). This reflected their residence in the central parishes. They were, however, significantly outnumbered as elders by ordinary writers. Moreover, compared with College members, writers tended to act as elders for longer. The longest-serving advocate was Gilbert Burnet who served as an elder on five occasions, first in the Tolbooth kirk parish in 1710, then in the New church parish in 1713 and, from 1717 to 1719, in the parish of the Tron kirk. Three writers to the signet served for as long as this or longer: James Baillie (ten years in two parishes), James Brisbane (six years as an elder of Haddo's Hold parish church), and John Russell (five years in Tron parish). Ordinary writers tended to serve longer still, however. Perhaps the most telling statistic from the data in this sample is that ten of the seventeen advocates who served as elders did so for only one year, whereas nine out of eleven writers to the signet and sixteen out of twenty-one writers served for longer.

College members were subject to the kirk session's parochial discipline no less than anyone else and they were not exempt from cases of scandal. The advocate William Copland, for instance, was assoilzied by the lord ordinary in a paternity action brought by his former housekeeper only because the gestation period, eleven months, was too long for him to be the father.[112] An interesting and suggestive case arose in 1712. On 16 September a servant girl, Janet Robertson, confessed to having committed fornication in her mother's house with Charles Menzies of Kinmundy WS. This had resulted in pregnancy. She was rebuked, ordered to attend the ministers for religious instruction, and told to inform the kirk session when Menzies returned to town.[113] The case dragged on, Menzies admitted his guilt privately but proved contumacious. At one stage, in March 1714, he was described as having been 'obldiged to go out of the way because of his bad circumstances'.[114] Interestingly, the kirk session, in April 1713, had even deputed one of its number, James Baillie WS, to speak privately to Menzies. Did professional solidarity keep him free from public condemnation (proceedings against him were eventually dropped) in return for his agreement to maintain Robertson and the child financially?

THE INTELLECTUAL AND CULTURAL MILIEU

The sources readily reveal, at least in numerical terms, the level of engagement College members had in Edinburgh's philosophical clubs and societies. It is much more difficult to assess the weight of their combined contribution to Edinburgh's intellectual flowering during the Enlightenment. Some individuals do stand out, chief among them, in terms of breadth of engagement, was undoubtedly Lord Kames.[115]

It was Kames who contributed to the important volume of *Essays* published by the Philosophical Society in 1754, at a time when Edinburgh's medical society had been attempting to reach out to other learned professions and expand its philosophical activities beyond the sphere of science and medicine.[116] There is a clear intellectual progression from this publication to the formation of the Royal Society of Edinburgh in 1783. Along the way, several clubs and societies were formed which met regularly for discussion and intellectual debate. A summary of what can be gleaned from published sources of the level of membership among lawyers, clerks and other College members, in five such societies, going back to the Rankenian Club (founded in 1716), is provided in Figure 4 (Appendix 1).

The men who attended these groups were not merely engaged in idle debate. As Roger Emerson noted in his study of the Select Society, its members were men who regarded civil society as being in need of leadership which they personally felt well placed to provide.[117] The minutes of that society demonstrate the practical questions that were debated, on social and political themes, alongside more aesthetic topics. Equally interesting is what is left out. In some cases, topics were left undiscussed that might all too easily have been encountered in the courtroom. For example, Emerson refers to the question of whether 'the laws of Scotland in relating to Coalliers and Salters promote the interest of this country?'[118] Why was discussion of this avoided? A generation before, judges had been asked the question whether it was lawful for one man to assign colliers to another.[119] Debate free from party or faction was a valuable commodity, and discussion did turn regularly to issues of wider legal policy such as the introduction of civil jury trials and the removal of entails.[120]

College members are prevalent in the list of members (preserved by the advocate George Wallace) of the pioneering Rankenian Club, founded in 1717. Wallace's father, minister of the new North kirk, had been a founding member and he himself had joined. The list contains twenty-three names, a small enough group for a club that existed for over fifty years until wound up in 1771.[121] It includes the names of eight advocates but no other College members. Of these, three, who joined by invitation, probably in the late 1750s, were sons of deceased members; perhaps only Alexander Murray had been a founder member, and the most successful of them professionally, Alexander Boswell, was not admitted to the bar until 1729.

George Wallace, also a leading light of the Select Society, was a member of the Royal Society of Edinburgh. John MacLaurin was in both the Rankenian Club and the Royal Society. The most clubbable advocate in eighteenth-century Scotland, however, was Andrew Crosbie (reputedly Scott's inspiration for the character of Paulus Pleydell in *Guy Mannering*).[122] Although never a Rankenian, Crosbie was a member of the Poker Club, the Select Society, the Philosophical Society and the Royal Society of Edinburgh.[123] Indeed, he was jocularly selected the Assassin of the Poker Club, should such be needed, with the philosopher David Hume his assessor, 'without whose assent nothing should be done', to reduce the prospect of murder.[124] Six advocates were among the forty-six founding members of the Philosophical Society in 1737.[125] By 1790 no less than 108 advocates, and six writers to the signet, were members of one, and sometimes of more than one, of these five organisations (see Appendix 1, Figure 3). These were often prominent figures, with thirty-one of the advocates becoming lords of session and a further six being appointed barons of exchequer. Yet, in the Select Society, only sixty-two of the eighty-two advocates proposed for membership were actually admitted, and some leading writers to the signet were also rejected. The rejects included successful lawyers, such as John Russell WS, John Mackenzie of Delvine WS, and the advocates Joseph Williamson and (much to his indignation) John MacLaurin.[126] On a single day in 1755 two future judges, Robert Craigie and James Veitch of Elliock, were both rejected. The latter perhaps gained revenge by becoming a founder member of the Royal Society; he was certainly very active as an office-bearer in its early years.

In fact, forty-three of the first 112 resident members of the Royal Society were College members though some were there *ex officio* and not because of their personal attributes.[127] As with membership of other societies, the balance in terms of College members was overwhelmingly in favour of the bar. Indeed, this underlines the respective standing of the bar and the bench, on one hand, and the lower-status profession of writer on the other. No less than seventeen of the advocates in the Royal Society were, or became, lords of session and three were, or became, barons of exchequer.[128] By June 1788 the late president (Arniston), the current president (Glenlee) and those destined to be the next three presidents (Succoth, Avonton and Granton) had been, or were, members of the Royal Society, and lawyers easily out-numbered any other professional group.[129] This dominance is reflected in the names of those appointed as general office-bearers in the Society's early years: Henry Dundas was vice president from 1783 (although he took little active part); Ilay Campbell was president of the literary class that year along with William Robertson and Hugh Blair, with Alexander Fraser Tytler appointed secretary.[130] Dundas and Tytler were still in office in 1789 and, in that year, Lord Dunsinnan was the other vice president; Lord Dreghorn, Lord Elliock, George Fergusson and Sir William Miller were all appointed to the twelve-man council, rubbing shoulders with men like the geologist James Hutton and the mathematician James Gregory.[131]

It can be difficult to gain a sense of the level of intellectual engagement by lawyers in the debates and concerns of contemporary Scotland. Because they became members of the Royal Society often simply because they ranked among the legal elite, this did not entitle them to a place among Edinburgh's literati. The best lawyers may have regarded themselves as too preoccupied to engage in literary pursuits of their own though some, most notably Kames, Monboddo and Hailes, certainly showed the way. Lawyers who published naturally tended to write about the law and this is largely true of men like George Wallace, Alexander Wight and John Millar. On the other hand, Hugo Arnot, James Boswell, John MacLaurin, and, of course, Walter Scott, were much more engaged in the literary scene. They made full use of the growing Advocates Library (the venue for meetings of the Select Society), and the keepers of that library, particularly David Hume (a great friend of the professor of philosophy, advocate and judge, Charles Areskine), were fully part of the wider literate culture.[132] Thomas Ruddiman, though not a debater, was involved in a rival club to the Rankenians which attracted the mischievous interest of young lawyers.[133] It is only natural to find connections between lawyers and men of letters because the written pleadings demanded of practising advocates give ample proof that the best of them were men of wide knowledge, literary, historical and scientific. For them, all knowledge was potentially useful and in the session papers they gave full vent to their passion for history and moral philosophy. Along with the liberal education which prepared them for the bar, this explains their propensity to engage intellectually with the fashion for literary and philosophical clubs and societies which were inspired by, and did so much to contribute to, the Enlightenment.

A glance at an advocate's library reveals a broad range of literary interests. In the diary he kept of books he had read, the young John Erskine, prior to his admission to the bar in 1781, listed books by Voltaire, Rousseau, Hume, Smith, Lords Hailes and Kames, alongside Burlamaqui's *Principles of Natural Law* (presumably the 1752 edition in English) and Halhed's recently published *A Code of Gentoo Laws* (1776).[134] As well as books on travel and geography, he had read works on Roman history (including Gibbon) and music, Goethe's novel *The Sorrows of Young Werter*, as well as Edmund Burke's *Philosophical Enquiry into the Origin of our Ideas of the Sublime and Beautiful* (1757) and William Hogarth's *The Analysis of*

Beauty (1753). The Advocates Library itself, though Sir George Mackenzie at its inauguration had advised filling it with law books and not works 'dealing with irrelevant subjects', had grown into a more general scholarly library during the eighteenth century.[135]

As well as through learned societies, lawyers contributed to Edinburgh's culture in more modest ways. Hugo Arnot's *History of Edinburgh* was a considerable scholarly achievement. Less remarkable was another advocate, David Fearn, who was in 1709 given permission by the town council to print the *Scots Postman* every Tuesday, Thursday and Saturday, on which days he had a monopoly on the printing of news in the town.[136] The nature of legal practice, involving the printing of multiple copies of pleadings, led to strong links between the bar and Edinburgh's printers and booksellers. Lawyers, of course, were prevalent among the customers of such firms as Hamilton and Balfour and Bell and Bradfute.[137] There were also family connections. The prominent JP, John Davidson WS, was the son of an Edinburgh bookseller.[138] Lawyers were also strongly interested in music and could count among their ranks some minor composers, such as Alexander Bayne, and members of the Musical Society of Edinburgh.[139] Advocates showed their interest by subscribing to the three-volume *Select Collection*, published by the Edinburgh-based Italian musician Domenico Corri, in 1779.[140]

Such interests may also be reflected in investments made by College members in theatres, particularly the Canongate Theatre and its successor, the Theatre Royal. It was because of the complex financial management of the Canongate Theatre after 1751 that it ended up in the ownership largely of members of the College of Justice. The theatre was conveyed to certain creditors in security of debts which its manager, John Lee, proved unable to pay. Hugo Arnot discusses this litigation and also mentions later actions that arose after the theatre was demolished during a riot.[141] The latter cases were dropped given that so many of the 'proprietors were since raised to the bench; hardly a quorum remained to decide the questions.'[142] Arnot does not name those 'of the long robe' caught up in the quarrel, but the session papers survive.[143] Among the owners of the theatre in 1767 were, on the bench, Thomas Miller of Barskimming, lord justice clerk, Lords Alemoor, Elliock and Monboddo; and, at the bar, David Moncreiffe, David Ross, John Dalrymple, Patrick Home, David Kennedy, and George Morison. It is worth noting that all of these men had belonged to the Select Society, with the exception of Elliock and Moncreiffe (both rejected as candidates for membership). Lawyers, of course, did occasionally have actors and musicians for clients but that is generally more indicative of an interest in the law of diligence than in musical theatre.[144]

CONCLUSION

While the College of Justice formed its own community within Edinburgh, it did not exist in a vacuum nor was it unaffected by the great changes that occurred between 1687 and 1808. Throughout that period lawyers made their presence felt intellectually, financially and physically. So ubiquitous were they, that it would have been possible in this chapter to analyse the contribution of lawyers to any number of areas of life, from freemasonry, to the early history of the Edinburgh hospitals, to the banking sector. Leading members of the College were involved in the affairs of the commission for disposing of the Equivalent, and a number of judges, clerks of session and advocates, not least Patrick Campbell of Monzie, Duncan Forbes and Andrew Fletcher, were even directors of banks.[145] Banking provided an element of patronage for those with political ties, particularly in the orbit of the Earl of Ilay. Any discussion of this, however, would run directly into political history and would reveal where the real political power lay: London, not Edinburgh.

John Shaw has referred to 'the mythology of the Edinburgh lawyers' importance in Scottish civil life'.[146] He is correct in terms of the wider politics, because College members were usually mere pawns in a system ultimately controlled from London. Appointments to banks, commissions for improvement, or to take one of Shaw's examples, the Board of Trustees for Manufactures, were strongly political. Six of the ten 'lawyers' on the Board of Trustees in 1749, for instance, were affiliates of the great political manager, Ilay (by then 3rd Duke of Argyll).[147] This was a context in which ability at the bar, or lack of it, counted for less than social position and political influence. It would indeed be wrong, therefore, to look to College members, even Lord Milton, Ilay's agent in Edinburgh, as in any sense political masters.

Although this chapter makes no attempt to discuss political history, this is a dimension in the relationship between the College and the town of Edinburgh which must always be understood.[148] Even outside the sphere of patronage and politics, a great deal can still be said about the importance of lawyers in the promotion of public works and the improvements that transformed the landscape of Edinburgh in the eighteenth century. Take, for instance, Robert Craigie's role as one of the commissioners for public improvement in the city from December 1752.[149] A mere month after his appointment, he had drafted a parliamentary bill permitting the compulsory purchases that would create space for 'erecting an exchange at the Cross' (the building that eventually became the Royal Exchange, now the City Chambers).[150] He was also involved in giving a legal opinion on how best the council might grant security to the Royal Bank of Scotland for a loan of £10,000 sterling to carry on public works.[151] This appointment lapsed when Craigie became lord president of the Court of Session in 1754. However, He was soon reappointed as commissioner as replacement for the late president, Lord Arniston.[152] After his death, Craigie, and his erstwhile colleague, the late baxter William Keir, were replaced by Lord Elliock SCJ and the ubiquitous Joseph Williamson, elected by the council as 'commissioners and trustees for carrying on the publick buildings and Improvements in this city'.[153]

The main commissioners under the Improvement Act, 1775 were again drawn heavily from College members, including the lord advocate Henry Dundas and Lord Braxfield.[154] Even if it usually stemmed from government patronage, there was a strong element of continuity in the involvement of lawyers in advancing the agenda of urban improvement in Edinburgh. As we have already seen, this agenda was sometimes taken forward on private initiative. James Erskine, Lord Barjarg, petitioned in 1763 for a public street to be built east from Candlemaker Row to allow access to the new buildings erected in the wake of the development of Argyll Square.[155] This would ease the prospect of obstructions in the Cowgate for traffic travelling east to west through the city. As owner of a house in Argyll Square, Erskine had since 1756 become involved in a complex plan to create this new passage; the council eventually approved of the legal arrangements he had proposed and indemnified him in regard to expenditure already made. The whole exercise involved Erskine 'in many meetings with the different members of the Councill especially those of the Committee of the Works'.[156] Not to be outdone, Lord Kames produced a proposal for building a passage north from the Nor' Loch. Recognising the progress Edinburgh had made in erecting new buildings, but that the areas to the south would soon be filled with houses, he strongly supported the city's advance northward.[157]

This chapter began by mentioning the fact that many prominent College members became vassals of the town council, appearing in the council minutes as petitioners for charters of confirmation to complete their infeftment. Lord Elchies, for instance, did so when he purchased a coach house and stable at the Cowgate port from the Earl of March and Ruglen in 1754.[158] The contribution of such men to the community was not unappreciated. The council was highly accommodating to the advocate Thomas Hope in 1749 when he wanted to build a gravel path through Hope Park.[159] Likewise, in 1757, the council generously agreed to assess the value of the composition payable by George Carre (Lord Nisbet), for a ruined tenement he had purchased thirty years earlier, on the basis of the 1727 value, rather than the current value.[160] The valuation reflected the fact that Carre had cleared the ground and built an attractive new house on the site.

Finally, it is important not to forget that Parliament House, the very hub of the College of Justice, belonged to the town council. Although the judges were not quite formal tenants (no rent was paid), it was the council that instructed repairs and improvements to the fabric of the building. There are regular examples of this in the council minutes, from the creation of a new judicial robing room in 1762 to frequent roof repairs and painting (the walls of the Inner House, for instance, were to be painted olive green in 1787).[161] In 1774 Bailie McQueen stopped the rain dripping through 'a small failure in the roof of the outer parliament house' by a timely repair.[162] Two years earlier, a far more serious risk was discovered. As the record put it, the lord president was informed:

> ... that a quantity of oil and other combustibles were lodged in the lumber room below the outer session house which the servants of the Town of Edinburgh could only come into with lighted candles as the room is of itself quite dark; and, in case of any accidental misfortune happening by fire, the advocates Library, public records and whole fabric of the session house, are in danger of being burnt.[163]

This called for an urgent meeting between members of the bench and the council. Co-operation of this kind did much to make the provision of justice in the central court run more smoothly. The next chapter will focus on those College members with particularly strong links to the town council. These were the men who lent their professional expertise to the administration of Edinburgh's affairs.

NOTES

1. ALSP, *Information for the Colledge of Justice against the town of Edinburgh*, n.d., Forbes collection, vol. 3, p. 4 (fo. 3456).
2. R. Chambers, *Traditions of Edinburgh* (Edinburgh, 1912), p. 96.
3. NLS, Erskine-Murray, MS 5076, fo. 18r.
4. C. B. Watson, ed., *Roll of Edinburgh Burgesses and Gild-Brethren 1701–1760* (Edinburgh, 1930); ibid., *Roll of Edinburgh Burgesses and Gild-Brethren 1761–1841* (Edinburgh, 1933).
5. TCM, SL1/1/102, fos 110–17.
6. Edinburgh had always had problems securing sufficient water. See M. Cosh, *Edinburgh: The Golden Age* (Edinburgh, 2003), p. 120; R. Houston, 'Fire and Filth: Edinburgh's environment, 1660–1760', 3 (1994) *Book of the Old Edinburgh Club*, pp. 30–1.
7. H. Arnot, *History of Edinburgh* (Edinburgh, 1779), p. 343.
8. TCM, SL1/1/65, fo 137–9.
9. Ibid., SL1/1/76, fos 90–2, 102; SL1/1/37, fo. 507.
10. H. Dingwall, 'The social and economic structure of Edinburgh in the late

seventeenth century' (2 vols, PhD thesis, University of Edinburgh, 1989), I, p. 48.

11. Ibid., I, p. 69.

12. Ibid., I, pp. 69, 126, 295; for Leggat, see NRS, RH15/136 (discharges, 1697, 1698).

13. Dingwall. 'Social and economic structure', II, p. 435.

14. Ibid., I, p. 336.

15. J. M. B. Alexander, 'The Economic and Social Structure of the City of London, *c.*1700' (PhD thesis, London School of Economics, 1989), p. 230.

16. Ibid, p. 231.

17. Berlanstein, *Barristers of Toulouse*, p. 29.

18. TCM, SL1/1/76, fos 192–3; the court record, on the next sedecunt day (12 Nov.), simply records that 'His Majesty King George the 2d departed this life the 25 of October': NRS, CS1/14/fo. 139v, although it does include a copy of the order in council recording George III's oath-taking.

19. The order of procession was: 1. the magistrates and council; 2. the council officers; 3. noblemen; 4. lords of session; 5. barons of exchequer; 6. commissioners of customs and excise; 7. the dean (James Ferguson of Pitfour) and several of the Faculty of Advocates; 8. the clerks (i.e. writers) to the signet; 9. officers of the army and the city's trained bands; 10. the town's constables.

20. Cf. NLS, Paul, MS 5156, fo. 67r: letter from Duncan Forbes (HMA) in London, intimating the death of George I, to the solicitor general, instructing him to inform the lord provost.

21. Forty-nine lords of session out of seventy-eight (six by right of their father: two Arnistons, Drummore, Alemore, Prestongrange and Henderland; one by right of his wife, Elchies); forty-five WSs (twelve by right of their father, ten by right of their wives).

22. On this, see chapter 5.

23. NRS, CS1/18, fo. 20r.

24. For the contract, see *Edin. Burgh Recs, 1689–1701*, pp. 151–2.

25. R. L. Emerson *Academic Patronage in the Scottish Enlightenment* (Edinburgh, 2008) p. 257. See also below, chapter 5.

26. For example, Pinkerton, ed., *Min. Bk, 1713–1750*, p. 148.

27. NRS, CS1/12, fos 35v, 61r; appointments were still recorded, e.g. in 1783 (CS1/16, fo. 159r) and 1793 (CS1/17, fo. 167v). Private persons might also be empowered to nominate bursars, e.g. Alexander McMillan of Dunmore WS, TCM, SL1/1/78, fos 166–7, 272.

28. Dundas demitted in favour of Adam Watt, second son of the Edinburgh town clerk, in 1727: TCM, SL1/1/51, fos 474–5, 497. He still occupied chambers in the university in August 1728 but died soon after: TCM, SL1/1/52, fos 10–11. After his death the council noted that, under several bonds, they owed him £1,760 sterling: TCM, SL1/1/52, fo. 175.

29. For example, TCM, SL1/1/76, fo. 341.

30. NRS, CS 1/14, fo. 72v.
31. Maidment, *Court of Session Garland* (Edinburgh, 1839), p. 23.
32. Cosh, *Edinburgh*, p. 84; J. Grant, *Cassell's Old and New Edinburgh* (3 vols, London, 1881–83), iii, p. 105.
33. NLS, Saltoun, MS 16551, fo. 142, where Royston is also mentioned fishing at Cramond; for the death of Barjarg's favourite hunting dog, ibid., Erskine Murray papers, MS 5083, fo. 98r.
34. TCM, SL1/1/132, fos 441–4.
35. Ibid., SL1/1/132, fo. 441. Earlier references include a competition to win a silver club in 1744: SL1/1/64, fo. 206.
36. For these offices, see the next chapter. For the trespass case, see ibid., SL1/1/142, fo. 63.
37. Grant, *Old and New Edinburgh*, p. 254. He was granted a water pipe for this lodging in 1745: TCM, SL1/1/65, fos 207–9. Strichen died at his country estate in 1775: CS1/15, fo. 169r. The close, latterly 66 High Street, was demolished in 1965–6.
38. TCM, SL1/1/123, fo. 285.
39. G. H. Ballantyne, *The Signet Library, Edinburgh and it Librarians, 1722–1972* (Glasgow, 1979), p. 67.
40. TCM, SL1/1/38, fo. 283.
41. NLS, Yester, MS 5072, fo. 137.
42. ALSP, *The Petition of Robert Reid, Writer to the Signet*, Arniston Collection vol 60, no. 17.
43. Ibid., *Petition of James Erskine of Alloa, Esq Advocate*, Miscellaneous ser., vol. 13 (1766–73), no. 13.
44. Ibid., *Answers for Arthur Wilson, writer in Edinburgh*, 20 Jan. 1785, Arniston collection, vol. 179, no. 15, p. 4. Mrs Shaw's late husband had been an Edinburgh chairmaster, presumably the owner or bearer of a sedan chair.
45. NRS, RH15/38/8. Somerville also painted two shop windows in the Lawnmarket owned by Forbes.
46. Ibid., Leith-Buchanan papers, GD47/1241/2.
47. R. A. Houston, 'Mortality in early modern Scotland: the life expectancy of advocates' 7 (1992) *Continuity and Change*, 62–3.
48. A convenient diagram of Edinburgh's closes is given in J. Gilhooley, *A Directory of Edinburgh in 1752* (Edinburgh, 1988), p. 113.
49. Both are listed in Williamson's *Directory* in 1773; as well as appearing in intermediate directories, Barclay (d.1811) was still in James' Court in the 1809 *Directory* and Buchan (d.1822) was there in the 1818 *Directory*.
50. Cf. remarks about Robert Dalrymple in NRS, Hamilton-Dalrymple papers, GD110/1306.
51. NRS, GD220/5/1734/11.
52. Ibid., GD220/5/1734/12.

53. A. J. Youngson, *The Making of Classical Edinburgh* (Edinburgh, 1966), pp. 226–8.
54. TCM, SL1/1/116, fo. 39.
55. Ibid., SL1/1/128, fo. 88.
56. Ibid., SL1/1/110, fo. 3.
57. Ibid., SL1/1/122, fo. 36.
58. Ibid., SL1/1/102, fo. 131; SL1/1/127, fo. 32.
59. Ibid., SL1/1/88, fos 285–6.
60. Ibid., SL1/1/117, fo. 245; SL1/1/121, fo. 294.
61. R. A. Houston, *Social Change in the Age of Enlightenment, Edinburgh 1660–1760* (Oxford, 1994), p. 66.
62. [D. Erskine], *Lord Dun's Friendly and Familiar Advices adapted to The various stations and Conditions of Life, and the mutual Relations to be observed amongst them* (Edinburgh, 1754), p. 6.
63. Chambers, *Traditions of Edinburgh*, p. 8.
64. TCM, SL1/1/100, fo. 243.
65. PKCA, B59/39/2/63. According to Aitchison's 1795 *Directory for Edinburgh, Leith, Musselburgh and Dalkeith*, three lords of session lived in St Andrew's Square, two each in George Square, Brown's Square and Argyll Square.
66. TCM, SL1/1/100, fo. 312.
67. W. Norrie, *The Annuity Tax* (Earlston, 1912), p. 5.
68. As later was evident in Glasgow, C. G. Brown, 'The Costs of Pew-renting: church management, church-going and social class in nineteenth-century Glasgow' 38 (1987) *Journal of Ecclesiastical History*, p. 350.
69. See Appendix 1. The pro forma printed paper receipts for payment of seat rent by the writer William Leggat in 1693 and 1694 survive: NRS, RH15/136.
70. TCM, SL1/1/65, fo. 80.
71. Ibid., SL1/1/93, fo. 164.
72. Ibid., SL1/1/54, fo. 138.
73. Ibid., SL1/1/93, fo. 334.
74. Ibid., SL1/1/51, fo. 190.
75. Ibid., SL1/1/65, fo. 80.
76. There were considerably cheaper seats. The wright, John Yeatts, repaired the seat he had in the Tron in 1741, spending 40 shillings, and was allowed by the council to rent it free for three years because he had increased its annual rental value to 10 shillings: ibid., SL1/1/62, fo. 158.
77. Ibid., SL1/1/56, fo. 272. For St Giles, see Taylor, *A Journey to Edenborough*, p. 106.
78. Ibid., SL1/1/56, fo. 299; SL1/1/53, fo. 232; SL1/1/72, fo. 325.
79. Ibid., SL1/1/48, fo. 157. Hume took another seat in the same church.
80. Ibid., SL1/1/65, fo. 288; SL1/1/65, fo. 87.
81. Ibid., SL1/1/71, fo. 144.

82. Ibid., SL1/1/80, fo. 65.
83. Ibid., SL1/1/51, fo. 358; SL1/1/56, fo. 290; SL1/1/68, fo. 231; SL1/1/61, fo. 214; SL1/1/63, fo. 273; SL1/1/67, fo. 243; SL1/1/72, fo. 166.
84. Ibid., SL1/1/49, fo. 451; SL1/1/68, fo. 231; SL1/1/76, fo. 196.
85. The deputes are Alexander Ross in 1775 and Allan Ross in 1765 (Old church); John Duncan in 1764 (New church); George Livingstone in 1731 (Tolbooth); David Home in 1720 (Tron): ibid., SL1/1/93, fo. 164; SL1/1/81, fo. 282; SL1/1/80, fo. 251; SL1/1/53, fo. 437. The principal clerks are William Kirkpatrick in 1755 (College kirk) and George Home of Kello in 1722 (South church or Old Greyfriars): SL1/1/73, fo. 167; SL1/1/49, fo. 423.
86. Ibid., SL1/1/68, fo. 243.
87. Ibid., SL1/1/105, fo. 202.
88. For example, H. M. Milne, *Boswell's Edinburgh Journals* (Edinburgh, 2003), p. 272.
89. Brown, 'pew-renting', p. 351.
90. TCM, SL1/1/56, fo. 252; Houston, *Social in the Change Age of Enlightenment*, p. 65.
91. Pinkerton, ed., *Min. Bk, 1661–1712*, p. 4; TCM, SL1/1/50, fos 117–20.
92. TCM, SL1/1/74, fo. 327.
93. NRS, CS1/14, fo. 97v.
94. TCM, SL1/1/74, fos 381–2; also fo. 352.
95. Ibid., fo. 396.
96. PKCA, B59/2/63.
97. NRS, CS 1/9, fo. 7r. This was not new. In 1634 Charles I ordered the lawyers and judges to take communion twice a year (as opposed to once as formerly) in the chapel royal in Holyroodhouse: ibid., CS1/15, fo. 75v.
98. TCM, SL1/1/58, fo. 64.
99. Ibid., SL1/1/64, fo. 166; SL1/1/86, fo. 52.
100. Ibid., SL1/1/76, fo. 388.
101. Ibid., SL1/1/49, fo. 268.
102. Ibid., SL1/1/52, fo. 446; SL1/1/67, fo. 37; SL1/1/60, fo. 104; SL1/1/64, fo. 173.
103. Ibid., SL1/1/65, fo. 87.
104. Finlay, 'The early career of Thomas Craig, advocate' (2004) *Edinburgh Law Review*, 312–13; M. Lynch, *Edinburgh and the Reformation* (Edinburgh, 1986), pp. 39–40, appendix iii; ALSP, *The Petition of Mr David Dalrymple Advocate*, 1 Feb. 1762, Meadowbank Collection, vol. 26, no. 2.
105. For example, ALSP, *Lt-Col Alexander Hay of Rannes and Mr William Robertson, advocate* v. *Hugh Hay preacher*, 24 May 1791, Arniston collection, vol. 181, no 1.
106. NRS, GD495/48/1/48. The Teind Court, set up by act of parliament in 1707 (*RPS 1706/10/315*), was a distinct court although the judges were the lords of session, sitting each Wednesday afternoon as Commissioners for

Plantations of Kirks and Valuation of Teinds (anglice tithes). They heard cases involving the valuation and sale of teinds, augmentation of ministers' stipends and other legal matters relating to churches and parishes.

107. ALSP, *Petition of George Trial of Hobbister*, 25 Nov. 1766, Arniston Collection, vol. 77, no. 7.

108. NRS, CS1/11, fo. 119v. For Swinton, see ALSP, *Hugh Buchan writer in Edinburgh against Mr Joseph Williamson advocate*, 28 Nov. 1769, Dreghorn collection, vol. 42, no. 28, p. 39. The king's solicitor was commissioned by the barons of exchequer.

109. ALSP, *The Petition of John Walker, one of the present Bailies*, 10 March 1763, Dreghorn collection, vol. 6, no. 13, p. 7.

110. See R. B. Sher, 'Moderates, managers and popular politics in mid-eighteenth century Edinburgh: The Drysdale "Bustle" of the 1760s' in J. Dwyer et al., eds, *New Perspectives on the Politics and Culture of Early Modern Scotland* (Edinburgh, 1982), pp. 179–209.

111. Williamson's description, in W. H. Goold, ed., *The Words of the Rev. John MacLaurin* (2 vols, Edinburgh, 1860), i, p. 37, reflects his large practice in the General Assembly; cf. also *Minutes of the General Kirk sessions of Edinburgh* (Edinburgh, 1763). Williamson and Graham were elders in the New church parish.

112. ALSP, *The Petition of Susanna Jack*, 6 July 1775, Miscellaneous Collection, vol. 3.

113. NRS, CH136/2, fo. 163; also fols 170–1, 174, 176.

114. Ibid., fo. 219.

115. W. C. Lehmann, *Henry Home, Lord Kames, and the Scottish Enlightenment* (The Hague, 1971); I. S. Ross, *Lord Kames and the Scotland of his Day* (Oxford, 1972).

116. N. Campbell et al., *The Royal Society of Edinburgh (1783–1983): the first two hundred years* (Edinburgh, 1983), pp. 2–5.

117. R. L. Emerson, 'The social composition of enlightened Scotland: the select society of Edinburgh, 1754–64', 114 (1973) *Studies on Voltaire and the Eighteenth Century*, pp. 296–7.

118. Ibid., 296. See also E. C. Mossner, *The Life of David Hume* (Oxford, 1980), pp. 281–2.

119. ALSP, *The Petition of Sir John Arnot of Arnot Baronet*, 2 Jan. 1731, Hamilton-Gordon Collection, vol. 3, no. 19.

120. Stewart, ed., *Min. Bk, 1751–1783*, p. 34, n. 61.

121. A. F. Tytler, *Memoirs of the Life and Writings of the Honourable Henry Home of Kames* (2 vols, Edinburgh, 1807, 1809), i, App. VIII. The list may be incomplete; Wallace compiled it from memory.

122. F. Miller, 'Andrew Crosbie, advocate, a reputed original of Paulus Pleydell in "Guy Mannering"', ser. iii, 7 (1921) *TDGNHA*, 11–32.

123. Ilay Campbell, William Nairn, Barons John Dalrymple and Cosmo Gordon are close behind, being the only other College members to be

members of three organisations: the Royal Society, the Poker Club and the Select Society.

124.   A. Carlyle, *The Autobiography of Doctor Alexander Carlyle of Inveresk*, ed. J. Hill Burton (Edinburgh, 1910), p. 441. See also Mossner, *Life of Hume*, p. 285.

125.   R. L. Emerson, 'The Philosophical Society of Edinburgh, 1737–1747', 12 (1979) *Journal of British Studies*, 154–91.

126.   On MacLaurin, see Mossner, *Life of Hume*, p. 366. He is not mentioned by Emerson.

127.   S. Shapin, 'Property, patronage and the politics of science: the founding of the Royal Society of Edinburgh', 7 (1974) *The British Journal for the History of Science*, 37.

128.   Of the thirty-eight, eighteen are recorded as members only of the Royal Society and not as members of the other societies examined in the sample.

129.   There were twenty surgeons and physicians (including six professors) and nine clergymen including, of course, William Robertson and Hugh Blair.

130.   *Transactions of the Royal Society of Edinburgh* (Edinburgh, 1788), vol. I, pp. 98–9; Shapin, 'Property, patronage and the politics of science', p. 37.

131.   *Transactions of the Royal Society of Edinburgh* (Edinburgh, 1790), vol. II, pp. 34–5.

132.   St Clair and Craik, *The Advocates Library*, pp. 41–7. For Hume and Areskine, see Mossner, *Life of Hume*, p. 181 and NLS, MS 5156, fo. 121.

133.   Duncan, *Thomas Ruddiman*, pp. 146–7; Emerson, 'The Philosophical Society of Edinburgh, 1737–1747', p. 156.

134.   NLS, Erskine Murray Papers, MS 5118.

135.   M. Townley, *The Best and Fynest Lawers and Other Raire Bookes* (Edinburgh, 1990), pp. 13–14.

136.   *Edin. Burgh Recs 1701–1718*, p. 173.

137.   W. McDougall, 'Gavin Hamilton, bookseller in Edinburgh' 1 (1978) *British Journal for Eighteenth-century Studies*, 14–16; Bell & Bradfute's invoice and exchange book (ECA, SL138/3/1) reveals the accounts held by advocates and writers to the signet, indicating a large number of legal texts for sale.

138.   His father was the bookseller, James Davidson, who was a JP for Edinburgh: NLS, Erskine Murray papers, MS 5130, fo. 68v.

139.   NRS, D and J. H. Campbell WS, papers, GD253/140/7.

140.   S. Baxter, 'Italian music and musicians in Edinburgh, c.1720–1800. A historical and critical study' (PhD, 2 vols, University of Glasgow, 1999), i, pp. 164–5.

141.   Arnot, *History of Edinburgh*, pp. 369–70.

142.   Ibid., p. 370.

143.   ALSP, *Petition and Complaint of Lord Algernon Percy and others*, 1767, Dreghorn collection, vol. 28, no. 46.

144.   For example, the actress Georgiana Bellamy, ALSP, *Memorial for Hugh*

Baillie, Esq; doctor of laws, 13 Feb. 1773, Miscellaneous collection, series 7, vol. 3 (also Meadowbank collection vol. 26, no. 15); the comedian West Digges, ibid., 7 Feb. 1763; Meadowbank collection, vol. 18, no. 19 (also Arniston collection, vol. 65, no. 21); *The Petition of William Hamilton*, 30 July 1766, Arniston Collection vol. 87, no. 6; ibid., *The Petition of Leonardo Piscatore Musician in Edinburgh*, 6 Dec. 1773, Miscellaneous collection, ser. 7, vol. 3. On Pescatore, see Baxter, 'Italian music and musicians', i, pp. 114–18.

145. For example, NLS, Yester, MS 7054, fo. 48.
146. Shaw, *Management of Scottish Society*, p. 124.
147. Ibid., pp. 68–73.
148. The best political studies remain Shaw, *Management of Scottish Society* and Murdoch, *The People Above*.
149. TCM, SL1/1/71, fos 7–8.
150. TCM, SL1/1/71, fo. 47.
151. Ibid.
152. TCM, SL1/1/72, fo. 13; NRS, CS1/14, fo. 12v. Thomas Gibson PCS signed the nomination paper.
153. TCM, SL1/1/76, fo. 317.
154. Youngson, *Making of Classical Edinburgh*, p. 49.
155. TCM, SL1/1/78, fos 359–68.
156. Ibid., fo. 361.
157. Ibid., fos 239–40.
158. Ibid., SL1/1/72, fos 153–4.
159. Ibid., SL1/1/68, fo. 150–1.
160. Ibid., SL1/1/74, fos 69–70.
161. Ibid., SL1/1/78, fos 130, 163; SL1/1/110, fo. 194.
162. Ibid., SL1/1/92, fo. 1.
163. NRS, CS1/15, fos 137v–138r. Punctuation added.

3

The College and Urban Administration

... therefore authorize Mr Davidson the citys agent to defend Baillie
Campbell in the foresaid Process at the expence of the City.[1]

As technically landlord and tenant, the relationship between Edinburgh's
councillors and the lords of session was in the mutual interest of both. The
capacity of the judges to provide advice on the law, and the requirement that
they regularly do so, were obvious benefits to the city and hardly to be
found elsewhere. In terms of governance, it ensured that Edinburgh had, by
some distance, the most sophisticated local administration in Scotland.

College members were strictly excluded from membership of the town
council which, though mainly consisting of merchants and tradesmen, was
dominated by the mercantile interest. The council was usually in thrall to a
political manager from the landed class, a role taken on across the
eighteenth century successively by the second and third Dukes of Argyll
(and the latter's agent, Andrew Fletcher, Lord Milton), James Stuart
Mackenzie, Sir Laurence Dundas of Kerse and Henry Dundas (with his
friend the Duke of Buccleuch) whose interests the councillors would
accommodate in return for patronage and defence of the town's interests in
London.[2] Apart from these, the political roles of the lord justice clerk and
the lord advocate were important and involved much direct correspondence
with London; similarly, the lord president, particularly former crown
lawyers with prolonged political experience such as Duncan Forbes, might
engage in lobbying and political projects of their own.

All of these might occasionally exert influence on the governance of
Edinburgh but the most important internal figure in Edinburgh politics was
the lord provost. Indeed, for much of the eighteenth century, it was from the
ranks of the magistrates (often the provost himself) that the burgh elected
its member of parliament. After the unconfirmed election of the advocate
James Stewart in 1713, the council ensured that lawyers were henceforth
excluded from representing Edinburgh which was the only single-
constituency burgh seat in Scotland.[3] Although the Dundas family was to
gain a tight grip on the neighbouring parliamentary seat of Midlothian,
that of Edinburgh itself was put beyond the reach of the lawyers who, after
all, were not local taxpayers, until Adam Fergusson of Kilkerran, a (non-

practising) member of the Faculty of Advocates was elected in 1784.[4] He was succeeded by Henry Dundas who had long given up his practice at the bar in favour of politics when he relinquished Midlothian in 1790 for the city seat.[5]

If a few College members had an indirect but important involvement in the political affairs of Edinburgh, and some – including advocates, such as Robert Dundas and Thomas Rigg, and writers like Thomas Tod WS and John Davidson WS – were local justices of the peace, many others had a significant impact on the town's internal government and administration.[6] The council, like any other corporation, needed the advice of lawyers to help it make decisions. It also required clerks to make and maintain its records, and law agents to bring prosecutions in the courts to ensure that its decisions were carried out. The council, quite naturally, took full advantage of having Scotland's most able lawyers and administrators on its doorstep. This chapter looks at how the town and College members were able to maintain a working relationship capable of meeting the legal and political challenges which Edinburgh, and Scotland, faced.

THE LORDS OF SESSION AND EDINBURGH TOWN COUNCIL

The most visible sign of the relationship between the College of Justice and the town council occurred twice in the year. At the beginning of the summer and winter sessions of the court, in June and November, the provost and magistrates, in their formal robes, appeared in 'salute' before the lords of session. This usually attracted the briefest of mentions. The clerk writing the sederunt book in 1771 said more than most, relating that the councillors 'congratulated their lordships on their happy return to the seat of Justice for the benefit of the lieges'. In the politically troubled days of 1793, it is recorded that the provost went a little further by reassuring the judges of the magistrates' efforts to suppress meetings 'among the lower classes of people under pretence of reforming our happy Constitution'.[7] This ritual salutation, going back at least as far as the early seventeenth century, was a cue for the judges to appoint a committee of their number each year to discuss with the magistrates issues of mutual concern.[8] This was effectively a standing committee, appointed in November to meet from time to time over the following twelve months, and concerned with 'the police of the city of Edinburgh'.[9] The number of judges on the committee varied, from as little as three to as many as seven, but experienced members of the bench were always there, cheek by jowl with the leading magistrates. Meetings took place, in the afternoons or evenings, in venues which including the council chamber and the Advocates Library.[10]

Issues for discussion varied. Often they were mercantile in nature. Thus, they conferred about the regulation of weights and measures within the burgh, and related issues, such as the quality and price of bread.[11] In December 1736 the judges instructed their members on the committee to make complaint about 'the exorbitant price taken of late for aquavite (whisky)'.[12] Similarly, when they desired the Inner House to be made more 'commodious & convenient', they brought this up with the council.[13] Issues of wider concern that reached the agenda reflected the council's request for the judges to advise them to help 'regulate any abuses in matters under their inspection'.[14] On particular issues the council sometimes took the initiative. In 1745 they sought advice from the lords on how best to deal with the traditional problem caused by chamber pots and other waste being emptied from windows into the streets.[15] In 1759 the regulation of fees in the tollbooth prison came under discussion; the following year, it was the town's supply of fresh water.[16]

If a matter was causing immediate concern, a special subcommittee of judges might be established. When, in 1780, the council sought advice on a proposal 'for removing the slaughterhouses in this city from the Westside of the New bridge to the east side', Lords Kames, Gardenstone, Kennet and Hailes were appointed to assist.[17] Beyond such formal arrangements, the council was not slow to take advantage of the judges' expertise. At the start of the Porteous affair in April 1736, when precognitions were being taken (by the town's procurators fiscal) following the shooting of Edinburgh citizens by the town guard, the lord justice clerk was invited to the council chamber to advise the council.[18] The following day, the lord provost waited on Lords Newhall and Strichen, experienced criminal judges in the high court of justiciary, to get their opinions.

Pressing questions of public concern occasionally led the judges and councillors to invite other interested College members to their discussions. In July 1731 the dean of Faculty, one of the principal clerks of session and the keeper of the signet, were invited to participate in the committee's discussions on measures for the poor.[19] A fuller committee, including the nominees of the barons of exchequer, also convened in 1754 to investigate replacing the building that marked the mercat cross of Edinburgh with a pillar, better suited to allowing traffic to pass to the Cowgate.[20] This resulted in an act of sederunt because of the legal standing of the mercat cross as the place where proclamations having legal effect were made. In this respect it is worth noting that, although the authority of the council to make and enforce its own enactments was unquestioned, the judges sometimes passed their own acts of sederunt to complement council regulations relating to issues such as the selling of flesh, the price of candles and the sale of beer and ale.[21] Occasionally this was at the council's invitation as when, during a period of food shortages in the winter of 1740, the judges were asked to 'add their authority' to an act of council concerning the importation of corn.[22] This may have stemmed from the practice of the Scottish Estates, before the Union, of passing enactments requiring certain things to be noted in the books of sederunt (as, for instance in 1691, a list of the debts owed by the town of Edinburgh).[23] At other times the committee made resolutions which were reported back for approval to the court or the council. For example, Lord Drummore reported to the lords in 1736 that the committee had resolved that certain exemptions be applied in the flesh market, a resolution which the lords then approved.[24]

Aside from regular committee meetings, and ad hoc meetings sometimes quickly arranged, the judges were involved in other formal interactions with the council. Every June, they appointed two of their number to oversee the management of the tax, imposed by statute in 1693, of two pennies per pint of ale sold within the burgh.[25] Annually in July judges were appointed to another committee concerning the operation of the charity workhouse in Edinburgh which opened in 1743. The legislation of 1686, aimed at clearing clamorous beggars from the town's streets, required the magistrates to present their proposals from time to time to the judges and, in the 1690s, annual meetings were held to discuss the issue.[26] A plan presented in 1738 for the creation of a workhouse, based on one 'practised with great success at Glasgow', was itself the product of a conference between the magistrates and judges and, from the start, along with the advocates and writers to the signet, they were involved in managing the new institution.[27] The College of Justice contributed eighteen out of its ninety-six managers.[28]

THE ADVOCATES AND EDINBURGH

The council, unlike its contemporaries elsewhere, directly employed advocates to acts as its assessors (or legal advisers).[29] It is true that the burgh of Stirling, apparently for reasons of economy, did appoint an advocate, Robert Colt, as its assessor in 1679. In doing so, the council complained that for several years, having lacked an advocate 'as the tounes ordinary assessor, they have been at great charges in consulteing evrie particular affair'.[30] Colt, however, died in 1694 and there is no evidence that the council made subsequent appointments.

Burghs sent commissioners to the meetings of the Convention of the Royal Burghs in Edinburgh, and the commissioners had 'assessors' who were sometimes advocates (or, indeed, judges or writers to the signet). In 1714, for example, Dumbarton nominated James Smollet as assessor to his father, whom it commissioned to attend a special meeting in Edinburgh.[31] Assessors of this kind, however, were political advisers, rather than legal advisers (although the convention itself had an assessor, often a leading lawyer).[32] If assessors did happen to be lawyers, particularly lawyers who worked in Edinburgh anyway (where the convention met), that was purely a matter of convenience, not necessity. Edinburgh itself normally nominated former magistrates, rather than professional lawyers, as assessors to the convention, despite its own administrators having an important role to play in convention business.[33]

When it came to legal matters, councils and other corporate bodies tended to instruct advocates only when their services were necessary. If an advocate with local connections could be employed, then that was an advantage, even if the council would largely have dealt with him via their law agent in Edinburgh. This seems to have been the practice of seventeenth-century Aberdeen.[34] Similarly, Dumfries town council in the 1770s consulted one of its sons, the eminent advocate Andrew Crosbie, whenever it was faced with difficult or 'kittle points'.[35] Crosbie had already been an adviser to the town council when he was formally appointed its 'ordinary lawyer' in 1775.[36] He retained that office until his death, when he was followed in turn by two other local men, Alexander Fergusson of Craigdarroch and Robert Corbet, son of a former provost.[37] In Crosbie's case, the town clerk, John Aitken, normally communicated with him via yet another man with local connections, Hugh Corrie WS, but the town provost also consulted him directly, particularly during vacations when he returned to Dumfries. Similarly, the University of Glasgow, in Principal Stirling's time, employed Walter Stewart as its ordinary advocate, with his younger half-brother, Archibald, his successor in 1721 (who, in turn, was succeeded in 1728 by Thomas Forbes, the son of the professor of civil law in the university).[38] The Stewart brothers, sons of the Renfrewshire landowner Sir Archibald Stewart of Blackhall – a man with strong links to Glasgow – often corresponded directly with Stirling but the university's litigation in Edinburgh was essentially managed through William Miller WS who later also acquired as a client the town council of Glasgow.[39]

Edinburgh was in a markedly different situation from provincial centres. Its council employed several (usually four) assessors simultaneously to deal with its legal business. Over the period 1700–99, it employed no less than forty-eight advocates in this capacity, among them some of the most prominent men at the bar. Edinburgh's assessorship was not an invention of the eighteenth century. Notable earlier assessors included such influential figures as Sir George Mackenzie of Rosehaugh and Sir John Nisbet of Dirleton.[40] In May 1689, declaring that too many assessors were on the payroll (there were seven at the time), the council decided to reduce them to 'such a competent number as is only necessary for advyseing of the Town processes'.[41] The assessorships were declared vacant until the council determined the appropriate number and, two days later, three were appointed at reduced salaries.[42] One of them was Sir John Lauder who had been an assessor since 1670. His removal would hardly have been politic because he had not long before travelled to London at the council's behest to deliver its loyal address to the Prince of Orange.[43]

The concept of an 'assessor' derives from Roman law and refers to those advocates who assisted magistrates and judges in their judicial activity.[44] This was a subject of interest to the classical jurists, with the Roman jurist Paul known to have written a monograph on the subject. Since little research has been done on this office in Edinburgh, and as it is important in the current context, it is worth giving a brief outline of it.

The business of an assessor for the town had at least six elements: 1 advising the lay magistrates in their courts; 2 providing opinions on issues arising from litigation involving the council and also parliamentary bills affecting the town; 3 pleading for the council in actions before the Court of Session, the Court of Exchequer, the High Court of Justiciary and on appeal to the House of Lords; 4 providing opinions in regard to administrative issues affecting the council; 5 taking trial of the qualifications of those writers seeking to become procurators in the burgh court; 6 acting as arbiter in cases involving the council which were submitted to arbitration. Not all opinions provided to the council came from assessors and, for obvious reasons, the assessors were not always involved in the council's arbitrations.

The first of these roles, advising the magistrates, was regarded as the most important in an act of council concerning the assessors in 1719. This made it clear that hitherto the assessors had fulfilled the role of 'retained lawyers' for the council, rather than proper assessors in the classical sense. Reorientation of the office was considered necessary to assist the magistrates, bolster the authority of the inferior courts and thereby greatly benefit the city.[45] A similar intention had underpinned an earlier act of council in 1698, drafted on the basis of an opinion by the then lord advocate (Sir James Stewart). By this measure the council encouraged attendance by at least one of its assessors at the bailie court (which sat in Parliament House) and facilitated this by altering the court's scheduled sittings.[46] The 1719 act went further in suggesting that attendance in the burgh's court was not merely a matter of convenience or propriety but the most fundamental requirement of the office. Four assessors were appointed and it was properly their business 'to sit on the bench with the Magistrats by turns and assist them in Judging of and determining all causes and questions brought before them whatsoever'.[47] Beyond that, all they were required to do was appear for the town before the lords of session in cases of suspension and advocation only (that is, to defend the judgments of the magistrates upon which they had advised). The phrase 'by turns' suggests some form of rota, or perhaps the allocation to each of the four assessors of a single court which they were to attend, such as the head court of south Leith or the Canongate or Portsburgh.[48] The latter interpretation is given strength by the record of the admission in 1727 of Thomas Erskine, elected one of the assessors in succession to the late Sir James Stewart of Goodtrees. As well as taking the usual oaths of office, Erskine specifically promised 'to aid and assist the Barron and assistant Bailies of Portsburgh in any matters wherein they were concerned in pursuing or defending the interest of the said Barrony, and particularly in advising any processes that may come before them'.[49] In 1772 John Stuart of Allanbank, by then at the bar for thirty-five years and an assessor since 1743, resigned the office of 'assessor for the Town of Leith' because of pressure of business.[50]

A sense of this advisory role can be seen from a newspaper report in 1741 concerning the trial of Peter Swan, before the lord provost as high sheriff of Edinburgh, for attempting to rob the Royal Bank of Scotland.

> His Lordship in his Robes was usher'd into Court by the City Sword and Mace carry'd by the proper Officers, &c. and Mr James Graham, Dean of the Faculty of Advocates, sat on the Left of his Lordship as Assessor. The Court being fenced, the Indictment was read, to which the Prisoner pled guilty, and petitioned for Transportation.[51]

James Graham of Airth was a busy man but, because the local courts did not sit constantly, the burden of attendance on assessors seems to have been reasonable, especially if each assessor was allotted only to one particular court. Yet the office was no sinecure. Under regulations for dealing with processes in the burgh court which took effect from 8 July 1736, as well as at formal diets of the court which were to occur at least one evening per week, the magistrates and assessors were to meet each Thursday at 6 p.m. during the months of June, July, December, January and February.[52] At these meetings they were to discuss all actions in which avizandum had been made and 'whereon the opinion of the whole four assessors had been demanded'.[53] In March, April, May, August and October only the assessor 'for the month', and any other of the assessors who happened to be in town, had to attend the diet of the court. In these months, no Thursday sessions for advising would take place. Unquestionably, however, burgh court business could take up a significant amount of time during the terms when the Court of Session was also sitting.

Under the 1719 arrangements, three advocates, in addition to the assessors, were to be employed as retained counsel 'whose office shall be to advise and plead in all Law cases which concern the Good toun'.[54] These were each to receive a retaining fee; that to be paid to the first named, the lord advocate Sir David Dalrymple of Hailes, was £300 Scots annually, that of the other two, Thomas Kennedy and Robert Dundas, was only £100 Scots per annum. It is worth noting the status of these men within the profession. Dundas was the serving solicitor general and Kennedy formerly held that office. The four assessors, themselves all experienced and eminent advocates, were to be paid a straight salary of £300 Scots per annum.[55] The expectation appears to have been that the retained counsel would carry on the second and third of the functions of assessors outlined above, that is, the provision of legal opinions and pleading before the Court of Session.

Several general points are worth making about the assessors. First, a division emerged between 'ordinary' and 'extraordinary' assessors. The latter term was generally applied to the lord advocate or the solicitor general if either, or both, held office as assessor but seems more generally to have been the term applied to retained counsel. This possibly stemmed from the resignation as an assessor of Robert Dundas in July 1721.[56] Dundas had been appointed lord advocate a year earlier but his resignation letter clearly indicates political tension with the council. Given that previous law officers, such as Sir George Mackenzie and Sir James Stewart of Goodtrees, had held office while employed as assessors, Dundas could not argue that there was any inherent incompatibility between the two offices. He did suggest that, since taking office as lord advocate, he had found some 'inconsistance' between his duty to the king and his role as an assessor 'in the present management' of the magistrates.[57] The underlying political issues were resolved (and Dundas was later consulted by the council) but the council's policy may have been from then on to regard crown lawyers as better suited to acting as extraordinary rather than ordinary assessors. This would have restricted them to being retained to provide opinions and plead cases in the Court of Session, rather than advising the magistrates in their courts.[58]

Weight is added to this interpretation by looking at the arrangements that were made on the respective elevations, in 1738 and 1760, of Duncan Forbes and Robert Dundas from lord advocate directly to president of the Court of Session. In January 1738 Forbes was replaced as a 'retained lawyer' by his successor as lord advocate, Charles Areskine.[59] The new solicitor general, William Grant, was also appointed a retained lawyer. Areskine, who moved from solicitor to advocate, saw his annual retaining fee from the city double to £200 Scots.[60] Similarly, Dundas was also succeeded as a retained lawyer for Edinburgh by his immediate successor as lord advocate, Thomas Miller.[61] In turn, Miller was replaced as solicitor general by two men, Francis Garden and James Montgomery, who were then retained as lawyers by Edinburgh.[62] The town council granted them 'the usual & ordinary fees annexed to these offices'. This suggests that the retained lawyers for the town were essentially the crown lawyers (appointed by reason of their office) and that normally they were referred to as extraordinary to distinguish them from the town's ordinary assessors.[63]

The crown lawyers could not spare the time to sit with the magistrates of Edinburgh. Nor was it possible for them to avoid, at least from time to time, having to appear against the interests of the council. Ordinary assessors would have been expected by the council to refrain from acting for other clients in a way that was contrary to the council's interest. Hew Dalrymple was removed as an assessor in February 1694 for appearing for a client in an action against the town.[64] This was an example not easily forgotten, though perhaps later regretted by the council when Dalrymple was elevated as lord president in 1698, a position he retained for almost thirty-nine years.

The council certainly did its best to keep on the right side of the crown lawyers. In 1742, for instance, an 'entertainment' was held for Robert Craigie HMA and Robert Dundas SG, and both were given retaining fees. Present was Robert Pringle, one of the ordinary assessors, and, according to what he later told Thomas Hay, the lord advocate had been authorised, by the London government, to say that places in or about Edinburgh that became vacant 'would be disposed of to such persons as the town desired'.[65] This is precisely what the council wanted to hear and Craigie, for once, was following the official line. Given the political importance of the role of the lord advocate, and the normally strong relationship between the advocate and those responsible for managing Scottish politics, the policy of retaining the services of the crown lawyers for the benefit of the town council made good sense. Because the assessors were generally men of the highest reputation at the bar, and many of them advanced to the bench, the relationship which it had with its assessors brought the council long-term benefits: it generated not only goodwill among the leading ranks of the legal profession and the bench but a clear appreciation among them of where the town's interests lay.

There is much evidence of the wide spectrum of legal issues – including matters of criminal law, feudal law, revenue law and administrative law – which the council referred to its assessors and other advocates. Only a few examples may be given. In 1754 the assessors were asked to consider how far the commissioners of Customs and Excise, the staff of the Stamp Office and the professors in the university were liable to the stent-masters in respect of their offices and lodgings.[66] The year before, when the town borrowed £10,000 from the Royal Bank of Scotland to fund improvements to the city, a committee of the magistrates required the written opinion of counsel on the best scheme for providing security to the bank and advice on how to relieve council members who had personally guaranteed the loan.[67] Advice was sought on whether the council was liable to the creditors of an army officer who had been imprisoned for debt in the Tolbooth and whom they had released on the grounds of ill health. Having recovered, the officer had absconded without repaying his debts. The legal opinion of two of the assessors, Robert Blair and James Oswald, was that the council should settle because it had no defence to an action for payment.[68] A more unusual question was whether the magistrates should still deliver, to the university's professor of anatomy, the corpse of a convicted murderer, sentenced in the High Court to death and public dissection, who had committed suicide in his cell. The assessors replied in the negative on the basis that it would be unlawful to perform the second part of the sentence (the dissection) without having carried out the first (the execution).[69]

Most of the issues were of a technical and administrative nature and they varied widely in importance. One minute the assessors might be advising on matters connected to the local presbytery, or on a dispute arising from one of the annual council elections, at another they might be framing an important bill for parliament.[70] In 1755, for instance, Peter Wedderburn was paid five guineas for drafting a bill for improving the harbour of Leith, a vital commercial measure.[71] Important legal opinions were sometimes copied into the council minutes, with the originals retained in the council's charterhouse. In 1755 the depute town clerk, George Lindsay, inventoried 'a great many memorials & querys made out for the City respecting the Import of certain clauses in acts of parliament, charters and other grants in favours of the good Town', which he then engrossed into a book.[72] This work may have stemmed from an inventory Lindsay had made by 1748 of papers in the possession of the late town solicitor, and joint town clerk, George Irving (d.1742).[73]

The role of the assessors was smoothly integrated into the management of council business. They could be consulted on behalf of the community not only by the full council, but also by the magistrates alone, or by the town's law agent or treasurer. The town's agent, whose role will be discussed below, generally had discretion about which assessors to consult. There were limits, however, and the council, displeased in 1718 with its agent, Ronald Campbell, running up a bill of £51 2s. 8⅔d. for consulting lawyers, promptly forbade him 'in all timecoming to give consultations to Lawers on the Goodtouns accompt'.[74] This unworkable prohibition did not last long. In 1751, for example, Ronald Dunbar, as agent, was free to select which assessors to consult on a question of jurisdiction.[75]

The tendency to employ as assessors advocates of prominence and experience had two almost inevitable consequences. The first was that assessors were obliged to resign, in some cases quite soon after appointment, when they were promoted to an office incompatible with that of assessor. William Calderwood was appointed assessor in 1699 to replace James Stewart who had been appointed joint principal town clerk of Edinburgh.[76] Calderwood himself had to resign when he was appointed lord of session in 1711.[77] John Lauder and Peter Wedderburn both resigned within a year of their appointments also because of being elevated to the bench.[78] Hugh Forbes, an assessor for over thirteen years, resigned on his appointment as a PCS; in 1799, Neil Fergusson resigned when appointed sheriff-depute of Fife.[79] Calderwood's resignation, at least, was probably welcome given that he was one of seven assessors at the time whom the council had the expense of maintaining. The council took the opportunity to ordain:

> That for hereafter when any of the said assessors shall be promoted Removed by Death or otherways Rendered unacceptable to serve the good town in the said station the office shall be sunk and none other shall be chosen in their Room and this to have place ay and while the said assessors be reduced to the usuall number of four allanerly [only].[80]

The second consequence of hiring prominent men was that pressure of business sometimes kept them from responding quickly to requests from the council. In 1754, on the appointment of William Wallace of Cairnhill as assessor, there was a complaint that 'such attendance as was necessary to be given by the several assessors [was] not regularly observed'.[81] This may be another reason why opinions from advocates who were not assessors sometimes had to be obtained. Regular attendance in Edinburgh, as a general rule, was always a necessary part of the assessor's role. In one case, the appointment of James Graham of Airth in 1739, so keen was the council to benefit from his considerable experience that it was prepared to make a partial exception. It dispensed with his attendance at the bailie court in consideration of 'the great fatigue and trouble he has by his business before the Court of Session and as being Judge of the High Court of Admiralty and dean of Faculty'.[82]

As the eighteenth century wore on the status of assessor began to decline and it grew less important as a potential route to a seat in the Court of Session relative to the office of sheriff-depute. Men with less experience or distinction at the bar began to be appointed assessors, culminating in the appointment of William Fraser Tytler (son of a previous assessor who had been promoted to the bench) in 1799 after only five months at the bar.[83] The controversial John Pattison, a former apprentice writer, was appointed in November 1793 after only six years as an advocate, having initially been rejected as a candidate for the bar by the Faculty of Advocates in 1785, apparently on the basis of his age and inferior social standing.[84] Overcoming this, he proved to be a success at the bar, perhaps aided by strong links to the town (he was probably nephew of the town clerk of Leith). The council particularly stressed his 'fitness and good qualifications' for the post.[85] Despite the apparent decline, Lord Brougham's nineteenth-century barb, that the assessors had little claim to distinction other than being 'the favourites of the corporation', could not properly be made of those who held that position during most of the eighteenth century.[86]

TOWN CLERKS

While assessors occasionally made important interventions to facilitate the administration and economic progress of the council, the role of town clerk was at all times indispensible. Because this office was held by a succession of College members (see Appendix 2), it was another important point of contact. The council's administrative history could easily fill a monograph of its own and cannot be narrated here. There was, however, a very important relationship between the College and the town council that was based partly on shared personnel (primarily the advocates and writers to the signet who gained important positions within the council's administration) and partly on the natural tendency to replicate, in the council's administration and minor legal jurisdictions, some of the offices and functions found in the College.

The most important council administrative position was that of principal common (or town) clerk. As early as the sixteenth century, this was a position which advocates were not averse to occupying.[87] Unlike the assessorship, the clerkship was never the exclusive privilege of those at the bar. Whether the town clerks were advocates, writers to the signet or ordinary writers, they needed knowledge of the notarial arts and it is no coincidence that, of the four advocates to have become notaries during the eighteenth century, two of them were town clerks of Edinburgh and another was town clerk of Glasgow.[88] The colourful Aeneas McLeod, appointed joint town clerk with Sir James Rocheid in 1687, was an Edinburgh writer and former keeper of the public registers under the lord clerk register who became a notary just prior to gaining the clerkship.[89] McLeod purchased the office directly from the council, paying 19,000 merks for it.[90] The office was for life, with the two joint (or conjunct) holders entitled, as their commissions stated, to 'all fees, profits, duties and casualties belonging thereto used and wont whereof any of the former Clerks were in possession'.[91]

In overseeing the council's affairs, and recording its minutes, the principal clerks directed a complex administrative organisation.[92] They were obliged to commission deputes (also known as their first servants) who, once approved by the council, would act in their absence and might themselves prepare and record council meetings.[93] Beyond that, the clerks commissioned other staff to carry out particular tasks. The full reach of the office was made clear in an action before the Court of Session in 1739.[94] The pursuer, Archibald Blair, set out the six categories of servants and subordinate office-holders, aside from the depute clerks, who were commissioned for life by the principal clerks and directly accountable to them. First, there was the keeper of the particular register of sasines for Edinburgh whose role it was to record services of heirs, instruments of sasine, and dispositions concerning heritable property. Second, they appointed a keeper to maintain the register of bonds and other moveable rights. Third, in the dean of gild court there was an extractor who made copies on demand of acts, warrants and decreets. It was also this man's job to write the burgess tickets. Another extractor was employed to attend the magistrates in the council chamber and when they acted as justices of the peace. A separate clerk was appointed to write the complaints and warrants for small debts in the justice of the peace court. Finally, the principal clerks also made direct appointments in the bailie court, nominating extractors and a keeper of that court. While the principal clerks might expect a consideration for granting these commissions, their fees were regulated by the council. Therefore, every time a lease was drafted for a shop, for example, or an act of council was drawn up granting a pew in an Edinburgh church, the principal clerks would receive a payment.[95]

So important was the common clerkship that its history was complicated by two competing interests: the council's desire to find the best qualified men for the job; and its need to raise revenue by selling the office to the highest bidder. The dangers of venality were highlighted by failed attempts in the 1690s to remove Aeneas McLeod, who brought an action in parliament to retain his office against hostile councillors who wanted rid of him on charges of malversation.[96] The crux of McLeod's argument was that, if the office were not held for life, it would never be a viable purchase because the holder would potentially be subject to removal after each annual council election.

To ensure that duly qualified candidates were in place, the council in November 1720 made a remarkable enactment by which it purported to bind its successors.[97] Recognising the danger of bias in appointing town clerks in an atmosphere subject to 'the solicitations of Friends and influence of persons of note and character', the council decided not to wait until vacancies arose.[98] They nominated George Irving WS to replace the advocate Adam Watt of Rosehill, and Matthew Brown DCS to replace the writer George Home of Kello.[99] Both replacements were to take effect on the death or resignation of the respective incumbent, at which point the relevant nominee would automatically acquire his half of the common clerkship. On 11 November 1720 the new appointees took the oath of office.[100] In 1728 Watt was permitted to demit as principal clerk to be reappointed jointly with Irving to the same office (with Home still holding the other clerkship). At the same time, citing the 'pernicious consequence' of people paying exorbitant sums in auctions for acquiring any office of trust for life from the council, it was enacted that a set of fixed rates be applied to various offices.

The amount to be paid by any new principal clerk was restricted to £400 sterling.[101] The council, ratifying the 1720 act in so far as it was consistent with the arrangements now set in place, permitted Irving and Brown to pay only £200 to the council on taking office although either remained free to make any private arrangement they wished with the incumbent. This was clearly intended as an exception. Future office-holders were not to 'give or promise any sum of money, gratuity, reward or other Consideration whatever to the person who last possessed the office, nor to any other person or persons on his account'.[102]

The acts of council of 1720 and 1728 were noble attempts to limit the effects of venality but both were doomed to fall at the first hurdle. In June 1742 the council, seeking to replace the late George Irving and faced, on the one hand with 'the present low state of the Good Touns revenue', and 'several well qualified persons offering their service' who were willing to pay more than £400, partly rescinded the act of 1728 and sought a payment 'not below One Thousand pounds Sterling'.[103] The bidding was won by the advocate Joseph Williamson who offered, in addition to the 'compliment' of £1,000, a further £400 towards building a workhouse for the poor and his promise to do his best to put the city's charterhouse and records in good order.[104] On providing surety for payment, and his oath that no private payments or acknowledgements had been made in consideration of the office (an oath required after 1718 by anyone taking lucrative offices under the council), he was sworn as joint town clerk for life with George Home.[105] Under this arrangement, each was solely responsible for his own acts of administration.

Home did not survive very long and, in deciding to overlook Matthew Brown DCS and elect as his replacement the writer William Forbes, the council in December 1742 annulled the acts of 1720 and 1728 as manifest violations of their right to dispose freely of the offices in their gift.[106] In his turn, Forbes, when elected in January 1743, promised to join with Williamson in putting 'the City's charter room and records in the best order in my power within such a short space as the nature of the thing will permit'.[107] As it turned out, both men had bid so much for their offices, and given bonds to guarantee future payment of these sums, that they had difficulty in paying the interest on these bonds.[108]

As a general rule, the town council tried to promote from within. Writers, like Archibald Blair, could spend over thirty years working in different parts of the clerks' office, rubbing shoulders with the magistrates and local procurators in the courts.[109] As men steadily gained promotion, careers can be traced through the council minutes. George Lindsay went from being one of the extractors to one of the depute clerks and then, in 1763, became one of the principal clerks.[110] Many similar examples exist but must give way to a single detailed illustration: it is a particularly important one, however, because it concerns George Irving who made his way not only to the common clerkship but also became, concurrently, the town's solicitor.

Irving, son of an usher to the privy council, trained as a writer in Edinburgh and became a notary in 1708.[111] Had the privy council not been abolished that same year, he might have expected to find work there but, by 1712, he was employed in the town clerks' chamber, writing and gilding burgess tickets.[112] Also in that year he was granted the pew in Lady Yester's church recently given up by George Buchan, a clerk in the Teind Court (later principal clerk there).[113] In 1717 the deacons employed him to attend the committee overseeing the parliamentary tax on ale sold in the burgh and he eventually became secretary to this committee.[114] It had probably been in connection with the legislation authorising this tax that he had earlier made a trip to London 'to negotiate the touns affairs'.[115] The following year the council employed him, and the writer, Alexander Baillie, to inventory the deeds in its charterhouse, this being one of many such efforts in the course of the century to improve the efficiency of the council's archive.[116] In 1720 he was admitted to the WS Society and it was nine months after this, as we have seen, that the council, expressing itself well satisfied with his qualifications, nominated him to replace Adam Watt as one of the principal clerks.[117] In 1725 he was elected by the council as clerk to the barony of Calton.[118] Following the death of Ronald Campbell WS, Irving was appointed solicitor or law agent for the council.[119] From 1728 he became one of the principal clerks, albeit nominally sharing the clerkship with Watt until the latter's death in November 1736. His own death occurred on 19 June 1742.[120] His successor as town clerk, Joseph Williamson, was appointed a week later and subsequently appears to have given up his seat in the Tolbooth church to Irvine's widow and sister-in-law.[121]

Irving was so ubiquitous that it is not always clear in what capacity he acted. In 1734 the council sent him to Stirling to cast a vote in the parliamentary election on behalf of the council which qualified as a freeholder through having acquired a superiority.[122] This was probably something he did as the town's agent. That was certainly the capacity in which he was involved in matters concerning the aftermath of the Porteous riot during the period 1736–7.[123] As solicitor he employed at least one clerk, John Snodgrass.[124] Having risen from the ranks to co-ordinate his own staff, Irving achieved such prominence and authority in Edinburgh's legal affairs that the historian George Menary assumed him to have been an advocate.[125] This was an easy mistake to make: the principal clerks of Edinburgh are generally not men to be underestimated. Joseph Williamson and Adam Watt were highly prominent figures. Watt left behind an impressive library of law books and he was well placed to influence the council, and delegates from the College of Justice, to appoint his younger son, also Adam, as joint professor of Universal History at the university in 1725 after the incumbent, Laurence Dundas, agreed to demit in his favour.[126]

AGENTS

As well as the role of assessors in advising magistrates, the fact that many cases heard before the inferior courts in Edinburgh were advocated to the Court of Session required council lawyers to develop working relationships with practitioners in the College. Those who made their living in the inferior courts would have been well-known faces on the legal scene because pursuing the council's business through the courts required joined-up thinking at all levels of its organisation, from the magistrates and the treasurer to the agent, the procurator fiscal and the assessors.[127]

In the context of the community of the College of Justice, the key attribute of the town's agents (they also used the title 'solicitor') is that, in the period of this study, almost all of them were writers to the signet and, therefore, College members.[128] Because much of their time was taken up dealing with actions advocated to the College, this made perfect sense, at least while writers to the signet retained a supposed monopoly over the management of actions in the central court.[129]

In many ways, the role of agent was no different from that performed by writers in regard to private clients. The office-holder did, however, have a number of special duties. The council, for instance, regularly granted warrants to their agent to bring prosecutions in their courts and the treasurer regularly paid significant sums to the agent to cover the cost of these and other litigation. The regular audits often refer simply to the 'agent's account' or, sometimes, to his account 'for sundry prosecutions at the instance of the City'.[130] Extensive advance payments were sometimes made. In 1803, the dean of gild persuaded the council that a better estimate of future costs should be obtained. The council ordered the agent in future to prepare and present

> a state of the processes presently in dependence before the Court of Session &c wherein the Council are interested, either as Pursuers or Defenders, as these stood at the conclusion of last session, with an account of the expences laid out on each of them; and at same time mentioning by whose authority these actions were entered into ...[131]

The actual salary paid to the town's solicitors is less clear from the record. In 1689 the salary was 100 merks.[132] Later it grew to £100 Scots (plus 200 merks for dealing with actions concerning the University of Edinburgh) but, in 1701, Ronald Campbell WS received £200 Scots.[133] It is difficult to establish what it was later in the century. New occupants were simply promised 'the usual salary, casualties, emoluments [and] profites due to the said office' in return for managing the city's legal affairs.[134]

Instructions to the agent are regularly recorded in council minutes. They often involve defending the judicial or administrative actions of councillors and magistrates. Thus, in 1774 the agent, John Davidson WS, was instructed to defend Bailie Tory in the ten-merk court.[135] The following year he was authorised to defend the kirk treasurer against a petition brought by Katherine Lyon, an Edinburgh schoolmistress, in conjunction with the town's procurator fiscal (whose formal assent to the prosecution was necessary).[136] Formal citations received by the council were often simply passed on to the agent with the general instruction that he look after the town's interests.[137] Periodically, particularly after elections when a new council was sitting, the agent was instructed to make up a memorandum (or 'state') of all actions in which the council was currently involved, so that they might be reviewed by a committee of councillors.[138]

While the council sometimes expressly authorised their agent to instruct counsel to plead a case, in general they relied on his judgement in doing so. For example, in July 1764 Davidson was required to instruct the assessor William Johnston in a case before the Court of Session relating to property in Black Friars' Wynd, and, simultaenously, to instruct the newly appointed assessor David Rae to argue 'the affair relative to the new wall lately built in Caltoun'.[139] It is likely that the councillors were simply following Davidson's recommendation in allocating these tasks to particular assessors. He would then either have met with the advocates to discuss these matters privately and gain their informal opinions, or simply have framed a written memorial for their opinions. Based on such a memorial, the four ordinary assessors in 1755 gave a joint opinion on the non-entry of feuars holding property directly of the town council.[140]

Much of the agent's time, as these cases suggest, was taken up advising on property matters within the burgh. This part of their function had always necessitated the retention of deeds belonging to the council and, because the office of agent was granted for life, when an agent died, one of the first tasks of the council was to gather in such deeds and ensure that they were passed on to the newly elected agent.[141] This gave the representatives of the deceased agent some leverage: they might retain these papers until they received any portion of unpaid salary.[142] At the same time, on taking office, an agent might have to recover papers in the hands of third parties, normally law agents who had borrowed them in the natural course of business. Thus, George Irving, shortly after his appointment, sought from John Buchanan WS some of the town's papers which he had borrowed from the late Ronald Campbell; on their return, Irving granted him a receipt.[143]

The material in their possession gives some idea of the preoccupations of the town's solicitors. Ronald Dunbar provided a written inventory to the council in 1747 of the seventeen documents in his custody, presenting them neatly in date order.[144] These ranged from a 1612 great seal charter concerning church livings granted to the council by James VI, to a decreet in an action in 1712 concerning the magistrates. Largely consisting of charters, these documents generally concerned grants of lands and jurisdiction to the town council, including areas such as Calton and Portsburgh. Dunbar handed the deeds over to the depute clerk and they were given to Walter Stewart, one of several men employed in the important work of inventorying in the charterhouse. Without easy and organised access to charters, the work of building the new Edinburgh that continued for much of the eighteenth century would have been even more difficult.[145]

Like the town clerks, the agents had a small staff working under them. Little is known about these men. We have already encountered one of them, John Snodgrass, who presumably spent much of his time preparing documents. Such assistance was needed because the agents were hard worked in a variety of courts. In 1753, for instance, Dunbar was authorised to assist the bailies of Leith in an action by them against the constables of Leith.[146] Although the Canongate had its own agent, he would no doubt consult his Edinburgh colleague from time to time.[147] The agent also had to work with the town's procurators fiscal. The latter's role included the defence of the magistrates in cases of alleged oppression (that is, where magistrates were alleged to have acted unjustly through making decisions ultra vires, or corruptly, or from personal motives). Such actions might involve them being called upon to defend their own conduct before the lords of session (or the privy council prior to 1708) or, at least, to co-ordinate the legal defence in conjunction with the agent and one or more of the assessors.[148] An example of this occurred in 1755 when bailies Stewart and Forrester, plus George Lindsay as clerk of the bailie court and Robert Gray as fiscal, were sued for damages for the alleged wrongful imprisonment of the merchant James Yuill.[149] Co-ordination, and knowledge of both College and council procedures, were paramount in the successful defence and prosecution of the council's legal interests.

CONCLUSION

This review of the administrative structure of the town council demonstrates a number of things. First, the council offered a range of employments and opportunities to College members. No less than the College itself, working for the council presented a means of promotion for young writers such as John Dunn who wrote to Lord Milton in 1733 that from his youth he had gone through all the 'stations in the town clerks chamber with ane eye to be promoted to be Deputt Town Clerk when ane opportunity offered'.[150] His chance never came. Adam Watt, on the other hand, secured employment for his son, John, in the dean of gild court and the same nepotism might have been at play in the appointment of John Forbes (possibly the son of the principal clerk, William Forbes WS), first as a servant in the office of the principal clerks and then as one of the joint keepers of the council records.[151]

Secondly, College members were heavily involved in managing the council's charterhouse. This reflects the demands of litigation: deeds had to be preserved securely and located quickly when needed. Without indexing work, undertaken over decades by the clerks and those they employed, the permission gained by the advocate Hugo Arnot in 1773 to access the council's records when writing his *History of Edinburgh* would have been much less meaningful.[152] Administrative experience gained in the College of Justice, particularly in the area of information management, was easily transplanted to the council chamber. Joseph Williamson, for example, was not only town clerk but also principal clerk in the Teind Court with an intimate knowledge of procedure there and in the horning office. He used his position to arrange for Hugh Buchan, who worked in the Teind Office and had acted for him as his advocate's clerk, to be made recorder of the town council minutes, despite having to overcome 'violent opposition'.[153] Ronald Campbell, the town's agent, was, towards the end of his life, also depute director of the chancery.[154] There is little evidence that those College members who worked for the council encountered any conflict of interest in doing so. In 1786 the town's agent John Davidson WS did decline to act for the council when the dispute over the tax exemption for College members flared up but his reason for doing so was his status as deputy keeper of the signet (an office holder within the WS Society).[155] His fellow WS, John Gray, who was one of the principal town clerks, handled the process for the council in his stead without any apparent conflict. In general terms, the relationship between College and council was harmonious after 1687, and conflicts did not result in major disruption. On the other hand, in times of crisis for the town, particularly the period surrounding the Porteous affair, College members readily came to the aid of the council.

Thirdly, the proximity of the College gave Edinburgh a distinct advantage in litigation and in the administration of justice locally. The advocate James Graeme of Buchlyvie acknowledged as much when, having been accused of assault and theft in 1738, he described the magistrates in the Canongate as being 'much better Judges than the Sheriff of *Stirling*, having always their Assessors at their Hand'.[156] Edinburgh's position can best be appreciated by comparison with other burghs. Glasgow was obliged to employ writers to the signet based in Edinburgh to act as its agents. In 1784 the council there elected Lawrence Hill WS to replace the aged John Russell WS as its agent for all lawsuits engaged in before the Court of Session.[157] Russell, who had latterly held office jointly with his son, was henceforth to restrict himself purely to administrative, rather than legal, matters. Although Glasgow's council records indicate payment to the town's Edinburgh agents, these are not particularly detailed. Both John Bogle WS and his successor William Miller WS received £100 Scots per annum for exercising the office and both annually rendered their accounts for any balances owing to them 'for Law suits and raising diligence against the Towns debtors'.[158] Payments to advocates may have been subsumed within these general payments to agents although fees paid to the macers are noted.

It is true that in Glasgow an advocate, John Orr, was for years both town clerk and clerk in the commissary court.[159] He never practised at the bar, however. Moreover, he may have come to dominate locally to an unhealthy extent. His annual income as town clerk was said in 1797 to amount to the impressive sum of £800 sterling. The sheriff-clerk objected to Orr as a candidate for the sheriffship in 1797 for fear that he would take cases away from the sheriff court to the burgh court in Glasgow 'where he acts in a Judicial character by determining every case that comes before that court'.[160]

Local archives elsewhere also provide evidence of other councils employing Edinburgh agents. Perth, in the first half of the century, retained William Cunningham of Bandalloch WS and then, later, John Dundas WS.[161] From the perspective of a WS, the offer of employment from a provincial town was, of course, to be welcomed, not only for its direct salary but also for any incidental income from additional clients which it might generate. Employment directly by Edinburgh was usually preferable to that of councils in the provinces, however. For a WS it was usually more convenient to work locally (that is, in Edinburgh) than with a distant employer and, because Edinburgh was involved quite heavily in litigation in the Court of Session, its business was greater with more opportunity to supplement the income of the office.[162]

The relationship between College members and Edinburgh town council, therefore, was one of mutual benefit. A good example is James Hamilton WS. His promotion in 1697 from town's agent to PCS in the College may have inspired others to see employment by the council as a means of increasing their profile in precincts of the central court with potential further promotion in mind.[163] The treasurers' accounts of Edinburgh indicate that considerable sums were passing through the hands of the town's agent and, though the salary is not known, the emoluments of the office are likely to have been substantially greater than its equivalent in other towns. This may explain why, no doubt to the chagrin of Glasgow, its agent John Davidson WS resigned in 1754 when he was elected agent for the town of Edinburgh.[164]

To conclude this chapter it might, indeed, be asked, given the proximity of the College of Justice, how well Edinburgh as a city was prepared to cope with the demands of eighteenth-century litigation. The town council employed staff to clerk its courts and to record transactions of a legal and administrative nature. To make those and past legal records useful, it ensured that efforts were made to catalogue and preserve them and to accommodate them securely in the clerks' chamber and the town's charter-house. Legal agents and procurators were employed directly to prosecute and defend actions in the inferior courts while, in the Court of Session, some of the leading men at the bar were retained to the same purpose. It was the interaction of the assessors, the guiding hands of the town's law agents and clerks, and the ability of the procurators fiscal to act in tandem with all of them, that helped ensure the smooth running of the town. If matters took on another dimension, Edinburgh had legal counsel, and corresponding solicitors on retainer in London, to deal with appeal cases to the House of Lords.[165] In short, there was nothing the town council was not fully able to do. The councillors (albeit not immune from external political interests) provided direction to a legal organisation made up of individuals who, though dependent upon them to take decisions and issue instructions, were capable of carrying out discrete tasks independently and of co-operating with each other and outsiders whenever circumstances required. It was the councillors' business to ensure that the major venal offices that existed within their administrative organisation, such as the town clerkship, were purchased by competent administrators, no less than it was their duty to ensure they employed assessors equal to the task of providing the best legal advice. As a public corporation, the town of Edinburgh, despite its regular need for money, always had the funds to defend its interests to an extent which most private individuals and organisations could only envy. Without the contribution of College members, almost none of this would be true.

NOTES

1. TCM, SL1/1/90, fo. 120.
2. For the political framework of Edinburgh, see A. Murdoch, 'The importance of being Edinburgh' lxii (1983) *SHR*, 1; ibid., *The People Above* (Edinburgh, 1980), esp. pp. 11–14; Sher, 'Moderates, managers and popular politics in Mid Eighteenth century Edinburgh', p. 180. The political importance of the Convention of Royal Burghs as a lobbying organisation, in which Edinburgh had an important role, should not be underestimated. See, B. Harris, 'The Scots, the Westminster parliament, and the British state in the eighteenth century' in J. Hoppit, ed., *Parliaments, nations and identities in Britain and Ireland, 1660–1850* (Manchester, 2003), p. 124 esp. at pp. 125, 133–5.

3. R. Sedgwick, *The House of Commons 1715–1754* (2 vols, London, 1970), i, p. 398; *Edin. Burgh Recs, 1701–18*, p. 256. For protests at the election of Stewart, see TCM, SL1/1/41, fo. 168.

4. TCM, SL1/1/105, fo. 233. He was the son of the judge, Sir James Fergusson, Lord Kilkerran.

5. For Dundas's elections, see ibid., SL1/1/114, fo. 225; SL1/116, fo. 10; SL1/1/137, fo. 121. The council used both men in the 1780s to forward its political business; e.g a letter for the king, reflecting the council's satisfaction at his recovery in 1789, was sent to Fergusson but, if he was not in London, it was to go to Dundas: SL1/1/113, fo. 209.

6. NLS, Erskine Murray papers, MS 5130, fos 67v–68v. This refers to the JP list for 1761.

7. NRS, CS1/15, fo. 17r; ibid., CS1/17, fo. 164r.

8. There is a reference in the sederunt books in Nov. 1637 to lords being deputed to meet the magistrates to discuss the price of 'vivers' (food): NRS, CS1/5, fo. 168v.

9. For example, TCM, SL1/1/76, fo. 53.

10. There is no particular pattern: e.g. a meeting was held in 'the new counsel chamber' on Friday, 29 June 1716 at 6 p.m. (NRS, CS1/10, fo. 188v); another at the same venue on Friday, 30 November 1722 at 6 p.m. (NRS, CS1/11, fo. 78v); another in the same venue on Friday, 29 June 1716 at 6 p.m. (CS1/10, fo. 188v); and another for the Advocates Library at 3 p.m. in June 1717 (CS/10, fo. 199r).

11. For example, ibid., CS1/17, fo. 149r; TCM, SL1/1/63, fos 333–4. For a complaint in 1800 about the removal of price controls on bread by the council with the advice of the lords, see *Letter from Thomas Smith Esquire occasioned by his Letter to the Lord Provost and Magistrates of Edinburgh* (Edinburgh, 1800), pp. 11–12.

12. NRS, CS 1/12, fo. 59v.

13. Ibid., CS 1/17, fo. 138r.

14. Ibid., CS 1/12, fo. 156v (18 Nov. 1741).

15. TCM, SL1/1/65, fos 262–5. The nastiness of the streets is often remarked upon, e.g. Taylor, *Journey to Edenborough*, pp. 129 (n.1), 135. See on this, Houston, 'Fire and Filth', pp. 25–7.

16. NRS, CS1/14, fo. 122v; TCM, SL1/1/76, fos 52–5.

17. NRS, CS1/14, fo. 122v; CS 1/16, fo. 87v.

18. *Eighth Report of the Royal Commission on Historical Manuscripts* (London, 1881), p. 311. For precognitions, TCM, SL1/1/57, fo. 50.

19. NRS, CS 1/11, fo. 220r.

20. Ibid., CS1/14, fo. 22r; *Acts of Sederunt*, pp. 489–90. For its removal, see P. Dunshea, 140 (2010) *Proceedings of the Society of Antiquaries of Scotland*, 'Another 18th-century reference to Arthur's Oven', pp. 207–8.

21. For example, NRS, CS 1/10, fo. 208r; CS 1/11, fo. 137r; *Acts of Sederunt*, p. 311

22. TCM, SL1/1/61, fo. 198.

23. NRS, CS1/9, fo. 36v.

24. NRS, CS 1/12, fo. 50r.

25. *RPS*, 1693/4/104.

26. For example, ibid., CS1/9, fos 23v, 41v, 57r,

27. TCM, SL1/1/59, fos 31–2; NRS, CS1/12, fo. 78r.

28. AL, FR339r/12, 'Heads of a Bill For granting an aid to the Funds destined for the support of the Poor of the City of Edinburgh; etc.', pp. 3–4.

29. Assessors in the sense of the legal office are not to be confused with the assessors for rates and duties (i.e. revenue officers) which the council appointed for the Canongate and Leith e.g. TCM, SL1/1/67, fos 204–5, or assessors to the markets e.g. SL1/1/35, fo. 105.

30. *Extracts from the records of the Royal Burgh of Stirling to 1752* (2 vols, Glasgow, 1887–89), ii, p. 25.

31. *Dumbarton Burgh Records, 1627–1746* (Dumbarton, 1860), p. 103.

32. For example, the lord advocate, William Grant, was assessor to the convention before his elevation to the bench in 1755; he was replaced by his successor as HMA: *Extracts from the Records of the Convention of the Royal Burghs of Scotland, 1738–1759* (Edinburgh, 1915), p. 485.

33. For example, George Home, town clerk, was general clerk to the Convention of Royal Burghs, and a later town clerk, Joseph Williamson, was joint general clerk to the convention.

34. G. Desbrisay, 'Authority and discipline in Aberdeen, 1650–1700' (PhD thesis, University of Aberdeen, 1989), p. 231.

35. F. Miller, 'Andrew Crosbie, advocate' (1921), p. 17.

36. Dumfries Archive Centre, Dumfries town council minutes, A2/19 (n.p. 9 Oct. 1775).

37. Ibid., for Ferguson's appointment is given at A2/21 (n.p. 14 March 1785); for that of Corbet, A2/23 (n.p. 1 June 1796).

38. Glasgow University Archives, MS 26634, p. 21 (3 March 1721, Archibald Stewart); MS 26635, p. 62 (14 Oct. 1728, Thomas Forbes). Walter Stewart's date of appointment has not been traced.

39. Ibid., MS 26631, p. 233 (13 Sept. 1716); GCA, Glasgow town council minutes, C1/1/37, fo. 369. Eventually it was Miller's son, Thomas, who was usually employed as advocate to act for the town council in Glasgow; he later became rector of the university.

40. *Edin. Burgh Recs, 1655–1665*, p. 246 (Nisbet, app. 19 June 1661); *Edin. Burgh Recs, 1681–1689*, p. 160 (Mackenzie, app. 6 Jan. 1686). For sixteenth-century traces, see Finlay, *Men of Law*, pp. 10–20, 40–2, 61, 117.

41. TCM, SL1/1/33, fo. 5r.

42. Ibid., SL1/1/33, fos 5r, 8r. The office-holders were Sir John Lauder, Sir Patrick Home and William Hamilton.

43. Ibid., SL1/1/32, fo. 313r. Lauder seems to have been replaced (by David Drummond) in Aug. 1686 but appears again as an assessor in July 1687,

along with Drummond and Robert Stewart: SL1/1/32, fos. 20v, 128r.

44. D.1.22; C.1.51,2.

45. TCM, SL1/1/48, fos 38–9.

46. *Edin. Burgh Recs, 1689–1701*, p. 239; TCM, SL1/1/69, fo. 91.

47. In 1687 the three assessors were also required to sit 'by turns that none of them be overburdened': SL1/1/32, fo. 128r.

48. On Edinburgh courts, see Cosh, *Edinburgh*, pp. 35–6.

49. TCM, SL1/1/51, fos 456–7.

50. Ibid., SL1/1/89, fos 65–6; his appointment is at SL1/1/64, fo. 36.

51. *The Daily Gazetteer* (Country edition), London, 15 April 1741, issue no. 1771. The jury returned a guilty verdict and Swan was sentenced to transportation. The papers in this case can be found at ECA, SL233/1/2. In 1686 the council determined that magistrates should wear black gowns: SL1/1/31, fo. 301v.

52. TCM, SL1/1/57, fo. 3.

53. Avizandum is a legal term meaning that the judge has determined to take time to consider before delivering his judgment. This is known as 'making avizandum'.

54. TCM, SL1/1/48, fo. 38.

55. They were John Elphinstone (adm. adv. 15 Feb. 1699, and a serving assessor since 23 Nov. 1705); Sir James Stewart (adm. adv. 22 Nov. 1704, formerly MP for the burgh and a former SG, a serving assessor since 16 Sept. 1715); John Mitchelson (adm. adv. 16 Nov. 1694) and Hew Dalrymple of Drummore (adm. adv. 21 Nov. 1710): ibid., SL1/1/48, fo. 39; also, for the dates of initial appointment of the serving assessor, SL1/1/ 38, fo. 438 and SL1/1/42, fo. 175.

56. Ibid., SL1/1, fo. 444.

57. G. W. T. Omond, *The Arniston Memoirs* (Edinburgh, 1887), p. 65.

58. This is not to suggest that ordinary assessors did not give opinions on cases involving the council before the Court of Session or plead in such cases on the council's behalf. They did both of these things. They alone, however, seem to have sat with the magistrates as their advisers, and it was primarily in respect of this that they received their salary.

59. TCM, SL1/1/59, fo. 1.

60. The payment of twice as much per annum for the lord advocate (still £200 Scots), as compared to the SG (£100 Scots), was also recorded in 1742 when Robert Craigie and his junior colleague Robert Dundas were given their retaining fees: NLS, Yester, MS 7049, fo. 81r.

61. TCM, SL1/1/76, fos 92–3.

62. Ibid; for appointments as SG, NRS, CS 1/14, fo. 134v.

63. As noted earlier Thomas Kennedy, as a former SG, is an exception. The phrase 'retained lawyer' seems to be applied in the minutes only to existing or recent crown lawyers. The sole exception of this is the retention of William Murray at the English bar to advise largely on House of Lords appeals.

64. *Edin. Burgh Recs, 1689–1701*, p. 142.
65. NLS, Yester, MS 7049, fo. 82r. Hay says both men were made burgesses. Only Craigie was made a burgess around this time, on 18 July 1742, and that is when the entertainment referred to probably occurred: Watson, ed., *Roll of Edinburgh Burgesses*, p. 44. Craigie became HMA on 4 March 1742 but is not recorded in the council minutes as being admitted as an assessor. Except for him, every lord advocate from the Restoration to Henry Dundas (adm. assessor 7 Aug. 1765) was an assessor. Henry Erskine and Ilay Campbell, however, were not.
66. Ibid., SL1/1/72, fo. 43. Also, notably, SL1/1/73, fos 405–8 opinion of Robert Pringle re liability of the collector of the window tax.
67. Ibid., SL1/1/71, fos 43–7. The advocates approached were Robert Dundas II (HMA), Robert Craigie and James Ferguson of Pitfour.
68. Ibid., SL1/1/132, fo. 333 (5 Feb. 1800).
69. J. MacLaurin, *Arguments and Decisions in Remarkable Cases, before the High Court of Justiciary, and other Supreme Courts, in Scotland* (Edinburgh, 1774), pp. 530–1. The case, from 1769, involved Mungo Campbell, who had shot the Earl of Eglinton.
70. E.g. TCM, SL1/1/98, fos 28–41; SL1/1/82, fos 216–18.
71. Ibid., SL1/1/72, fo. 350.
72. Ibid., SL1/1/73, fos 79–84. The book, unfortunately, does not survive in ECA.
73. Ibid., SL1/1/67, fo. 220
74. Ibid., SL1/1/46, fo. 49.
75. Ibid., SL1/1/69, fo. 284.
76. Ibid., SL1/1/36, fo. 396.
77. Ibid., SL1/1/40, fo. 258.
78. *Edin. Burgh Recs 1689–1701*, p. 20; TCM, SL1/1/73, fo. 18.
79. TCM, SL1/1/64, fo. 36; SL1/1/131, fo. 128.
80. Ibid., SL1/1/40, fo. 258.
81. Ibid., SL1/1/72, fo. 119.
82. Ibid., SL1/1/60, fos 94–5. Apparently this was not his first appointment as assessor but I have not identified any earlier appointment of Graham in that role.
83. Ibid., SL1/1/131, fo. 128.
84. NRS, Papers of the Dundas family of Melville, GD51/957/6; Stewart and Parratt, *Min. Bk 1783–1798*, p. xxxv, n.113; Maidment, *Court of Session Garland*, pp. 52–7.
85. TCM, SL1/1/122, fo. 156. John Pattison, the putative uncle, was appointed town clerk of Leith in 1774 and was still in office in 1793: SL1/1/91, fos 318–22; SL1/1/126, fo. 414. He might conceivably have been Pattison's apprentice-master. Pattison the assessor was also son-in-law to one of the Edinburgh ministers.
86. Henry, Lord Brougham, *Speeches on Social and Politics Subjects* (2 vols, London, 1857), ii, p. 368. 'Corporation' is used here in the sense of burgh

council. See also Henry, Lord, Cockburn, *Letters Chiefly Connected with the Affairs of Scotland* (London, 1874), pp. 394–5.

87. James Henryson and Adam Otterburn were both town clerks, although both are better known as lord advocates: J. Finlay, 'James Henryson and the origins of the office of king's advocate', 79 (2000) *SHR*, p. 24; J. C. Inglis, *Sir Adam Otterburn of Reidhall* (Glasgow, 1935).

88. The Edinburgh clerks referred to were Adam Watt (adm. NP, 15 Feb. 1704) and Joseph Williamson (adm. NP, 22 Dec. 1742); and, for Glasgow, John Orr (adm. NP, 16 June 1781). The fourth advocate was John Belshes (sheriff-clerk of Midlothian, adm. NP, 31 July 1745). Biographical details of these men will be found in *ARNP*.

89. *Edin. Burgh Recs, 1689–1701*, introduction, p. xxviii; NRS NP2/15 (entry dated 25 Jan. 1687).

90. ALSP, *Answers for Aeneas McLeod Town Clerk of Edinburgh*, n.d., Forbes collection, vol. 3, fo. 2337.

91. ALSP, *Memorial for Archibald Blair Extracter in the town-clerks chamber of Edinburgh*, 27 July 1739, Drummore collection, vol. 2, no. 896, p. 1.

92. Their duties included acting as electoral returning officer, e.g. SL1/1/118, fo. 64.

93. The council reiterated the need for them to give consent to the appointments of deputes by their clerks in 1736: TCM, SL1/1/57, fos 106–7. The depute clerks were to maintain custody of processes in the bailie and other courts: SL1/1/34, fo. 105. One of them seems to have audited the kirk treasurers' accounts: SL1/1/122, fo. 151. See also ALSP, *Memorial for George Lindsay Deputy Clerk of the Good Town of Edinburgh*, 12 Dec. 1739, Drummore collection, vol. 3, no. 911.

94. *Memorial for Archibald Blair*, p. 2.

95. For the new table of fees drawn published in July 1743, see TCM, SL1/1/64, fos 23–7.

96. ALSP, *Answers for Aeneas McLeod*, fo. 2337.

97. TCM, SL1/1/48, fos 275–8.

98. Ibid., SL1/1/48, fo. 275.

99. Brown's patron, Lord Pollock, recommended him in 1716 as agent for the University of Glasgow, citing the competence he had shown in his employment 'about the Session house': GUL, Murray, 650/2/2. William Miller, however, gained the appointment.

100. TCM, SL1/1/48, fo. 294.

101. Ibid., SL1/1/52, fo.34.

102. Ibid., SL1/1/52, fo. 37 (punctuation added); for the act see fos 32–40.

103. Ibid., SL1/1/63, fos 75–6. Payments to anyone other than the council remained prohibited.

104. Ibid., SL1/1/63, fos 77–8. He paid in instalments as did a later clerk, John Dundas WS: SL1/1/89, fo. 23.

105. Ibid., ECA, SL1/1/63, fos 87, 90. The oath of 10 Sept. 1718 is much referred to subsequently; it is found at SL1/1/46, fo. 48. This was the oath sworn in 1720 by Irving and Brown.

106. Ibid., SL1/1/63, fo. 266. This William Forbes is not to be confused with his contemporary William Forbes WS. The town clerk became NP in 1743 (*ARNP*, no. 1211; his cautioner was Ronald Dunbar WS). He was neither a WS nor a College member. William Forbes (adm. WS in 1720) became NP in 1725 (ibid., no. 691). He was employed by the council in 1726 as one of a series of men tasked 'to put the goodtouns charter house in order': TCM, SL1/1/51, fo. 217. Neither man should be confused with the three contemporary advocates of the same name! The act of Dec. 1742 appears at SL1/1/63, fos 266–8.

107. Ibid., SL1/1/63, fo. 282.

108. Forbes had promised to pay £1,410 sterling: ibid., SL1/1/63, fos 280–3.

109. ALSP, *Memorial for Archibald Blair* (*supra*, n. 94), p. 4.

110. TCM, SL1/1/57, fo. 34 (depute clerk); SL1/1/78, fos 274–9 (principal clerk).

111. Finlay, *Admission Registers*, no. 256. His cautioner was the Leith merchant, William Bryden.

112. TCM, SL1/1/40, fo. 493. He continued to write burgess tickets, or more properly to collect the fees for having them written, until at least 1728: SL1/1/52, fo. 230.

113. Ibid., SL1/1/40, fos 493, 496. If this was by arrangement with Buchan, it is possible Irving also worked in the Teind Court. Writing burgess tickets suggests he was extractor in the dean of gild court. For further references to Irving, see SL1/1/40, fo. 493; SL1/1/41, fos 174, 227; 1/1/43, fos 61, 157; SL1/1/45, fo. 71.

114. Ibid., SL1/1/45, fo. 30. For the 1693 Act, see above, n. 23. For Irving as secretary, SL1/1/50, fo. 89.

115. Ibid., SL1/1/44, fo. 83. He received 30 guineas in expenses.

116. Ibid., SL1/1/45, fo. 106. In 1726 Baillie's widow received £25 in respect of his share of the work carried out: SL1/1/51, fo. 172. Baillie, employed by successive lords clerk register, also inventoried the records in the Laigh Parliament House: A. L. Murray, 'The Lord Clerk Register' 52 (1974) *SHR*, 146.

117. *History of the WS Society*, p. 109.

118. TCM, SL1/1/50, fo. 427.

119. Ibid., SL1/1/51, fo. 191. At the same time, the council admitted Matthew Brown as a burgess and gild brother, free of charge in consideration for his good service to the town. Since he was already one of the depute clerks of session, he cannot have been Irving's rival for the post: NLS, Mackenzie of Delvine, MS 1505, fo. 8.

120. *History of the WS Society*, p. 109.

121. TCM, SL1/1/63, fos 77, 273.

122. Ibid., SL1/1/55, fos 108, 128. This was in respect of lands in Powis to

which the council took sasine in 1717: SL1/1/44, fo. 159; see also NLS MS 17532, fos 185r–v.

123. Ibid., SL1/1/58, fos 88, 90; SL1/1/59, fo. 77. Irving received 200 guineas for his services in regard to this matter, which indicates his involvement was as solicitor, not principal clerk.

124. Ibid., SL1/1/52, fo. 188; SL1/1/64, fo. 28. Snodgrass may have been related to a later procurator fiscal, and sheriff-clerk, of Renfrew, on whom, see J. Finlay, 'Pettyfoggers, regulation and local courts in early modern Scotland' (2008) 87 *SHR*, p. 61.

125. G. Menary, *The Life and Letters of Duncan Forbes of Culloden* (London, 1936), p. 107

126. NRS, Wills and Testaments, CC8/99, fo. 320; TCM, SL1/1/50, fo. 573.

127. For an example of the council ordering the chamberlain directly to employ assessors, see ibid., SL1/1/38, fo. 312.

128. The only exception to this is the last one, the writer John MacRitchie, appointed on 6 Dec. 1797 as successor to the late John Davidson WS: ibid., SL1/1/128, fo. 58. It was a sign of the times that MacRtichie, in the 1800s, went into partnership with James Little, such partnership arrangements becoming prevalent in the nineteenth century (see, e.g. SL1/1/145, fo. 112; SL1/1/146, fo. 96). See Appendix 2 for a list of the town's agents.

129. See chapter 7 below.

130. For example, ibid., SL1/1/100, fo. 297.

131. Ibid., SL1/1/138, fo. 17.

132. Ibid., SL1/1/33, fo. 21r.

133. Ibid., SL1/1/36, fo. 879. From 1699 Campbell held in his person the offices of 'writer' and 'agent' for the town and petitioned for an increase in salary given; formerly each of these office-holders had been paid £100 Scots (with an additional subvention from the university for the latter). The council responded by saying that expenses of actions had diminished and were 'not a fourth part of what they were in use to be' because so many were settled out of court; therefore, having determined to pay him 200 merks they raised this to £200 Scots. Thereafter, there seems to be no separation between the town's writer and the town's agent.

134. For example, TCM, SL1/1/51, fo. 191 (punctuation added); cf. SL1/1/135, fos 103–4. For office-holders, see Appendix 2.

135. Ibid., SL1/1/92, fo. 73. Little is known of this inferior court, though it evidently dealt with low-value claims.

136. Ibid., SL1/1/92, fo. 175.

137. For example, ibid., SL1/1/80, fo. 245.

138. For example, ibid, SL1/1/76, fo.182.

139. Ibid., SL1/1/80, fo. 70.

140. Ibid., SL1/1/74, fos 437–40.

141. For example, ibid., SL1/1/51, fo. 217 (representatives of Campbell to

Irvine, 1726); SL1/1/63, fo. 214 (representatives of Irvine to Dunbar, 1742; SL1/1/72, fo. 45 (Dunbar to Davidson, 1754).

142. Ibid., SL1/1/63, fo. 202.

143. Ibid., SL1/1/52, fo. 480.

144. Ibid., SL1/1/67, fos 30–3. Dunbar, was also, at one time, substitute keeper of the register of hornings (on which, see chapter 8): ALSP, *Hugh Buchan writer in Edinburgh* (*supra* p. 71, n. 108), p. 35.

145. Youngson acknowledges the contribution of advocates and writers to the signet in the process of architectural renewal, but the debt is more widely owed: *The Making of Classical Edinburgh*, pp. 49–50.

146. TCM, SL1/1/71, fo. 42.

147. Ibid., SL1/1/76, fo. 212. The Canongate's agent required a council warrant to look for deeds in Edinburgh's charterhouse.

148. For the defence of a bailie before the privy council in 1694, see ibid., SL1/1/35, fo. 9.

149. Ibid., SL1/1/72, fo. 324.

150. NLS, Saltoun, MS16553, fo. 21.

151. TCM, SL1/1/63, fo. 268; SL1/1/71, fos 153, 158–60.

152. TCM, SL1/1/93, fo. 281.

153. ALSP, *Hugh Buchan writer in Edinburgh* (*supra* p. 71, n. 108), pp. 13, 35. The Edinburgh writer, John Robertson senior, was Williamson's first clerk in the period 1743–8: ibid., pp. 63, 67–8.

154. NRS, Great seal register, C3/17, fo. 44, no. 39.

155. TCM, SL1/1/108, fo. 58.

156. ALSP, *The Petition of Mr James Graeme of Bucclivie, Advocate*, 27 July 1738, Kilkerran collection, vol. 2, no. 59, p.1. On Graeme, see chapter one above.

157. GCA, Glasgow town council minutes, C1/1/37, fo. 369.

158. Ibid., C1/1/28, fos 67, 179.

159. He was also dean of the Faculty of Procurators in Glasgow where he seems to have had local family connections. The minute book contains Orrs going back to the seventeenth century: J. S. Muirhead, *The Old Minute Book of the Faculty of Procurators in Glasgow, 1668–1758* (Glasgow, 1948). There is a plaque dedicated to Orr in Glasgow cathedral.

160. NRS, Dundas of Melville papers, GD51/5/396.

161. SCA, B66/25/585.

162. The income was 100 merks per annum in 1689; it is not clear how much it was in the eighteenth century.

163. *Edin. Burgh Recs, 1689–1701*, p. 216. Hamilton was appointed agent in 1689 at a salary of £133 6s. 8d. Scots: *Edin. Burgh Recs, 1681–1689*, p. 258.

164. *Extracts from the Records of the Burgh of Glasgow* (11 vols, Glasgow, 1876–1916), vi, p. 382. Glasgow replaced him with John Russell Sr, WS.

By 1749 Davidson was son-in-law of William Miller WS, previously agent for Glasgow, making him brother-in-law to the advocate and judge Thomas Miller: NRS, Memorandum book of John Mair, RH15/134, fo. 16.

165. J. Finlay, 'Scots lawyers and House of Lords appeals in eighteenth-century Britain', 32 (2011) *Journal of Legal History*, 249.

4

The Lords of Session

As one looks over the record of coarseness and stupidity and debauchery which filled so large a part of some of their lives, one wonders how so high spirited a people as the Scots allowed such men to have the power, in the sacred name of the law, of deciding all-important questions of life, liberty, and property.[1]

It was largely the lords of council and session – or senators of the College of Justice – who developed Scots law into the distinctive legal system that it remains today. To their role in legal decision-making, every office in the College was subordinate. The lords also supervised the conduct of the lawyers and clerks who acted in their court, ensuring they obeyed the acts of sederunt and respected the obligation (imposed under the oath *de fideli administratione*) to carry out their roles faithfully.[2]

A formal oath swearing, though no longer specifically recorded in the books of sederunt, apparently took place whereby 'if not each Session at least annually' the lords enjoined writers and clerks 'to observe the Regulations'.[3] Punishments were certainly meted out, not only to wayward College members but also to any misbehaving clerk, notary or procurator from the local courts.[4] As Scotland's 'superior tribunal', the Court of Session could review the decisions of any inferior judge who had suspended a local court procurator or deprived him of office.[5]

Apart from details of some individuals given in the *Dictionary of National Biography*, the standard work of reference for biographical data on the senators of the College of Justice remains that of Brunton and Haig, published in 1832.[6] This is a valuable and scholarly work. Away from the sphere of political history, however, much of what has been written about the eighteenth-century lords of session, particularly by near contemporaries, is anecdotal and preoccupied with their general tendency for hard drinking and other individual traits of character. Like nineteenth-century writers on the English bar, the focus in Scotland has often tended to fall on individual 'great men', even if some were later acknowledged to be, as Cockburn said of Lord Polkemmet, 'not much above an idiot'.[7]

As befits a study in community, the approach in this chapter is to examine the lords as a group. Given the relatively small number of them, this is quite feasible.[8] From (and including) the elevation of Sir George Lockhart of Carnwath in 1686 to that of Robert Blair of Avonton in 1808, 115 lords of session were appointed. This figure includes two lord chancellors and ten extraordinary lords. Following the parliamentary Union in May 1707, and the emergence of a strict *cursus honorum* for the appointment of ordinary lords of session, sixty-eight of the sixty-nine ordinary lords of session who were appointed prior to 1800 were drawn from the ranks of the bar.[9]

The eighteenth century saw significant developments in law reporting, and recent scholarship has cast new light on the significance of judicial decisions as the main means of developing Scots law in the early modern period.[10] Neither subject can be explored here although it is worth remembering that the quality of judicial decisions varied with the intellectual strength of the bench. According to Hill Burton, *Kilkerran's Decisions* were 'quite distinct' from other Scottish reports because of the large number of leading cases they contained, making them more important in the case law of the Court of Session than the decisions taken by Mansfield in respect of the King's Bench in England.[11] Since the period of the reports coincided with a low level of litigation, this might reflect the greater time judges had to consider the arguments in important cases.[12] Or it might simply mean that, at this period, the bench was particularly strong (and the reports do coincide with the presidencies of Culloden and Arniston).

There was certainly an ebb and flow. Lord Stair felt the need to defend the intellectual rigour and honesty of his colleagues (some of whom certainly needed defending) but, by the time of his death in 1695, it could reasonably be argued that the bench was a strong one.[13] By the time of the death of Sir Francis Grant (Lord Cullen) in 1726, Robert Wodrow expressed the view that not only were many of those judges promoted since the Revolution dead or dying but that 'such as are brought in in their room are generally not of the former stamp'.[14] Wodrow, no jurist, meant that the late generation, though not necessarily the best lawyers, were men of integrity who had managed to 'keep the bench in great respect'.

Few shared Lord Dun's idealised vision of the judge as God's viceregent, untainted by 'sinful practices and vicious habits'.[15] Most judges, particularly those who openly kept mistresses, could never hope to achieve such a standard.[16] Yet all agreed on the central role of the judges in developing Scots Law. In 1707 Sir Francis Grant even argued that there was no need for a legislative function in Scotland because the College was 'one of the best constitute bodies in the world'.[17] The Union meant fewer reforming legal statutes in Scotland, particularly in the sphere of private law.[18] Case law, the product of rational legal reasoning, could easily be comprehended within the empiricist direction that was taken by Scottish Enlightenment philosophy which, in jurisprudence, superseded the rationalist natural law theories of writers like Pufendorf.[19]

Lord Kames took up a version of moral sense theory influenced by Adam Smith's impartial spectator, preferring judicial decision-making to the will of parliament. The legislator, no matter how well informed, was acting prospectively and creating rules of general application; the judge, responding to particular facts, was creating rules which were more in tune with societal development, and Kames viewed his judicial colleagues as the primary means of modernising Scots law.[20] In the same tradition, Professor John Millar made his own distinctive contribution in his lectures at the University of Glasgow.[21]

By the second half of the eighteenth century, modernisation was required because legal reformers were intent on positioning Scotland to compete commercially within the British Empire. Whether the College of Justice could achieve such a task without reducing the size of the bench was questioned more than once. By implication, Adam Smith regarded institutions with so many judges as less able to work efficiently.[22] Others held similar views. In 1742 the president, Duncan Forbes, indicated privately that he would go further than his colleague, Lord Arniston, who wished to reduce the number of judges to nine, and make the court even smaller and more accountable because a wrong opinion, given through ignorance or corruption, passed more easily 'Unheaded, and Uncensured in a Crowd' than it would do if there were fewer judges.[23] Such plans for reform, along with a more famous proposal to reduce the size of the court supported by Henry Dundas and Ilay Campbell in the 1780s, came to nothing until 1808.[24]

Because their judicial function was its *raison d'être*, this chapter will examine the lords as a group and identify their significance within the College.

GROUP PORTRAIT

Published data suggest that a slight majority of the lords of session were eldest sons and that a third of them were second sons.[25] This is broadly comparable with the bar as a whole.[26] Most were from wealthy backgrounds. Almost one in three were the sons of lawyers; one in five were the sons of earls or baronets, and two-fifths were the sons of lairds. Apart from Lord Polton, the rest were the sons of professional men, such as doctors of medicine and kirk ministers.[27]

Wealth enabled foreign education. It is possible to identify the universities attended by thirty-one of the forty-one advocates, admitted in the period 1700–49, who were subsequently promoted to the bench. No less than twenty-seven can be placed with reasonable certainty in the Netherlands at Leiden, Utrecht or Groningen (in John Sinclair's case at both Leiden and Groningen). The last of them chronologically, David Dalrymple, went to Utrecht in 1744 where his studies have left some trace in the record.[28] The lack of matriculation lists in some Dutch universities renders our knowledge incomplete although this was certainly not the only route to the bar or bench. In Henry Home's case, for instance, his father's economic circumstances prevented legal study abroad.[29]

As mentioned in the introduction, a lord of session was more likely than an advocate in general to have married the daughter of a fellow College member and to have been the son-in-law of another judge.[30] This certainly brought career advantage. For instance, William Honyman (Lord Armadale) made a quick start at the bar with help from his father-in-law, Lord Braxfield. Having married in 1777, the same year as his admission, by 1781 he was the tenth most active advocate in the Outer House and, by the summer of 1786, had been appointed sheriff of Lanarkshire. Twenty years later, Colin Mackenzie recounted that Armadale originally made slow progress at the bar until, 'under the auspices and instruction of the celebrated Lord Braxfield … he got at length into considerable practice'.[31] Professor Prest, in his study of seventeenth-century English barristers, noted the importance for any lawyer seeking to attract clients beyond his own immediate community or kin network to be popularly recognised as a judge's favourite (typically through a blood or marriage relationship).[32] Braxfield's eminence gave Honyman a distinct advantage.

Others shared similar benefits though they did not necessarily appreciate them. As James Boswell (son of Lord Auchinleck) complained to William Temple in 1767, the year after he entered the bar:

> the absurdity of mankind makes nineteen out of twenty employ the son of the judge before whom their cause is heard. And you must take it along with you that I am as yet but a very raw counsellor, so that a moderate share of business is really a load to me.[33]

In terms of family background, the bench was becoming increasingly homogeneous compared to the 1600s. About one in eight lords ordinary appointed in the eighteenth century followed their fathers on to the bench. Despite what is often thought about legal dynasties, however, it was difficult for any family to achieve a long pedigree on the bench. The prolific Dalrymples managed four generations of judges (Stair, North Berwick, Drummore and Westhall). The family of Dundas of Arniston had three generations on the bench (including, like the Dalrymples, two presidents).[34] These families, however, were exceptional. Men like William Grant (Lord Prestongrane), son of Lord Cullen, did not have a successor on the bench nor did Gilbert

Elliot, James Erskine or Andrew Pringle although all followed their fathers there. The names that had dominated the bench in the 1600s could not easily sustain their presence in the 1700s, and new family names, such as Erskine, Pringle, Ferguson, Grant and Boswell, began to appear.

A sign of homogeneity, however, is the fact that the forty-eight advocates who became lords ordinary in the seventeenth century shared thirty-nine surnames, while the sixty-eight advocates who did so in the following century shared only forty-six surnames.[35] Eighteenth-century judicial gowns were being shared within a narrowing social spectrum even if identity of surname did not always mean a close family relationship. While the most common eighteenth-century judicial surname was Campbell, each Campbell lord of session came from a separate branch of the kindred.

Because Scotland was a small jurisdiction, the backgrounds of the judges were well known to many litigants. This necessitated a long history of measures being taken in the College to prohibit undue solicitation.[36] Henry Home, when at the bar, thought himself justified in the public interest (rather than his client's private interest) in approaching judges extrajudicially. As counsel in *Bell of Blackwoodhouse* v. *Gartshore* – a fundamental case in the development of what conveyancers now call the 'offside goals rule' – he solicited the judges privately to ensure they were fully aware of the conseq-uences of not guaranteeing the security of infeftment.[37] Lord Arniston, recently appointed to the bench, favoured the uninfeft first disponee over the second disponee who had taken infeftment but, thanks to Home, the other judges disagreed. This, he later claimed, was 'the first stroke to his [that is, Arniston's] reputation', pricking the aura of invincibility which had surrounded his legal opinions.[38]

James Boswell once wrote that appointing judges from different parts of the country 'diffuses and divides that private and imperceptible influence which must ever be in a narrow country'.[39] It did not, however, altogether remove the problem of men seeking to influence their kinsmen on the bench. Alexander Mackenzie of Coul, for instance, in a letter to John Mackenzie WS in January 1745, related that their clan chief regretted the death of Lord Royston (James Mackenzie) but 'does not despair of seeing some of his name with a purple gown'.[40] Coul had replied that this would be impossible unless the chief himself were the tailor.[41] In one of Montrose's legal processes against Rob Roy Macgregor, his agent George Robertson related the advice of the duke's ordinary lawyer that he should write to his friends on the bench to take notice of the affair because the evidence was weak.[42] Likewise, in a prosecution for murder in May 1745, advocated from Lord Lovat's regality court, Lovat wanted to influence the advocate-depute, Andrew Pringle, and was willing to write directly to the lord advocate (Robert Craigie) and his friends in the court of justiciary, Lords Strichen, Tinwald and Drummore.[43]

Despite recurrent attempts to prevent solicitation, a custom that was thought to create mistrust among those who 'have not acquaintance or friends to recommend them', efforts to influence litigation were not restricted to the great and the good.[44] Compared to the seventeenth century, however, there is relatively little evidence of outright attempts to corrupt the bench. Janet Carnegie in 1734, for example, wrote to Lord Milton asking him to intervene in the case of her poor female relation who was being harassed by vexatious litigation in the Outer House before Lord Royston. This was not open ended. She asked Milton to interpose with Royston 'to be as favourable as the justice & merits of the cause will allow' and to do the same himself should the matter come before him in the Inner House.[45] While highly irregular by modern standards, this is hardly sinister. Likewise, Lord Elibank wrote to Milton in 1732 asking him, 'as far as justice will allow', to expedite a relatively small claim against his wife's cousin and her second husband for payment of a bill subscribed by her late first husband.[46] In this case, Milton was the lord ordinary but Elibank's only concern was expedition, given the modest sum involved, otherwise 'attendance in town, expences of lawers &c will very soon exceed the claim'.

In 1730, when he had an action pending before the Court of Session, Lord Lovat, in the company of a hundred of his kinsmen, happened to encounter David Erskine (Lord Dun SCJ). Lovat claimed that 'I never did nor would solicit any judge', but as 'a known & faithfull servant to all the Erskines in the world' he did ask for Dun's friendship.[47] Dun, not yet having studied Lovat's cause, did no more than promise that, if the law was for him, he would not be against him. Although in this case Lovat baulked at direct solicitation, he urged his advocate, Dun's kinsman Charles Areskine, 'to convince that nice judge that I have law on my side'.

Lord Milton received a number of requests to act judicially in a way consonant with his friendship for the writer.[48] On one occasion, the Marquis of Lothian even asked him what agent to employ in an action coming before the court.[49] The University of Glasgow's agent, William Miller, wrote to Principal Stirling in 1725 listing five judges who were 'the friends of the Colledge', chief among them Lord Pollock, a former rector and long-time confidant of Stirling.[50] Yet this does not always mean impropriety. Pollock himself was described as acting in a 'very fair and equall' way by George Robertson, in a letter to his client, the Duke of Montrose, in 1713.[51] The following year, when the action was still continuing, Pollock wrote to Montrose that if he could do anything for his service 'in that affaire, ye may be assured I will laye my self out to the outmost'.[52] That need not be taken to mean he would act unfairly or improperly. On the other hand, judges were occasionally suspected of being corrupt or partial.[53] Boswell disliked their tendency to waver in their opinion and, at least once, feared they were not impartial.[54] Judges were certainly not above the workings of patronage. In September 1714, for instance, Lord Cullen approached the Duke of Montrose's advocate and asked him to inform the duke that, if there was a vacancy among the clerks to the commissioners of trade, he would like his brother-in-law (probably the writer Thomas Fordyce), to be considered for it.[55]

Nor was the process for appointing lords of session beyond the influence of corruption, even in the eighteenth century. It is worth bearing in mind Ramsay of Ochteryre's view of Lord Haining; a man of 'very slight knowledge of law ... made a judge by the interest of potent friends'.[56] Even when Henry Dundas was in the ascendant and claimed to eschew political placemen in favour of appointing men to the bench on merit, he pointedly excluded his political opponents.[57]

BECOMING A LORD OF SESSION

The College of Justice contained two kinds of judge: ordinary lords and, until their appointment ceased in the 1720s, extraordinary lords. Extraordinary lords were direct political appointees and often had no legal training (the Leiden-educated Earl of Ilay is the best-known exception to this).[58] There are notorious cases from the sixteenth and seventeenth centuries of corrupt and ignorant men raised to the bench as extraordinary lords.[59] Prior to a new procedure being introduced in 1674, the trial which had to be undertaken by new ordinary lords of session, who were always crown nominees, was described by Professor William Forbes as being 'very perfunctorious, and in effect a mock'.[60]

Under this procedure, the nominee was to sit beside the lord ordinary in the Outer House for three days.[61] He was then to make the report of any interlocutors sent to the lords in the Inner House for advising. The final stage of the trial involved the nominee taking a seat in the Inner House and, in respect of disputes advised that day, to be the first to give his opinion.[62] The 1674 act of sederunt was drafted at the invitation of Charles II who approved of this method of trial.[63] To enforce it, the lords sometimes made ad hoc arrangements. In 1766, for instance, a lord ordinary had to make a special sitting so that David Dalrymple, who had been nominated in March at the end of the session, could sit beside him as probationer.[64] The same occurred in 1796 when Lord Meadowbank was admitted on the last day of the session; a single cause was 'taken up by authority of the Court to be called before Lord Dunsinnan Ordinary on Acts & Regulations & to be reported by Mr Maconochie Lord Probationer'.[65] Unusually, in November 1793, Lord Dunsinnan had to call two actions 'in order that they may be reported to the Court by the two Lords Probationers', William Baillie of Polkemmet and David Smith of Methven, who were then appointed on consecutive days.[66]

A special arrangement also had to be made in 1689 when twelve new lords of session were appointed (one of whom, Sir Robert Sinclair, did not take up his seat). The only existing judges to be reappointed were Sir George Lockhart (lord president until his murder in October 1689), Alexander Swinton of Mersington (who had been excused the requirement to take the Test oath in 1687 before replacing Lord Edmonstone in 1688) and Sir John Dalrymple. Because the bench was entirely vacant, pending all these appointments, it was enacted that the royal nominees were to be tried by the Estates who, in the absence of existing lords of session, had the right to admit or reject them.[67] The alternative, an extension of the royal prerogative, was unacceptable to contemporary opinion.[68] It was also argued that the Crown lacked the power to renew Stair's appointment as lord president and that this position should be determined by election by the lords of session once constituted.[69] This was strongly tinged with anti-Dalrymple sentiment, a feeling common enough to lead to condemnations of the new bench as consisting of 'the dross of the nation'.[70]

The 1689 statute also confirmed earlier legislation concerning the lords of session, including a 1579 Act which punished attempts to bribe them and also provided the existing lords with the power to examine and reject any unsuitable royal nominee.[71] An act of parliament of 1592 confirmed this and also required that new lords of session be at least twenty-five years old and, to discourage bribery further, have an independent minimum annual income.[72] The Union negotiations produced, in article 19, the requirement that ordinary lords of session be drawn exclusively from the ranks of the advocates, writers to the session or clerks of session. Royal nomination was confirmed but only those who had 'served in the colledge of justice as advocats or principal clerks of session for the space of five years, or as writers to the signet for the space of ten years' were eligible for promotion to the bench.[73] This was subject to the proviso that a WS would first have to undergo 'privat and publick tryal on the civil law before the faculty of advocats, and be found by them qualified for the said office two years before he be named to be a lord of the session'.[74]

A particular consequence for advocates of promotion to the bench was that annual pensions or retaining fees which they received from clients were discontinued provided the payments concerned were for their 'management of law affairs'. The phrase is significant because there was no legal presumption that a bond in favour of an advocate for services done and to be done related exclusively to services as an advocate. Lord Pitmedden, for example, continued to receive a pension while on the bench but this was not viewed as incompatible with his status because the services for which the pension was paid involved management responsibilities over and above acting as an advocate.[75] The wording used in the deed constituting the right to the pension was therefore central in determining whether it could survive the payee's transition from advocate to judge.

The matter was litigated in the late 1720s by the advocate Alexander Lockhart, as assignee from his father of the unpaid pensions of his grandfather, Sir George Lockhart, former president of the court. Called to the bar in 1656, Sir George, described by Mackenzie of Rosehaugh as another Cicero, had a hugely successful career and was granted a number of annual pensions, including one in 1669 by Lord Drumlanrig for 300 merks, one in 1673 by the Duke of Gordon for £20 and one in 1684 for £100 by Sir William Purves.[76] After his appointment as president, direct from the bar in 1685, he had not sought payment of any of these pensions, even though the evidence suggests he could have done with the income.[77]

Lockhart's arguments in these cases, which raised points based on the law of prescription as well as issues of interpretation of the bonds in question, were generally unconvincing.[78] Perhaps his best prospect was the 1669 obligation which was to last all the days of Sir George's life, and appears to have arisen partly because of past services and partly in recognition that Sir George 'was ready to give his best Assistance' to Drumlanrig in future. Drumlanrig's grandson, Charles, Duke of Queensberry and Dover, like defenders in the other two cases, denied liability. Because the pension was not unambiguously related to service as an advocate, he argued that it was *contra bonos mores* because, to continue the payment of such pensions once the advocate became a judge, threatened judicial impartiality and opened a door to corruption. It was the fact of becoming a judge that was seen as decisive; an advocate who ceased practising at the bar, but who then entered upon a chamber practice, was still entitled to his pensions because he would still be useful to his clients.

THE PRESIDENCY OF THE COURT

The president was a key figure in the court. This was reinforced in 1808 when the judges implied that his position was protected by the Act of Union. They viewed a plan to split the court into three chambers, each under a presiding judge, as subversive of the privileges of the office, stating that the 'Lord President of the Court of Session is not only President of the Court but is also President of the whole College of Justice, and as such the office cannot be abolished or divided'.[79]

The president directed the advising of judgments and personally authenticated the interlocutors and acts of sederunt, subscribing them '*in praesentia dominorum*'.[80] Like any good chairperson, his role could be pivotal in ensuring the speedy dispatch of business. Lord Arniston, for example, has been credited with removing a five-year backlog in less than three months after his appointment as president in 1760.[81] This was achieved by force of personality, chairmanship and the respect his colleagues had for him as a lawyer.[82] Equally important was his almost constant attendance; indeed 'the great weight of the labour & attention, that belongs to the President's Chair' was what had purportedly secured Arniston's promotion over the veteran Lord Justice Clerk Tinwald (who had been beaten to the chair in 1748 by Arniston's father).[83] In 1761 Arniston attended 97.4 per cent of sederunts. His father, as president, had attended only 64.4 per cent in 1751. Like other judges, presidents grew old and less able to attend or to impress their personalities on colleagues. Duncan Forbes, soon after he took over as president in 1737, is also credited with clearing a substantial backlog.[84] His predecessor, Hew Dalrymple, had similarly often been unable to attend in his final years (in 1736 he attended only 70 per cent of sederunts); Forbes, on the other hand, was much more vigorous and attended over 95 per cent of sederunts in 1741.

A forceful president could sway his colleagues and, according to Colin Mackenzie WS, this was a defining feature of Ilay Campbell's presidency. In January 1807 Mackenzie criticised Campbell as being too eager that his opinion rule the decision of the court. This made him 'apt to make exertions (bearing the semblance of partiality) to carry a majority of the court along with him' and any resistance, he alleged, made him 'peevish and fretful'.[85] This is perhaps borne out by Campbell's unrealistic suggestion in 1807 that, if the court was split into two divisions (speeding up business by doubling its capacity to get through the workload), the president should preside in both of them.[86] On the other hand, Campbell in 1790 had perhaps made advising easier by imposing a rule whereby counsel should no longer be allowed to interrupt the judges as they delivered their opinions, even when a judge made a factual error. If a later judge did not correct the error, there was to be an interval following the deliberation during which counsel could clear up such errors of fact as had been raised.[87]

There is no room here for a detailed history of the office of president.[88] The full description under which he was appointed at the start of the eighteenth century, that is, 'constant president in absence of the lord chancellor', does, however, contrast with the short-lived early seventeenth-century practice of appointing presidents for a single session only.[89] The lord chancellor, whose office was abolished in 1708, did occasionally attend the court. In that capacity the Earl of Marchmont attended almost a third of sederunts in 1701. Even in the presence of the chancellor, the 'praeses' (or presiding judge) was always the president of the court and, when the president was absent, the lords elected a temporary praeses who was not necessarily the most senior available judge. Earlier practice had been to nominate a vice president in terms of the 1579 Act.[90] According to this, the role of the vice president, until the return of the chancellor or president, involved the 'calling of maitaris, repeating of allegeances proponit be the advocattis at the bar, collecting of the lordis voitis and pronunciatioun of thair decreitis and interloquitouris'.[91] The practice of appointing a vice president can still be found after the Restoration. In the absence of President Stair in 1679, having consulted previous legislation and considered past practice, the lords elected Lord Gosford to be vice president to preside whenever Stair was absent. Gosford was not the next most senior judge.[92] Likewise, when Stair died on 25 November 1695, then holding office for the second time as president, James Falconer (Lord Phesdo) was next day elected praeses for the week.[93] Phesdo was neither the most experienced lawyer nor the senior judge. Until March 1698, when Stair's son Hew (by then in his mid fifties) moved from dean of the Faculty of Advocates to become constant president, the presidency varied in accordance with regular elections by the lords.[94]

The occasional need to appoint a temporary praeses potentially weakened the court because it led to a succession of ad hoc 'presidents for the week' who had varying skills as chairmen. For instance, in the absence of the president in June and July 1751, seven lords were elected to preside for various periods – normally a week although the most senior of them, Lord Dun, presided for three days and Lord Justice Clerk Tinwald did so for twelve days. This is unlikely to have been particularly effective and, moreover, presidents of the week were susceptible to making mistakes. Drummore, for example, made an error in not leaving blank the penalty clauses in Lord Chancellor Hardwicke's draft bill for preventing clandestine marriage in Scotland in 1754. His error was understandable, not least because referring draft legislation to judges was an English practice little known in Scotland. The lords had delayed carrying out the House of Lords's instructions because the president had been 'in a langwissing (languishing) condition', Lord Dun had just resigned, and the absence or illness of other judges had left the bench depleted by a third.[95]

Dalrymple's unprecedented elevation in 1698 directly from dean of Faculty to president was not repeated until the appointment of Robert Blair in 1808. The six presidents appointed in between had all been lord advocates (three being appointed immediately from that office to president) and four of them had also been solicitor general.[96] The holders of these two Crown offices required parliamentary seats as a matter of course and, while a political career was an advantage in gaining a seat on the bench, it seems to have been virtually essential in reaching the presidency of the court. It was certainly not beyond a president, or any lord of session, to play politics with their office. Hew Dalrymple himself provides a good example. When he died in 1737, he was lauded as the longest-ever serving president, having spent 'longer than any is known to have been att the head of a Court of Judicatorie with the same soundness of Judgement to the last'.[97] Whether he had the same vigour towards the end may be questioned. He had petitioned the lords for permission to step down, on the final day of the session in February 1731, making reference to the 1587 legislation concerning aged and infirm senators of the College.[98] Citing (unspecified) precedents, he sought to retain the privileges of College membership while being excused the burden of attendance. Lord Milton saw a hidden agenda in this 'unprecedented novelty'. The Earl of Ilay agreed, suspecting a plan to place his son, Hew Dalrymple of Drummore, in the president's chair. By April, the scheme had come to nothing, Dalrymple claiming that he had intended only to stand down at some future time for the public good if something might be done for his children. Ilay, reasonably, regarded this as 'gibberish'.[99] Dalrymple continued to attend, featuring in 112 out of 124 (90.3 per cent) sederunts in 1731 although, inevitably, his physical vigour declined. In his last full calendar year in office, 1736, he attended only eighty-seven sederunts (70 per cent).

THE LORDS AND THE COMMUNITY

Like advocates, the lords either owned houses in Edinburgh, or its environs, or lodged in dwellings where they worked and entertained socially.[100] Much business was done at home where informations were read late into the evening, committee meetings were sometimes held and acts of sederunt drafted. For instance, the act of sederunt regulating the trial of intrant advocates, published by the court on 28 February 1750, had been the subject of a meeting over dinner two days earlier between the lord justice clerk (Charles Areskine) and Lord Elchies, probably at the former's home in Milne's Court.[101] John Gibson Lockhart, on meeting Adam Rolland in 1819, heard him describe the eighteenth-century informal style of visiting which involved the laborious ascension of Old Town staircases leading up to snug supper parties, sometimes organised at short notice.[102]

The sources certainly indicate that strong friendships existed between judges, particularly between those who shared the same politics. The correspondence between Elchies and Milton, for instance, reveals a close intimacy between their respective families.[103] At the same time, there were inveterate rivalries and disputes, such as that in 1751 between the neighbouring landed proprietors William Grant (lord advocate and future Lord Prestongrange) and Lord Drummore, which came to a head on the pretext of a dispute over a local turnpike road.[104] Lord Whitehill, disappointed at not becoming president in 1698, is said to have bitterly lampooned in the press his rivals in the Dalrymple family.[105] Clashes of personality could not always be resolved.

The fierce antipathy between Lords Hermand and Meadowbank became less public only when they were allocated to separate divisions after the court was split in 1808.[106]

It was a strength of the College that its most lauded members should be drawn from across the country. In examining the seventy-six ordinary lords of session and the two lord chancellors (the Earl of Seafield and the Marquis of Tweeddale) appointed in the period 1700–99, it is nonetheless noticeable that almost a third held estates within a 20-mile radius of Edinburgh and another third held estates within a 40-mile radius. Lord Murkle's estate in Thurso, some 180 miles to the north, was by far the most distant (despite Orkney being a source of prominent advocates). Lord Milton at Brunstane, the Dundases at Arniston, Lords Kames, Drummore, Eskgrove, Prestongrange and Polton, all held seats within a few miles of Parliament House. The average judge, returning home for the vacation, faced a journey of just over 40 miles. In about 10 per cent of cases, including those of Culloden, Ankerville, Forglen and Gardenstone, the journey exceeded 100 miles.

It was undoubtedly important for the College that judges, despite spending their careers at the bar in Edinburgh, remained strongly identified with their local areas. Many served as local justices of the peace, such as Lord Strichen who was a JP both in Aberdeenshire and in Inverness-shire, or Lord Elliock in Dumfriesshire. They were also, as estate owners, interested in land improvement and estate management. Lord Barjarg, for example, sought to sell timber from his local woodland and to develop coal-mining.[107] In 1769 his local agent, obliged to collect money in Dumfries banknotes, advised Barjarg that Lord Elliock, his neighbour in the south-west, would help him get those notes exchanged for sterling without having to discount them.[108] As well as those who sought agricultural improvement and the development of salmon fisheries for their own estates, some College members took more than a professional interest in the building of canals and roads; as John Mackenzie WS told a client, his personal maxim 'is to be a friend to all Turnpike Bills'.[109]

Spending vacations at a significant distance from Edinburgh did, however, pose problems at times of crisis. Duncan Forbes of Culloden, when lord president, was relatively inaccessible for significant periods of time during vacations, and this was a particular issue during the rebellion of 1745. A good politician, Forbes later presented his presence in the Highlands at the time as a virtue. Certainly, holding an estate near Edinburgh was not necessarily an advantage. While this could mean commuting daily to work, this was at the mercy of the weather. Law agents can be found paying chairmen to deliver petitions and answers to judges at their houses. An account of William Macdonald WS in 1780, for example, records sums paid for carrying documents out of Edinburgh to Lord Hailes at Newhailes and the two-mile trip to Lord Covington at Craighouse.[110]

Given their habit of leaving Edinburgh for the vacation, the question of where lords of session were lawfully domiciled arose in several cases. In the event of death, did the commissary court of Edinburgh have jurisdiction over their moveable estate or was it the local commissary court where their family estates were situated? Roman law favoured the view, as Robert Craigie pithily argued, that 'Rome was the Domicil, not of the Senator but of his Office'.[111] Therefore, Edinburgh should not be presumed to be the legal domicile of a lord of session. This was the argument he presented in a dispute among creditors of the late Lord Kimmerghame in 1732. The *jus gentium*, according to Dutch commentators, such as Voet and Leeuwen, followed the Roman rule closely. If a man held an office in The Hague, and worked and died there, succession to his goods was appropriately regulated by his family's domicile wherever that happened to be.[112] This principle was apparently followed in 1708 in a case (never reported) concerning the goods of Lord Mersington, who had died at his estate in Dalkeith in 1700. By adhering to it in 1732, the lords rejected the idea that a lord of session, by accepting office, could impliedly be taken to have declared Edinburgh to be his domicile or that a man who had seats in several counties might have no settled domicile at all. In session time, the late Lord Kimmerghame had habitually brought his family with him to Edinburgh where he leased handsome lodgings to accommodate them for the year (sometimes taking a lease for more than a year). Unlike Mersington, he died in Edinburgh. It was decided that none of this was enough to give those who had sought to bring confirmation of his estate in Edinburgh any preference: jurisdiction lay with the commissary court of Lauder.

PRECEDENCE

The question of precedence preoccupied judges no less than it did university professors.[113] The normal rule adopted in the College, that precedence was determined by date of admission to the bench, mirrored that of every major court of justice in Europe.[114] There was doubt, however, about the relative positions of lords of session and barons of exchequer. This was largely resolved in November 1729 by Queen Caroline.[115] The president of the College was to have precedence over the chief baron of the Court of Exchequer, and the latter was to enjoy precedence over the other senators of the College of Justice and the remaining barons. The other judges, senators and barons alike, had place according to the date of their commission or appointment.[116] Therefore

> Every senator of His Majesties said College of Justice whose Commission or appointment to his said office is of ane Elder date shall take place and

have the rank and precedency of and above all Senators of his majesties said College of Justice and Barons of his majesties said Exchequer whose commissions or appointments are of a later Date[117]

and vice versa. If both were appointed on the same day, a senator was to take precedence over a baron. This was declared an unalterable rule, with the only exception being that no peer, or the son of a peer, could be deprived of the precedence afforded by his title merely by holding one of these offices.

This rule was applied (for the first time) in 1761 when James Erskine was appointed, as Lord Barjarg, to replace Lord Shewalton.[118] Erskine resigned as a baron of exchequer in order to be nominated as a lord of session. His nomination raised a delicate point of principle. If he were to be regarded as the most junior lord ordinary, this might be perceived as a slight on the exchequer court. Although Baron Maule became involved in discussions in London about it, the matter was, in fact, easily resolved under the rule set out in 1729. The Duke of Argyll, Lord Hardwicke, and Lord Mansfield, in agreement with English practice, determined that Erskine should take precedence in the session according to the date of his appointment to the exchequer court. Gilbert Elliot (the son of second Lord Minto), lord of the treasury, reported to Milton that this had been settled, adding that no remonstrance against it would change anything.[119] The only ones with reason to remonstrate were those lords demoted by Erskine's appointment: Prestongrange, Edgefield, Coalston, Alemoor and Elliock. There is no evidence that any of them actually complained.

ATTENDANCE

Regardless of the judges' official seniority, the most successful legal practitioners understood the court and knew which judges had the most influence with their colleagues. They knew that 'pleasant words' in the right direction might 'multiply friends and pacify enemies', as the thirteenth-century proceduralist Durand put it.[120] Working out the mathematics of pleading, however, in a court with an Inner House of fifteen judges (with nine required for a quorum), was effective only when the right judges were physically present to influence the outcome. A number of cases came down to very narrow votes which might have gone differently if a single judge had been present or absent.[121] Pleaders would subsequently note such cases, because these circumstances affected their standing; as Ilay Campbell remarked of a 1739 case, 'the authority of it will be the less, when it is remembered, that it proceeded upon the narrowest majority, and when four of the Lords were absent'.[122]

Several factors affected the composition of the court. Sudden outbreaks of illness, such as the 'present resigning distemper' which prevented a quorum forming in June 1782, could have a short-term but severe impact.[123] The strategists, and everyone else, knew that the beginning of a session could be particularly slow and that the court might not immediately achieve a quorum. In June 1751, when the court recommenced with a Saturday sitting following the vacation, only eight judges appeared.[124] By the next sitting, on Tuesday, they were all present except the long-term invalids, Dun, Monzie and Haining. Something of a crisis occurred on 1 June 1738 when only seven judges appeared in Edinburgh.[125] The various excuses proffered, some given second-hand, were recorded. These ranged from a headache to a cold; Arniston had remained in the Highlands taking goat's whey while Milton was recuperating in Bath; Drummore, heading south from Aberdeenshire, was delayed at the Dundee ferry by contrary winds. Those judges present determined that in future no excuses would be accepted unless produced in writing.

Problems were exacerbated when illness was compounded by delays in filling vacancies on the bench. On 20 June 1764 the court had only nine fit judges and, because one of them had to sit in the Outer House, no Inner House business could be done.[126] The late Lord Edgefield's recent replacement, Pitfour, failed to appear, and two other judges, Woodhall (d.5 May) and Prestongrange (d.23 May), had still not had their places filled. The president was obliged immediately to write to the government and, remarkably, within a fortnight two new judges, Gardenstone and Kennet, had been nominated and admitted as replacements.[127]

Short of making the court inquorate, age and infirmity took their toll on judicial attendance.[128] Elderly judges languished for months barely, if at all, attending proceedings. Indispositions were routinely accepted as excuses by the court in the eighteenth century in marked contrast to earlier practice. When Lord Craigie sought to repair to Bath in June 1675, for example, the king issued a letter instructing the lords to excuse him and to make alternative arrangements so that his duties may be discharged.[129] An act of royal grace had become an administrative matter for the lords themselves.

In April 1733, the *Edinburgh Evening Courant* reported that the administration of justice in Naples was being seriously hampered by the large number of common colds that had afflicted lawyers and judges.[130] In Scotland, too, colds might routinely lead to extended absences, sometimes for weeks.[131] In November 1722, the writer George Robertson was so severely affected by a cold that he remained housebound for a fortnight and his son had to write his correspondence for him.[132] It was because of a cold in March 1723 that Lord Arniston decided not to go to London during the vacation, and the president, North Berwick, then resolved not to go without him.[133] His son (the third Lord Arniston) managed to hear causes in the Outer House when 'indisposed by the cold and hoarse' in 1737, but his colleagues allowed him to sit at the side bar where it was quieter.[134]

There is a general correlation between the increasing age of a judge and a decrease in his attendance in court. In analysing a sample of attendance consisting of every fifth year from 1691 to 1806, the year of lowest judicial attendance (1781) coincided with the highest average age of those on the bench. In the case of individual judges, it is generally true that the older they became the lower their attendance was but experiences varied. Tables 3(a–c) compare the attendance of some contemporary judges. Table 3(a) shows a similar pattern of uniformly declining attendance over time in the cases of Kames and Auchinleck, both of whom died in 1782. Tables 3(b) and 3(c) demonstrate a less uniform picture which is probably to be expected given the unpredictability of illness and the varying pressure of private affairs and other official business. Lord Dun (d.1758), whose length of service (forty-seven years) was greater than any judge in the eighteenth century, enjoyed a high rate of attendance in three sample years prior to 1726 as follows: 1711 (99.2 per cent), 1716 (97.6 per cent), 1721 (95.2 per cent). His full attendance in 1746 is slightly misleading because this represents only seventy-seven sederunt days. In 1751 he was aged seventy-eight but still attended more often than not. Lord Stonefield was on the bench for almost thirty-nine years, and his attendance was also volatile. In 1771 he suffered a series of short absences in January, July and November whereas, in 1791, he was excused on the basis of indisposition on 10 March and did not sit again until the commencement of the following winter session on 12 November.

Table 3(a) *Attendance (percentage of sederunts)*

Year	1756	1761	1766	1771	1776	1781
Kames	91.4	94.9	99.11	92.9	87.5	85.7
Auchinleck	100	100	96.46	97.3	91.1	30.3

Table 3(b) *Attendance (percentage of sederunts)*

Year	1726	1731	1736	1741	1746	1751	1756
Dun	100	96	98.4	97.4	100	62.7	–
Milton	85	92.7	87.1	94.9	88.3	91.5	55.6
Minto II	–	92.8	94.3	84.7	98.3	97.4	90.7

Table 3(c) *Attendance (percentage of sederunts)*

Year	1761	1766	1771	1776	1781	1786	1791	1796	1801
Elliock	100	99.11	74.3	99.1	88.4	44.7	–	–	–
Monboddo	–	–	94.7	97.3	99.1	95.6	94.7	100	–
Stonefield	–	100	72.5	97.3	98.2	93	57.9	97.4	85.5

RETIREMENT

It was only in 1808 that judges obtained a statutory right to a pension, worth three-quarters of their salary, provided they had been on the bench for fifteen years or were too ill to serve.[135] Until then, unless some other arrangement could be made, they generally remained in office until they died. Even after 1808, judges did not always retire in time. John Clerk of Eldin noticeably declined while on the bench; Lord President Granton, on seeing this, wrote out his own resignation, put it in an envelope, and gave it to his wife and eldest son with the instruction that they produce it as soon as his faculties began to fail.[136]

Contemporaries criticised judges who went on too long. The most extreme example was Lord Dun, who served for forty-seven years. Towards the end of his life, Dun was described by Lord Drummore as 'a living ghost, tho he has no ailment, but Age'.[137] This certainly may have affected the quality of the court but so long as a quorum was nine then the particularly aged members could not, by themselves, greatly affect its efficiency.

Nonetheless, the advising of causes was a labour-intensive business. Despite the periodic proposals for reform (notably in the 1740s and 1780s), it was in 1808 that change finally took place with the introduction of two separate divisions within the Inner House. Requiring at least nine judges to sit together was one thing but a quorum of four lords in each of two divisions (eight and seven judges respectively) might have led to problems had the change not coincided with the introduction of the retirement pension to clear out the more aged judges.[138] Since each division had to supply lords ordinary for the Outer House, it was conceivable that one of them might be disproportionately affected by illness and thereby unable to form a quorum. This problem was addressed when permanent ordinaries were introduced in 1810, and the divisions of the Inner House completely separated from the Outer House. Three out of five judges in each division now formed a quorum and, in the event that the number of judges in a division fell below three, one or more permanent lords ordinary could be called in from the Outer House to make up the number.[139]

CONCLUSION

Although they were a small group, the lords of session were, professionally and socially, the key figures in the College. Their decisions moulded the reputation of the court. Social and family relations between individual judges were often close as were such relations between judges and other leading College members. The judges also developed strong connections to Edinburgh, with many of them dying there while the court was in session. In some cases, particularly the funerals of Lord Newhall in 1736 and President Arniston in 1787, the court and the town took great pains to mark the funeral almost as a civic occasion (in the latter case, the magistrates and university professors joined the procession from Parliament House to the president's house in Adam Square).[140] In fact the only president, between James Dalrymple of Stair (who died in 1695 'in his house at the entrie to the parliament close') and Ilay Campbell, known to have died outside Edinburgh, was Glenlee, who died at his estate in Ayrshire in 1789.[141]

Able advocates who had connections to sitting judges were in high demand. An attempt to prevent a son pleading before his father on the bench, or a brother pleading before his brother, was defeated in 1681: thereafter advocates continued to maximise the use of such advantageous connections.[142] A poem in 1700 refers to those who 'Their cause to promote, Employ the son to get the father's vote'.[143] Armadale's connection to Braxfield has already been noticed. The young James Boswell and his cousin Claud were given instruction by Lord Auchinleck (who had, himself, as a young man, been permitted to attend his father's consultations); later, when Auchinleck was nearing eighty and in decline, Boswell noticed how his business fell away when his father was absent from the court.[144] When it was mooted in 1742 that his son become joint solicitor general, Lord Arniston replied that this meant 'tying him to teach him his duty' (that is, he would have to train him in the office).[145]

The significance of social relationships can be seen in the contract in 1725 arranged upon the marriage of Mary Kinloch and Alexander Hamilton WS.[146] This was witnessed by the leading advocate James Graham of Airth along with twenty others, including the lord president (North Berwick), Lord Milton, four other advocates, and one principal and one depute clerk of session.[147] Social occasions such as weddings would not only have underlined the standing of the judges but reinforced the mutual sense of community between the bar, the bench and the other prominent members of the College. Of course, that is not to say that every connection worked well. Lord Strichen's marriage to the daughter of the late Duke of Argyll, for instance, may, in professional terms, have seemed a good idea but it was roundly lamented by her brother as 'a bad bargain for them both'.[148]

Twenty-nine eighteenth-century lords of session had a son at the bar but in only seven cases did the son follow the father on to the bench.[149] What counted for promotion, increasingly, was professional experience. William Calderwood of Polton gained promotion to the bench in 1711 despite what John Hamilton WS considered his 'very mean parentadge' (his father was a bailie in Dalkeith).[150] Not only had Calderwood benefited from an excellent education and made a useful marriage, he had been an assessor of Edinburgh, was linked early in his career to wealthy clients among the nobility (including the Kerrs of Lothian and the Buccleuch family), and was able, as he told the Earl of Breadalbane, to count on recommendations from 'a great many of our countreymen'.[151] His son, in turn, was admitted to the bar on the same day as Joseph Pringle, the son of Lord Newhall.[152] If Polton was not a judge of great reputation, he did have influence on the development of the law, not least because combined figures, drawn from the years 1711, 1716, 1721, 1726 and 1731, demonstrate that he was present in an impressive 97.8 per cent of sederunts (527 out of 539 over five years).

Political factors counted in promotion but ability and experience were essential. Of the seventy-six ordinary lords appointed in the period 1700–99, sixteen (including Calderwood) had been Edinburgh assessors. Eight had been lords advocate (of whom six had been solicitors general).[153] Only four had been deans of the Faculty of Advocates. Of these, two (James Ferguson and Alexander Lockhart) were noticeably short of experience of public office because of their reputed Jacobitism.[154] The abolition of heritable jurisdictions, which led to the greatest scramble for patronage of the century, did not greatly change the dynamic although it did lead to judicial experience becoming a criterion often looked to in promotion of prospective lords of session. Of the first forty-five lords appointed after 1748, twenty had served as sheriff-depute (in itself an office the candidates for which were subjected to a rigorous assessment of political orthodoxy by the government).

Commonality of experience, however, did not prevent personal or political differences arising on the bench, and there was certainly factionalism. Even trivial disputes could create lasting rancour. One such incident, on the road south to an appeal in London, led William Nairn (Lord Dunsinnan) later to suggest that he had never known anyone 'so impetuous and so destitute of *common sense*' as Alexander Lockhart (Lord Covington).[155] Advocates and experienced agents knew exactly how relations stood between individual judges and the types of argument that might appeal to them. Notes of judges' comments that were scribbled on session papers during advising give a sense of how sharp some retorts might be. In one case Lord Kames is noted as complaining that he had heard 'nothing but quibbling' from his colleagues.[156] In another, Lord Eskgrove acknowledged that he had changed his opinion from that which, as counsel, he had entertained in earlier cases.[157]

Not all the judges present actually participated in the debate (or, at least, said anything worth noting). Some were content simply to follow. According to Colin Mackenzie WS in 1807, for instance, Lord Dunsinnan was a cipher whose vote was 'generally attached to the opinion of the President'.[158] On the other hand, Lord Cullen was 'extremely indolent' and very slow to form an opinion in the Inner House, and Lord Hermand was 'loud and boisterous in his manner and rash and headstrong in the matter of his opinions'.

Above all, as we have seen, after the Union, the bench was filled from the ranks of the Faculty of Advocates. In 1744 it was plainly said that the Faculty was the 'nursery' of the bench, and this metaphor was repeated by Henry Erskine, as dean of Faculty, in 1790 when he asserted that the Lords were regarded 'as having a paternal jurisdiction over the Faculty'.[159] In 1804, the Lord Advocate applied the same metaphor to describe the office of sheriff-depute which, for over half a century, had been filled exclusively by advocates.[160] On his graduation from the 'nursery' to the bench in 1782, John Swinton informed the dean that the change was a desirable one at his time of life but that he did not leave his brethren 'without a sensibility difficult to be exprest'.[161] Boswell, as usual, has expressed something of it when his friend Alexander Lockhart, after fifty-three years as an advocate, had made the same transition in 1775 following an eight-year period without a vacancy on the bench: 'At the bar he had the notion of ending. As a judge he would think of beginning.'[162] Certainly, the 'drudgery of great practice' was not to everyone's taste and it was to this that Ramsay ascribed Francis Garden's acceptance of a judicial gown after nearly two decades at the bar.[163] Robert McQueen was not alone when, aged fifty, he made known his desire to 'retire' from practice to the bench.[164] It is to the advocates within the College that we must turn in the next chapter.

NOTES

1. *New York Times*, 14 Feb. 1915, review of W. Forbes Gray, *Some Old Scots Judges: Anecdotes and Impressions*.
2. For sixteenth-century oath swearing, see J. Finlay, 'Advocates unlimited: the *numerus clausus* and the College of Justice in Scotland' 82 (2009) *Historical Research*, 209–10.
3. ALSP, *The Petition of John Murray of Conheath*, 9 Dec. 1721, Hamilton Gordon collection, gol. 41, no. 29, p. 2.
4. See generally J. Finlay, 'Pettyfoggers, regulation, and local courts in Early Modern Scotland' (2007), *Edinburgh Law Review*, 54–63; ibid., 'Ethics, etiquette and the early modern Scots advocate' (2006) *JR*, 161–5.
5. ALSP, *Information for the Rev. Mr James Wemyss*, 22 April 1785, Miscellaneous Collection, ser. 6 (1785–6), p. 6.

6. G. Brunton and D. Haig, *A History of the Senators of the College of Justice* (Edinburgh, 1832). A new edition of this work, by Athol Murray and the late Peter McNeill, may soon appear.

7. Miller, *Cockburn's Millenium*, p. 310. As Cocks points out, some of the great men discussed in England were, in fact, Scots: R. Cocks, *Foundations of the Modern Bar* (London, 1983), p. 27.

8. This, of course, is a small number only relative to courts in civilian systems. In England, Duman found only 105 judges appointed in the courts of Chancery, the three common law courts and the ecclesiastical courts, in the period 1727–1820: D. Duman, *The Judicial Bench in England* (London, 1982), p. 3 n. 7. In the Court of Session in the same period seventy-one lords of session were appointed although the court structures and procedures were very different and the jurisdictions differed greatly in size. The *Parlement de Paris* had 240 judges in 1715 alone and about 1,200 judges in supreme appellate courts as a whole; the *Reichskammergericht* varied in the size of its membership, from seventeen to thirty-two, at any one time between 1495 and the 1650s but always significantly outnumbered the contemporary Court of Session: J. P. Dawson, *A History of Lay Judges* (Harvard, 1960), pp. 70–1, 111.

9. For discussion of the rules, see text below at p. 99. The exception was James Hamilton of Pencaitland WS who was, in 1712, elevated from PCS apparently without ever having become an advocate.

10. On law reporting, see D. M. Walker, *A Legal History of Scotland* (7 vols, Edinburgh, 1988–2004), v, pp. 5–13; on judicial decisions, see J. D. Ford, *Law and Opinion in Seventeenth-century Scotland* (Oxford, 2007) esp. 282–91; J. W. Cairns, 'Adam Smith and the role of the courts in securing justice and liberty' in R. P. Malloy and J. Evensky, eds, *Adam Smith and the Philosophy of Law and Economics* (Kluwer, 1994), p. 31; ibid., 'Attitudes to Codification and the Scottish Science of Legislation, 1600–1830' 22 (2007) *Tulane European and Civil Law Forum*, 1.

11. *Decisions of the Court of Session, from the year 1738 to the year 1752, collected and digested into the form of a dictionary, by Sir James Fergusson of Kilkerran* (Edinburgh, 1775); J. Hill Burton, *The Lives of Simon Lord Lovat, and Duncan Forbes, of Culloden* (London, 1847), pp. 359–60. Tytler, *Life of Kames*, i, pp. 52–3. Lord Kilkerran was on the bench from 1735 to 1759.

12. Cf. D. Lemmings, *Professors of the Law: Barristers and English Legal Culture in the Eighteenth Century* (Oxford, 2000), p. 318.

13. Ford, *Law and Opinion*, p. 390.

14. Wodrow, *Analecta*, iii, p. 281.

15. Erskine of Dun, *Friendly and Familiar Advices*, cap. 1.

16. To give just three examples: Lord Grange who kept a mistress and famously exiled his wife to St Kilda; Lord Gardenstone whose behaviour revealed him to be less than a paragon of virtue; and Lord Drummore

whose mistress bore him children and was known to Carlyle: Ramsay of Ochtertye, *Scotland and Scotsmen*, i, 373–5; Carlyle, *The Autobiography*, pp. 7–15, 667.

17. F. Grant, *The patriot resolved* (Edinburgh, 1707), p. 10; on this work, see K. Bowie, *Scottish Public Opinion and the Anglo-Scottish Union, 1699–1707* (Woodbridge, 2007), pp. 110–12.

18. J. Innes, 'Legislating for three kingdoms: how the Westminster parliament legislated for England, Scotland and Ireland, 1707–1830' in J. Hoppit, ed., *Parliaments, Nations and Identities in Britain and Ireland, 1660–1850* (Manchester, 2003), pp. 21–7. But general legislation could still have pronounced economic effects in Scotland, cf. B. Harris, 'The Scots, the Westminster parliament, and the British state in the eighteenth century', in ibid., pp. 127–8, 132, 137–8.

19. J. W. Cairns, 'Legal Theory', in A. Broadie, ed., *The Cambridge Companion to the Scottish Enlightenment* (Cambridge, 2003), p. 231; D. Lieberman, *The Province of Legislation Determined* (Cambridge, 1989), pp. 162–3; generally, K. Haakonsen, *The Science of a Legislator: The Natural Jurisprudence of David Hume and Adam Smith* (Cambridge, 1981).

20. See, generally, Lieberman, *The Province of Legislation Determined*, pp. 162–3.

21. J. W. Cairns, 'Legal Theory', pp. 233–4; generally, Lehmann, *John Millar of Glasgow*.

22. Cairns, 'Adam Smith' pp. 51–2.

23. NLS, Yester, MS 7053, fo. 24r.

24. Phillipson, *Reform of the Court of Session*, pp. 62–3; J. Boswell, *Letter* (Edinburgh, 1785); J. Thomson, 'The old fifteen' (1921) *JR*, 239–42.

25. Of the eighty-three advocates admitted in the period 1700–99 who went to the bench, there are data for sixty of them: of these thirty-two (53.3 per cent) were eldest sons, twenty (33.3 per cent) were second sons and the remainder (13.4 per cent) were third or later sons. This is based on F. Grant, *The Faculty of Advocates* (Edinburgh, 1944).

26. Although Grant's data are incomplete, analysis of them suggests that about 60 per cent of eighteenth-century advocates were only or eldest sons.

27. For Polton, see p. 111.

28. See, generally, John W. Cairns 'Legal Study in Utrecht in the Late 1740s: The Education of Sir David Dalrymple, Lord Hailes' (2002) *Fundamina*, pp. 30–74.

29. G. Scott and F. Pottle, eds, *The Private Papers of James Boswell* (20 vols, New York, 1928–34), vol. xv, p. 269; Ross, *Lord Kames*, pp. 19–20; Lehmann, *Henry Home, Lord Kames*, p. 9.

30. Six SCJs elevated in the eighteenth century had been sons-in-law of sitting SCJs: Armadale (son-in-law of Braxfield); Covington (Edgefield); Coalston (Drummore); Hailes (Coalston); Meadowbank *secundus* (Avonton); Nisbet (Kimmerghame).

31. British Library [BL], Althorp G/64. I am grateful to Dr David J. Brown for this reference. Honyman's father, Patrick, was a confidante of Charles Areskine as justice-clerk.

32. W. R. Prest, *The Rise of the Barristers: A Social History of the English Bar, 1590–1640* (Oxford, 1986), p. 27.

33. *Letters of James Boswell*, ed. C. B. Brewster (2 vols, Oxford, 1924), i, p. 115. In modern practice, a judge in Scotland should not normally sit on a case in which a member of his family appears as advocate: *Statement of Principles of Judicial Ethics for the Scottish Judiciary* (Judicial Office for Scotland, 2010), para. 5.6.

34. This excludes the promotion of Robert Dundas (called in 1779) to lord chief baron of exchequer in 1801.

35. Note that his number of sixty-eight represents specifically those who went from bar to bench.

36. For example, NRS, CS 1/4/2, fo. 251v; D. Parrat, The *Development and Use of Written Pleadings in Scots Civil Procedure* (Edinburgh, 2006), pp. 22h3; [John Swinton], *Considerations concerning a Proposal for Dividing the Court of Session into Classes or Chambers* (Edinburgh, 1789), pp. 13–15.

37. ALSP, *Information for William Bell of Blackwoodhouse*, Feb. 1737, Kilkerran collection, vol. 1, no. 38; Mor. Dict., no. 2848. The case refers to the old principle which, in modern practice, conveyancers call the 'offside-goals rule'.

38. Scott and Pottle, eds, *Private Papers of James Boswell*, vol. 15, p. 279.

39. Boswell, *Letter to the People of Scotland*, p. 66.

40. NLS, Mackenzie of Coul papers, MS 1336, fo. 46.

41. Cf. Ford, *Law and Opinion*, p. 283, cites Mackenzie's claim that, in 1661, each great man was allowed to appoint 'a friend or two' to complete the bench.

42. NRS, GD220/5/1720/1.

43. HMC, *Report on Laing MSS*, pp. 308, 311, 314.

44. NRS, CS1/9, fo. 26v; *Acts of Sederunt* (11 Nov. 1690), p. 188.

45. NLS, Saltoun, MS 16557, fo. 64. This is similar in tone to correspondence sent to Lord President Craigmillar in the 1660s: H. M. Paton, ed., 'Letters from John, Earl of Lauderdale, and others, to Sir John Gilmour, President of Session' in *Miscellany of the Scottish History Society, Fifth volume* (Edinburgh, 1933), no. lxxxiv, pp. 190–1.

46. NLS, Saltoun, MS 16550, fo. 281.

47. NLS, Paul, MS 5156, fo. 93r.

48. For example, ibid., Saltoun, MS 16551, fos 36, 41.

49. Ibid., MS 16754, fo. 146.

50. GUL, Spec. Coll., Murray 650/2/119.

51. NRS, GD220/5/1711/2.

52. Ibid., GD220/5/1714/15.

53. For the period prior to Duncan Forbes, Hill Burton is particularly scathing, describing the judges as 'the avowed partisans of political sects or great families, and would have considered that they did their friends injustice by a vote against them': *Lives of Simon Lord Lovat and Duncan Forbes, of Culloden*, p. 358. The evidence suggests that this may be an exaggeration for the post-Union period. See also A. D. Gibb, *Judicial Corruption in the United Kingdom* (Edinburgh, 1957), chapter 4, where most of the evidence discussed is drawn from the seventeenth century when, as Simpson suggests, judges might rig the order of hearing cases to 'oblige their friends and surprise their enemies': J.M. Simpson, 'The Advocates as Scottish trade union pioneers', G. W. S. Barrow, ed., *The Scottish Tradition* (Edinburgh, 1974), p. 169.

54. Milne, ed., *Boswell's Edinburgh Journals*, p. 443.

55. NRS, GD220/5/372/7; Admission register of notaries public, NP2/16, no pagination, 25 Feb. 1691.

56. Ramsay of Ochtertye, *Scotland and Scotsman*, i, p. 323.

57. Phillipson, *Reform of the Court of Session*, p. 7.

58. For the origins of extraordinary lords, see Hannay, *College of Justice*, 128. On Ilay, see Shaw, *Management of Scottish Society*, 43. The last extra-ordinary lord was the marquess of Tweeddale in 1721.

59. For example, Hannay, *College of Justice*, pp. 114–18; Omond, *Lord Advocates*, pp. 172–3; some secondary references are given in B. I. Manolescu, 'George Mackenzie on Scottish Judicial Rhetoric' 20 (2002) *Rhetorica*, p. 281.

60. Forbes, 'Great Body', University of Glasgow, Sp. Coll., MS Gen. 1249, fo. 1745.

61. For the nomination and trial of Kames, see Ross, *Lord Kames and the Scotland of his Day*, pp. 117–18.

62. Advising, in general, did not take place in order of seniority. This is clear from manuscript notes on session papers in various collections. The president, however, would normally sum up at the end.

63. *Acts of Sederunt*, p. 115.

64. NRS, CS 1/15, fos 23r–24r.

65. Ibid., CS1/18, fo. 66v; CS90/1/10 (8 Mar. 1796).

66. Ibid., CS1/18, fos 3r, 4v, 4r.

67. *RPS*, A1689/6/18.

68. Cf. Brunton and Haig, *Senators of the College of Justice*, pp. xxxvii–xxxviii.

69. *Late Proceedings and Votes in the Parliament of Scotland*, pp. 31–2. Stair was nonetheless appointed president after Lockhart's murder. The three-year gap in nominating Stair's successor after 1695, however, is worth noting.

70. P. W. J. Riley, *King William and the Scottish Politicians* (Edinburgh, 1979), p. 23.

71. *RPS*, A1689/6/18; 1579/10/55.

72. Ibid., 1592/4/72. The Roman age of majority was also the requirement of judges elsewhere, for example, J. de Langle, *Semestria* (Paris, 1611), vii, X (p. 390).

73. *RPS*, 1706/10/363.

74. This provision is found neatly summarised in NLS, Saltoun, MS 17538, do. 109r.

75. ALSP, *The Petition of Charles Duke of Queensberry and Dover*, 7 Jan. 1730, Elchies collection, vol. 3, no. 46, p. 2. Alexander Seton of Pitmedden (d.1719) was elevated in 1677 and removed in 1686.

76. Brunton and Haig, *Senators of the College of Justice*, p. 420. The pensions are described in three cases collected in the same volume of papers: ALSP, *The Petition of Sir William Purves of that Ilk*, 29 July 1729, Elchies Collection vol. 3., no. 1; *The Petition of Charles Duke of Queensberry and Dover*, 7 Jan. 1730, ibid., no. 46; *Information for his Grace Cosmos-George [sic] Duke of Gordon, against Alexander Lockhart Advocate*, 9 July 1730; ibid., no. 127.

77. NRS, Correspondence of the dukes of Hamilton, GD406/1/9220.

78. ALSP, *Answers for Mr Alexander Lockhart Advocate to the Petition of his Grace Charles Duke of Queensberry and Dover*, 11 Jan. 1730, Elchies collection, vol. 3, no. 46.

79. NRS, CS1/19 (unpaginated), 7 March 1807.

80. 'In the presence of the lords' (I.P.D. for short). On the earlier history of the presidency, see Hanny, *College of Justice*, pp. 107–10.

81. Brunton and Haig, *Senators of the College of Justice*, p. 524.

82. Cf. The comment of Kames about Arniston, *supra*, p. 96.

83. NLS, Erskine-Murray papers, MS 5081, fos 25r, 50v. Henry Pelham made clear that Areskine was not given the chair in 1748 because Lord Milton resigned as lord justice clerk only on condition Areskine succeed to that office, rather than replace Forbes as president: ibid., MS 5076, fos 23r, 25r.

84. Omond, *Lord Advocates of Scotland*, i, pp. 355–6. Omond ascribes the clearance rate to a procedural change whereby delays were not to be granted simply because lawyers were absent or not prepared for debate.

85. BL, Althorp, G/64, fo. 3. I owe this reference to Dr David J. Brown.

86. Phillipson, *Reform of the Court of Session*, p. 115.

87. AL FR339r/1/1 (Campbell to Henry Erskine, dean, 9 Oct. 1790).

88. Cf. Brunton and Haig, *Senators of the College of Justice*, pp. xxxiv–xxxvi.

89. E. B. Fryde et al., eds, *Handbook of British Chronology* (3rd edn, London, 1986), p. 199; *Introduction to Scottish Legal History* (Stair Society, 1958), p. 460.

90. *The Records of the Parliaments of Scotland to 1707*, eds K. M. Brown et al., 1579/10/55.

91. That is, 'calling of matters, repeating of allegiances proposed by the

advocates at the bar, collecting of the lords' votes and pronunciation of their decreets and interlocutors'.

92. NRS, CS 1/7, fo. 129v.
93. Ibid., fo. 113v.
94. Ibid., CS 1/9, fo. 156r.
95. NLS, Erskine-Murray papers, MS 5078, fo. 15.
96. These were Culloden (1737), Arniston III (1748), Glendoick (1754), Arniston IV (1760), Glenlee (1787), Avonton (1789).
97. NRS, CS 1/12, fo 62v.
98. Ibid., CS 1/11, fos 215v–216r; NLS, MS 17538, fo. 34. Dalrymple was excused in order to go to Bath in July 1723 to recover from a bout of illness: NLS, Mackenzie of Delvine, MS 10851, fos 41r–v. The legislation is at *RPS*, 1587/7/31.
99. NLS, Saltoun, MS 16545, fos 76, 82.
100. Monboddo was particularly known for his conviviality during the session: [J. Maidment], ed., *Kay's Edinburgh Portraits* (2 vols, Edinburgh, 1842), pp. i, 32.
101. NRS, CS 1/13, fo. 139r; NLS, Saltoun, MS 16671, fo. 26. Areskine, then an advocate, lived there in 1718: ibid., Erskine-Murray papers, MS 5072, fo. 137.
102. J. G. Lockhart, *Peter's Letters to his Kinsfolk*, ed. J. Ruddick (Edinburgh, 1977), p. 28.
103. For example, NLS, Saltoun, MS 16675, fo. 73.
104. Ibid., fo. 77.
105. C. A. Malcom, 'The lord justice clerk of Scotland, II' xxvii (1915) *JR*, 383.
106. Maidment, ed., *Court of Session Garland*, p. 72.
107. For example, ibid., fos 27r, 45r, 60r.
108. NLS, Erskine Murray papers, MS 5083, fo. 33r.
109. NLS, Airth papers, MS 10858, fo. 145r. On this theme, see Ross, *Kames and the Scotland of his Day*, chapter 16.
110. NRS, Macdonald of Sanda papers, GD92/162.
111. ALSP, *Information for Mr William Hall of Whitehall, one of the principal Clerks of Session*, 15 Nov. 1732, Elchies collection, vol. 5, no. 29, p.2.
112. J. Voet, *Comment. Ad senatus consult. Tertullian* s.34, de judiciis n. 98; S. van Leeuwen, *Censura Forensis theoretico-practica* (Leiden, 1662), 3.12.
113. For example, GUA, MS26635, fo. 16 (Professor William Forbes's protest re precedency).
114. For example, J. de Langle, *Semestria*, vii. VII, p. 358.
115. NRS, CS 1/11, fos 196v–197v.
116. Cf. the rule in English law whereby puisne justices in King's Bench and Common Pleas ranked *inter se* according to the date of their patent of appointment, not according to the court in which they sat: J. H. Baker, *The Order of Serjeants at Law* (London, 1984), p. 57.

117. NRS, CS1/11, fo. 197r.

118. Ibid., CS1/15, fo. 151r. Shewalton died at Drumlanrig on 31 March 1761.

119. NLS, Saltoun, MS 16720, fo. 60v.

120. Proverbs 16: 24. Durand, *Specul.* 1 bk.1. Partic.IIII. Tit. de Advocato, 1.4.5.9.

121. NLS, Saltoun, MS 16551, fo. 119 is an example of a bare quorum that was finely balanced; as one judge declined to vote because he personally had a similar plea *in pendente*, this left seven judges to vote plus the president: the vote was four to three.

122. ALSP, *Memorial for Murdoch McLaine of Lochbuy*, 23 Sept. 1786, Robertson collection, vol. 6, no. 1, p. 11.

123. NRS, CS1/16, fo. 134v.

124. Ibid., CS1/13, fo. 153v.

125. Ibid., CS 1/12, fos 79r–80r. Lord Minto's excuse, that his son had suffered a dislocated arm, was communicated by Lord Royston but was not accepted as reasonable although no punishment for non-attendance is recorded.

126. Ibid., CS 1/14, fo. 198r.

127. Ibid., CS 1/14, fo. 198r–200v

128. The same is true in the Court of Exchequer, see Murray, 'Post-Union Court of Exchequer', pp. 117–18.

129. Ibid., CS 1/7, fo. 10v.

130. *Edinburgh Evening Courant*, no. 1489 (5–9 April 1733).

131. For example, Lord Dun in Jan. 1742, LJC Barskimming in Jan. 1771: NRS, CS 1/12, fo. 163r; CS1/15, fo. 109r.

132. NRS, GD220/5/1737/7–12.

133. NLS, Yester, MS 7044, fo. 22.

134. NRS, CS1/12, fo. 74v.

135. 48 Geo. III. c.145; Phillipson, *Reform of the Court of Session*, p. 112. Legislative changes to judicial salaries affected Ilay Campbell who tried to have his pension increased retroactively: GCA, Campbell of Succoth papers, TD219/6/25.

136. Heriot Watt University Archive, Riccarton campus, 4/D/33 (handwritten notebook).

137. NRS, Hamilton-Dalrymple papers, GD110/916/57.

138. 48 Geo. III, cap. 151, s.7.

139. 50 Geo. III, cap. 112, s.32; 53 Geo. III, cap. 65, s. 14. Ivory, *Form of Process*, ii, 71.

140. NRS, CS 1/12, fo. 59v; CS1/17, fo. 61r. Omond., ed., *Arniston Memoirs*, p. 198. Members of the bar, as a general rule, did not attend judicial funerals: Pinkerton, *Min. Bk, 1713–1750*, pp. 160–1

141. Ibid., CS1/9, fo. 113v; Hew Dalrymple also died in Parliament Close in 1737: CS 1/12, fo. 62v. Glenlee's death is noted at CS 1/17, fo. 101v.

142. Sir John Lauder of Fountainhall, *The Decisions of the Lords of Council and Session from June 6th 1678, to July 30th, 1712* (2 vols, Edinburgh, 1759, 1761), i, p. 153.

143. Cited by Thomson, 'The old fifteen', p. 234.
144. ALSP, *Memorial and Observes for Captain John Chalmer of Gadgirth*, 12 June 1745, Falconer collection, vol. 1, no. 191, p. 3; Milne, *Boswell's Edinburgh Journals*, pp. 35, 368. The latter comment was made on 20 Jan. 1780. Auchinleck, who had attended 91.1 per cent of sederunts in 1776, attended only 30.3 per cent in 1781. He died in Aug. 1782.
145. NLS, Yester, MS 7046, fo. 71r.
146. NRS, Brooke of Biel papers, GD6/2234.
147. Graham of Airth was son-in-law to Lord Pencaitland. His grandaughter, Graham [*sic*], married George Fergusson (the future Lord Hermand) in 1793: J. Fergusson, 'Lord Hermand – A biographical sketch' in F. P. Walton, ed., *Lord Hermand's Consistorial Decisions 1684–1777* (Edinburgh, 1940), p. 14.
148. NLS, Saltoun, MS 16545, fo. 106.
149. Archibald Campbell (son of Succoth); Robert Dundas (son of Arniston); David Dalrymple (son of Drummore); James Erskine (son of Tinwald); George Fergusson (son of Kilkerran); William Miller (son of Glenlee); and Andrew Pringle (son of Haining).
150. NRS, Correspondence of the dukes of Hamilton, GD406/1/5713.
151. NRS, Barcaldine papers, GD112/39/251/9. This collection is no longer in the NRS.
152. NRS, CS1/11, fo. 209v.
153. In total, 10 solicitors-general became lords of session, 4 of whom without first being promoted to lord advocate.
154. The other two, Robert Dundas (Armiston III) and Robert Dundas (Arniston IV), had been solicitors general, lords advocate and MPs.
155. NLS, Acc 4796/38/2. His emphasis.
156. ALSP, *Information for Sir John Philp, Auditor of the Revenue in Scotland*, 13 Dec. 1758, Arniston collection, vol. 40, no. 8.
157. ALSP, *Information for Sir James Grant of Grant Baronet*, 16 Jan. 1786, Arniston collection, vol. 183, no. 4.
158. BL, Althorp G.64.3. I am grateful to Dr David J. Brown of the NRS for this reference.
159. ALSP, *The Petition of Mr James Catanach, LLD, Advocate in Aberdeen and Ors*, 27 July 1744, Falconer collection, vol. 1, no. 7, p. 16; Signet Library Session Papers, *Answers for Henry Erskine (Dean) to the petition of Mr Robert Forsyth*, 15 Dec. 1790, 357: 28.
160. D. J. Brown, 'Henry Dundas and the Government of Scotland' (PhD thesis, University of Edinburgh, 1989), p. 360.
161. AL, FR339/1.
162. Milne, *Boswell's Edinburgh Journals*, p. 191.
163. Ramsay of Ochtertyre, *Scotland and Scotsmen*, i, p. 372.
164. M. Fry, *Dundas Despotism* (Edinburgh 1992, repr. 2004), p. 59.

5

Advocates

What is an advocate? He is a good man, learned in the law, who, having been admitted to his office by public authority, is called upon by litigants to explain their case orally or in writing, to prove it and to defend it by his skill.

Ulric Huber[1]

The Faculty of Advocates did not emerge overnight. By the time the College was endowed in 1532 advocates can be found acting together in their collective interests.[2] John Shairp was described in 1582 as 'dene of the advocattis of the sessioun', although the phrase 'dene of the Faculty' does not appear until 1619, when an act of sederunt required all intrants to present a book to be chosen with his advice.[3] Why advocates should call the leader of their group 'dean', from the Latin *decanus*, is a matter for conjecture. The link between 'dean' and 'Faculty' strongly suggests, however, that it was taken from the university environment. The word also had a classical significance in the Roman army and connotations within the medieval church. It is an apt word to describe their leader because, in legal literature, advocates were metaphorically regarded as equivalent to knights or soldiers (as protagonists in the courtroom), priests (as confessors; in the same vein they were also compared to physicians) and university professors (as figures of great learning).[4] Assuming that the title of dean was inspired by university practice, it seems unlikely that Shairp would be described as dean without the corresponding idea of a Faculty of Advocates. Although sixteenth-century records remain silent, advocates as a group had considerable social and political weight, particularly after the 1550s when their numbers expanded.[5]

The earliest surviving regulations of the Faculty date from 28 June 1655, in a short document entitled 'Constitutions for ordering the Government of Advocattis amongst themselves'.[6] These are concerned with internal organisation. For instance, advocates were required, on pain of a fine, to attend Faculty meetings when personally cited. If any failed to pay the fine, then 'his servant shall be debard by command of the dean from ent[e]ring the bars until his master give satisfactioun', that is, a contribution to the Faculty's poor box. Should an advocate 'commit any miscarriage or reflect uncivily against his brother' he would be called before a 'committee', censured, and fined. The same applied to advocates' servants. The committee, rather than an embryonic dean's council, seems to mean one of several ad hoc committees intended to deal with particular issues.

These 'constitutions' highlight three further points. First, advocates had to keep personal minute books in which they recorded which processes they had borrowed, including the names of the parties and 'the number of pieces' (that is, the total number of documents). Second, advocates, their servants and expectant advocates, were at the end of the session to pay a minimum sum to the poor box by way of charitable donation; not only that, but the amount payable depended on when they were admitted, with more recent intrants paying less. This recognised that it took time to make money at the bar. Third, there is mention of a clerk and a treasurer, as well as the dean. The treasurer was accountable for ensuring that funds collected, as set out in the clerk's records, were to be applied 'for the releife of decayed Advocatts there [that is, their] wyfes children and known servants and upon utheris pious uses as the said Committee shall appoint'.

These early regulations do not represent the formal incorporation of the Faculty. They were simply the consequence of a reorganisation of the basis upon which advocates interacted as a group and supported members in difficulty. Indeed, though the Faculty could sue in its own name through its officers, it was not incorporated. This was not unique. Barristers in Paris did not incorporate their order either, and the Inns of Court in England remained voluntary associations, managing to hold property through trustees and to sue through office-holders.[7] Since the Faculty met in Parliament House (owned by the council) and held no heritable property in its own name, it had no need to enter contracts for repair or maintenance.[8]

In Scotland, incorporation did not always lead to positive results. For example, the Incorporation of Surgeons and Barbers of Edinburgh, granted its Seal of Cause in 1505, developed a fractious relationship with the physicians. The surgeons quickly developed rules for the conduct, examination and admission of their members, had their own lending library, and developed an apprenticeship system not dissimilar to that of other crafts in Edinburgh.[9] By the later seventeenth century, the surgeons enjoyed first rank among the crafts on the town council and had long used political influence to ensure that the physicians were not granted corporate status; indeed, it was only through royal support that the physicians managed finally to achieve this in 1681.[10] If the advocates had avoided incorporation in a bid to avoid local politics, that attitude had evidently changed by 1701 when a draft act appears, apparently under the hand of the dean, Robert Bennet. The draft, which was never enacted, sought formal incorporation by the establishment of a free Collegiat Society, with power to them to appoint and hold their Meetings from time to time, anent the ordinary usual concerns of the said Faculty, and to Name their own Dean of Faculty, Thesaurer and Clerk, and other Officers and members: And to appoint Examinators for Trial of Intrants, to uplift their Compositions, to receive Liberalities, Donations and Gifts from others, to prosecut [sic] and pursue for the same, to erect Libraries, and these already Erected to advance, to settle, appoint and establish a Fond for a Profession of Law ...[11]

The desire of the advocates to have a properly funded chair in law in Scotland had long been expressed and would soon be fulfilled with the foundation of the first chair at Edinburgh in 1707.[12]

BECOMING AN ADVOCATE

The process of admission raises a number of important themes in connection with the office of advocate and the way in which it was viewed by contemporaries.[13] Before discussing these wider issues, it is useful to begin simply by describing the process. Comparing two intrants, several generations apart, allows elements of continuity and change to be more readily identified.

The first, John Mackenzie of Delvine, petitioned the lords for admission in January 1681.[14] After he narrated his time overseas, hearing 'the publick profession of the Lawes in the universitie of Bourges in France and other places', they recommended that the dean take trial of his qualifications and report back. Two days later, the dean remitted him to the 'private examinators' who were appointed by the Faculty on an annual basis. At this point there was a delay. Mackenzie petitioned the court in July, complaining that he had 'manie days agoe' paid the treasurer 500 merks of entry money, as required by the Faculty, but that the examinators 'for causes unknowne to your petitioner absolutelie refused to examine me at all'. On 9 July the lords recommended to the dean and the examinators that Mackenzie be examined the following week, although his private examination actually took place on 28 July 1681. He was found qualified to proceed to a further trial, the public examination, and on 9 November a title from the Digest, D.19.2 was assigned to him. On 6 December, having been examined on that title and found qualified, it was recommended to the dean that a title be assigned to him for his public lesson. The title assigned was D.19.2.39.1, taken from the jurist Paul, which stated that advocates should not return their fees if they were not responsible for failing to plead in a case. By custom, following a set introduction, the public lesson was read in Latin, to the judges, members of Faculty and the audience in court, from the position where one of the judges normally sat.[15] For this procedure, the candidate symbolically wore a hat.[16] Mackenzie read his lesson and was admitted on 20 December.[17]

The second example is Neil Menzies. On 13 January 1801 the lords, having heard Menzies's petition, which narrated that he had for several years applied himself 'to the Study of the Civil law, and of the Municipal Laws of this Kingdom', remitted him to the dean to take trial of his skill in the law in the usual way and to report. A month later, he was remitted to the private examinators on the civil law for trial upon promising 'on his honour to give no Treat or Entertainment on account thereof' and certifying that he was at least twenty years of age. Two days later, on 16 February, he was assigned the nineteenth of that month for his examination, at which time he was found qualified and the seven examinators recommended that the dean proceed. On 16 February 1802 the dean remitted him to the private examinators on Scots law who, on the same day, assigned him the twenty-sixth of the month for his examination. The six examinators having found him qualified, on that same day the dean assigned him a title from the Digest, D.5.4, which he was 'to distribute on Saturday the 27th Current and assigns him the Saturday immediately following for the Diet of his publick Examination'. On 6 March he was found qualified by the three public examinators and on their recommendation the dean assigned him D.5.4.pr (dealing with claims for part of an inheritance) as the subject of his discourse to the lords and to the Faculty. On 9 March the lords admitted him

> into the office of an Advocate with all the priviledges and immunities there-unto belonging, to be enjoyed by him Sicklike and as freely in all respects as any other Advocate does enjoy the same Likeas the said Mr Neil Menzies did take and swear the Oaths of Alledgeance and Abjuration and subscribe the same with the assurance and gave his *Oath de fideli administratione* to be obedient to the Lords in his station and to maintain the priviledges of the College of Justice.[18]

At some point, probably in January 1801, Menzies would have paid (or provided caution for) his entry money of £150 sterling, although there is no specific note of this.

The first difference between these two examples is that when Mackenzie became an advocate there was no single method of admission. In fact, the particular process he underwent had only existed for a generation. Demonstration of knowledge of Roman law had long been a mode of admission as an advocate. The conjunction of a private examination, followed by a public examination and a public lesson before the lords, dates in outline from the Commonwealth period and in detail from at least 1664.[19] At the same time, aspiring intrants had for generations been admitted solely on the basis of their knowledge and experience in Scots law. In 1683 Aeneas Macpherson, in his bill to the lords, set out the two modes of admission:

> ... ther hes beine alwayes tua wayes of entering to bee Advocats in this Kingdome one by going abroad and studying the civil and common lawes and another by long attendance on this House and studying the Municipall Law of the Nation And as the one way of entrie is by a publick tryall so the uther hes always bene by the Lords allowance ...[20]

He was granted admission by the latter route. This was also the means by which advocates' servants had often entered the bar in the seventeenth century, sometimes helped by personal recommendations from the dean or others.[21] The 1664 act of sederunt had permitted the lords to dispense with examination in Roman law; if moved to do so, they could admit any candidate, be it a servant, friend or relative, without need of any proof of merit. The system was abused, particularly in the 1680s. Although in theory the entry money, the 500 merks Mackenzie paid to the Faculty, was doubled for those entering by bill, it was difficult to enforce this since the Faculty had no role in the process of admission by bill.[22] The judges in 1679 had declined to enforce by act of sederunt the Faculty's own decision which established the differential rates of entry money.[23]

These rates reflected on the status of the intrant. Mackenzie was undoubtedly taking the more 'honourable' route to the bar. According to John Spotiswood, those who entered following examination on Roman law were 'more respected'.[24] Because this required an expensive foreign education, it was the preserve of the wealthy, though even they normally spent no more than two years studying abroad.[25] The cost of study in the Netherlands at the turn of the eighteenth century, estimated at about £100 to £120 sterling per annum, was substantial compared to the average income of a Scots estate.[26] This was compounded by the fact that it typically followed on from years spent studying the arts curriculum at a Scottish university.

In 1688 the lords made an act of sederunt ratifying the two modes of admission. In doing so, they tightened the procedure by requiring those who entered under the extraordinary procedure by bill to be examined in the presence of the lords concerning 'their knowledge of the styles, the forme of process, and of the principles of our law'.[27] Continuing disaffection with the system of admissions based on Scots law is clear from a further act, in 1691, which required near relations of lords of session to take the ordinary trial in Roman law.[28] The judges thus tacitly acknowledged their vulnerability to importuning relatives. Dispensations could still be made, however, and this was addressed in June 1692 by further reform. The lords determined to make no future dispensation unless 'they be first well informed of the persones integrity, good breeding, honest deportment and fittnes for exercising the office of ane advocat and that he has attended the hous a considerable tyme for qualifieing himself in order therto'.[29] Such candidates were no longer to be tried by the lords but were remitted for trial to the dean and Faculty of Advocates who were to examine their 'knowledge of the practique of our law, the styles and form of proces'. The question of 'breeding' was assumed not to be an issue for those entering by examination on Roman law. The Faculty, for its part, devised a system for examining these candidates on Scots law which reflected the existing procedure on admission by trials in Roman law.[30] It was not used only because entry by trial on Scots law soon fell into desuetude and candidates came to be admitted exclusively by trial in Roman law.[31]

This leads to the second difference between the experiences of Mackenzie and Menzies. Unlike Mackenzie, Menzies was examined in both Roman law and Scots law. This change arose at the desire of a Faculty committee.[32] An examination in Scots law, along broadly similar lines to the private examination in Roman law, became an additional requirement of admission in February 1750 but it was not a mode of entry in itself; it operated in conjunction with the examinations and lesson in Roman law.[33] Professor Cairns refers to the latter as admission 'on an entirely academic model' and this is important because it reflects wider developments which will be discussed below.[34] The Faculty took this change seriously, at the expense of the unfortunate Lockhart Gordon who had spent years preparing for his trials in Roman law. Despite having 'planned out his studies' on the basis of admission by trial purely on Roman law, and having had already been remitted to the private examinators, his plea to the Faculty for exemption from the new examination in Scots law was ignored and he seems to have abandoned his attempt to become an advocate.[35]

A third difference between Mackenzie and Menzies was that the admission process took longer for Menzies than it did for Mackenzie (despite the latter's complaint of delay). Learning Scots law took time. By 1750, it no longer relied on observation of court practice, private reading, drafting exercises and, perhaps, lessons under the eye of an experienced advocate. It meant attendance at university classes. The Faculty endorsed this by recommending a gap of one year between the private examination on Roman law and examination on Scots law.[36] It also specified in 1750 a minimum age for legal practice (hence the production of a certificate by Menzies). In 1785, it even toyed with (but did not enforce) an upper age limit of twenty-seven, to prevent intrants from first engaging in lesser professions and to discourage them from 'contracting Habits of life' thought improper for the profession.[37]

From 1795 a candidate gained the right to appeal to the lords of session if he were initially found unqualified, either by failing to produce certificates confirming he had received a regular university education or by not meeting the integrity and good breeding criteria established in 1692.[38] Moreover, the 'syllogistic mode' of impugning theses was discontinued in the same year, in favour of a more general questioning of the candidate , although there is no evidence that this was any more rigorous than what it replaced.[39] Henry Home (adm. 1723), who was not educated abroad, had a particularly low opinion of the 'common mechanical preparation' for the bar.[40] Even in his day, the technical standard of knowledge required was not high; he later confessed to feeling surprised when he momentarily forgot the answer to one of the questions that was commonly put.

A significant difference between Menzies and Mackenzie was the amount of entry money each had to pay, since this had increased dramatically in the course of the eighteenth century. The lower rate of 500 merks that Mackenzie paid would, at the time of the Union, have amounted to just under £28 sterling. This rate more or less continued (with slight augmentations to assist the poor) until 1720 when it increased to a flat rate of £40 sterling, with further rises introduced from the 1760s leading eventually to the sum of £150 being charged from 1790.[41] The Faculty gave, at various times, two justifications for these increases: its need for money to support its poor and to supply its library with books.[42] The lengthier, more expensive, process of admission which Menzies undertook also helped to maintain exclusivity, particularly once a legal education abroad had given way to a cheaper domestic one. As formal private tuition in Edinburgh was introduced, followed by the endowment of chairs in Law in both Edinburgh and Glasgow, and as the exodus to the Dutch law schools began to subside after the 1720s, education in Roman law, especially after 1750, was no longer necessarily the preserve of the elite.[43]

Roman law nonetheless remained fundamental because becoming an advocate continued to be seen in academic terms. According to counsel for the advocate Charles Hamilton-Gordon in 1744, Scotland

> ... in place of Doctors, has established the Faculty of Advocates as the highest Barrister Rank of Lawiers in this Kingdom: They are now our Doctors of Law, or a Degree above them, and therefore are qualified in the Letter as well as in the Meaning of the Foundation to be Professors of Law.[44]

He might have added that the hat, worn by intrants when giving their public lesson before the court, had descended from the traditional doctor's cap worn by law graduates.[45]

FROM FOREIGN TO DOMESTIC

That advocates received an education in Roman law, and relied so heavily on (particularly northern) European literature, was important for the outlook of the College of Justice and the way its members viewed its standing as a supreme court. Their voluminous written pleadings indulge freely in references to a wide spectrum of learned authors. Legal education as it developed in Scotland's universities was modelled on the Dutch experience which many advocates and lords of session had undertaken. Professors in the Netherlands had prospered most when, in addition to their public lectures, they catered to demand by offering students, in return for fees, collegia (small private classes) in subjects that were of most relevance to them.[46] John Millar's teaching in Glasgow after 1761 offered an expanding array of classes on subjects including the *Institutes*, the *Digest*, Scots law, criminal law and English law.[47] At the same time, the Faculty could influence student demand as, for example, by its promotion of the study of public law and the law of nature and nations in 1760, and its decision in 1762 to examine intrants in that subject, 'in so far as it is connected with the Civil Law or the Law of this Country'.[48]

As education became less of a hurdle to admission to the bar, other factors gained increasing relevance. In 1692 there had been no need to question the 'good breeding' and 'honest deportment' of candidates undertaking their trials in Roman law but, by the 1780s and 1790s, such issues had come to the fore and the focus shifted towards social exclusivity.[49] The petitions for admission of John Wright (a private teacher of law and mathematics who had trained as a shoemaker) in 1781 and in 1790 Robert Forsyth (son of a shoemaker who held a licence to preach from the Church of Scotland) were particularly controversial.[50] There was an element of snobbery in the Faculty's attitude, though Cockburn (who was not unbiased) later suggested that the real ground of objection to men of lesser origins was their inherent Whiggism.[51] On the other hand, if a man were admitted to the bar who, because of social or other factors could not possibly develop a viable practice there, the Faculty could argue it had an interest in preventing his admission for two reasons: first, in order to restrict inevitable future claims upon its poor fund and, secondly, to preserve, in the public interest, the independence of its members. As a general rule, men with private means were regarded as more independent and less corruptible.

The 1785 proposals relating to age and 'habits of life' were never enforced and, by the late 1780s, with the careers of John Pattison (admitted, not without controversy, in 1787) and Thomas Walker Baird (admitted in 1793) the path seems to have been cleared for ordinary Edinburgh writers not only to enter the Faculty but to begin to capitalise on their obvious advantages. These men, the 'mushrooms' or new arrivals without pedigree in the College, had practical experience and groups of existing clients some of whom might continue to employ them when at the bar.[52] Their career profiles bear a similarity to that of Joseph Marie Duroux in Toulouse who spent a dozen years as a *procureur* before, very unusually, entering the profession of *avocat* where he immediately became one of the leading pleaders.[53] Duroux was competing against a high proportion of young and inexperienced men, because the bar in Toulouse at the time was expanding and the average age of practitioners was declining.[54] The same can be said of Edinburgh in the 1790s; Pattison and Baird had many competitors but few had their experience or contacts and those that did were generally undistinguished.

The only agent in the College of Justice to be admitted an advocate in the eighteenth century was David Armstrong in 1763.[55] Apart from him, and possibly Robert Mackintosh, between the 1690s and the 1780s established writers did not proceed to the bar. The pattern followed by men in the seventeenth century, such as John Frank WS and the writers Robert Park and Alexander Ferguson of Isle, who went from one branch of business to another, was simply not followed.[56] Ferguson, in particular, was successful at the bar but his training meant, in the words of Lord Grange, that he was 'no Civilian tho he understands Scots business well enough'.[57]

On the other hand, aspiring advocates did gain practical experience in legal offices, and they may be responsible for some of the commonplace books, abridgements and manuscript collections of decisions which still survive. Duncan Forbes (adm. 1709) and James Burnett (adm. 1737) attended writers' chambers prior to studying Roman law at Leiden and Groningen respectively.[58] Henry Home attended the office of the writer John Dickson, without undertaking a formal apprenticeship; Robert McQueen (adm. 1744), apparently apprenticed with John Goldie WS.[59] Allan Maconochie (adm. 1770) is said to have completed an apprenticeship with Thomas Tod WS while also attending university classes in divinity, church history and even medicine before going to London and Paris to observe the workings of foreign courts.[60] Walter Scott, apprenticed to his father as a WS aged fourteen in 1786, ultimately preferred to go to the bar (which he did in 1792). He had a reasonable practice there before becoming sheriff-depute of Selkirkshire in 1799 and a PCS in 1806.[61] James Graham, admitted a WS in 1788 and then as an advocate in 1795, changed direction more fundamentally by being ordained in England where he also became a poet.[62] The obvious benefit which a career as a writer or WS in Edinburgh might bring prior to going to the bar makes it highly likely that other advocates who had fathers or other relatives with writing chambers in Edinburgh spent time there as young men, gaining knowledge and practical experience and making contact with potential clients.[63] The 1780s do seem to have been a turning point, stimulated perhaps by the debate surrounding the admission of John Wright.

A detailed discussion of academic and practical legal education, an important subject in its own right, is beyond the scope of the present work.[64]

There was a close link, however, between education and admission as an advocate, and the Faculty maintained a keen interest in the educational standards attained by intrants to the bar. At the same time, practising advocates often advised younger relatives on where to study, which texts to purchase and which professors to employ as teachers. Their attitude was generally hard-headed and practical. In 1695 George Dunbar wrote to John Mackenzie about his young nephew, Kenneth Gordon.[65] Dunbar had taken advice from Sir Robert Gordon, after Kenneth had spent an unprofitable period at St Andrews University:

> His opinion was that he should be a session or two at Ed[inbu]r[gh] in a writeing chamber & then sent abroad to studie the Law ... He wishes him above all that he be master of the Latin tongue ... This is the great thing wherein most of our young scholars are defective, qch [which] is rather to be attributed to the decay of schools than to them.[66]

Gordon, who matriculated at Leiden in 1699, seems to have followed this advice. By contrast, Mackenzie's own son, another Kenneth, made excellent progress at St Andrews.[67] The best-documented foreign education of the period is that of John Clerk of Penicuik.[68] In 1694 his uncle, David Forbes, detailed his preferred method for studying law. His opening remarks are instructive:

> Considering that you are not to profess the practice of the pure Common Law [sc. jus commune] bot to dispose your self for the understanding of or practizing in our own Municipale Law with regard to the principalls of Common Law I think it absolutely proper that you doe first by yourself read the pure text of the Institutes once or twice.[69]

The linkage between the practical application of Scots (municipal) law and the principles of the jus commune is suggestive. Forbes was educated in the Netherlands at a time when the trend began to favour the more practical jus hodiernum and the arguments presented in the session papers confirm this view of the efficacy of Roman law.[70] The Faculty might point to it as evidence of status, of a learning and culture at the very least comparable to any bar in contemporary Europe; but advocates needed only enough Roman law to allow them, when required, to construct reasoned arguments that would convince Scottish judges to grant remedies to Scottish litigants.

ADVOCATES AND LEGAL PRACTICE

However rigorous the admissions process may or may not have been, the profession of advocate remained oversubscribed. The limit of ten, originally imposed in 1532, lasted barely a generation.[71] Having gained admission, advocates were free to set up in business and hope that clients began to appear. Adam Smith doubted that a twentieth of them even recovered the cost of their education.[72] According to Camic:

> ... unless one was sufficiently well connected to draw an ample clientele early on, the private practice of law in so small a country did not generally bring adequate financial and social returns for many hard years.[73]

Advocates faced strong competition, not only for the public offices of profit in the gift of the Crown but other offices which their status reasonably entitled them to hold. As the demand for such offices outstripped supply, some were reduced to touting for patronage.

Building a practice required four things: ability, social or political connections, patience and luck. An independent means of support was also important because professional income often materalised slowly. In 1799 George Dempster wrote that his nephew, poorly employed at the bar, 'must not despair but attend, attend, attend'.[74] This, he advised, might procure him some business and even raise him to the bench; it would certainly bring him into contact with the best morals and manners in the country.

The correspondence of Kenneth Mackenzie illustrates life at the bar. He certainly had a good foundation to his career. After his successful studies in St Andrews, noted earlier, he took colleges on Roman law at Leiden under Antonius Schulting and Gerhard Noodt.[75] By studying in the Netherlands he was following in the footsteps of his father and his uncle.[76] As the son of John Mackenzie of Delvine, a former advocate and retired PCS, he had an entrée into the legal world. This might have been stronger still had not his brother George, who went to the bar in 1710, been obliged to leave it having supported the Jacobite rising in 1715. Even so, in a letter to his father in March 1722, barely four weeks after admission as an advocate, Kenneth saw where his best prospects lay:

> Since my last to you I saw Huntington who promised to procure me a dozen or fourteen causes against the next session, tho I do not reckon much on it, but as an introduction to business. Yet I thought fit to let you know what weight your word has with him, & likewise, if you'll allow me so much liberty, that your absence has been a very signal disadvantage to me, which makes me apply more closely for my uncles countenance, for with a great many *plus est in opinione quam in veritate*.[77]

The uncle referred to as 'Huntington' was Alexander Hay, a successful advocate (and an episcopalian allegedly much employed by Jacobites) who could afford to offload a few cases.[78] Alexander was the son of Thomas Hay PCS, brother to John Mackenzie's third wife, Margaret, of the family of Hay of Alderston in East Lothian.[79] He was also the father of another advocate, also Thomas, who was to become depute keeper of the signet and, eventually, a lord of session.[80]

For the remainder of 1722 Kenneth Mackenzie, not unusually, had no business.[81] On his father's instructions, he spent his time observing his brethren at the bar and developing his knowledge of the law through the study of printed and manuscript sources. In June, he wrote the following

> En un môt me voil quattre mois un Avocat, sans que quelque un m'a encore graissé la patte, that bodes none of the best, but I have laid up a stock of patience instead of guineas, have got Stair's Institutions for business, & especially mentem sanam in corpore sano, all which with a walk now & then about the town & agreable company at home, make my time pass easily & pleasantly enough.[82]

It was not until the following February that he had some legal business, albeit a case on behalf of his father. At the end of that month, he contemplated heading north with the criminal circuit where, perhaps, 'a Client or two might be picked up'.[83] Seeking criminal cases was a feature of many young advocates' early careers; Henry Brougham, for example, seems to have enjoyed modest success on the criminal circuit on the occasions he did not choose to attend Ayr races instead.[84]

Mackenzie's business must have been improving because, in March 1723, he was looking for a servant. Even this was no easy task, because servants seemed 'as ill to be had as Wives', although he reflected that he might ride north with one and discard him, rather than take him for better and for worse.[85] Eventually he employed the writer James Edgar though only on an occasional basis.[86]

His clientele derived from his primary contact network, in particular his family: kinship and neighbourhood connections were as important in Scotland as at the English bar.[87] Mackenzie's clients consisted largely of friends and relatives, neighbours on the family estate and men directed to him on the advice of his father. It was to the latter he wrote, in June 1723, that 'I saw the highland Chieftan you sent me for a Client who with our other north countrey friends has kept me pretty busy this week'.[88] A year later there is reference to a client from Glenshee, again recommended by his father, whose case had been advocated to the Court of Session. Kenneth wrote to his father requesting 'the pieces of the process' (that is, the legal papers including the summons) because his client had failed to send them or reply to an earlier letter.[89] At the end of the year, having returned to Edinburgh from a visit to his father, he drew a contrast between Delvine, where his father had had a new client waiting for him, and the capital where no client awaited his return.[90]

Mackenzie's career had not taken off. In 1726 he happened to meet the writer George Robertson, the law agent whose clients included the Duke of Montrose. Robertson, a friend of his father's, gave him 'a consultation as a mark that he would be glad to continue it [that is, the friendship] from father to son'.[91] These were not important cases, however, and, if difficult points arose, John Mackenzie still directed his son to obtain the opinion of more experienced counsel. In one case on behalf of their kinsman, Alexander Robertson of Faskally, he told him to instruct Alexander Hay and James Graham of Airth.[92] Meanwhile, Kenneth continued to study and, in November 1723, with half a dozen others, he took a private college with Professor Alexander Bayne at the university.[93] Bayne wrote his own *Institutes* on the basis of those of Sir George Mackenzie which essentially he updated for use in his own teaching.[94] His student was clearly interested in Mackenzie as a model.[95] He had his own copy of Mackenzie's *Institutions*, and his published pleadings he regarded as 'masterpieces, & the justest models for the bar I ever saw onely allowing something for the change that time makes on every thing.'[96] He procured a copy of the published works of Mackenzie for his father in 1725 and then borrowed them for further study.[97]

In addition to the leading authors on Scots law, Kenneth read some of the printed pleadings of his colleagues at the bar, sending the best of them to his father when copies were available.[98] A well-drawn session paper was clearly something that brought attention within the profession. This is what the author of the *Idea Juris Scotici* meant when he described pleadings as being 'drawn by the ablest of the Council [that is, counsel], and perused and approved by the rest'.[99] He also spent time making searches of the registers in the Laigh Parliament House on behalf of his father. This was a learning experience of sorts but one more useful to the training of a writer than of an advocate. His lack of income is reflected in the fact that, in October 1724, he had to ask his father to send him money for clothes and a wig because life in Edinburgh had, as he put it 'bared my cloaths & emptied my pockets'.[100] Generally, Kenneth was careful with money, refusing to advance any on behalf of clients in the exchequer for fear he would not be repaid.[101] He was still suffering a lack of clients in February 1727 when he resolved to leave Edinburgh as soon as the session ended because of the expense of living there without business.[102]

Though his father lived until 1731, this run of Kenneth Mackenzie's correspondence seems to end in 1728. One of the last things he mentions – which must have made an impression on him – was a challenge to a duel made in July 1728 by James Graham of Kilmannan to Robert Dundas following 'some hard words utter'd at the bar about two years agoe'.[103] Graham and his brother were imprisoned on the basis of a warrant Dundas obtained from the justice-clerk. The Faculty of Advocates became involved and demanded heavy punishment, appealing to the judges' own sense of self-preservation:

> ... What we complaine of is a thing of a very extraordinary nature we apprehend it touches us all that have the honour to wear a gown & plead before your Lo[rdshi]ps And that indeed it touches your Lo[rdshi]ps in as strong a Degree for if Lawyers are to be challenged to fight and threatened with Death by every person against whom they plead in the strongest manner that they can and ought to doe in causes of that kind Your Lordships may meet with the same treatment.[104]

Mackenzie's career at the bar was long and steady but not particularly successful. In March 1745 he was chosen by Edinburgh town council, ahead of his younger contemporary Alexander Boswell of Auchinleck, to replace Thomas Dundas as professor of civil law at the university there.[105] Other university professors are also known to have been less than successful at the bar. Glasgow's first professor of civil law, William Forbes, was once described by Lord Grange as having 'more Law & Learning than twenty others who make more noise at the bar. But he is not a ready man at all nor a good pleader.'[106] Alexander Irving, professor of civil law at Edinburgh from 1800, was a sound lawyer but 'a man of the most invincible shyness, diffidence and reserve ... [and therefore] little calculated to be a Barrister'.[107] Fraser Tytler, sole professor of Universal History, Greek and Roman Antiquities at Edinburgh from 1786, did practise at the bar and (following William Wallace, professor of Scots law) became the second current holder of a chair at the university to be appointed an assessor to the town council.[108] In 1807, five years after his elevation to the bench, he was privately described by Colin Mackenzie WS as a man 'more apt in quotations from antient commentators than able in the application of them'.[109] Criticisms of this kind could not, of course, be made of all professors or former professors but Mackenzie may have been in the same mould. After all, as Lord Elchies pointed out, legal practice and academic life were distinct enterprises.[110]

If the shy, stuttering and bookish types were, indeed, more fitted for an academic life than for cut and thrust at the bar, it is important to remember that it was rare for an advocate, however brilliant, to become an overnight success. The session, as Boswell put it, was 'a court of papers'; the absence of civil juries made it difficult for individual renown to spread quickly.[111] Henry Mackenzie, in his eulogy of Lord Abercromby, drew a sharp distinction between the English bar and Scotland, where 'a speech, however remarkable, is rarely followed by those important consequences to a barrister's future business, of which there are daily instances in Westminster-hall'.[112] This did not stop men from trying. Soon after his admission in 1800, Henry Brougham regretted that his client had confessed to sedition because he had prepared 'a long and learned harangue, for the express purpose ... of bringing himself into notice'.[113] It is notable that his friend, Andrew Clephane, was present in court, given that he himself was not admitted to the bar until the following year.

Eloquence and rhetoric certainly had their place. Pleading in Scots law had been largely oral in the sixteenth century.[114] A visitor in 1629 suggested that the Scots practice was for the advocate to proceed, at greater or lesser length, according to the weight of the coins the client placed in his hand as he spoke.[115] The balance had shifted towards written informations by the end of the eighteenth century. John MacLaurin agreed with the view that 'in Scotland, a lawyer wrote all he spoke, and printed all he wrote'.[116] Although advocates had to subscribe papers they submitted to the court (and were therefore responsible for their content), there was initially no rule requiring them personally to have composed any papers to which they added their subscription.[117] In fact, an entry in the books of sederunt in 1738 makes it clear that it was acceptable for an advocate to sign a paper written by another.[118] This is worth quoting in full:

> This day [15 June 1738] the dean of Faculty was called and told by the President that the lords observed lawiers names at papers putt into their boxes and bills & answers in which the facts were misrepresented which they did interpret to proceed from ane abuse of lawiers signing papers brought to them by agents without reading & considering them; that for hereafter the lawiers must understand that whatever is signed by a lawier or his name subjoined therto is a deed of the lawier and that he restes his character upon what is therein advanced. The dean of Faculty undertook to acquaint the Faculty of the caution the lords gave them that they might conform themselves therto in time coming.[119]

By 1801 the lords clearly regarded it as an abuse for a lawyer to subscribe a paper depending in an action without either having drafted or revised it.[120] At all times, subscribing advocates were held accountable for what appeared in papers they signed unless they could convince the court that they were misinformed by their client.[121] In 1758, for instance, James Knox was fined £5 for misleading his counsel, and comments in his petition were excised.[122] The lords, exasperated by the frequency of poor orthography in pleadings, determined in 1768 that agents submitting papers would be fined for giving in papers which included 'imperfect quotations or typographical errors'.[123] This was renewed in 1808 when the lords expressed their exasperation at the submission of incorrect and incomplete papers that were 'unfit to remain as original and authoritative records of the Court'.[124]

The young Robert Blair is said to have written papers for other advocates; Henry Brougham certainly wrote papers for Henry Erskine though he received none of the fees from Erskine's clients.[125] Cockburn said of Thomas McGrugor, whose early success did not last, that 'some of the great guns of the profession got considerable praise for successful shots which McGrugor had loaded and pointed for them'.[126] Writing papers was seen as a way of gaining experience and acquiring business; it was a good opportunity for the gifted early career advocate. Leading advocates did not necessarily have time to draw their own papers and, as with seventeenth-century English barristers, applying a signature to a pleading drafted by another may sometimes have been a formality.[127] In his youth, Boswell likened the composition of law papers to writing essays for newspapers; but he appreciated the labour involved.[128] In 1778 he recorded that he had written fifteen pages of an information before bed and completed it the following morning.[129] Boswell likened the judges to sponges, soaking up these written arguments, and compared Lord Alemoor to a large melon and Lord Alva to a small lime.[130]

Henry Cockburn, in his *Journal*, described something of the drudgery involved in drafting informations. Taking the example of Robert Forsyth, he described the labour of men (the 'clerk-killers') who spent their days dictating pleadings.[131] This could keep one or two clerks, 'thin, wiry, black creatures, with sleepless eyes and elastic fingers' occupied for sixteen hours a day. Cockburn regarded Forsyth, in particular, as a fount of knowledge on many subjects, if not always an original thinker.[132]

The best advocates had retentive memories and an encyclopaedic knowledge of cases and legal authorities. Men like 'the living library', Lord Cullen, could quickly turn when necessary to the appropriate page of anything in the civil or canon laws or in the acts of parliament.[133] Some were unduly long-winded, which could draw complaints from the bench. In 1743, the president objected to the length of a fifty-five-page pleading which Thomas Hay notably described as having been 'signed by William Grant' rather than written by him. Grant defended himself, referring to an eminent lawyer he had heard at the bar

> not many years ago plead three hours without interruption & spent two hours of that time in stating the fact & that such pleading if put in writing must have made a long paper. That a long case could not be told in few words & he did not know if he was more prolix than other people; that he did his best & believed there was nothing in his paper that could be omitted.[134]

The suggestion that several hours might be spent in argument before the judges is certainly borne out by other sources. George Robertson referred in 1713 to a pleading that began 'a little after three a clock and continued till near half ane hour after six'.[135] A skilled pleader could persuade the bench of the justice of his client's cause. John Mackenzie WS admitted as much, acknowledging that outcomes sometimes depended 'more on the choice of the lawier than the Agent' and, in the matter concerned, recommending to his client Alexander Lockhart as 'a fit man to explain it at the Barr'.[136] That such explanation might be given in an atmosphere of surprising informality is suggested by some of James Boswell's notes on cases in which he pleaded.[137]

Lockhart had a particular reputation for eloquence but, in the view of some, he had too passionate a style of pleading, even shedding tears in his client's cause, which lost effect with overuse.[138] The aim was always, as the thirteenth-century proceduralist Guillaume Durand noted, to behave so as to please the judges rather than offend them.[139] The key to achieving this was to get to know the judges and to frame arguments that would appeal to their own views and prejudices or, as Sir George Mackenzie put it, 'soften and sweeten humours' on the bench.[140]

A number of other advocates enjoyed high regard as effective speakers. Alexander Carlyle regarded Andrew Pringle (Lord Alemoor) as the finest secular speaker in the country.[141] In 1813 William Erskine (elevated as Lord Kinedder in 1822), a man of 'shewy talents', would have been well regarded as a speaker, according to the president and justice-clerk, were he less conceited.[142] Fine eloquence, however, might be lost on the lords of session. As Boswell quipped, wasting golden words on them was akin to playing Italian allegros to a 'parcel of strong ploughmen dancing in a barn'.[143]

THE LEADERS OF THE BAR

In any court where there is no *numerus clausus,* or artificially imposed limit on entry to the bar, then, assuming reasonable demand to practise, some advocates will prosper and some will fail.[144] That is why the English bar was regarded as something of a lottery.[145]

The number who succeed, and the extent to which they monopolise business, depend largely on the level of litigation. The more cases there are the larger the bar that can be sustained and, at the same time, the smaller the proportion of business which falls to the most successful advocates. Where litigation is contracting, fewer advocates make a living exclusively from the bar and those who are most successful tend to have a larger, even dominant, share of business. This pattern was seen in the College of Justice in the sixteenth century. It was no less apparent in the eighteenth. As he himself noted, Lord Kames laboured for a decade at the bar without making £10 because there were at that time (the 1720s) several great lawyers who 'closed the bar and let no young Man forward'.[146] He included in their number Arniston, Duncan Forbes, Robert Craigie, James Boswell and James Graham of Airth.

We have already seen that litigation in the Court of Session was contracting in the middle of the eighteenth century.[147] To determine the size of the working bar from the court records, and to identify its leading figures, a clear methodology is needed. That adopted here is based on a survey of sample years of two rolls, the roll of ordinary causes and the roll of suspensions and advocations, both of which record parties and their advocates. By calculating the number of advocates employed, and the rate of employment of each of them, it is possible to identify the leaders of the bar.[148]

Because it is based on lists of names, this methodology must overcome two problems. First, a small number of names are illegible. In the present study, this was so small as to be statistically irrelevant. Second, while the clerk will have known which 'Murray' or 'Ferguson' he meant when recording their name, the historian is, in a few cases, faced with having to identify which of the five Murrays or three Fergusons, who were contemporaries as members of the Faculty of Advocates, were being referred to. A particular problem arises when, for example, a reference such as 'Hay' ceases to refer to Alexander Hay and begins to refer to Thomas Hay, because both had careers at the bar which overlapped. Since 137 of the 820 advocates admitted between 1690 and 1800 had a unique surname, the clerk might be forgiven for sticking to established usage and forgetting to differentiate properly a new practitioner whose name was as yet rarely heard in the court. Thankfully, there is sufficient evidence from a range of sources to help identify the most important practising advocates and assist in providing a sense of what proportion of new Outer House business they attracted. Having identified them, it is also possible to establish how long the leading practitioners had been at the bar and how many of them then proceeded to the bench.

These data (see Appendix 3) allow several conclusions to be drawn. First, there was a high level of continuity. Once an advocate gained a good practice then, health permitting, there was no reason why this might not be sustained for years. Two very different characters, Andrew Macdouall and Alexander Lockhart, are good examples of long-lasting success at the bar. Macdouall (later Lord Bankton), is not given the most flattering portrait by John Ramsay of Ochtertyre. Ramsay does admit, however, that 'with all his oddities, he was much employed'.[149] The Outer House rolls bear this out even if, as Professor Gordon noted in his brief survey, analysis of his career from the reported cases in *Morison's Dictionary* is inconclusive.[150] In 1711, after three years at the bar, Macdouall was involved in nineteen causes in the Outer House; this compares to Alexander Hay, admitted in 1697, who had twenty-five causes in 1711 (by 1721, Hay had become the best-employed advocate). Macdouall had also progressed and by 1731 had overtaken Hay to become leader of the bar. This was no small achievement though it pales in comparison to Alexander Lockhart who was the busiest practitioner in 1751, 1760 and 1761; in 1741 he was second only to Henry Home (by then prospering) and he was still one of the most active pleaders in 1771. Lockhart, according to Home, got into business early thanks to his influential relations and his willingness to act for 'rascals' (mainly Jacobites).[151]

Secondly, there is a relationship between the size of the practising bar, the level of litigation, the tendency of a small group to dominate the business of the court and the trend for promotions to the bench to be made from that small group.[152] Domination of the bar by a relatively small group is not uncommon; this certainly reflects the experience in England where practice at the bar was unevenly distributed, and also in Toulouse where the career structure has been likened to a pyramid with a narrow pinnacle and wide base.[153] The size of the practising bar in Scotland fluctuated substantially and was at its lowest in 1761 (Table 4).[154] The men at the top in that year had been at the bar for about twenty years and would have entered the Faculty in the early 1740s, known to be a low point in terms of litigation. As litigation picked up during the remainder of the century, and advocates' admissions increased, the practising bar also grew in size. As it did so, the dominance of its leaders decreased and men with less experience at the bar could reach the top of the profession more quickly.[155]

Table 4 *Size of the working bar (estimate)*[156]

1701	1711	1721	1731	1741	1751	1761	1771	1781	1791	1801
92	91	77	83	74	66	51	59	84	89	89

Table 5 *Average experience of the ten busiest practitioners (in years)*

1701	1711	1721	1731	1741	1751	1761	1771	1781	1791	1801
13	17.3	18.1	24.3	19.7	20.9	19	16.4	15.2	19.4	11.9

Table 6 *Dominance of the top advocates*
(per cent of ordinary cause business per grouping)

	1701	1711	1721	1731	1741	1751	1761	1771	1781	1791	1801
Top 5	20.9	31.7	30.8	32.5	33.7	52.5	37.1	29.1	20.9	19.3	20.5
Top 10	34.9	49.2	48	52.5	52.6	52.6	55.6	47.6	36.9	34.6	40.2

At the pinnacle of the profession in 1801 were four men who at the beginning of 1791 were not yet members of Faculty. This contrasts with the dominant figures in 1751, men who had already been working at the bar in the 1720s. One of the more notable meteoric rises in the 1790s was Thomas Walker Baird. The natural son of an Edinburgh wright, in 1787 Baird had inherited property in the Cowgate and this might have given him the wherewithal to train for the bar which he entered early in 1793.[157] By the beginning of 1801, a year which would see him involved in more ordinary actions than any other advocate, he could afford to move to more plush surroundings in Queen Street.[158] Baird was not a notary though he worked as a writer prior to coming to the bar and, in 1790, was registered as first clerk to the advocate John Macfarlane.[159] This may have been a useful experience though Macfarlane himself was new to the bar (he was admitted on 15 January 1789). Baird's rise was not unprecedented. John Pattison, of course, made a similar leap in 1787 from writer to advocate.[160] Just three years later Pattison had the third largest number of clients in the ordinary cause roll of anyone at the bar, having quickly exploited his professional contacts in Edinburgh.[161]

Despite numbers burgeoning in the 1780s and 1790s, the bar was not regarded as filled with particularly able men. Good contacts, joined with a modicum of talent, might go a long way: far enough for plain writers like Pattison and Baird to turn themselves into leading counsel. They might simply have been good while others were mediocre. In 1813 the President (Granton) and Lord Justice Clerk (Boyle), writing confidentially to Henry Dundas, assessed the bar candidly. In their opinion

> ... the period which elapsed from 1780 down to the year 1793 or 4, did not produce men of very superior abilities. If there were any, they are already taken out of the way by death or promotion, and all who remain, we consider only as men of second rate abilities and knowledge, and some of them stand perhaps not so high.

As Hope was admitted in 1784 and Boyle at the end of 1793, those whom they held in low regard were very much contemporaries. In the period 1780–94 inclusive, 122 members of Faculty were admitted. Of those, about eighty-five were still living in November 1813, with seven having been promoted to the bench. Over the next thirteen years, a further six of them would be promoted, down to Alexander Irving (Lord Newton).[162] Unless they were late bloomers, they fall within the category of 'second rate' or worse.

This leads to the third conclusion. There was a correlation between ability at the bar and promotion to the bench. Very few of the top advocates in 1701 and 1711 ended their careers as judges. By 1741 very few did not. This might in part be linked to living longer: the mortality of advocates improved considerably towards the end of the seventeenth century and at the beginning of the eighteenth.[163] Good lawyers lived long enough to want a change of direction. Because the Union all but guaranteed promotion from the bar to the bench, there were more judicial gowns to be had than ever before and more spaces to fill. When the bar had more practitioners, at the beginning and end of the eighteenth century, the range of choice was wider (even if some were second-rate or worse) and judges might be drawn from beyond the leading advocates. When the practising bar was smaller, as it was in the 1740s, advocates fit for the bench could realistically be drawn only from this narrower group. It may be worth adding that the average age of the judges in 1741 was 55.8; in 1771 it was 59.1 and by 1796 it had gone up to sixty-six. The average length of service on the bench of those who were sitting judges in 1741 (29.4 years), 1771 (30.5 years) and 1795 (27.8 years) did not vary greatly notwithstanding that lords of session were, on average, getting older.

A survey of cases involving litigants surnamed Mackenzie in the Hamilton-Gordon collection of Session Papers in the Advocates Library provides incidental, if unscientific, support for these conclusions. The 129 papers in these cases (arranged alphabetically), dating from 1717 to 1747, were subscribed by twenty-nine advocates, eleven of whom later became lords of session. James Graham of Airth subscribed twenty-one of them, followed by Henry Home (fifteen) and William Grant (ten) with five advocates, including Alexander Lockhart and Duncan Forbes, subscribing seven papers each. The uneven distribution of business is clear from the fact that 46.5 per cent of the papers were subscribed by only five advocates and ten subscribed an even higher proportion, 71.3 per cent. These are higher percentages than Figure 4 would suggest but the figures, drawn from a single collection of session papers, are less representative. What is suggestive, therefore, is not the numbers but the overall pattern: in a random collection of pleadings, over a thirty-year period, a large proportion was drafted by a small number of advocates who are known to have been among the leading practitioners.[164]

NON-PRACTITIONERS

At the other end of the scale from the leaders of the bar were those men who joined the Faculty with no intention of practising law. According to William Forbes, many men with good estates sought admission to the Faculty 'with no other view than the Honour of becoming Members of it'.[165] Henry Mackenzie also thought that the eldest sons of the gentry went there to gain 'a sort of fashionable distinction' because of the polite education that entry to the Faculty required. According to him, there was in the 1760s 'an elegance of manners, joined with a degree of knowledge and information, among the Faculty of Advocates in Scotland, not to be met with in any similar body of men in any other country'.[166] An English visitor, Edward Topham, took a more disparaging view. Writing in 1775, he said that the advocates were 'almost innumerable' because 'every man who has nothing to do, and no better name to give himself, is called Advocate'.[167] He thought very few of them practised and gained business, however. Moreover, some of those who did brought honour to their country by making their bar 'a school of eloquence, and not, as I am sorry to say with us, a jargon of barbarous and almost unintelligible words, and who preserve, in their debates, the manners and sentiments of Gentlemen'.

Among the Faculty's membership, therefore, it is important to distinguish those who practised law from the kind of gentleman who entered advocate, in the words of Boswell, 'merely to have a feather in his cap'.[168] Doing so largely requires a close examination of the court records although extraneous sources can sometimes be helpful. For instance, the 1694 Edinburgh poll tax records note the names of some advocates who no longer practised, such as James Brown who 'doeth not follow his Employment as ane advocat'.[169] Electoral rolls also sometimes recorded advocates who did not practise. Out of the 129 advocates mentioned in Adam's *Political State of Scotland* in 1788, only ten are described as not in practice and two are described as having little practice. That does not mean that 117 must have been practising. Most of the comments indicate advocates' political allegiances, the size of their estates and the number of votes they held. Many describe men in terms incompatible with practice at the bar because they held administrative or other offices or lived in England. On the other hand, forty-two members of Faculty are described as 'a lawyer', sometimes of eminence, or in great or moderate practice, and sometimes as being ambitious for professional advancement. Thus, of George Buchan-Hepburn it was noted that '[h]e wants a Judge's gown'; the same was said of James Ferguson of Pitfour. In a similar vein, William Honyman sought promotion at the bar while Sir John Belshes-Wishart wanted a clerkship of session.

This reflects the clear division in contemporary parlance between 'advocates' and 'lawyers'. One of Lord Milton's papers, titled 'Marks to Advocates 1763' contains fifteen categories and reflects a method of classifying Faculty members though, unfortunately, no actual list of advocates applying the classification is attached. The first four categories are as follows: '1. Good Lawyers 2. Young men that promise well & fitt to be sheriffs 3. advocates but not lawyers 4. non attendants retired to the country'.[170] This paper was written from the viewpoint of the government's need to fill vacant sheriff-deputeships with the right candidates. This, and other sources, indicate that an 'advocate' was any Faculty member whereas a 'lawyer' was an advocate who actively engaged in legal practice. This was the sense in which it could be said that Fife had 'more advocates, & fewer Lawyers in it, than any County of Scotland'.[171] Lord Kames even suggested that the Faculty's examinators might helpfully provide new intrants with some hint as to whether or not they were actually thought qualified to make a living at the bar.[172]

Non-practising members of the Faculty of Advocates could be relatively unknown in Edinburgh. Because advocates generally enjoyed above-average lifespans, they might spend many years in retirement.[173] Thus, the character of William Montgomery of Magbiehill (father of James Montgomery, lord advocate and chief baron) was described to Tweeddale in some detail by Thomas Hay in 1742.[174] A mercurial or light-headed man, he was 'by profession a lawyer but without knowledge or practise' and Hay had no memory of him attending Parliament House.[175]

Private correspondence assists in distinguishing those advocates who practised from those who pursued some alternative career or who simply managed their family estates. One of the objections to advancing John Orr, already both town clerk and commissary of Glasgow, to the office of sheriff-depute of Lanark in 1797 was that he had never actually been a practising lawyer.[176] Charles Anstruther is another example. Admitted advocate in 1729, he built up a tolerably good practice, helped by family connections (his brother Philip had been at the bar since 1711 and was not the first Anstruther to practise there). He then entered the marines, however. In 1738 Philip married into the family of Hay of Sprott, and it was from a member of this prominent family that Lord Milton later received a request to assist Charles who aimed to purchase a captaincy in a regiment based in Minorca. His decision to change career, despite establishing a practice at the bar, had been based on the fact that his friends had persuaded him to study the law but that, in reality, 'the bent of his inclinations and what he aimed at most was in the military'.[177]

Was it possible to leave the bar (as opposed to being removed by order of the court) and lose the privileges of College membership? The 1694 poll tax curiously describes Patrick Smith as 'late advocate, at present out of town'. This probably means he was retired from practice but it also raises the question of whether an advocate who did not practise retained any of his privileges. In 1768 Alexander Duncan, who had joined the Faculty in 1755, argued in the positive. As a petitioner, Duncan styled himself simply 'advocate'; in the Answers, however, he is designed 'Advocate; Lieutenant in the Royal First Regiment of Foot'. This action was an election case brought by the advocate Robert Mackintosh and others against the magistrates and town council of Cupar.[178] Its context was a wider political struggle between Mackintosh and the sitting Member of Parliament for Fife, George Dempster.[179] It was a typical case of alleged municipal bribery and corruption, with Duncan cited as a witness by complainers who wanted him to answer questions about discussions he had had with his friend Dempster.[180] According to the pleadings, Duncan had 'attended' the bar for some years but found it (probably financially) 'expedient' to join the army. He refused to reveal the contents of any conversations with Dempster on the basis that Dempster had sought his advice and spoken freely to him in his character as a friend and also as a lawyer. The pleadings, written by John MacLaurin, are worth quoting:

> It is well known to your Lordships, that many gentlemen enter lawyers who have no intention of attending the bar for life, or making a livelihood by their practice: They study the law, and put on the gown, to enable them the better to manage their own estates, advise their tenants, friends and neighbours in the country, and qualify themselves for the lucrative and honourable offices which can be conferred only upon gentlemen of the law. And it was never before doubted, that lawyers, tho' not practising, but residing in the country on their estates, or elsewhere, were intitled to all the privileges of the gown; and accordingly many of them have been promoted to the highest offices in the law.[181]

It was further argued that an advocate who followed a profession not incompatible with the bar should retain all the privileges and immunities of the College of Justice.[182]

One of the difficulties in distinguishing advocates in general practice from those who acted on an occasional basis is the fact that advocates appeared quite often as party litigants. In the sixteenth century advocates sued for their fees.[183] By the eighteenth century this was seen as mercenary and incompatible with their status.[184] The actions they brought differed little from those of other landowners, and merely because they retained the services of a fellow advocate to act for them does not negate the possibility that they themselves were in practice. Some eminent and skilled practitioners were sensible enough not to have themselves for clients.

CONCLUSION

Advocates, in Scotland and elsewhere in Europe, had a grasping reputation and must have developed a thick skin to deal with the threats and verbal abuse that might come from litigants. In one instance in 1776, John MacLaurin even had shots fired through the window of his house.[185] When, during a deposition in 1749, Sir John Houston took advantage of Lord Minto's temporary absence in the Inner House and angrily called the advocate George Brown 'Ane impertinent puppie', it was not Brown but the clerk who later complained to the judge.[186]

Of everyone at the bar, it was Alexander Lockhart, that 'clever, bitter fellow' as Lovat called him, who was a lightning rod for complaints.[187] To Robert Dundas, Lockhart was 'always for the subject' (against the government), for General Bland, he was 'the great Jacobite Lawyer … who is always employed against the Crown'; to Boswell, he was 'a prodigy in his profession', and, to Henry Home, he was the man who 'took all the rascally causes'.[188] Bland was particularly furious with Lockhart for attacking the character of a witness, one of his soldiers, in the trial of the alleged murderer of an army sergeant in 1749. He was disappointed that the lords of justiciary had not intervened to protect the witness from being 'abused by that foul mouth'd advocate'. When the witness later threatened Lockhart, who then obtained a warrant against him, Bland took the view that Lockhart, for his behaviour in this and other cases, deserved a good beating. He alleged that although his fellow advocates were obliged to support him publicly, in private they were sorry the witness 'had not beat him heartily, as he fairly deserved it'. Whether engaging in a violent dispute with his neighbour, or getting petty revenge on a brother advocate by inserting offensive words about him in a decreet arbitral, Lockhart had a lively career. It was one which, in later life, he was reluctant for James Boswell to publicise through writing his biography.[189] Yet he reached the pinnacle of his profession; so revered was he that, after his death, his admirer Lord Newton is said to have worn Lockhart's old gown until it was in tatters.[190]

Putting aside his pedigree as the grandson of a lord president, Lockhart was one of those men who benefited from a useful marriage, in his case to Margaret Pringle, shortly after his admission to the bar. Initially, however, the marriage was the talk of Edinburgh because Margaret did not get on her with her female in-laws.[191] Her father, Thomas Pringle WS, was by no means their match socially. Within the legal profession, however, he was a leading agent who had not only trained a string of influential writers and became depute-keeper of the signet but had placed a son at the bar (the future Lord Edgefield).[192] Short of marrying a judge's daughter, Lockhart had hit the jackpot professionally: by gaining a wife, he also gained connections to many prominent agents.[193] Living with his wife at his father-in-law's house, as he found himself in August 1726, therefore did no harm to his professional prospects.[194] It is no surprise that, as dean of Faculty, Lockhart later expressed support to John Davidson WS for a plan (never put into effect) to unite the libraries of the advocates and writers to the signet, combining their resources and placing them in Robert Adam's new General Register House.[195]

The relationship between advocates and writers to the signet was always fundamental. When in 1692 the advocate David Dunmuir persuaded the Lord Ordinary on the Bills to issue a warrant to the macers to incarcerate the advocate Charles Gray, together with his servants and William Panton WS, for having retained process papers for years, refusing to return them, the latter were subjected to the same hazard as Gray.[196] No doubt it was part of an agreed strategy to cause delay because this was not the first complaint Dunmuir had been obliged to make. At the same time, shared hazards could bring shared rewards. James Boswell mentions a visit to the home of Robert Syme WS in 1775 when the latter, suffering from a cold, sat in his nightgown surrounded by court processes.[197] The visit was necessary because Syme provided Boswell with a great deal of his business, just as English barristers often credited their early success to the friendship and patronage of solicitors.[198] Walter Scott, like Kenneth Mackenzie, owed many of his earliest fees to his father, who was also a WS, and to his father's former apprentices.[199] It is to writers to the signet, therefore, that we shall turn in the next chapter.

NOTES

1. Huber, *Praelectionis* (3rd edn, 2 vols, Utrecht, 1711), vol. 2, III.1 (p. 143): 'Quid est advocatus? Est vir bonus, Jurisperitus, a litigantibus rogatus, ut voce vel scripto causam suam Judici exponat, probet, atque ex arte defendat, ad hoc officium publica auctoritate admissus'.
2. Finlay, *Men of Law*, chapter 4.
3. M. H. B. Sanderson, *Mary Stewart's People* (Edinburgh, 1987), p. 23; Hannay, *College of Justice*, p. 150.
4. For example, M. Berlich, *Pars prima conclusionum practicabilium* (2 vols, Leipzig, 1651), IX, 15 (vol. 1, p. 34); J. Wissenbach, *In libros iv priores Codicis Justiniani repetitae praelectionis* (Franeker, 1660–3), II, 5, 7.
5. Finlay, 'Advocates unlimited', p. 206.
6. AL, FR 339r/11(i).
7. J. H. Baker, *The Legal Profession and the Common Law* (London, 1985), pp. 45–74.
8. TCM, SL1/1/89, fo. 47; SL1/1/92, fo. 297; SL1/1/39, fos 692–4.
9. H. Dingwall, *Late Seventeenth-Century Edinburgh* (Aldershot, 1994), pp. 229–31.
10. Ibid., p. 229; *eadem*, *Physicians, Surgeons and Apothecaries: Medical Practice in Seventeenth-Century Edinburgh* (East Linton, 1995), p. 111.
11. NRS, Supplementary parliamentary papers, PA7/17/1/121.
12. J. W. Cairns, 'The Origins of the Edinburgh Law School: the Union of 1707 and the Regius Chair' 11 (2007) *Edinburgh Law Review*, 300.
13. This subject has rightly deserved significant attention in recent years. See Cairns, 'The formation of the Scottish legal mind in the eighteenth century'; ibid., 'Rhetoric, language, and Roman Law: legal education and improvement in Eighteenth-Century Scotland'; and, ibid., 'Alfenus Varus and the Faculty of Advocates: Roman visions and the manners that were fit for admission to the Bar in the eighteenth century', 28 (2001) *Ius Commune*, 203–32.
14. NLS, Papers relating to the Signet, MS 1505, fo. 103.
15. In 1728 it was discussed whether to afford a role in disputes at public examinations to the students of civil law in Edinburgh. No recommenda-

tion appears to have been made: Pinkerton, ed., *Min. Bk, 1713–1750*, p. 110; AL FR339r/9.

16. The symbolism is explained fully in J. W. Cairns, 'Advocates' Hats, Roman Law and Admission to the Scots Bar', pp. 24–61.

17. NRS, CS1/8, fo. 14v. His admission is essentially identical to that of Archibald Stewart in 1718. Stewart's petition is dated 27 Feb. and his admission was on 17 Dec. the same year: NRS, Court of Session processes, Carmichael and Elliot, CS181/7086; CS1/10, fo. 218v

18. NRS, Menzies of Menzies papers, GD1/337/40/2.

19. J. W. Cairns, 'Advocates' Hats, Roman Law and Admission to the Scots Bar', esp. pp. 30–2, 41–2.

20. NRS, CS1/8, fo. 41v.

21. For example, the admission of John Cunningham, former servant of Lord Woodhall, was supported by the dean in 1642: ibid., CS1/5, fo. 134r.

22. Cairns, 'Advocates' Hats', pp. 46–7.

23. *Acts of Sederunt*, p. 181.

24. Spotiswood, *Form of Process*, p. xxxix.

25. K. van Strien and M. Ahsmann, 'Scottish law students in Leiden at the end of the seventeenth century: the correspondence of John Clerk 1694–1697' p. 19 (1992) *Lias*, p. 284. John Clerk, unusually, spent three years in Leiden: J. M. Gray, ed., *Memoirs of the Life of Sir John Clerk of Penicuik, Baronet, Baron of the Exchequer, Extracted by himself from his own Journals 1676–1755* (Edinburgh, 1892), pp. 14–19.

26. Shaw, *Management of Scottish Society*, pp. 27–8; Cairns, 'Alfenus Varus and the Faculty of Advocates', p. 211.

27. *Acts of Sederunt 1553–1790*, p. 181.

28. Ibid., p. 195; Pinkerton, ed., *Min. Bk, 1661–1712*, introduction, p. x.

29. Pinkerton, ed., *Min. Bk, 1661–1712*, pp. 116–17; *Acts of Sederunt*, p. 200; NRS, CS 1/9, fo. 61v. Black was admitted on 26 July 1692: ibid., CS 1/9, fo. 64v.

30. Pinkerton, ed., *Min. Bk, 1661–1712*, p. 164.

31. Cairns, 'Alfenus Varus and the Faculty of Advocates', p. 208.

32. Shaw, *Management of Scottish Society*, p. 27; Pinkerton, ed., *Min. Bk, 1713–1750*, p. 241.

33. *Acts of Sederunt*, p. 451.

34. Cairns, 'Advocates' Hats', p. 48.

35. Pinkerton, ed., *Min. Bk, 1713–1750*, p. 240. There is no evidence of what happened to Gordon's entry money, assuming this had been paid.

36. NRS, CS1/13, fo. 139r.

37. NLS, FR339r/23/3, *Report of the Committee, appointed to prepare Regulations respecting the Course of Studies necessary to be followed, and the other Qualifications which ought to be required in those who wish to become Members of the Faculty, 1785*. See, for a similar sentiment, J. C. Watt, *John Inglis: A Memoir* (Edinburgh, 1893), pp. 54–5.

38. Pinkerton, ed., *Min. Bk 1661–1712*, pp. 180–1.
39. Ibid., p. 182, n.306.
40. Scott and Pottle, eds, *Private Papers of James Boswell*, xv, p. 271.
41. Pinkerton, ed., *Min. Bk 1661–1712*, p. 29. In 1762 it went up to £60 then in 1769 it was augmented again to £80. Fifteen years later it increased still further to £100 and, in 1790, to £150.
42. Cf. NRS, CS 1/14, fo. 169v (1772) and CS1/16, fo. 177r (1783). CS1/15, fo. 90r (1769) is similar. CS 1/17, fo. 123r mentions specifically the salaries of those in charge of the library.
43. This is largely the thesis of Cairns, 'Importing our lawyers from Holland', esp. pp. 139, 152–3.
44. ALSP, *Information for Mr Charles Hamilton-Gordon, Advocate*, Elchies's Papers, 1744, vol. 15, no. 7, p. 21. For discussion, see R. L. Emerson, *Professors, Patronage and Politics: The Aberdeen Universities in the Eighteenth Century* (Aberdeen, 1992), pp. 65–9; J. W. Cairns, 'Lawyers, law professors, and localities: the Universities of Aberdeen, 1680–1750', p. 46 (1995) *Northern Ireland Legal Quarterly*, pp. 321–3.
45. Cairns, 'Advocates' hats', p. 49. It has been suggested that the public lesson before the lords may have ended after 1795, except for special occasions: Stewart and Parratt, eds, *Min. Bk, 1783–1798*, p. 182, n. 306.
46. See generally M. Ahsmann, 'Teaching the *ius hodiernum*: Legal education of advocates in the Northern Netherlands (1575–1800)' 65 (1997) *Tijdschrift voor Rechtsgeschiedenis*, p. 428.
47. J. W. Cairns, 'John Millar's lectures on Scots criminal law' 8 (1988) *Oxford Journal of Legal Studies*, p. 367.
48. Stewart, ed., *Min. Bk, 1751–1783*, pp. 94, 119.
49. The wording of the 1692 act was revived in a draft in 1785: cf. Pinkerton, ed., *Min. Bk, 1661–1712*, p. 116, and Stewart and Parratt, eds, *Min. Bk, 1783–1798*, pp. 28–9; see also, Cairns, 'Alfenus Varus and the Faculty of Advocates', pp. 229–30
50. Discussed at length by J. W. Cairns, 'The face that did not fit: race, appearance, and exclusion from the bar in eighteenth-century Scotland' (2003) 9 *Fundamina*, p. 11; ibid., 'Alfenus Varus and the Faculty of Advocates', esp. pp. 214–20. See also Stewart, ed., *Min. Bk 1783–1798*, pp. xxxiv–xl.
51. Cairns, 'Alfenus Varus and the Faculty of Advocates', p. 230; H. Cockburn, *Journal* (2 vols, Edinburgh, 1874 ?), ii, p. 153. See also Miller, *Cockburn's Millennium*, p. 310, for Cockburn's description of Wright and his dismissive description of his annual class in which, he claimed, 'the first lecture generally ended the course'. Forsyth was by far the more successful practitioner.
52. J. Dwyer and A. Murdoch, 'Paradigms and politics: manners, morals and the Rise of Henry Dundas, 1770–1784' in J. Dwyer et al., eds, *New*

Perspectives on the Politics and Culture of Early Modern Scotland (Edinburgh, 1982), pp. 226–7.

53. Berlanstein, *Barristers of Toulouse*, p. 22.

54. Ibid., p. 13.

55. Discussed in Finlay, 'Corruption, regionalism and legal practice in eighteenth-century Scotland' (forthcoming).

56. NRS, CS1/9, fos 59v–60r. See, generally, Finlay, 'Lower branch of the legal profession', pp. 42–6.

57. NRS, Mar and Kellie papers, GD124/15/981.

58. Hill Burton, *Lives of Simon Lord Lovat, and Duncan Forbes*, pp. 276–7; J. Ramsay of Ochtertyre, *Scotland and Scotsmen in the Eighteenth Century*, ed. A. Allardyce, 2 vols (Edinburgh and London, 1888), i, p. 351.

59. Ross, *Lord Kames*, p. 11; Lehmann, *Henry Home, Lord Kames*, p. 8; B. D. Osborne, *Braxfield: The Hanging Judge?* (Argyll, 1997), p. 86. Ross is wrong to regard Dickson as a WS. He may be identified with a twenty-eight-year-old Edinburgh writer who was admitted notary public on 28 March 1688: NRS, Admission register of notaries public, NP2/15 (unpaginated).

60. [Lord Brougham], *Memoir of the late Hon. Allan Maconochie of Meadowbank one of the Senators of the College of Justice* (Edinburgh, 1845), p. 7. He had, apparently, already taken the classes in civil law and Scots law.

61. Dickson, 'Sir Walter Scott and the Parliament House', xlii (1930) *JR*, 1–2.

62. Grant, *The Faculty of Advocates*, p. 86.

63. The same is largely true for England too: D. Duman, *The English and Colonial Bars in the Nineteenth Century* (London, 1983), pp. 82–3.

64. P. Nève, 'Disputations of Scots Students Attending Universities in the Northern Netherlands', in W. M. Gordon and D. Fergus, eds, *Legal History in the Making* (London, 1991), pp. 95–108; R. Feenstra 'Scottish-Dutch Legal Relations in the Seventeenth and Eighteenth Centuries', in T. C. Smout, ed., *Scotland and Europe, 1200–1850* (Edinburgh, 1986), pp. 128–42; R. Feenstra, 'Teaching the civil law at Louvain as reported by Scottish students in the 1430s (MSS. Aberdeen pp. 195–7) (1997) *Tijschrift voor Rechtsgeschiedenis*, pp. 245–80; J. W. Cairns, 'Importing our Lawyers from Holland: Netherland's Influences on Scots Law and Lawyers in the Eighteenth Century', *Scotland and the Low Countries, 1124–1994* ed. G. G. Simpson (East Linton, 1996), pp. 136–53. These articles by Professor Cairns appear as part of a two-volume collection, published by Edinburgh University Press in 2014. See also my chapter in the *Edinburgh History of Education*, to be published in 2015.

65. Gordon counted as a nephew despite the fact that Mackenzie's marriage to his aunt lasted less than a month before she died: J. Munro, 'Clansmen and clients', 12 (1965) *Scottish Genealogist*, 38.

66. NLS, Delvine papers, MS 1103, fo. 56.

67. Munro, 'Clansmen and clients', p. 42.
68. See, generally, Van Strien and Ahsmann, 'Scottish law students in Leiden'.
69. NRS, Clerk of Penicuik papers, GD18/2301.
70. See, generally, Ahsmann, 'Teaching the *ius hodiernum*'.
71. J. Finlay, 'Advocates unlimited', pp. 209–13.
72. Cited by C. Camic, *Experience and Enlightenment* (Edinburgh, 1983), p. 201.
73. Ibid. The picture was precisely the same in Westminster and Dublin, e.g. D. Hogan, *Legal Profession in Ireland* (Dublin, 1986), chapter 6.
74. J. Fergusson, ed., *Letters of George Dempster to Sir Adam Fergusson 1756–1813* (London, 1934), p. 280.
75. NLS, Delvine, MS 1209, f. 191r. On Noodt, see G. C. J. J. Van den Bergh, *The Life and Work of Gerard Noodt (1647–1725): Dutch Scholarship between Humanism and Enlightenment* (Oxford, 1988).
76. NLS, Delvine, MS 1332, fo. 69. His uncle was Colin Mackenzie of Coul, on whom see *Album Studiosorum*. col. 748 and also R. Feenstra and C. J. D. Waal, *Seventeenth-century Leyden Law Professors and their influence on the development of the Civil Law* (Amsterdam and Oxford, 1975), p. 85n. Kenneth's cousin appears to have been killed during his return from Holland in 1693: W. K. Dickson, ed., 'Letters to John Mackenzie of Delvine from Revd. Alexander Munro, 1690 to 1698' in *Miscellany of the Scottish History Society, Fifth volume* (Edinburgh, 1933), p. 249.
77. NLS, Delvine, MS 1209, fo. 16r. The Latin means 'there is more in opinion than in truth' and the sense is that many would credit Huntington's opinion even if Mackenzie were in truth unworthy of it. Henry Home, as a young man, was a cousin of Alexander Hay and found his assistance rather limited: Scott and Pottle, eds, *Private Papers of James Boswell*, xv, p. 279.
78. On his background, see NLS, Erskine Murray, MS 5078, fos 110v–11r. Hay was Kenneth Mackenzie's uncle by marriage.
79. On John Mackenzie, see D. Watt, 'Chiefs, lawyers and debt: a study of the relationship between Highland elites and the legal profession in Scotland *c.*1550 to 1700' (PhD thesis, University of Edinburgh, 1998), pp. 174–6; and J. Munro, 'Clansmen and clients', pp. 36–40.
80. NLS, Yester, MS 7045, fo. 45r; NRS, CS1/14, fo. 32r.
81. Cf. Walker, ed., *Correspondence of Boswell and Johnstone of Grange*, p. 226, n. 7.
82. NLS, Delvine, MS 1209, fo. 22r. The French means 'in a phrase, four months as an advocate see me remain without anything having greased my palm'.
83. Ibid., fo. 30r.
84. *Brougham and his Early Friends: Letters to James Loch, 1798–1809*, ed. R. H. Buddle Atkinson and G. A. Jackson (3 vols, London, 1908), vol. I, pp. 187, 245.

85. NLS, Erskine Murray, MS 5078, fo. 33r.
86. This may be the same Edgar who, as servant to Lord Minto, was admitted a burgess of Edinburgh on 8 March 1710. Minto died in 1718, leaving him free to be employed elsewhere.
87. Prest, *Rise of the Barristers*, pp. 25–6; Duman, *English and Colonial Bars in the Nineteenth Century*, p. 90.
88. NLS, Delvine, MS 1209, fo. 44r.
89. Ibid., fo. 67r.
90. Ibid., fo. 96r.
91. Ibid., fo. 133r.
92. For example, ibid., fos. 49r, 193, 197. Robertson was Kenneth Hay's brother-in-law. He refers to Alexander Hay as Robertson's 'uncle' though, in fact, he was uncle to Robertson's wife. The 'Mr Graeme' in this letter is not specified but, because these are described as 'old' lawyers and the letter is dated 1723, Airth is the only possibility.
93. Ibid., fo. 55r.
94. On Bayne, see W. Menzies, 'Alexander Bayne of Rires', p. 36 (1924) *JR*, p. 60; Cairns, 'John Millar's Lectures on Scots Criminal Law', pp. 383–6.
95. On Mackenzie's pleading, see B. I. Manolesu, 'George Mackenzie on Scottish Judicial Rhetoric', p. 20 (2002) *Rhetorica*, p. 275.
96. NLS, Delvine, MS 1209, fo. 122.
97. It is clear that other works on rhetoric and pleading were studied by Scots' advocates. In one case, for instance, Claude Gaultier's book on pleading was cited as an authority: ALSP, *Copy of the Process of Separation and Aliment, before the Commissaries of Edinburgh, At the Instance of Mrs Anne Montgomery*, Pitfour, vol. 6, no. 13, p. 46. This probably refers to the two-volume 1688 quarto edition in the Advocates Library: C. Gaultier, *Les plaidoyez de Monsieur Gaultier avocat au Parlement* (Paris, 1688).
98. For example, ibid., fo. 69.
99. *Idea Juris Scotici* (London, 1733), p. 8. This work appears to have been written by James Innes but, in fact, was not (see chapter 6, n. 162).
100. NLS, Delvine, MS 1209, fos 95r–v; also fo. 139v.
101. Ibid., fos 151r–v.
102. Ibid., fo. 159r.
103. Ibid., fo. 188r. This challenge was not unique, e.g. J. Finlay, 'Ethics, etiquette and the early modern Scots advocate' (2006) *JR*, pp. 174–6.
104. NRS, Court of Sessions unextracted processes, first arrangement, CS236/A/1/39, 13 July 1728. George Robertson does not discuss this episode, but does provide a possible context: ibid., GD220/5/1733/3.
105. TCM, SL1/1/65, fo. 130.
106. NRS, Mar and Kellie papers, GD124/15/981.
107. NRS, Papers of the WS Society, GD495/48/1/8. His appointment, as joint professor with John Wilde who was mentally ill, is recorded in TCM, SL1/1/132, fos 365–7.

108. Wallace, appointed to the chair in 1765, became an assessor in 1772: TCM, SL1/1/81, fos 268–71; SL1/1/89, fo. 195. Tytler, having been appointed joint professor with John Pringle in 1780, became sole professor of universal civil history in 1786 and then an assessor in 1789: ECA, SL1/1/98, fo. 262; SL1/1/114, fo. 274.

109. BL, Althorp G/64. I am grateful to Dr D. J. Brown of the National Archives of Scotland for this reference.

110. NLS, Saltoun, MS 16549, fo. 270r. For Kames seeking support in Aug. 1732, see H. R. Duff, ed., *Culloden Papers* (London, 1815), no. clxii. For the appointment of Dundas, see TCM, SL1/1/54, fos 235–6.

111. Milne, ed., *Boswell's Edinburgh Journals*, p. 238; Cairns, 'Attitudes to codification and the Scottish science of legislation', p. 60.

112. *The Works of Henry Mackenzie* (8 vols, Edinburgh 1808), vii, p. 113.

113. Buddle Atkinson and Jackson, eds, *Brougham and his Early Friends*, pp. 144–5.

114. Cairns, '*Ius Civile* in Scotland,ca. 1600' 2 (2004) *Roman Legal Tradition*, p. 142.

115. C. Lowther, *Our Journall into Scotland, anno domini 1629* (Edinburgh, 1894), p. 31. See MacQueen, 'Two visitors in the session, 1629 and 1636', p. 155.

116. MacLaurin, *Works*, ii, p. 4.

117. Advocates were warned in 1709 to use only 'decent and respectfull expressions towards the Judges and parties' otherwise they would be debarred from Parliament House; but this did not require informations and memorials to be written by advocates: NRS, CS1/10, fo. 92r.

118. The rule was the opposite for writers to the signet although they could subscribe documents drawn by their servants or apprentices.

119. NRS, CS1/12, fo. 81r. Punctuation added. Cf. G. W. T. Omond, *The Lord Advocates of Scotland* (2 vols, Edinburgh, 1883), i, p. 356.

120. NRS, CS1/19 (unpaginated), entry dated 7 Feb. 1801.

121. On the content of papers, and potential punishment, see Finlay 'Ethics, etiquette and the early modern Scots advocate', pp. 162–5, 17–1.

122. ALSP, *Answers for Charles Hamilton-Gordon*, 26 Jan. 1758, Arniston collection, vol. 41, holograph gloss.

123. NRS, CS1/15, fo. 56v.

124. Ibid., CS1/20 (unpaginated), entry dated 11 March 1808.

125. Buddle Atkinson and Jackson, eds, *Brougham and his Early Friends*, p. 245.

126. Miller, *Cockburn's Millenium*, p. 314.

127. Baker, *The Legal Profession and the Common Law*, p. 115.

128. Milne, ed., *Boswell's Edinburgh Journal*, 49. Dr Johnson furnished content for one of Boswell's (unsuccessful) pleadings: J. Boswell, *Life of Samuel Johnson, LLD* (1791 edn), ii, pp. 407–8 (4 June 1781).

129. Ibid., 329.

130. Ibid., 231.

131. H. Cockburn, *Journal* (2 vols, Edinburgh, 1874), ii, pp. 151–8.

132. According to Archibald Alison, Henry Cockburn was indolent which prevented him from achieving a larger general practice at the bar: cited by J. M. Pinkerton, 'Cockburn and the Law' in A. Bell, ed., *Lord Cockburn: A Bicentenary Commemoration* (Edinburgh, 1979), p. 108.

133. R. Wodrow, *Analecta, or Materials for a History of Remarkable Providences* (4 vols, Edinburgh, 1842–3), iii, p. 282. Wodrow thought his pleadings 'dark and intricat'.

134. NLS, Yester, MS 5073, fo.180r. Some punctuation added.

135. NRS, GD220/5/1711/4. The books of sederunt rarely indicate sittings in the afternoon.

136. NLS, Airth, MS 10863, fo. 104v.

137. F. Brady, *James Boswell: The Later Years* (New York, 1984), p. 45.

138. Scott and Pottle, ed., *Private Papers of James Boswell*, xv, 280–1. John Scott, at the English bar, was lampooned for shedding tears on behalf of clients: R. A. Melikan, *John Scott, Lord Eldon, 1751–1838* (Cambridge, 1999), p. 12.

139. *Speculum Judiciale*, 1.4.5.

140. Mackenzie, 'What Eloquence is fit for the Bar' p. 12; Manolescu, 'George Mackenzie on Scottish Judicial Rhetoric', p. 281.

141. Carlyle, *The autobiography of Dr Alexander Carlyle*, p. 263; Ramsay, of Ochtertyre, *Scotland and Scotsmen*, i, pp. 323–5; Somerville, *My Own Life and Times 1741–1814*, p. 108.

142. NRS, GD495/48/1.

143. Milne, ed., *Boswell's Edinburgh Journals*, p. 291.

144. On the early *numerus clausus* in the College, see Finlay, 'Advocates unlimited', 206–7.

145. J.-M. Schramm, '"The anatomy of a barrister's tongue": rhetoric, satire, and the Victorian bar in England' (2004) *Victorian Literature and Culture*, 285.

146. Scott and Pottle, eds, *Private Papers of James Boswell*, xv, p. 271.

147. See chapter 1.

148. Insofar as advocates' surnames only are sometimes given, it may be impossible to distinguish precisely which of several contemporaries is being referred to. Evidence from session papers and other sources can help to eliminate some advocates who are known not to have practised. But definitive figures based on these sources are probably impossible to achieve.

149. Ramsay of Ochtertyre, *Scotland and Scotsmen*, i, p. 128. Ramsay was neither an advocate nor WS, but spent time around Parliament House, presumably in a writer's office..

150. A. McDouall, *An Institute of the Laws of Scotland* (Stair Society, 1995), ed. W. M. Gordon, introduction, pp. xiii–xiv.

151. Scott and Pottle, eds, *Private Papers of James Boswell*, xv, p. 271.
152. By 'practising bar', in this context, is meant court practitioners rather than any advocates who had only a chamber practice, that is, those drafting or revising papers and giving opinions rather than presenting cases in the Outer House. The number of chamber practitioners is likely to have been very small.
153. Prest, *Rise of the Barristers*, pp. 30, 58; Berlanstein, *The Barristers of Toulouse*, pp. 14–16.
154. In calculating the figures in Appendix 3, only advocates who made more than five appearances were included as members of the practising bar.
155. A 'list of Gentlemen of the Faculty present 10 March 1786' gives fifty-four names, but another list, perhaps those summoned to the meeting, records eighty-seven names: Stewart and Parratt, eds, *Min. Bk, 1783–1798*, p. 44, n. 71. Another dozen advocates are mentioned.
156. In making this estimate, only advocates who acted for five or more clients were included as members of the practising bar.
157. He was heir of provision to Miss Thomas Louisa Baird: TCM, SL1/1/109, fos 26–7.
158. Ibid., SL1/1/134, fo. 374.
159. For example, NRS, *Act of Factory in favour of Thomas Walker Baird*, 23 Dec. 1789, CS111/42; Adv. Lib., Register of Advocates' First Clerks, FR 34B, fo. 56. On first clerks, see chapter 8.
160. See chapter 3, n. 81.
161. Less successful was James Graham (adm. 1795), also a former WS. He was later ordained in the Anglican Church.
162. This must exclude Francis Jeffrey, appointed SCJ in 1833 but admitted to the bar on 16 Dec. 1794.
163. R. A. Houston, 'Mortality in early modern Scotland: the life expectancy of advocates' 7 (1992) *Continuity and Change*, pp. 51–2.
164. The litigants were all Mackenzies but only nine papers were drawn by advocates named Mackenzie: Kenneth Mackenzie (four papers), James (two), Colin (two), Alexander (one).
165. W. Forbes, *The Journal of the Session* (Edinburgh, 1714), p. viii.
166. H. Mackenzie, *Account of the Life of Lord Abercromby* (Edinburgh, 1796), p. 108.
167. E. Topham, *Letters from Edinburgh, written in the years 1774 and 1775* (London, 1776), p. 315.
168. J. Boswell, *Letter to the People of Scotland* (Edinburgh, 1785), p. 47.
169. M. Wood, ed, *The Edinburgh Poll Tax Returns for 1694* (Edinburgh, 1951), p. 7.
170. NLS, Saltoun, MS 17537, fo. 166r. Other categories include 'foolish & silly'; 'Jacobite not attended since 1745'; 'madman'; 'a good inoffensive man, but no deep lawyer' and 'never had business but capable'.

171. Ibid., MS 17537, fo. 162r.
172. Scott and Pottle, eds, *Private Papers of James Boswell*, xv, p. 275.
173. Houston, 'Mortality in early modern Scotland', p. 55.
174. NLS, Yester, MS 7049, fos 122v–123r. William Montgomery was admitted advocate on 11 March 1707: NRS, CS1/10, fo. 48v.
175. His father was apparently a writer: ALSP, *The Petition of Dames Helen and Jacobina Hamiltons*, 3 Dec. 1762, Meadowbank collection, vol. 26, p. 9.
176. NRS, Dundas of Melville papers, GD51/5/413.
177. NLS, Yester, MS 7049, fo. 118r.
178. ALSP, *Answers for Mr Robert Mackintosh, Advocate and ors*, 3 Aug. 1768, Dreghorn collection, vol. 31, no. 20.
179. *The Letters of George Dempster to Sir Adam Fergusson 1756–1813*, ed. J. Fergusson (London, 1934), pp. 65–8; A. M. Laing, *A Life of George Dempster, Scottish M.P. of Dunnichen* (New York 1998), pp. 68–74.
180. Dempster and Duncan both entered the Faculty in 1755.
181. ALSP, *The Petition of Mr Alexander Duncan, Advocate*, 26 July 1768, Dreghorn collection, vol. 31, no. 19, p. 5.
182. Non-practising advocates were eligible for the office of sheriff-depute in 1748.
183. Finlay, *Men of Law*, pp. 43–4.
184. For example, A. Macdouall (Lord Bankton), *Ane Institute of the Law of Scotland* (3 vols, Edinburgh, 1751–53), ii, pp. 484–5.
185. TCM, SL1/1/94, fo. 198. The town council offered a reward in a bid to catch the perpetrator.
186. NRS, CS1/13, fo. 105r. Examples abound. Hew Dalrymple of North Berwick, when a commissary of Edinburgh, accepted a challenge to a duel by his fellow advocate, Aeneas McPherson, in 1684. Both were briefly imprisoned: Fountainhall, *Decisions*, i, p. 270.
187. HMC, *Report on Laing MSS*, p. 295; cf. the remarks of Ramsay of Ochtertyre, *Scotland and Scotsmen*, i, pp. 133–6 and those of Henry Home in Scott and Pottle, eds, *Private Papers of James Boswell*, xv, pp. 280–2.
188. NLS, Yester, MS 7051, fo. 38r; Milne, ed., *Boswell's Edinburgh Journals*, p. 124; Scott and Pottle, eds, *Private Papers of James Boswell*, xv, p. 280; NRS, RH2/4/379.
189. NLS, Minto papers, MS 11033, fo. 31r; NRS, Montague-Douglas-Scott, dukes of Buccleuch, papers, GD224/377/6 (the offended advocate was Kenneth Mackenzie); Milne, ed., *Boswell's Edinburgh Journals*, pp. 193, 365, 368–9.
190. W. O. Steuart, 'The Lockharts of Lee' xl (1928) *JR*, p. 148.
191. NLS, Delvine, MS 1209, fo. 143.
192. Grant (*Faculty of Advocates*, p. 125) suggested Lockhart was married to Edgefield's daughter. This is impossible.

193. Relationships with attorneys were also key to success in the English bar: Duman, *English and Colonial Bars in the Nineteenth Century*, pp. 91–4.
194. NLS, Delvine, MS 1209, fo. 145.
195. NLS, MS 1493, fo. 9; see Stewart, ed., *Min. Bk, 1751–1783*, pp. 200, 208–9; I. G. Brown, *Building for Books* (Aberdeen, 1989), chapter 5.
196. NRS, Dunmure papers, RH15/143.
197. Milne, ed., *Boswell's Edinburgh Journals*, p. 216.
198. For example, Duman, *English and Colonial Bars in the Nineteenth Century*, p. 92.
199. T. P. McDonald, 'Sir Walter Scott's fee book' lxii (1950) *JR*, pp. 297, 313. The same is true of William Bannatyne McLeod: Maidment, ed., *Kay's Edinburgh Portraits*, ii, p. 234.

6

Writers to the Signet

[My son] judges most proper for his purpose to be with a writer to the signet for a season, Therefore, I beg it as a favour of you, with all your former kindnesses the help to settle him with a known man of good Employment ...[1]

The early history of the Society of Writers to the Signet has been recounted by Hannay.[2] Writers to the signet were firmly identified with the College of Justice from its foundation in 1532, and their surviving records go back further than those of the Faculty of Advocates.[3] The formal head of the Society was the keeper of the signet which, traditionally, had been held by the royal secretary and then by the secretary of state for Scotland until that office was abolished in 1746. Thereafter, separate keepers of the signet were appointed until 1817 when the office was combined with that of lord clerk register.[4]

In any decisions of importance for the Society, the keeper acted with the advice of a governing body of commissioners. This was indefinite in number but never contained less than five members drawn from the most experienced practitioners.[5] In addition to general meetings of the members, the first Monday each month was appointed in 1691 as the regular meeting time of the commissioners.[6] Like the Faculty of Advocates, the WS Society made provision for members and their dependants who had fallen on hard times. It also kept a library. In 1722, a general meeting resolved to buy for members' use all the Scots law books in print, and the (pre- and post-Union) acts of parliament, and to do so annually thereafter.[7]

THE ROLE OF THE WS

The Society regarded itself as always having been a 'body political and corporall'.[8] Writers to the signet should therefore be carefully distinguished from ordinary writers who were unconnected to the Society. Anyone acting as a legal agent might be referred to colloquially as someone's writer or 'doer'. Only a WS, as a College member, enjoyed the general privileges of such membership and, equally importantly, the particular privileges, discussed below, in relation to Court of Session actions. These actions, of higher value and importance than most of the business dealt with locally, reflected their higher status in the legal world than mere Edinburgh writers.[9]

This difference in status did not mean that individual writers to the signet never had to work with local writers; in fact, it was quite common for them to farm out copying duties to ordinary writers when necessary. Thomas Tod WS, in his account book, records debts incurred to a number of Edinburgh notaries and writers for this purpose.[10] It was also common for a client to employ both a local agent and a WS who would regularly correspond not only in regard to litigation in the Court of Session but more generally in respect of conveyancing and estate management.

Such relationships, though they might involve long-term correspondence, had their limits. Any attempt by a WS to share his exclusive privileges with anyone outside the Society, by means of forming a business partnership, was strictly prohibited.[11] A WS was in no different position from the member of any Edinburgh incorporation when it came to dealing with unfreemen in breach of corporation privileges.[12] Similarly, any WS who fraudulently extended College privileges to an ordinary writer, for instance by subscribing the latter's letters as though they were his own, risked having all his letters stopped at the signet by authority of the keeper.[13]

It was competent, or at least tolerated, for an ordinary writer to manage an action in the College of Justice. In 1739, in declaring Neil McViccar infamous for various misdeeds, the lords of session described him as 'a writer & ordinary practicer in managing of Causes before this Court'.[14] George Robertson, whose correspondence provides a valuable insight, was an ordinary writer who managed cases in the College on behalf of clients including the Duke of Montrose. Three categories of business, however, could not be conducted by such men, and the WS Society constantly struggled to maintain these exclusive privileges for their own members.[15]

First, only a WS could raise a summons in the name of the Crown to initiate action in the Court of Session and only a WS could write letters to enforce the decreets of that court or inferior courts. Secondly, all signatures (deeds bearing to pass under the hand of the king or the barons of exchequer) and all charters passing under the signet, privy seal or great seal, were traditionally prepared by writers to the signet. Following the Union, however, some of this work was undertaken in the secretary of state's office in London. In 1672, the writers to the signet also lost their exclusive right to officiate as clerks at apprisings (sales following diligence) carried on within Edinburgh. This followed the introduction of a new system of adjudication which placed this business firmly in the hands of the clerks of session.[16] Nonetheless, in the case of anyone who had gained admission as a WS, the depute keeper of the signet fell under an obligation:

to pass under the Signet, all such formal Letters, Precepts, summonses, and others known to pertain to the said Office [of WS], which shall be by him presented, under ther subscription, during his lifetime.[17]

The subscription of lengthy documents (summonses excepted) was supposed to appear 'upon the margine at the Juncture of the sheetes', just as was the case with extracts signed by the clerks of session.[18]

Nothing prevented a WS from engaging in court practice as a procurator in an inferior court (where, at least prior to 1748, they might also preside) though this was done only occasionally.[19] For instance, in 1773, Samuel Mitchelson WS billed a client for defending him in a prosecution.[20] The office of procurator, however, like that of ordinary writer, was of lower status: during the eighteenth century no WS sought admission, for example, as a procurator in the bailie court of Edinburgh. If necessary, a WS could easily engage a procurator, experienced in pleading in lesser courts, to act for his client.

Depositions in 1766 provide a picture of what happened in an action of debt in Edinburgh sheriff court in 1753 brought by William Hogg against the Earl of Buchan.[21] John Pringle WS, on the earl's behalf, undertook a co-ordinating role. He instructed the procurator Robert Dick to act in court, obtained the advice of an advocate on strategy and, ultimately, removed the case to the Court of Session. In the same way, Samuel Mitchelson would not personally carry out diligence against his client's debtor but would pay a writer to do it and add the cost to his client's account.[22]

ORDINARY WRITERS

Writers deserve attention because of their prominence in Edinburgh and their connections to College members. Unlike the admission registers kept by the WS Society and the clerk to the admission of notaries, no registers of writers were maintained. Anyone might describe himself as a 'writer'. Even an 'improvident thoughtless young Man', like the feckless Charles Hay who was heading for Jamaica as an indentured servant by the time he was thirty-four, could describe himself as both a 'writer and accomptant'.[23] Writers might usefully be placed in three categories: the urban writer, the country writer and the local court procurator. Many writers were also notaries public, an office which required some knowledge of legal forms, although the examination procedure was not always rigorous.[24]

Arthur Wilson's career provides an illustration of the opportunities available to the urban writer. Having served an apprenticeship with a writer in Haddington, Wilson came to Edinburgh. He had gained the patronage of Lord Coalston who recommended him to a place in a 'public office' (that is,

probably the office of a PCS or the Bill Chamber). After working as a writer
there for some time, he served John Welsh WS before becoming clerk to
Robert Trotter WS.[25] In this last capacity, he managed Trotter's business for
a time before, in 1784, being recommended as first clerk to an advocate (a
role which automatically qualified him to act as an agent before the Court
of Session). Even at that stage, he described himself as having 'little other
than a fair character, and habits of sobriety and industry'.[26]

Increasingly, it was urban writers such as Wilson with whom members
of the WS Society had to compete when it came to the management of legal
actions. Strictly speaking, only advocates' servants were the proper managers
of such processes because, traditionally, they were the only agents in the
College. Yet writers to the signet had encroached on this area of business
and, to a growing extent, ordinary writers were doing the same.[27] The latter
were a more serious problem because writers were entirely 'unlicensed' in
contrast to writers to the signet who at least had privileges and standing
within the College.[28] In 1701, the WS Society had successfully opposed the
desire of agents to be created into a separate society and to become College
members, but this did not stem the tide.[29]

It was a counsel of despair when, from 1754, the lords of session began
formally to admit ordinary writers to act before them as 'agent or solicitor'.[30]
The WS Society maintained its privileged monopoly over certain types of
business but, by 1800, some 192 writers had been admitted as agents
capable of managing legal actions within the College.[31] A complaint in 1788
from the Faculty's barkeeper makes it clear that some, such as Nathaniel
Grant and Alexander Paterson, had been attending the Outer House even
before they were formally admitted as agents.[32] The formal distinction
between writers who were admitted to the College and those who were not
soon became regularised and is evident in the early Edinburgh and Leith post
office directories. The act of sederunt authorising the licensing of agents,
however, failed to solve the problem of interference by unlicensed men, as the
lord president emphasised to a meeting of writers which he called in 1771.[33]

In the same year, Alexander Orr WS sent some hints to John Mackenzie
WS concerning agenting in the College. He drew a distinction between
Edinburgh writers and local procurators in local courts who were only
admitted by an inferior judge after some form of trial (usually by a local
society of procurators). Then he continued:

> From the Multitude of people, who, under the General name of writer in
> Edinburgh attend and do business in the Court of Session, many of them
> without any regular education or Institution, it is matter of wonder that
> more irregularities are not committed … When that happens [that is,
> irregularity], a reflection naturally follows on the whole body who agent at
> the Barr, in the nature of things it is impossible to distinguish, so that the

name of writer to the signet, writer in Edinburgh or agent, do all fall under the Censure especially in the eyes of Spectators, who seldom know any other distinction among the Practitioners but that of Lawier and agent.[34]

He proposed that a roll of names be kept on the walls of the Inner and Outer Houses of those writers admitted as agents there.

One local group in the capital, the Society of Solicitors before the Commissary, Sheriff and City Courts of Edinburgh, had a particular reason for complaining about their status as compared to writers to the signet. The Society, whose articles of association date from 1707, gained a seal of cause in 1765 from Edinburgh town council. It subsequently obtained a royal warrant and was recognised by the lords of session in 1772.[35] Its members' complaint stemmed from legislation in 1785 by which every solicitor or attorney residing in certain cities, including London, Westminster and Edinburgh, was obliged to pay a higher rate of stamp duty than practitioners who resided elsewhere.[36] Each practitioner had to obtain an annual certificate of enrolment, on stamped paper, from the clerk of the court in which they were admitted. The Solicitors' Society, in a memorial written in 1792, alleged that this was unfair because their practice, which involved a large number of small actions of low value, obliged its members to live in the centre of the city. The writers to the signet, on the other hand, conducted fewer cases of higher value. Because these yielded them a greater income, they could easily afford to live outside the city.[37] Indeed, the majority of writers to the signet and College agents, so it was claimed, resided outside the city limits.[38] Because the solicitors in Edinburgh competed with the writers to the signet in drafting certain documents for which stamped paper was required, they regarded themselves as worse off than mere country practitioners who, they claimed, enjoyed a higher income than they did.

THE WS SOCIETY

The formal leader of the writers to the signet was often based in London and it was a strange fact of eighteenth-century life that when great men gained high office of state in Scotland, they often started from a position of absolute ignorance. There was no blueprint; no handbook of essential information was passed on to allow a smooth transition. Each new office-holder was tied into his own patronage network and his men on the ground in Edinburgh had quickly to find out how his new office functioned, how it could make money and where its boundaries lay. They did so by exploiting their existing contacts in the offices of relevant clerks and other College functionaries.

When he took over as secretary of state in 1742, the Marquis of Tweeddale appointed Thomas Hay as depute keeper of the signet. According to his enemies, this was the moment Hay thought it prudent to remove pictures of the Pretender that were hanging in his house.[39] His immediate priority, however, was to discover who had the right to make which appointments to office and who should countersign which documents.[40] Similarly, on the appointment of Sir Gilbert Elliot of Minto as keeper of the signet in 1766, John Mackenzie WS (later appointed depute keeper) got hold of copies of the commissions of Elliot's predecessors in order to work out some of the same details. These proved of limited help. Mackenzie was particularly confused to discover that while the depute keeper of the signet, as an appointee of the secretary, was a member of the College of Justice entitled to its privileges, the secretary himself, were he to reside in Scotland, was not.[41] The Duke of Newcastle and Lord Harrington, as joint principal secretaries, made life easier in 1731 by simply asking the WS Society to send them a memorial setting out their principal business. This the Society did, furnishing a very full account of the activities of its members who were described as 'the principall and most experienced conveyancers in Scotland'.[42]

In general meetings, called by the keeper, the WS Society made regulations governing the proper conduct of its members.[43] Committees of the Society also regulated matters such as the fees to be charged in the chancery or procedures to be followed in the Bill Chamber.[44] The lords of session often sought the opinion of the Society. In 1748, for instance, they did so when drafting an act of sederunt regulating the fees of clerks and other officers in the sheriff and stewart courts, and the clerks and macers in the circuit courts.[45] The Society's members were not above ignoring its own internal rules. An example is the practice engaged in by some of subscribing letters, summonses and other documents which fell within their exclusive purview, while discounting the fee.[46] Fees for such activities were stipulated and could not be reduced but only remitted in full. Remission might be considered appropriate where the document was required at the instance of a secretary of state or a member of the College of Justice – be he a lord of session, or a macer or even an apprentice WS. Remission of fees was also allowed where the writing was for someone on the poor roll. In every case where fees were remitted, the word 'gratis' had to be added to the subscription.

The WS Society's affairs did not always run smoothly. They had awkward members, one of whom objected in 1742 to John Dickie, a candidate for membership of the Society.[47] Dickie was of good character and might have been thought unobjectionable. Hew Crawford, however, 'a religious observer' of the Society's regulations, noticed that Dickie was clerk to the Hammermen of Edinburgh, an office for life worth £50 annually. On scrutinising the Society's records, Crawford found an act from 1656 by which any WS accepting office as clerk to one of the Edinburgh crafts, regarded as a base occupation, was to be dismissed from the Society. Thomas Hay, and the

Society's commissioners, called a meeting at which, after lengthy debate, they repealed the 1656 act because such clerkships were no longer looked down upon. Three members, however, objected since repeal of the act was a matter for the members and not the commissioners whose powers derived from those of the general body. The matter was put off for twenty-four hours and Hay, fearing that the objectors were stirring up dissension for political reasons, had his brother, James Hay WS, check the Society's records. Based on what his brother found, Hay formed the opinion that the law-making power in the Society resided not in the members but in the Secretary of State and, under powers they derived from him, the keeper and commissioners.

At the subsequent debate seven members were opposed to Hay's opinion, among them significant figures such as John Mackenzie, Hew Crawford, Ronald Dunbar and Andrew Hay of Montblairie. No one disputed that the act was inappropriate or should be repealed; the only question was who had the power to repeal it. Hay won the debate by his casting vote, emphasising that, because the act was in desuetude and no longer in force, this particular question did not, in fact, arise. He retained concerns that this might be the first sign that a group antagonistic to the keeper was emerging. He reported that John Lumsden had subsequently been described as being 'of the Keeper's party' by Hew Crawford.[48] On the day of Dickie's examination and admission, however, the ceremony went smoothly and the affair appears to have blown over.

Responsibility for oversight of ethical and professional standards was maintained by the Society through two means. First, it appointed a procurator fiscal to prosecute complaints against members before the keeper and the commissioners.[49] Secondly, two ordinary members, each serving half a year, were nominated to visit offices and observe the conduct of business, bringing misdemeanours to the attention of the fiscal.[50] More serious transgressions were dealt with by the lords of session.[51] Occasionally this included fines and imprisonment, as when Lord Henderland's clerk was defamed and assaulted by Archibald Milne WS in 1790 and the latter was fined and ordered to spend a week in the Tolbooth prison.[52] Serious cases of misconduct, such as defrauding the public or defaming the court, might lead to suspension or deprivation of office.[53] Dilatoriness, or errors in papers, might lead to a small fine for the agent, although this was often overlooked, wrongly in Sir Walter Scott's opinion.[54]

APPRENTICESHIP

The writing chamber of the WS was the engine room of the College of Justice. During the eighteenth century at least forty members, in the course

of their careers, are known to have trained four or more apprentice writers to
the signet. Samuel Mitchelson senior, WS (d.1788) and Samuel junior (d.1793),
between them trained no less than twenty-two Society members. If the
apprentices of their apprentices are included, then it is possible to trace the
professional descent of more than sixty writers to the signet from the office of
Mitchelson senior alone. He himself had trained with Alexander Stevenson of
Montgreenan who, in turn, was trained by Thomas Pringle; both Stevenson
and Pringle were also prolific in training new writers to the signet.

Not every apprentice intended to seek admission to the WS Society. John
Mackenzie of Delvine WS, for example, had at least twenty apprentices but
only six of them became writers to the signet.[55] William Henry, indentured
as Mackenzie's apprentice in 1744, went on to practise as an ordinary writer
in Edinburgh in which capacity he witnessed the indenture of another of
Mackenzie's apprentices in 1767.[56] Clearly, Henry remained prominent in
Mackenzie's professional life though he was not himself a WS. Likewise,
Robert Drummond, who rose no higher than writer, worked for over a
dozen years in the chamber of Charles Farquharson WS and, after his early
death, in that of Farquharson's father Alexander, another WS.[57] Using the WS
admission register to measure the activity of apprentice-masters, therefore,
provides incomplete results. It ignores apprentices who went on to work as
ordinary writers and does not reveal the full influence a leading WS might
have within the legal profession in Edinburgh.

The process of apprenticeship naturally began with an agreement by a
writer to take on an apprentice, often arranged through a mutual acquain-
tance. In October 1711, Bailie John Mackenzie of Inverness, by prior
arrangement, sent his son south to the care of the advocate John Mackenzie
of Delvine.[58] Their agreement stipulated that an (unnamed) apprentice-master
was to have 600 merks over three years, for training the boy and providing
bed and board. If the master and the boy could not agree an indenture
beyond a year (a provision allowing for the possibility that they simply did
not get on), then the master was to have 250 merks for the year and, after
that, the boy would be free.

Whatever the terms of the final agreement between a master and his
apprentice's guardian, its existence was intimated by petition to the keeper
and the commissioners who would formally authorise the practitioner to take
on the apprentice. This provided a check on the suitability of a practitioner
to act as apprentice-master. An indenture was then drawn up and registered
in the books of council and session, with the clerk to the Society adding an
entry in its own register of indentures.[59] The apprentice's father, typically,
would then pay the apprentice fee. The date of entry to the apprenticeship
could be backdated, perhaps again indicative of an initial trial period. For
example, John Hay's indenture with his master, Hew Crawfurd WS, was

dated 15 August 1722 but the commencement of his three-year apprentice-ship was therein backdated to 1 June of that year.[60] A similar practice was adopted in the indenture between Alexander Glass WS and John Horsburgh in 1723. Horsburgh had already entered into an indenture with William Alves WS but Alves had died. The terms of both indentures were identical.[61] Interestingly, Horsburgh had written them both, probably copying Alves's office style; the first indenture may have constituted an early drafting exercise for him.[62]

It was reasonably common for some apprentices to have, consecutively, more than one apprentice-master. This might result from the death, retire-ment or promotion of the original master. When Lawrence Hill WS died in 1792, his three apprentices (including his younger brother Robert) seem to have been transferred wholesale to Harry Davidson. It is not obvious why Davidson, rather than someone else, took them on. Nor is it clear why Alexander Keith was transferred to John Mackenzie WS a few months after the death of his master, Hugh Crawford, in February 1756.[63] The apprentice fee of £350 Scots paid under the original indenture in August 1754 was repaid by Crawford's heirs to Keith's father and then paid to Mackenzie who agreed to complete the training.

The level of apprentice fee varied. In respect of his own son, John Mackenzie of Delvine agreed in 1726 to pay the Perth writer John Mercer 600 merks for a three-year indenture, the same sum as mentioned above for the son of the bailie of Inverness in 1711.[64] After that, young John Mackenzie was apprenticed to Hew Somerville WS in 1729 for three years at a cost of only 300 merks and it was this apprenticeship which he mentioned when he petitioned for entry to the Society in 1737.[65] Mackenzie himself, during the 1740s and 1750s, generally charged £25 sterling (the equivalent of 300 merks) for training apprentice WS members. After 1755, with one exception, Mackenzie took on no more apprentice writers to the signet, but he did take on apprentice writers, charging them 500 merks Scots for five-year apprentice-ships (except on two occasions when he remitted his fee).[66] In 1782 Archibald Tod charged £80 sterling for a five-year WS apprenticeship.[67]

As well as the apprentice fee, the apprentice had to provide a cautioner who would guarantee that he would faithfully attend his master and not absent himself without leave. A liquidate penalty clause was included whereby a specified sum was payable in the event of default. In John Hay's case this was £40 Scots, and John and his cautioner jointly bound themselves that he would not:

> wittingly or knowingly permit or allow of any Harm or Detriment to his said Master in his name or Goods But shall hinder and impede the same to his power and timeously Acquaint his said Master thereof And That he shall

not under the said penalty reveal or divulge any writs or Business wherewith he is instructed by his Master.[68]

In addition, both were bound to pay any costs and damages incurred by his master in the event that John failed to adhere to the agreement. This was important because the level of damages an apprentice-master might have to pay a client could easily outweigh the contractual penalty. The case of James Scott in 1717 provides an example.[69] James was indentured to William Cunningham WS for the space of two years from 22 February 1716 (again on the basis of a pre-existing engagement between the master and the apprentice's father). The apprentice fee was £200 Scots, payable in two equal instalments. Nine months prior to the end of the apprenticeship, before the second instalment was paid, James was incarcerated for fraud. It seems, among other things, that he had been using the signet seal to falsify letters, and the WS Society's commissioners had complained to the lord justice clerk. In July 1717, after two months in the Tolbooth, James was released but the lords of session declared him incapable of ever becoming a member of the College or holding any public office. As cautioner, his father Walter was required not only to pay the outstanding amount of the apprentice fee, but also another £100 as the contractual penalty. Cunningham also sued for a further £100 as the cost of a replacement servant for the remaining nine months of the indenture period, plus £24 10s. 8d. Scots which he had advanced to James and which the latter had misapplied. The biggest part of Cunningham's claim, however, was for damages; it had cost him £500 Scots to have new seals made up for some of his clients to replace those which James, allegedly, had removed for his own nefarious purposes. Faced with a potential bill in excess of £800 Scots, Walter sought an arbitrated settlement and the parties agreed to submit the case to John Mitchelson, advocate.[70]

Under an indenture, the apprentice-master for his part was typically bound to instruct the apprentice in the 'art and vocation' of writing or 'the science and vocation as clerk to the signet' and, in the words of Crawfurd's indenture with John Hay, 'to conceal no part thereof from him so far as his capacity is able to receive'. Normally the master was also placed under a contractual penalty in the event of non-performance.

The apprentice would work at one of the letterns (desks) in his master's writing chamber, drafting and copying documents. He might also be required to deliver messages to writers' offices, attend the signet office, examine the minute books in the Bill Chamber or look for sasines in the registers kept in the Laigh Parliament House. There was more to his role than this, however. In a legal action in 1743, the Edinburgh writer David Couper wrote the following of William Ruthven, a writer he had employed in his chamber:

The only Use he found him fit for was to copy Papers, and to carry a Process from or to a Clerk's Office, or a Lawyer's Lodging, or to put Papers into the Lords Boxes, or the like. He cannot say with Truth, that ever he made a Note of a Process, or consulted a Lawyer, or wrote a Memorial or Representation in a Cause, or performed any other part, as Agent or Manager of a Process, where your Petitioner had any Concern. Nor can he say that he used to be present at Consulting, consequently he could not have the Trust of managing Processes.[71]

This case is particularly interesting because the judges referred a matter for the opinion of two experienced writers to the signet, John Lumsden and Hew Crawford, who made it clear that their own servants and apprentices were allowed to manage processes on their behalf. This they did not for payment (unless there was a contractual arrangement permitting this) but only 'for the Benefit of Instruction'.[72]

Apprentices worked long hours. In the case of Alexander Keith, though this was not unusual, his indenture bound him to attend his master from 8 a.m. to 8 p.m., and at other times, day or night, as necessary, with the only exception (provided he was not unwell) being his dinner hour.[73] The truth of this can be seen from George Robertson's correspondence; one of his letters was written at one o'clock in the morning after a conference with counsel.[74] Over and above this, there might have been duties of a more household nature. For instance, John Telfer, an Edinburgh writer, tutored his master's son during his apprenticeship.[75] Notably Telfer, a weaver's son from Wigtown, was so proficient that he was asked to teach Latin, arithmetic and writing to a young man who was himself destined for a career in the law.[76]

The integration of apprentices into the master's household meant that adherence to appropriate moral conduct was often clearly stipulated in their indentures. John Mackenzie's indenture in 1729 provided that should he defile his body with fornication or adultery, or become a 'carder, dicer, night-walker', or bear company with such persons, then he and his cautioner would be bound to pay a penalty to his apprentice-master.[77] This was not very different from the indenture entered into by Andrew Robertson in 1630; Robertson would immediately lose all the benefits of his apprenticeship should he engage in any 'abominable act'.[78] As well as maintaining secrets, apprentices were not to take business from their masters. It was alleged in 1783 that James Smith, apprentice to Thomas Adair WS, was acting in defiance of the WS Society regulations by attempting to act as agent in his own right in a process of his master's.[79] Had this been true, he would as a penalty have been debarred from entering the Society (he did, in fact, enter as a WS in 1789).

The general good behaviour of the apprentice was fundamental both to maintaining his master's reputation and furthering his own future prospects.

At the institutional level, the College had an interest in maintaining appropriate behavioural standards of the clerks, servants and apprentices of its members as well as the members themselves. The lords of session were prepared to maintain discipline, not only within the court precincts but well beyond, and not only in regard to the conduct of men in their professional roles. They readily acquiesced in a request from the town council, at the beginning of the winter session in 1715, to provide lists of clerks and servants of College members and, in regard to writers to the signet, 'to make lists of all those that writes in their severall chambers'.[80] The request was linked to unruly mobs that had been causing problems within Edinburgh during the summer. On 9 June 1714 the council had issued a proclamation which, in the light of past abuses and seditious gatherings, prohibited crowds forming on the streets, particularly on 10 June (the Pretender's birthday).[81] On 10 June itself, the lords narrated that some who depended on the court had been reported to have participated in mobs and riots in Edinburgh. Anyone found to have done so was 'declared incapable of managing affairs of any sort and of any manner of Imployment in or about the said Court of Session' for a period of at least three years.[82] To reinforce this message, it was to be repeated in the Outer House at noon and then printed and displayed at the mercat cross and in Parliament House. The town council appointed a committee for securing the public peace on 27 July and, in late August, a force of men was raised, at the council's expense, to keep the peace.[83] In the following months, powder and guns were borrowed from naval vessels cruising the coast, an extra bailie depute was appointed to keep the peace in Leith and, after a surprise Jacobite assault on Edinburgh castle, the town's defences were improved and barricades were erected.[84]

Unfortunately, the lists provided by the College have not survived. The entries in the books of sederunt and town council minutes do, however, reveal a glimpse of the fact that young legal apprentices were very much part of the functioning of the College. This episode reveals them to have been, perhaps like the clerks of the *Basoche* in Paris, a potentially volatile group.

THE EDUCATION OF APPRENTICES

Education was largely gained through acquiring familiarity with the styles of writs and securities commonly used in legal practice. Guiding literature was available, most notably the *Stile* book published by George Dallas WS in 1697 though it was an expensive text to purchase.[85] One of the early private teachers of law at the start of the eighteenth century, the advocate John Spotiswood, had himself been apprenticed to a WS and tailored some of his teaching to the needs of such apprentices.[86] This included aspects of conveyancing which led him to publish his own style book (revised by a committee of the WS Society) in 1708 for the use of his students, as well as, later, his *Forme of Process*.[87] Spotiswood expected his students to be skilled in languages, grammar, rhetoric and logic; he also provided them with teachers of history and philosophy.[88]

Formal teaching of apprentices was something which was perhaps envisaged when Alexander Bayne was appointed professor of Scots law at the University of Edinburgh in 1722. The town council saw how much it was in the national interest (as well as the town's interest) to have a professor 'not only for teaching the Scots law But also for qualifying of wryters for His Majesties signet'.[89] Apprentices needed a good general education and might supplement this by attendance at university classes, including those on Scots law.[90] In 1742 John Murray told the lords that he had undergone an apprenticeship with Hew Crawford WS and had, for some time since, been 'studying the Scotch law with the professor thirof'.[91] Henry Home certainly attended lectures by James Craig, professor of Civil law at Edinburgh. Though he found them dull, for him this was nothing compared to the drudgery of what passed for education in a writer's chamber; he condemned the slowness, the routine and the 'want of variety' there, all of which influenced his views on legal education.[92]

University attendance became increasingly common for apprentices as time went on. James Waugh, whose application for membership of the Society of Solicitors was rejected in 1793, had eighteen years practical experience and had also attended the Scots law class in the University of Edinburgh.[93] According to his indenture in 1782, one of Archibald Tod's apprentices had not only gone through a regular course in the High School of Edinburgh but had attended Professor John Hill's public humanity class in the university and had also 'studied mathematics and other branches of education'.[94] By then additional texts were beginning to appear. An example is Anthony MacMillan's *Forms of Writing* in 1784 which quickly went into a second edition with an additional supplement.[95] This was followed by another substantial work by the same author, specifically on conveyancing, originally composed at the end of 1784 but rewritten after the printer lost the manuscript.[96] MacMillan, originally a writer from Kirkcudbright, moved to Edinburgh to be trained in the chamber of a WS and at one stage seems to have contemplated writing his own *Institutes*.[97]

An attempt to provide direct formal teaching of apprentices emerged towards the end of the century. In 1783 and 1784 Walter Ross twice delivered a private course of lectures on conveyancing and legal diligence. Owing to pressure of business (which seems to have taken him away from Scotland) Ross was unable to continue teaching after 1784 but his justification for doing so at all makes interesting reading.[98] So varied were the branches of business, he claimed, that specialisation meant that men in some offices had little experience of some aspects of practice, be it conveyancing, agenting or estate management.[99] If the medical profession should have instructors in all the separate branches of the discipline, rendering 'the education of Students scientifically compleat', then why should not the legal profession?[100] It was his plan to explain the terminology of legal practice, to analyse the deeds that were used and to trace the progress of every branch of the profession, both for the advantage of young apprentice writers and also for young advocates.[101]

In 1793 the WS Society appointed Robert Bell WS (at an annual salary of 60 guineas) to give a series of lectures on 'the theory and practice of conveyancing' and to collect the decisions of the Court of Session, particularly those relating to the province of writers to the signet.[102] Bell's determination to collect decisions independently was controversial and met resistance from the judges.[103] The plan to teach apprentices also seems to have met some resistance.[104] In May 1793 it had been proposed that, once the lectures began, every apprentice be expected to attend at least one course of lectures and that every candidate for admission to the WS Society should produce a certificate demonstrating that he had attended a full session. This was, however, removed from the final motion. These lectures were initially given in the Signet Hall from January 1795 until May. Despite the enthusiasm of the lord provost, the council was slow to provide accommodation and referred the matter to the university. Despite its 'very sincere respect' for the Society, the Senatus Academicus refused in August 1795 to provide accommodation.[105] The plan to provide lectures in conveyancing was also supported by the lord president though there was opposition from the Faculty of Advocates to a proposal that a university chair in conveyancing be established.[106] Nonetheless Bell was lecturing to apprentices in 1802 though he was disappointed with his fee income.[107] At the same time, in Glasgow, John Millar's replacement, Robert Davidson, is noted for little more than meeting the needs of the local society of procurators in teaching them the practical rudiments of Scots law.[108]

Despite the WS Society strongly reiterating in 1684 the view that qualification as a notary was a necessary step on the road to becoming a WS, this was not true in practice.[109] Only about three-quarters of writers to the signet were admitted as notaries during the eighteenth century and a number of these became notaries only after admission as a WS.[110] It was a sign of solidarity that a new notary public who was already a member of the WS Society was more than twice as likely as other new notaries to have a fellow WS stand as cautioner for him.

At the end of the apprenticeship, the candidate would seek admission to the Society by making application to the keeper of the signet. There are many instances where a number of years passed between the end of training and entry to the WS Society. For instance, George Dunlop was placed in the chamber of David Balfour WS in October 1793 but he did not become a WS himself until 1807.[111] On receiving the application, the keeper and the commissioners would, if he was of acceptable character, refer the candidate to the Society's nominated examinators who would then test his knowledge.[112] At this stage the candidate would also be expected to make a contribution to the Society's poor fund and to provide 'library money'.[113] In 1731 it was asserted that each of the five commissioners nominated as examinators would question the candidate on a different branch of knowledge, from clauses in deeds, securities and conveyances, to the form of summons and the execution of bonds, bills and decrees of the Court of Session or other courts in Scotland.[114] He might be asked supplementary questions by the keeper or other commissioners and would then be required to write or repeat the form of any instrument or security required by the examinators.[115] The candidate would then leave and a majority vote of those present in his favour would lead to admission.

This was largely the procedure used in the case of John Mackenzie of Delvine. On 1 March 1737 he was remitted to take his trial in the Signet Office on 14 March in front of only four examinators plus the keeper and the commissioners. On being asked to vote 'Qualifyed or Not', they found him qualified.[116] Archibald Tod, in 1781, underwent a similar but lengthier process which involved two examinations, one private and one public.[117] On 8 March he was remitted to three private examinators who examined him five days later and reported that he was qualified to undergo a public trial. This was considered at a meeting of the keeper and the commissioners on 25 June when he was remitted to the public examinators on 3 July in the Signet Hall where, after a vote, the keeper and commissioners found him qualified. Like Mackenzie, he would then be expected to pay his entry fee. In 1755 Thomas Tod noted in his end-of-year accounts the payment of £90 sterling, 'for entering Clerk to the signet', which he had paid in February.[118]

THE ACTIVITIES OF WRITERS TO THE SIGNET

Despite the lengthy apprenticeship (the expectation by 1808 was that an apprenticeship would last five years or be subject to additional stamp duty), the pressure of professional life really began at the point of becoming a WS.[119] It was alleged that Robert Syme, immediately after his admission in 1735, had nothing but 'what his industry and abilities' might bring him.[120] He was already in arrears to his landlady, and it was suggested he might contract marriage with the relatively well-to-do daughter of the clerk of the regality of Dalkeith. For men like him, a good marriage may have been a necessary means of gaining working capital. Not every recent apprentice, after all, was as fortunate as Thomas Tod. An assiduous recorder of income and expenditure, Tod's accounts reveal that his father, Archibald, an

Edinburgh writer, had given him £200 sterling to start him in business in 1755.[121] He also inherited his father's office in the exchequer.[122] After his apprenticeship as a writer, James Waugh, let down by 'a weak father and tyrannical stepmother' who squandered his slender family inheritance, took years of 'servitude before the inferior courts' before he could afford the entry money for the Society of Solicitors.[123] This may have been a relatively common experience, explaining why a WS often delayed his admission. Some men, for financial or other reasons, were obliged to give up the law altogether. Alexander Cunningham's former apprentice, Michael Ancrum, simply disliked the law and went to the American colonies.[124] William Clerk who, at his uncle's desire, had apprenticed to Nicoll Hardie WS, is even more unusual. Having apprenticed, he went abroad and entered holy orders; when he died in Madrid in 1743, he had spent thirty years as confessor to the king of Spain.[125]

In order to flourish, the one thing a WS had to do was form relationships with fellow lawyers (whether advocates or other writers), keepers and underkeepers of registers and the clerks working for judges and carrying out administrative functions in the precincts of the court. Information of value to a client might be gleaned from relatively casual social contact making it, in short, part of a WS's task simply to know things. To achieve this end, writers would occasionally make personal visits to offices and other repositories of information. Let us take a few days in the life of George Robertson, an ordinary writer, as recounted in a letter to his client, the first Duke of Montrose, dated Tuesday 27 January 1713.[126] First, he had spoken to Robert Boyd in the commissaries' chamber where he heard Boyd order an eik (an addition) to be made to the testament of one of Montrose's creditors so that his widow might be entitled to uplift the debt and settle the matter. Second, he had called to meet Montrose's debtor, Lord Blantyre, but missed him; he had since spoken to the young advocate John Stewart, Blantyre's brother, who informed him that the first money coming in from the family estates was earmarked for payment to Montrose. Third, he had spoken to David Watson in the Bill Chamber and received an account of dues which would be payable to Montrose (as keeper of the privy seal) at Candlemas.[127] That things did not always run so smoothly is shown by another letter from Robertson, written in May 1725. Having received a warrant from the duke to install a minister in the kirk of Cardross, Robertson went to the writer to the privy seal's office where he had a formal presentation written out on parchment. He then went to John Buchanan's office to have it sealed. Buchanan, who kept the privy seal for the then keeper, the Earl of Ilay, had temporarily gone to Glasgow, much to Robertson's chagrin. These kinds of activities, and frustrations, were very much part of the life of the busy writer and WS. To minimise effort, he might simply put in an appropriate word and arrange to be kept informed. Thus, in 1721 Robertson relates that he had spoken to Hercules Scott in the Signet Office to enquire whether any warrants for diligence against one of his client's debtors had recently arrived to be signeted; finding none, he arranged for Scott to let him know should any appear.[128]

Professionally useful contacts were particularly needed when it came to finance. Space does not permit a full discussion of the ways in which lawyers were involved in matters of commerce. Apart from their connections to the banks and the wider economic infrastructure, however, they can be found advising clients on trading ventures and investment. The Edinburgh writer Ludovick Grant was entrusted by many foreign merchants to transact their business in Scotland.[129] Thomas Erskine, a merchant based in Gothenburg, is one of many Scots abroad who employed agents in Edinburgh, in his case William Lumsden WS.[130] In dealing with money, lawyers needed an understanding of exchange and, at times, even obtaining hard currency could be a challenge. During the South Sea crisis, a client of Alexander Hamilton of Dechmont WS, writing from London in November 1720, advised him to 'take care upon whom you draw in such times as these are, the fall of south sea has undone almost every body'.[131] During this run on credit, George Robertson experienced difficulty in drawing on lenders in London who, at one stage, were unable to provide guineas at all.[132] The two most regular and important aspects of finance were the handling of clients' monies and the conveyancing of land.

HANDLING CLIENTS' MONIES

When Samuel Mitchelson WS left Edinburgh for London in March 1775 for the hearing of a House of Lords appeal, he was obliged to leave behind a letter of procuratory empowering one of his apprentices, David Balfour, to act in his absence. This document sets out in some detail the powers Balfour was to have not only to act for Mitchelson but also on behalf of those clients who had empowered Mitchelson to deal with their affairs.[133] He could receive monies, and grant receipts and discharges, accept bills drawn or to be drawn on Mitchelson and pay any such bills which fell due. At the same time, he was to keep a regular book of accounts 'in the same manner as he has done for some time past', recording all his dealings so that, when he submitted the accounts, he would receive credit for his proper expenditure and necessary expenses.

These powers were the standard repertoire of the Edinburgh writer and allowed him to put clients' monies to best use. The accounts Mitchelson prepared for his client, Dr William Sinclair, a physician in Thurso, demonstrate his own meticulousness.[134] On 16 June 1766 he received £480 sterling from a Mr Elliot, in part payment of a debt owed to Sinclair by the late Mr Budge. Elliot was presumably Budge's executor. Mitchelson immediately lodged that money in the hands of a banker at 4 per cent interest and then, on 8 July, he withdrew it when he lent £500 to Captain Charles Congalton. The latter had made out a bond in Sinclair's favour which was, no doubt, at a more favourable rate. The interest paid on the brief bank deposit just about covered the guinea which Mitchelson charged for receiving and banking the money, settling accounts with Mrs Budge (presumably the widow) and writing a letter of reference to John Bell WS, who was dealing with the estate, regarding the interest chargeable on sums lent to the late Budge. This is a good example of how a law agent acted as a middle man, receiving money on behalf of a client and then arranging for that money to be lent at interest to borrowers. If a borrower defaulted, the agent would then take steps to exercise diligence.

Money received was normally in the form of rents, loan interest, and feu-duties in respect of properties which the client held as feudal superior. To perform this task well, the agent needed a clear record of what his client's assets were. A well-organised writer would prepare a rental book which might contain abbreviated descriptions of the farms or estates belonging to his client, the names of tenants, the dates and duration of each lease, the amount of the contractual and casual rents, and a list of any particular obligations between tenant and landlord. In most estates an annual process was gone through of granting or renewing leases and setting rents. Alexander McMillan WS, for example, was employed to oversee this on the Buccleuch estates in 1755.[135] Not every client was meticulous about record keeping and it was specifically at the request of his client, James Murray of Broughton, that John Syme WS undertook the labour of compiling a book of this kind in the 1760s.[136]

Anyone seeking knowledge of a deceased relative's finances could generally rely on that relative's writer to provide an accurate account. A clear picture was not always possible, especially when clients used different writers throughout their lives. In 1757 Archibald Tod assisted Sir James Clerk in understanding some transactions entered into by his late father, Sir John, the baron of exchequer.[137] Tod had worked for both Sir John and another of his sons, and clarified some questions concerning debts owed to the estate, but his account books were incomplete and a measure of reconstruction was necessary. Sometimes Tod had only dealt with particular aspects of wider transactions; so, for instance, it was possible to connect dispositions he had drafted to certain bonds but he was unable to confirm whether the bonds had actually been paid. Tod advised Sir James to speak to his own cousin, William Forbes WS, who had also been his father's agent. In another instance, he admitted to his own 'want of exactness to book [a document] when received'.[138] The letter also hints at a friendship between Tod and the baron (who was probably his senior by about fifteen years) in respect of which Tod had preserved some correspondence from the latter out of 'vanity'.[139] Sir John had once generously paid him two guineas for the laborious pursuit, over a two-year period, of unpaid rent; on another occasion, he had gifted him some perch for his pond.

Gifts of this kind, from clients to their agents, were not unusual. The sending of plants and seeds, and the giving of general gardening advice, are a particularly common feature of correspondence between lawyer and client in this period (lawyers, including Sir John Clerk, were among Scotland's garden theorists, helping to bring Dutch ideas to Scotland).[140] It went both ways partly because lawyers, as city dwellers for much of the year, had relatively easy access to imported goods. Alexander Mackenzie of Coul, for instance, asked John Mackenzie WS to help him improve his land by sending some grass seeds with the next ship sailing from Leith to Inverness.[141] He wanted sufficient rye grass and clover seeds to cover 4 acres, advising Mackenzie to check among farmers of his acquaintance about the quantity required. A couple of weeks earlier, he had asked the same lawyer to send him enough linen to make two shirts 'fitting for a Ross Laird'.[142] Two months later, Coul complained that commissions for his wife had arrived (including a pair of stays) but not his linen.[143] Lord Lovat also asked for cloth to be sent north to him, sending a sample south to be matched by a good tailor.[144] He even instructed his agent to supply him with a butler – suggesting one he had experience of who was in the service of the family of Dundas of Arniston – plus an unmarried coachman and a clerk who knew how to use cipher.[145] In return, he was kind enough to send a cow to Edinburgh as a gift to his agent.[146]

Writers acting for noblemen sometimes dealt with substantial sums. George Robertson, for example, was heavily involved with the finances of the Duke of Montrose, in consultation with the duke's factor, Mungo Graeme of Gorthie. Because he was based in Edinburgh, Robertson was on hand to receive Montrose's quarterly salary as keeper of the signet and also received precepts for salary payments when the duke was briefly lord clerk register between July and December 1716.[147] Robertson had probably done the same when Montrose received dues as keeper of the privy seal: he certainly did so when the duke held the great seal from 1716 to 1733. In general, Robertson applied this income to paying off some of the duke's creditors and to making other payments in accordance with instructions directly from the duke or from Gorthie. His practice reflected considerable forward planning. Whenever income was received on the duke's behalf, Robertson would draft a discharge which he would arrange in advance to have ready and subscribed at the appropriate term date.

By the end of the eighteenth century writers were finding a safe investment for clients' money in annuities purchased from Edinburgh town council. The popularity of this apparently began in April 1787 with a letter from the writer, James Stewart, on behalf of a lady in London who wished to lay out £1,000 at 10 per cent per annum for life.[148] Stewart did his best to make the offer irresistible, pointing out that the lady concerned was 'of a weakly constitution forever complaining, and last winter much afflicted with rheumatisms'. The council duly accepted, granting a bond for 9.5 per cent. The following year another Edinburgh writer, David Lothian, sunk £700 at 10 per cent and, in 1791, Alexander Keith WS negotiated 9 per cent for his client, Robert Scott.[958] Such annuities contributed to servicing the council's debts and became a regular occurrence.

CONVEYANCING

The WS was a 'species' of lawyer who specialised in conveyancing (the buying and selling or heritable, or real, estate), so the American visitor, Nathaniel Carter, was informed in 1825.[150] Negotiating the purchase price of property was indeed an important branch of business for any WS, and one requiring perseverance, knowledge of the market and the ability to make a decisive end to a negotiation.

The underlying principle of conveyancing was that the purchase price be a multiple of the annual rental value of the property concerned. Teinds were a special case because the sale price was fixed by law in 1629 at the rate of nine years' purchase.[151] Even so, a negotiation involving the Duke of Montrose's lawyers in 1711 demonstrates that a hard bargain might still be struck. The writer Gabriel Napier was instructed by a client to purchase the teinds of Kilcreuch but baulked when asked to pay twelve years' purchase rather than nine.[152] George Robertson, for Montrose the seller, held out for at least ten and this led to a conference in the advocate James Graham's chamber. Although the law prescribed nine years, in practice some 'titulars' held out for more and Robertson thought the buyer might be 'inclinable to give a years purchase more to free himself of the expence he might be at in a process'.[153] When he stuck at nine-and-a-half, Robertson, insisting on ten, pointed out that securing a decreet of sale in court would cost him three times the difference. Finally, the matter was referred to the advocates on both sides (Graham and Sir James Dalrymple) to determine, the buyer agreeing to accept whatever price they agreed. A different negotiation, in 1714, involved the same offer of ten years' purchase which this time was accepted.[154] Robertson himself, and Robert Boyd agent for Viscount Kilsyth, decided to adjust the details among themselves on the basis of old rentals and other papers produced by Kilsyth although, not unusually, complications emerged.[155]

Local knowledge was important. The purchase prices in Edinburgh when the New Town was being built, for instance, were at a quite different rate from rural property. As well as the number of years' purchase, rental value was another variable factor. In 1788 John Graham WS was able to get the council to increase the rental value of houses in Bull's Close which the council were forcibly purchasing for demolition to make way for new building.[156] While the sale price, in those distressed circumstances, was only five years' purchase (as assessed by a jury formed for the purpose), the rental value was increased from £7 to £8, a negotiation which augmented the sale price substantially. In contrast, the following year, Thomas Tod WS was able to sell his house in Miln's Square for twenty years' purchase.[157]

The removal of wardholding in 1748 was the most important change in eighteenth-century conveyancing practice.[158] This form of tenure was traditionally subject to a number of casualties which the skilled conveyancer would seek carefully to avoid.[159] For safety's sake, cautious writers would often ask advocates to revise documents concerning ward and nonentry to ensure they were accurate.[160] When the reform took place, the legislation empowered the Court of Session to provide for compensation to superiors for the fact that clauses *de non alienando* were discharged in favour of vassals.[161] This was a general matter of public importance and, in 1756, the judges sought the advice of the Faculty of Advocates and the WS Society, obtaining reports from them on the question of how much additional feu-duty vassals should pay.[162]

CONCLUSION

According to a story related by Andrew Mitchell in 1742, James Innes, supposed author of *Idea Juris Scotici* (published in London in 1733) had resorted to London after being refused entry to the WS Society.[163] The refusal was prompted by his having committed a fraud in the management of a minor's estate. According to Mitchell, Innes stole the text from his apprentice-master, presented it to 'some of the foolish benchers in Gray's Inn', and was called to the English bar.[164] He then went to Jamaica where he came up with a scheme to remove the attorney general and to take the post for himself, with a suitable bribe being paid. Innes matriculated arms in Edinburgh and described himself in the register as 'advocate general' of Jamaica.[165] We may therefore doubt the sincerity (if not the plausibility) of the preface to his supposed book which he claimed to have written for the information of a gentleman who had studied English law and wished to be informed of the law in north Britain.[166]

If true, this story represents the ultimate breach of faith between a master and his apprentice. Innes was not the only apprentice seeking to better himself nor was he unique in falling foul of the discipline of his master. At the same time, his master's stolen work, probably written to benefit his own apprentices rather than an English readership, reveals a keen interest in the branches of his profession. Innes, by nefarious means, bridged the substantial divide between an apprentice WS and a member of the English bar. Had he been more honest and less bold, rather than in Jamaica he might have ended up acting as an unregulated local agent in Scotland, exactly the kind of man the WS Society was wary of throughout the eighteenth century.

In June 1738 the Society made a stand against these unlicensed agents. Its members appeared in court, 'according to antient custom' dressed in their gowns, desiring 'to know the lords pleasure as to any injunctions they thought fitt to give them in the execution of their office'.[167] They again referred to 'ancient custom' in 1750 when they formally requested judicial permission to wear their gowns in court.[168] These were attempts to remind the judges of their proper place as College members and the privileges this gave them at a time when the scarcity of business made the threat from unlicensed agents all too real. The wearing of a gown was symbolically very important. For advocates, the gown was a mandate to act for their clients; its removal, as the judges acknowledged in 1687, would in effect 'break their imployments'.[169] For writers to the signet, however, it had become a desperate gesture since it was clear that they were fighting a losing battle.

The major defeat came in 1754 when the privilege of 'agenting' causes was extended beyond writers to the signet and advocates' first clerks to any other person found by the judges to be qualified.[170] This was ratified in 1772 when the Society of Agents in the College was, de facto, recognised.[171] The judges instructed that this Society hold an annual meeting on 1 July and appoint a *praeses* (president) and eight examinators each year whose names were to be reported to the clerks of session and recorded in the books of sederunt.[172] Sixteen years later came a rearguard action when an advertisement was placed in newspapers declaring that only advocates and writers to the signet were to be permitted to sit on the benches in the Inner House (these having been erected to allow lawyers to hear pleadings from the bar and advising on the bench).[173] The Society of Agents objected and sought an explanation from the judges. They pointed out that the 1672 regulations of court did not specify that writers to the signet had the right to act as agent in causes (this was restricted to advocates' first clerks) though the 1754 act of sederunt did do so.[174] Moreover, they asserted that there was no difference, when it came to acting as agents, between them and writers to the signet:

> The Agents conduct an equal proportion of the poors Causes, bear the same expence on business, pay the same taxes to Government, and the same fees to the macers of Court at admission as Writers to the Signet do …[175]

The books of sederunt certainly bear this out in terms of the separate annual nominations of writers to the signet and agents to act for the poor.

The efforts of the WS Society to differentiate themselves from the agents were doomed. Edinburgh writers had long been significant competitors to College members, and the difficulties in holding them back in the 1780s were akin to the difficulties faced by the Faculty of Advocates in holding back more humble applicants from membership. The 1754 act simply recognised the reality that the agents, writers to the signet and advocates formed a nexus within the legal practice of the College and the agents, no less than the personnel in the College's chambers must have their place if the court was to function.

NOTES

1. John Mackintosh to John Mackenzie, advocate (spelling modernised), 9 Nov. 1692, NLS, MS 1104, fo. 175.
2. Hannay, *College of Justice*, pp. 273–324.
3. *History of the WS Society*, pp. xx–xxi. Note that the phrase 'clerk to the signet' is often used by contemporaries and has the same meaning as writer to the signet. For consistency, I shall use only the latter phrase.
4. Ibid., p. xxxix.
5. Ibid., p. 391.
6. *History of the WS Society*, p. 334.
7. Ibid., 389. On the development of the Signet Library, which at the time was situated in Writers' Court, see Ballantyne, *The Signet Library*, esp. pp. 28–36.
8. *History of the WS Society*, p. 390.
9. In 1672 it was enacted that a WS may be punished for drawing a summons for any action worth less than 200 merks. Such actions normally belonged in the inferior courts: *RPS*, 1672/6/50, cl. 16.
10. NRS, Leith-Buchanan papers, GD47/1241/17–18.
11. For example, *History of the WS Society*, p. 423.
12. For example, a shoemaker who formed a partnership with a tanner to make shoes for foreign export was criminally prosecuted and expelled for breaching the privileges of the incorporation of shoemakers: ALSP, *The Petition of William Murray, Shoe-maker in Edinburgh*, 28 Feb. 1766, Arniston collection, vol. 83, no. 1.
13. For example, *History of the WS Society*, p. 337.
14. NRS, CS1/12, fo. 96r.
15. See NLS, Minto, MS 11033, fos 21r–v.
16. *RPS*, 1672/6/55; Sir George Mackenzie of Rosehaugh, *Works* (2 vols, Edinburgh, 1716, 1722), ii, p. 312. The modern law of adjudication, which has not changed hugely since the seventeenth century, is contained

in G. L. Gretton, *The Law of Inhibition and Adjudication* (2nd edn, Edinburgh, 1996).

17. NRS, Leith-Buchanan papers, GD47/416.

18. NRS, CS1/7, fo. 30r.

19. For example, James Ure WS presided in a baron court in the 1730s: ALSP, *The Petition of Mr James Graeme of Bucclivie, Advocate*, 27 July 1738, Kilkerran collection, no. 59, p.1.

20. NRS, Sinclair of Freswick papers, GD136/1090/14. This was the younger Samuel Mitchelson.

21. ALSP, *Mr William Hogg v. Henry-David earl of Buchan*, 21 Nov. 1766, Arniston Collection, vol. 85, no. 9, pp. 18–21.

22. NRS, Sinclair of Freswick papers, GD136/1090/14. In this case, from 1773, he paid William Walker for carrying out diligence. Walker was an Edinburgh writer, a notary (from 1760), and a procurator in the bailie court (from 1765): TCM, SL1/1/80, fo. 274.

23. ALSP, *Petition of Alexander Hay, Wright, burgess of Edinburgh*, 21 Jan. 1760, Arniston collection, vol. 49, no. 32, pp. 2, 4.

24. *ARNP*, introduction (forthcoming).

25. By public office was probably meant the office of a clerk of session or the clerk to the bills.

26. ALSP, *Answers for Arthur Wilson, writer in Edinburgh*, 20 Jan. 1785, Arniston collection, vol.. 179, no. 15, pp. 1–2. On advocates' clerks, see chapter 8.

27. An attempt to block them was made in the 1672 regulations; for comments, see J. Thomson, 'The Old Fifteen' (1921) *JR*, p. 232.

28. The impression given is that the number of ordinary writers was significantly outstripping the number of WS Society members. The index to the last published volume of the Register of the Great Seal (admittedly, in this context, a far from perfect source) suggests a roughly even number of writers in Edinburgh and writers to the signet in the 1660s. This was not the pattern of the eighteenth century during which almost 1,500 'writers in Edinburgh' were admitted as notaries.

29. *History of the WS Society*, pp. 361–2; J. Barclay, *The SSC Story: Two Hundred years of Service in the College of Justice* (Edinburgh, 1984), p. 8.

30. *Acts of Sederunt*, pp. 480–1; NRS, CS1/14, fo. 24r. The first two were not admitted until 21 Jan. 1755: CS 1/14, fo. 36v.

31. Technically, they were not College members but they assumed the privileges of members: *Bruce v. Clyne* 5 (1833) *The Scottish Jurist*, p. 197, no. 144.

32. AL, FR339/1. Grant (who was six sessions in arrears of the dues payable to the doorkeeper in 1788) was admitted notary in 1791 and agent in the College in 1794: *ARNP*, no. 2671; CS1/18, fo. 12v. Paterson (ten sessions in arrears) was admitted agent in the College in 1786: CS1/17, fo. 32r. On the doorkeeper, see chapter 8.

33. NLS, Delvine, MS 1505, fo. 144.
34. Ibid., MS 1505, fo. 145. Contractions expanded.
35. The seal of cause is found at TCM, SL1/1/81, fos 7–10. The 1772 act of sederunt is at NRS, CS 1/15, fo. 126r; *Acts of Sederunt*, pp. 575–7. This was a forerunner to the SSC Society.
36. 25 Geo. III, c.80, s.1. Advocates were exempt from stamp duty because they swore an oath recorded in the books of sederunt and no certificate of fitness was issued to them. By 1785 this had long been controversial. See my forthcoming article on the impact of this legislation to appear in the *Journal of Scottish Historical Studies*.
37. According to the 1785 Act, the rate was £5 for those residing in Edinburgh and £3 for others.
38. NRS, GD495/48/1/10.
39. NLS, Alva, MS 5078, fos 112–13.
40. For example, NLS, Yester, MS 7050, fos 8r–8v.
41. NLS, Minto, MS 11033, fo. 96v.
42. *History of the WS Society*, pp. 389–94.
43. The keeper had power to call and adjourn meetings; unlike the Faculty of Advocates, there were no anniversary meetings: ibid., p. 391.
44. For example, NLS, Papers relating to the Signet, MS 1505, fo. 178–v.
45. NRS, CS1/13, fos 66r–69r.
46. NLS, Papers relating to the Signet, MS 1505, fos 76r–v.
47. NLS, Yester, MS 7048, fos 116r–119r.
48. Ibid., MS 7049, fo. 1r.
49. *History of the WS Society*, p. 391. I intend to say more about this office in a future book on legal practice.
50. Ibid.
51. Finlay, 'Pettyfoggers, regulation and local courts', 54–5.
52. NRS, CS 1/17, fo. 115r.
53. For example, *Acts of Sederunt*, pp. 239–40, 457; 10 Feb. 1710 (David Ramsay); 8 Dec. 1750 (James Hay).
54. For example, the lord ordinary was authorised to issue a moderate 'amand', of at least 40s, when a party delayed submitting an information at the date he had appointed: NRS, CS 1/12, fo. 82v; D. Douglas, ed., *The Journal of Sir Walter Scott* (New York, 1891), p. 135.
55. This is based on indentures recorded in NLS, MS 1173, plus data drawn from the WS admission register.
56. NLS, John Mackenzie WS papers, MS 1173, fos 36r, 201r. Henry already described himself as 'writer in Edinburgh' when he became a notary in 1743: *ARNP*, no. 1226. His three-year apprenticeship with Mackenzie did not add to his status but gave him considerable experience of legal forms used in the College; his presence in 1767 suggests a continuing working relationship.
57. ALSP, *Memorial for Robert Drummond Writer in Edinburgh*, 10 July

1744, Elchies Collection, vol. 15, p.2. The published information suggests Charles was the son of John Farquharson of Inverey. This appears to be mistaken: *History of the WS Society*, p. 66.

58. NLS, Delvine, MS 1104, fo. 172. The apprentice-master is not named.
59. NLS, John Mackenzie WS papers, MS 1173, fo. 34.
60. NRS, Dundas and Wilson, C.S., papers, GD236/2/14.
61. NRS, Horsburgh papers, GD178/3/5/91, 93.
62. Cf. an earlier, also identical, indenture of apprenticeship between Alves and Alexander Ferguson of Craigdarroch: NRS, Fergusson of Craigdarroch papers, GD77/195. Neither Ferguson nor Horsburgh, though both apprenticed writers to the signet, actually became a WS although Ferguson, at least, certainly completed his apprenticeship.
63. NLS, John Mackenzie WS papers, MS 1173, fo. 114.
64. Ibid., MS 1173, fo. 1.
65. Ibid., MS 1173, fos 3v, 12r–13r. The cost of being turned from a complete novice into a trained writer seems generally to have been higher than the additional cost of being turned from a writer into a WS.
66. The two exceptions were for close connections, the son of the late Alexander Mackenzie of Lentron in 1761 and the son of the late Prof. Kenneth Mackenzie in 1767: ibid., MS 1173, fos 160r–v, 200v–201r. The latter, Andrew Mackenzie, became a WS.
67. NRS, Leith-Buchanan papers, GD47/418.
68. NRS, Dundas and Wilson, C.S., papers, GD236/2/14.
69. NRS, British Records Association papers, GD2/392. See also *History of the WS Society*, p. 387.
70. On arbitration, see J. Finlay, 'Arbitration in eighteenth-century Scotland' (2011) *JR*, 277–91.
71. ALSP, *The Petition of Mr David Couper Writer in Edinburgh*, 24 Feb. 1743, Elchies collection, vol. 14, no. 60, p. 4.
72. Ibid., p. 5.
73. NLS, John Mackenzie WS papers, MS 1173, fo. 114v. Journeymen tailors were in the same position, although this was subject to complaint to the Court of Session: ALSP, *State of the Process, the Incorporation of Taylors of Edinburgh*, July 1762, Dreghorn collection, vol. 6, no. 26.
74. NRS, GD220/5/1725/12a.
75. NLS, Minto, MS 11033, fo. 118v.
76. Telfer's origins are revealed in *ARNP*, no. 1783.
77. NLS, John Mackenzie WS papers, MS 1173, fo. 3v. This contrasts with the indentures of articled clerks in England which generally did not require abstention from fornication: C. W. Brooks, *Lawyers, Litigation and English Society since 1450* (London, 1988), pp. 62–3.
78. NRS, Henderson of Fordell papers, GD172/2398.
79. ALSP, *Answers for John Grant*, 4 Dec 1783, *Miscellaneous collection* (1782–85), p. 7. A 1678 act of sederunt prescribed that writers' servants

who added their master's subscription to any bill normally drawn by a writer was to be punished as a forger: *Acts of Sederunt*, pp. 139–140.

80. NRS, CS1/10, fo. 183r–v.
81. TCM, SL1/1/41, fos 419–20.
82. NRS, CS1/10, fo. 160r.
83. TCM, SL1/1/42, fos 127, 146–7. A further force is later mentioned for Leith, ibid., fo. 149.
84. E.g. ibid., SL1/1/43, fos 1, 7–8, 19, 36. See also D. Szechi, *1715: The Great Jacobite Rebellion* (London, 2006), pp. 102–3.
85. Ballantyne, *Signet Library*, p. 28.
86. J. W. Cairns, 'John Spotswood: A Preliminary Sketch' in W. M. Gordon, ed., *Miscellany III* (Stair Society, 1992) pp. 136–7, 142, 144.
87. *An Introduction to the Knowledge of the Stile of Writs, Simple and Compound, Made Use of in Scotland* (Edinburgh, 1708); *The Forme of Process, Before the Lords of Council and Session* (Edinburgh, 1711); *History of the WS Society*, p. xxxv.
88. Cairns, 'Spotswood', pp. 145–6.
89. TCM, SL1/1/49, fo. 424.
90. For training, see also Finlay, 'Lower branch of the legal profession', pp. 46–9, 60–1. On legal education see, generally, J. W. Cairns, 'The origins of the Glasgow Law School: The professors of the Civil Law 1741–61', *The Life of the Law*, ed. P. Birks (London, 1991), pp. 151–94; ibid., 'William Crosse, Regius Professor of Civil Law in the University of Glasgow, 1746–49: a failure of enlightened patronage' (1993) xii, *History of Universities*, pp. 159–96; ibid., '"Famous as a school for Law, as Edinburgh ... for medicine": Legal Education in Glasgow, 1761–1801 in A. Hook and R. B. Sher, eds, *The Glasgow Enlightenment* (1995), pp. 133–62; 'From "speculative" to "practical" legal education: the decline of the Glasgow Law School, 1801–1830' (1994) *Tijdschrift voor Rechtsgeschiedenis*, pp. 331–56; ibid., 'The formation of the Scottish legal mind in the eighteenth century', pp. 253–77; ibid., 'Rhetoric, language, and Roman Law', pp. 31–57; ibid., 'Lawyers, law professors, and localities', pp. 304–31.
91. NRS, CS1/12, fo. 161v.
92. Scott and Pottle, eds, *Private Papers of James Boswell*, xv, p. 270; Lehmann, *Henry Home, Lord Kames*, pp. 8–9; Ross, *Lord Kames*, p. 12. On education, see esp. Henry Home, Lord Kames, *Historical Law Tracts* (Edinburgh, 1758), preface, pp. v, vii; ibid., *Elucidations concerning the Common and Statute Law of Scotland* (Edinburgh, 1777), preface, p. xiii.
93. TCM, SL1/1/121, fos 36–7, 39.
94. NRS, Leith-Buchanan papers, GD47/418.
95. A. MacMillan, *Forms of Writing used in the most common cases in Scotland, with such part of the principles of the law as appear connected therewith* (Edinburgh, 1784).

96. A. MacMillan, *A Complete System of Conveyances of, and Securities upon Lands; or, of heritable rights, according to the present practice of Scotland* (Edinburgh, 1787); the mishap is described at p. viii.

97. T. Murray, *Literary History of Galloway* (2nd edn, Edinburgh, 1832), pp. 164–5. Macmillan was designed 'writer in Edinburgh' on becaming a notary in 1780: *ARNP*, no. 2229. He never became a WS. In the preface to *Forms of Writing* (pp. xvii–xviiii) he indicates dissatisfaction with existing legal treatises which he did not think suitable for laymen. He does, however, in the preface to the *Complete System* mention with approval Alexander Wight's book on election law published in 1773.

98. *History of the WS Society*, p. cviii; see also Cairns, 'The face that did not fit', p. 24.

99. W. Ross, *Lectures on the Practice of the Law of Scotland* (2 vols, Edinburgh, 1792), preface, p. x.

100. Ibid., p. xi.

101. Ibid., p. xviii.

102. *History of the WS Society*, pp. 420–1.

103. See Lord Cockburn, *Memorials of His Time* (Edinburgh, 1856), p. 165; and Lord Brougham, *Memoir of the late Hon. Allan Maconochie of Meadowbank*, pp. 14–15.

104. David Hume, as professor of Scots law, was certainly against it: G. C. H. Paton, ed., *Baron Hume's Lectures 1786–1822* (6 vols, Edinburgh, 1939–58), vi, pp. 340–1.

105. TCM, SL1/1/124, fos 67–68, 99–100.

106. *History of the WS Society*, p. 424; also, NRS, CS 1/18, fos 76v, 80v.

107. *History of the WS Society*, p. 426.

108. Cairns, 'From "speculative" to "practical" legal education', p. 339.

109. Finlay, 'Lower Branch of the Legal Profession', p. 47.

110. The figures are: 556 WS admitted, 329 of whom were notaries by 31 Dec. 1799. Of these at least 223 were notaries before becoming writers to the signet. On notaries generally, see the introduction to J. Finlay, *The Admission Registers of Notaries Public in Scotland 1700–1799* (2 vols, Scottish Record Society, 2012).

111. NLS, Acc. 4796/1.

112. Poor character was used a reason for rejection: *History of the WS Society*, p. 392.

113. For example, NRS, Leith-Buchanan papers, GD47/416.

114. *History of the WS Society*, p. 392. Examinators were remunerated. Thomas Tod WS received £4 as annual salary acting as one in Jan. 1757: ibid., GD47/1241/4. Assuming service from 1 Jan. to 31 Dec., he would have examined four successful candidates.

115. Ibid.

116. NLS, John Mackenzie WS papers, MS 1173, fo. 14v. It is unclear whether the keeper and commissioners made the determination having viewed the

examination, or whether it was the examinators alone or, indeed, both groups together.

117. NRS, Leith-Buchanan papers, GD47/417. When the two-step process of public and private examination was introduced has not been identified.

118. Ibid., GD47/1241/2, entry dated 31 Dec. 1755.

119. 48 Geo. III, c.149, sched. 1.

120. ALSP, *Information for Elizabeth Sutherland,* 23 Jan. 1772, Arniston collection, vol. 109, no 26, p. 1.

121. NRS, Leith-Buchanan of Ross and Drummakil papers, GD47/1241/2. This is marked 'got from my father but not to be returned'.

122. Ibid. He paid £135 to secure the survivancy of the office of depute usher which Archibald Tod obtained under Lord Bellenden in 1743: NLS, Yester, MS 7056, fo. 40r. For Tod, see Murray, 'Post-Union Court of Exchequer', p. 115.

123. TCM, SL1/1/121, fo. 37.

124. ALSP, *The Petition of Alexander Cunnynghame, one of the Clerks to the Signet,* 13 Dec. 1763, Arniston collection, vol. 58, no. 31.

125. *The London Daily Post,* no. 2788 (29 Sept. 1743). According to this report, his father, William Clerk, advocate, was nominated SCJ but died in 1695 before his commission was completed. If true, it is not obvious which vacancy this was intended to fill.

126. NRS, GD220/5/1711/8. Robertson seems to have been in practice at least as early as 1695: ALSP, *Answers for the representatives of James Robertson,* 24 June 1760, Pitfour collection, vol. 16, no. 11, p. 5.

127. Watson was one of the depute clerks to the bills: NRS, Scrymgeour/ Wedderburn papers, GD137/3571; Exchequer Papers, E603/32.

128. NRS, GD220/5/1729/7.

129. ALSP, *The Petition of David Bruce, writer in Edinburgh,* 18 June 1762, Meadowbank collection, vol. 26, no. 13.

130. ALSP, *Petition of Thomas Erskine of Gottenburg, merchant,* 18 July 1788, Arniston collection, vol. 179, no. 4

131. NRS, Montgomerie, earls of Eglinton, papers, GD3/14/1/13.

132. NRS, GD220/5/1725/13, 14. The economic effects of the South Sea Bubble are played down by J. Hoppit, 'The Myths of the South Sea Bubble', 12 (2002) *Transactions of the Royal History Society,* 141–65. Robertson may have experienced particular problems because Montrose was paid from the civil establishment and the effect of the collapse of the South Sea Company was mainly felt on public credit; R. Saville, *The Bank of Scotland: A History, 1695–1995* (Edinburgh, 1996), pp. 89, 95–6.

133. NRS, Innes of Stow papers, GD113/5/295.

134. NRS, Sinclair of Freswick papers, GD136/1084.

135. NLS, Saltoun, MS 17358, fo. 95. This employment was distinct from that of Archibald Campbell WS who was employed to manage the duke's lawsuits.

136. NRS, *Hamilton-Dalrymple papers*, GD110/1422.
137. NRS, *Clerk of Penicuik papers*, GD18/5683. Archibald Tod the writer should not be confused with his grandson, Archibald Tod WS (adm. WS, 1781).
138. Goldie was writer to the privy seal; see chapter 7.
139. Clerk (b.1676) was admitted advocate in 1700; Tod, admitted NP in 1717 (*ARNP*, no. 494), was probably born in the early 1690s.
140. P. Davidson, 'Paper gardens: garden ideas and garden poems in Scotland and the Netherlands in the seventeenth century' in A. Adams and M. van der Weij, eds, *Emblems of the Low Countries* (Glasgow, 2003), pp. 171–83.
141. NLS, *Mackenzie of Coul papers*, MS 1336, fo. 7v.
142. Ibid., MS 1336, fo. 5v.
143. Ibid., fo. 15.
144. HMC, *Report on Laing MSS*, p. 273.
145. Ibid., pp. 289–91.
146. Ibid., p. 274.
147. NRS, GD220/5/1720/4; ibid., GD220/5/1935/1
148. TCM, SL1/1/109, fos 236, 238.
149. Ibid., SL1/1/110, fos 209, 214; SL1/1/117, fo. 203.
150. N. H. Carter, *Letters from Europe* (2 vols, New York, 1827), i, p. 260.
151. Stair, *Inst.*, II .8. 11.
152. NRS, GD220/5/1704/27; 1705/12; 1705/18–19; 1705/22; 1706/15–16. Teinds, originally a tenth of the produce of a parish for the support of the clergy, later came to be held by laymen as a fixed burden (no longer in kind) on lands, which the landowner could redeem. For their valuation, see Erskine, *Inst.*, II. 10. 31–2.
153. Ibid., GD220/5/1705/19. A 'titular' meant the owner of the teinds, as opposed to a tacksman or leaseholder.
154. Ibid., GD220/5/1714/6.
155. For the points in dispute, see ibid., GD220/5/1714/8.
156. Ibid., SL1/1/111, fo. 169; SL1/1/113, fos 14, 181, 363. The jury assessed the value of Bull's Close in 1788 where private bargains could not be made: ibid., SL1/1/110, fo. 350.
157. TCM, SL1/1/115, fos 276–8.
158. 20 Geo. II, c.50.
159. MacMillan, *Complete System of Conveyances*, p. v.
160. NRS, GD220/5/1740/8.
161. Discharging the clause *de non alienando sine consensu superiorum* (of not alienating without the consent of the superior) technically prevented wardship from arising. Since the superior lost the right to prevent alienation, and could thereby no longer profit from a wardship, some compensation was to be paid for potential loss of income.
162. *Acts of Sederunt*, p. 495.

163. NLS, Yester, MS 7050, fo. 113r. Mitchell was Tweeddale's undersecretary of State and was also his private secretary.
164. J. Foster, ed., *Register of Admissions at Gray's Inn, 1521–1889* (London, 1889), p. 371. He was called to the bar in 1734: R. J. Fletcher, *Pension Book of Gray's Inn* (London, 1910) pp. 220, 223.
165. Lyon office, Public Register of all Arms and Bearings, 1/169. I am grateful to the Lyon clerk, Mrs E. A. Roads, for this information.
166. J. W. Cairns, 'Institutional Writings in Scotland Reconsidered' in A. Kiralfy and H. L. MacQueen, eds, *New Perspectives in Scottish Legal History* (London, 1984), pp. 91–2.
167. NRS, CS1/13, fo. 80v.
168. Ibid., fo. 140v. The custom actually dated back to a regulation dated 8 Nov. 1609: *History of the WS Society*, p. xlvii.
169. Sir John Lauder of Fountainhall, *Historical Notices of Scotish* [sic] *Affairs* (2 vols, Edinburgh, 1848), ii, p. 805.
170. *Supra*, p. 160.
171. This Society, not to be confused with the Society of Solicitors in the inferior courts, was the forerunner of the SSC Society: Barclay, *The SSC Story*, p. 7.
172. *Acts of Sederunt*, p. 576. It is probably no coincidence that the WS Society's advertisement mentioned in the next note was dated 1 July.
173. AL, FR339r/23 (iii), 5 Aug. 1788, 'Memorial for the Society of Agents or Solicitors admitted and enrolled in terms of the Acts of Sederunt 1754 and 1772'. The text read: 'On Monday the Writers to the Signet came to the resolution of using their Gowns in future, both in the Outer and Inner House; and the Court of Session have issued an order prohibiting any person to sit on the Benches of the Inner House, except Advocates and Writers to the Signet in their Gowns.'
174. The lords in July 1754 instructed macers to apprehend any persons 'confabulating' together or noisily disturbing the court, 'particularly att the Back of the Benches in the Innerhouse': NRS, CS1/14, fo. 21r.
175. AL, FR339r/23 (iii), 'Memorial for the Society of Agents or Solicitors'. I intend to say more about representation of the poor in a future book on legal practice.

7

The Working Chambers of the College

I have served in a publick office fourteen years, Ten of which Closs at an Extracters latran; No wonder then if I should expect a bit of bread in a publick office when my service for that time can be vouched with honestie diligence & obedience ...[1]

Behind the scenes in the College were a series of private chambers where summonses were drafted, records copied, deeds registered and men passed their lives often in apparently grim and uninspiring circumstances. These offices brought the kind of steady income to which many local writers could merely aspire, making them so attractive that men were sometimes willing to overextend their credit to acquire them. The focus in this chapter is on these office-holders whose work facilitated the judicial activity of the lords of session and many of the functions of the writers to the signet.

THE CLERKS OF SESSION

College offices which generated fee income, such as that of principal clerk of session, were often purchased as an investment. They were not necessarily, however, wise investments. The Oliphant family provides a cautionary example. Charles Oliphant, having purchased the office of PCS from William Moir of Hilton, obtained in July 1691 a great seal commission in favour of him and his eldest son, a young advocate named James. Oliphant, formerly one of the depute clerks, intended to hold office as PCS jointly with his son, so that both would work in an office alongside James Dalrymple as 'ordinary clerks of session, parliament and convention of estates'. He had planned this promotion carefully and his son was included in the new commission in the light of good precedents for the office being held on a joint basis.[2]

Despite the precedents, however, the purchase proved a bad bargain. Within a generation, the Oliphants had lost their estate and James was destitute. They had failed to take into account a 1685 act of parliament which required the clerks of session to be organised in three offices, with no more than two clerks in each office.[3] The judges, given that limitation, interpreted the king's commission in 1691 to be in favour of a single individual only. Whether that was to be the father or son was a decision they left up to Charles Oliphant who, at the opening of the new session in November 1691, chose to occupy the office himself. As a result, James never became a clerk of session. The closest he came was the office of depute clerk to the bills in 1713 although this he retained only briefly before having to sell it.[4] The sale was forced because James continued to labour under the obligation to make an annual payment to William Moir, stemming from the sale in 1691, for an office which, as events unfolded, he never held. Having already disposed of his estate to meet other debts, James eventually had to resort to the Faculty of Advocates in 1716 for financial assistance.[5]

So far as the Oliphants are concerned, timing was everything, and the confused recent history of the office of PCS perhaps explains their mistake. In 1676 the king had ordered the lords to nominate only three principal clerks, indicating that there should in future:

> bee only thrie ordinary Clerks of session besides the Clerke of the Bills according to the ancient Constitution, and that of the Number that now serve yow make choyse of the thrie that shall still serve and that you modifie such satissfactioun to be payed by those that remaine to those that are to goe out as you shall find just and reasonable ...[6]

Faced with selecting only three, the lords decided to continue in office one clerk 'in everie one of the thrie Chamberis'.[7]

The 1676 royal letter, however, was recalled in June 1678 as a mark of favour to the new lord clerk register, Sir Thomas Murray of Glendoick. The king empowered Glendoick, during his tenure of office, to appoint clerks of session and to commission in that office 'any qualified person'. This he did, commissioning the advocate Harry Mackenzie senior, on the judges' recommendation, as early as November 1678 after John Hay demitted office.[8] As a result, the limit imposed in 1676 of three clerks no longer applied; by 1686 there were six clerks in the Inner House (including William Moir) and six in the outer (including Charles Oliphant).[9] This became the norm. Indeed, by 1750, the clerks themselves regarded this arrangement as having existed since 'Time immemorial', even though there had still only been two principal clerks in 1652 and no more than three in 1662.[10]

Becoming a principal clerk of session

The fact that Charles and James Oliphant paid a sum that eventually bankrupted them was, at least in theory, no longer possible after further reforms introduced in the *Articles of Regulation concerning the Session* in

1695.[11] From that date, all new principal clerks of session had to swear that they had not given more than one year's salary as consideration for their office. Moreover, no clerk was to be appointed without having served as an advocate or WS for three years. The thirty appointments made between 1709 and 1806 show that this rule was followed. Between John Dalrymple, in 1709, and Walter Scott, in 1806, thirteen advocates and seventeen writers to the signet were appointed. On average, advocates were appointed about fourteen years after their admission to the Faculty while writers to the signet waited until almost twenty-one years had elapsed from their admission to the WS Society. The average figures, however, conceal a considerable range because patronage might determine how quickly the office was gained.[12] These articles also required a 'strict Tryal of the Ability and Integrity of all Clerks' to be undertaken before admission and the requisite oaths of admission could be administered. The nature of the trial can be seen, for example, in reference to the admission of James Robertoun in 1712, who having:

> reported a petition with the ansuers in presence as a part of his tryal in order to his being admitted clerk and having writ a minute of debate in presens & therefter withdrawn & extended the debates immediately returned and read the same in presence and being then examined by the Lord President upon the maner of extracting acts & decreets according to the forme he took the oath appointed by the last act of Regulations to be taken by the clerks of session before ther admission ...[13]

The oath included a statement that he had promised no money or favour in gaining the office, beyond the year's salary permitted by legislation. The misfortune of the Oliphants is further illustrated by the admission of Alexander Mackenzie WS as a PCS in December 1718. Mackenzie, who had 'been upwards of three years writer to the Signet', directly succeeded to the office which had been demitted by his father, John Mackenzie of Delvine. Alexander was admitted 'in conjunction and in the same chamber or office with Sir James Justice as the same was formerly possessed by the said Mr John Mackenzie'.[14]

The trial of new principal clerks echoed the form of trial which new lords of session had to undertake. Its main feature was attendance at a hearing, minuting the debate and reporting on this to the court. In 1778 Alexander Menzies was admitted 'having reported a petition and answers, and minuted a debate in presence'.[15] The examination by the president on the manner of extracting (digesting) acts and decrees which Robertoun underwent, described above, is not so clearly attested in most cases.

A minute of debate could be a lengthy document depending on how many advocates participated in the debate and the complexity of the points discussed. The initial representation would be made for the pursuer, or the crave of a bill put forward by a suspender; then there would be answers by the opposing advocate followed by a reply for the pursuer or suspender; in turn, this would be followed by a duply from the other side which, if necessary, would be answered by a triply, and so on. Two, three or four advocates would normally be involved but, in one case, nine are mentioned.[16] A debate between two advocates could be quite lengthy, particularly on procedural points. In 1772, for example, the debate between Ilay Campbell and Robert Blair, over whether the Roman law concerning the transmission of penal actions to heirs should apply on the particular facts of the case before them, extended to four closely printed pages. The only legal sources cited in the debate were Mackenzie's *Institutions* and Spotiswood's *Practicks*.[17] The lengthy process involving the Duke of Montrose and the Laird of Ardincaple in 1713, involved an unusual proceeding. One of the advocates at the debate, Sir James Dalrymple, a former PCS, obtained

> ... the minuts of debate in order to putt in ther alleadgeances [allegations] conform to ther informations & pleadings (tho Mr Alexander the clerk had made the minutt as full as was possible of all that was materiall) Sir James would need have his own way formeing ther pairt of the debate and this as it did take up some time so has made the Minut some[what] longer ...[18]

Evidently, Sir James did not wish to have any of his historical observations on the Lennox charters omitted from the minute. Although a serving clerk of session was precluded from representing parties before the lords (but not from giving general legal advice), Sir James had demitted office in favour of his son, John, in 1709 and thereafter returned to the bar. Clearly, however, he had not entirely let go the reins.[19]

The business of the clerks of session

Shortly after his appointment as a PCS in 1743, the advocate Hugh Forbes received a congratulatory letter from Andrew Mitchell which referred to his recent shift 'from the active part of a Lawyer to the more serene employ-ment of a Clerk'.[20] The clerks might not have agreed with this view even though vacancies in their ranks usually inspired many applications from the bar (more than twenty men had competed in 1743 to replace the late Sir John Dalrymple).[21] Forbes had joined the small band of principal clerks responsible for running offices which formed the archive of the court. The business of the clerks was to record and maintain the interlocutors, minutes of debate, condescendences and other papers generated by the activities of the College as a court of record. Lord Dun emphasised 'that the Clerk be painful, faithful, and distinct, in the discharge of the duties of his office'.[22] An error made in drawing up an interlocutor, after all, might lead to an appeal and further expense.

One of the most important duties of the principal clerks was to maintain the books of sederunt. The book currently in use remained in the custody of one of the clerks.[23] No entry was to be made without the warrant of the lords of session as they made painfully clear in December 1738 to three of the clerks, Sir John Dalrymple, William Hall and Thomas Gibson, who had all been privy to an unsigned protest finding its way into the book of sederunt in July. The protest (in Dalrymple's hand), against a regulation concerning 'the manner of entering and booking decreets into the register', had not been made in the judges' presence and its inclusion had been unauthorised. It was struck out and the three clerks reprimanded in open court. The regulation which displeased the clerks had complained about their delay in recording decreets, a process which was then taking several years. The delay was a serious problem; it had led to extracts of decreets not being conform to the record and even to two extracts of the same decreet being inconsistent.[24]

It was also the clerks' responsibility to maintain a register of deeds to allow the recording of personal and real rights, either to preserve them or to found legal diligence. Connected to this, James Hamilton PCS applied in 1703 for payment of two year's 'fire money' from Edinburgh town council. This payment, which went back to 1686 at least, was a fee (of £60 Scots and, later, £10 sterling) for lighting fires in the Laigh Parliament House to heat up the room, presumably to preserve from damp the public records and registers that were stored there. In return for the fee, the council obtained free access to those records on demand.[25] The public records included the registers of deeds which, as entries began to multiply in frequency, were maintained by substitutes. In 1687 there was one substitute in each clerk's office for recording deeds; during the eighteenth century, two substitutes came to be appointed in each office.[26] The WS Society complained in 1774 that the substitutes, who normally purchased their offices from the clerks and held them for life, were themselves appointing young men to write extracts for them whose orthography was poor and whose documents contained errors. All the principal clerks had to do was subscribe extracts from the register, without correcting them, and because their substitutes drew little income from this task, errors remained commonplace.[27]

An example of the function of the clerks of session can be seen in the new procedure, adopted by the lords in 1739, for intimating to the parties interlocutors on bills.[28] This involved the principal clerks preparing a book of enrolment. Every sederunt day, before the court rose, the clerk was to insert the names of the parties and any decisions made in regard to their case, by marking them in one of four ways.[29] Once the court rose, the book would be passed to one of the depute clerks. These would take it in turns to make out rolls, based on the deliverances of the court, which were affixed to the walls of the Inner and Outer House. Once this was done, the enrolment book was to be returned to the custody of one of the principal clerks. The principal clerks took it in turns to keep the book in their office and the depute clerk, in affixing the roll to the wall in Parliament House, would mark upon it which clerk held custody of the book at any given time. The parties were permitted to look at the enrolment book free of charge to ascertain the state of the case.

One of the principal clerks was commissioned to act as clerk to the king's processes. He received an emolument of £40 for doing so and, in turn, might commission a depute (with a salary of £20); an extractor was also given a small salary (£10) for dealing with such cases.[30] An example of this rather low-level patronage is the commission by Thomas Gibson PCS, as king's clerk, in favour of the writer Peter Low in July 1752.[31]

THE DEPUTE CLERKS OF SESSION AND THE CLERKS IN THE BILL CHAMBER

There were two categories of clerk of session: the six principal clerks in the Inner House and the six depute clerks (or underclerks) in the Outer House. The principal clerks were responsible for paying the rent for their office and the costs of coal, candles and other necessities.[32] The depute clerks, who were commissioned by the principal clerks, took the minutes in actions before the lords ordinary who sat, by rotation, in the Outer House. They also had the task of calling the processes, one which often took place in far from serene circumstances. In 1710 the lords issued a warning to those who were cursing and uttering profane expressions when the presiding clerk was calling the processes, or reading from the minute book, in the absence of the lord ordinary; bystanders were even encouraged to inform against them anonymously.[33] Depute clerks might also be instructed by a lord ordinary to take depositions; Lord Barjarg so commissioned Robert Leith DCS in 1766.[34]

Like the principal clerks of session, the two principal clerks in the Bill Chamber came to be commissioned by the Crown under the great seal and they then commissioned, between them, three deputes. As noted in chapter 1, among other things, this office dealt with diligence and bills of suspension and advocation. When David Watson was admitted an underclerk there in 1715, he was specifically to deal with 'loosing arrestments, receiving caution in lawburrows & recording abbreviats of adjudications being offered in presence'.[35] He would seem to have been in charge of the register of abbreviats of adjudications which, in 1793, was in the custody of James Kerr, another depute clerk in the Bill Chamber.[36] Substantially the same business, as dealt with by Watson, was still being dealt with in the Bill Chamber in 1803.[37]

David Watson is an interesting character and demonstrates the lack of care, or perhaps, the potential for bribery in the appointment of deputes in some of the offices. Watson is alleged to have fraudulently contracted credit on the basis of his public position.[38] In particular, 'raising his Credit by the grossest deceit', he persuaded his intending father-in-law to inflate the value of what he would receive under his marriage contract in order to persuade his own creditors that his financial worth was higher than it was. So desperate was he to secure himself a position within the College, Watson allegedly promised in the marriage contract to pay his wife an annual rent for life from an estate he did not own but merely leased. His eventual sequestration showed up the fraud but, by then, he had sold such land as he owned, deserted his family and left the country.

One area of potential malpractice, which the lords were determined to regulate, was the abuse of clerks giving out legal processes to unlicensed agents. Shortly after Glendoick's appointment as lord clerk register in 1678, the lords clamped down on this, prohibiting such processes to be given out except to advocates or 'their knowne servants'.[39] As we saw in chapter 6, writers to the signet later asserted the right to act as agents, and others were licensed to do so from the 1755. In 1682, however, to avoid 'dangerous consequences', clerks of session had to obtain bonds from their servants that they would not 'negotiate in or manage processes' as some had presumed to do in the past.[40]

SALARY AND REGULATION OF THE CLERKS

The 1695 articles of regulation, mentioned above, contained further provisions concerning the dues of the clerks and underclerks. In particular, they made clear that, while all clerks were entitled to their salaries and fees, they should take nothing beyond this; any 'undue taking' would lead to the loss of office plus a fine of one year's salary. This was reflected in the oath they took when they assumed office and at the commencement of each subsequent session. By way of salary, the principal clerks were to receive 4,000 merks annually and the depute clerks 1,500 merks. This was to be paid out of the money collected on their behalf by an officer called the collector of the clerks' fees (discussed below). In the event of a shortfall, payment was to be made proportionately out of such sums as had been collected. Also from this fund was to be paid (at the rate of 1,800 merks annually) the collector, who was to be appointed by the lords and was to ingather all lawful dues in respect of the work of the clerks and their servants. Because he was in receipt of funds, and responsible for payments, the collector had to find a cautioner who would guarantee payment in the event of default. He also had to sign all acts, decreets and other writs otherwise no payment upon them would be due; at the same time, once a week, the collector was supposed to sign the clerks' minute book.

As payments to clerks were made out of dues, and depended purely upon fee income, they were not salaries in the proper sense, being much more precarious than salaries paid from the civil establishment. That this caused concern is clear from a failed attempt by the clerks in 1721 to have such a salary annexed to their office.[41] Some found it difficult to make ends meet when the amount of business in the court was low. Hugh Forbes PCS, for instance, died in debt in 1760 with his affairs disordered.[42] The account book of one of his creditors, the Edinburgh writer John Mair, records a number of loans that he made in the 1740s and 1750s to macers and extractors and also to Alexander Finlayson DCS.[43] As early as 1734 Lady Newark (Jean Leslie) reported that the business in the Bill Chamber was much less than it used to be and was decreasing daily.[44] Her husband, Sir Alexander Anstruther, a clerk in the Bill Chamber, was hugely in debt and her son, David, who became one of the clerks there in 1730, would not have been able to maintain himself if he did not live with her.[45] Few had problems as severe as James Justice PCS whose career is discussed later in this chapter.

The principal clerks took responsibility not only for directing what went on in their offices but also for seeking redress from the lords of session on behalf of those affected by irregular practices among agents and parties who sought to evade paying their dues. A good example is a petition presented in 1753 complaining of an 'ingeneous device to evade payment' of their fees in a case that had been litigated for almost a decade.[46] This referred to the practice of borrowing a process, after a decreet had been pronounced, to use it to draft a discharge and renunciation of the sum ordered to be paid. Normally, the clerks could withhold an extract of the decreet until all their fees were paid and, without the extract, no party could enforce the decreet. Collusion to avoid the need for an extract deprived the clerks of any means of insisting on their fees. The lords found the parties in this case liable for the fees, conform to the certificate produced by the collector of the clerks' dues, and also for the expenses of the petition.

The lack of salary raised issues in 1748 when the lords were charged with administering claims for estates forfeited by Jacobites.[47] Again, the clerks sought a remedy because the legislation made no mention of payments to them for their pains in dealing with questions arising from these claims.[48] In response, the lords ordered £3 Scots to be paid to the collector when every claim was given in, and for any answer that was made where the claim was disputed, and a range of ancillary fees was also set out.

THE COMMUNITY OF CLERKS

While co-operation between the three separate offices of clerks was the norm, it had its limits. A notable attempt in 1733 by four of the principal clerks to argue that the 1695 regulations had, by implication, created a 'society' of clerks of session, was unsuccessful. From 1696 the principal clerks had undertaken regular meetings to consider their common interests and oversee the management of their income. In 1725 this had extended to entering a 'Contract of Communication' by which all dues were to be pooled and divided between all three offices. Minutes of these general meetings were taken until 1727 when a dispute arose. Under the contract, servants in each office (who were mainly the extractors, discussed below) were to be regarded as the servants of all the principal clerks regardless of who controlled the chamber in which they actually worked.

The dispute occurred because two of the principal clerks, Alexander Mackenzie and James Justice, refusing to co-operate with the other four, allowed some of their servants to charge higher fees for extracts than the regulations permitted. A particular accusation of misconduct was made against the extractor Alexander Tytler.[49] Although exonerated, he was nonetheless suspended briefly for exhibiting discourtesy when arguing in the High Street with Thomas Gibson PCS. The case provides insight into the workings of the clerks' offices and the tensions which existed there. Evidently Mackenzie attended the office only every second fortnight and, presumably, a similar practice normally pertained in the other offices. It transpired that Tytler had been doing a favour for James Armour WS whose clients required a decreet to be copied quickly to defeat the claims of competing creditors. Having received it at about 4 p.m., he and his servant stayed up most of the night and had copied all fifteen pages by the start of business next day. As a reward, he was paid 30 shillings, more than was due but less than Armour said he would have paid had his clients had greater means.[50]

The main allegation against Tytler was that he had 'compendised' the decreet. This refers to a fraudulent practice whereby an extractor would deprive the clerks of income by producing a shorter deed than was strictly warranted. Two things affected the income of the clerks: one was the number of times a party might reclaim against an interlocutor (this affected the number and size of papers in the court); the other was the size and content of extracts.[51] If extractors missed out essential elements or, alternatively, drafted extracts with unnecessary detail, they would harm the interests of their employers either by reducing their income directly or, in the longer term, discouraging litigants through adding significantly to their legal costs. It was found, however, that neither circumstance applied in Tytler's case and Mackenzie and Justice argued more generally that the regulations did not create a society of clerks and that they remained better off working in independent offices. In this way, they would remain liable only for the misdeeds of their own servants whom they had an exclusive right to appoint and discipline without interference.[52] Nothing more is heard of this idea of a 'society' of clerks of session though the clerks continued to co-operate where common interest dictated.

EXTRACTORS

The extractors were employed in the clerks' chambers to carry out writing and copying tasks, an extract being an authenticated copy of a legal instrument normally, as in this case, 'extracted' from a register. As well as writing out blank pro forma summonses and preparing written states of cases (copies of the amalgamated documents in a process), the extractors, upon application by lawyers, made copies of interlocutors, judicial acts, warrants and documents in the register of deeds. They were not mere copyists, however, because drafting decrees involved blending the summons, interlocutors and final judgment into a single continuous narrative: a sometimes lengthy process which required some expertise.[53] Their activities were under the direction of a clerk in the sense that one of the clerks had to sign each extract for it to be valid. That did not mean, however, that the clerk necessarily paid much attention to the content or accuracy of any extract which he subscribed.

In 1687 the extractors were certainly regarded as College members. In an action in 1741, however, the judges seem to have reached a different conclusion.[54] This case had arisen after a number of extractors had been dismissed for refusing to abide by regulations laid down by the principal clerks of session in 1739. The lords determined that an extractor was no more than an amanuensis who held his office at the clerk's pleasure. The show of defiance, in their refusal to accept the regulations, hints at a sense of community among the extractors which is also evident from the fact that it was the custom for them and the clerks' other servants to dine together at the end of every session.[55]

This is not the only evidence of occupational solidarity. The extractors in the clerks' offices, for example, had so organised themselves that they had their own poor fund, as did the clerks themselves.[56] There was a clear sense of mutual obligation. James Wright, an extractor in Hall and Gibson's office, received a sum in 1728 from Alexander Hamilton WS, representing the extractors' compounded dues in a process which he then paid to the widow of Alexander Baillie who had been the extractor during the hearing of the process.[57]

Extractors were not well off and often faced difficult circumstances particularly when the courts were less busy. One way to relieve this would have been for extractors to gain the privilege of managing actions (which sometimes they seem to have exercised informally). They certainly lobbied for this in 1754, arguing that most of them had been apprenticed to writers, had served in positions of trust in public offices for a significant period, and had intimate knowledge of the forms and procedures of the court.[58] These arguments were not successful, probably because acting as agents might undermine their position of trust as disinterested custodians and copyists of papers in legal actions.

Unable to make money as agents, extractors therefore had a precarious living. In 1754 an experienced extractor, Patrick Baillie, complained to Hugh Forbes PCS because he had been asked to surrender the key to his 'latron' (that is, his lettern, or writing desk) in the office shared by Forbes and John Murray PCS.[59] Baillie, a writer from the Highlands, had trained in Inverness with the town clerk and had, in the past, received help from Hugh's kinsman, the late Duncan Forbes. After fourteen years in public office and ten as an extractor, he was now confined to his room, having suffered chronic illness, in fear that the other extractors were combining against him. Though each extractor and a servant had, as of right, a key to only one lettern in an office, in fact, Baillie claimed, they may accumulate several keys (presumably to preserve to themselves as much work as possible) because there were more letterns than extractors in the office. He argued that he had better title to the lettern, having been granted it by the clerks themselves, than any fellow extractor could enjoy on his own authority. His entreaty probably went unheeded because the man to whom he was required to surrender his key, James Leslie, did become an extractor. Indeed, when he was later working in the office of Home and Tait (Alexander Tait having succeeded Hugh Forbes), the lords punished him for acting as an unlicensed agent.[60]

Extractors' fees, never generous, were always controversial. A committee of the lords was appointed in February 1791 to review them, along with the macers' fees and those of the keeper of the Inner House rolls.[61] While changes were made to the latter categories, nothing was done for the extractors.[62] An insight into how they earned their fees is given by a 1796 memorial which they drafted for the court, setting out the formal disciplines of their trade.[63] By regulation of the court, extracts had to be written in what was called 'close writing', that is, with at least thirty-six lines in the page and nine words per line. The failure to meet this standard (which, of course, added to costs) might lead to objection being taken by agents which would suspend the effect of the extract. If that happened, the opposing agent would refuse to pay the extractor's fee and, though extractors argued that they were writing more compactly and carefully than at any time over the preceding forty years, occasional complaints were still being made to the clerks of session.

Seventeenth-century regulations, in 1606 and 1672, referred to a pattern copy which was probably written rollwise, not bookwise, and made no mention of any requirement of so many words per page. The extractors, thinking an average of six words per line reflected actual practice, and conjecturing that this had always been the appropriate standard because it reduced the need for contractions and reflected earlier documents, asked the court to confirm this.[64]

Just as the extractors were under the direction of the clerks, so the extractors' servants were ruled, with a rod of iron, by the extractors themselves. Charles Melville recounted a chance meeting in 1781 with an old schoolfriend of his in Edinburgh who worked in an extractor's office in the New Town.[65] He was notionally paid £26 per annum but, because he had to pay 10 shillings to the woman who washed and sanded the office, and his master kept back £1 10s. for the Christmas vacation, he received only about £24. His master, 'a rugged fellow', had maintained six clerks in his chamber but, at the time, kept only four 'out of avarice'. Melville's friend was so hurried with overwork that he never slept more than four hours and rarely went to bed for fear of oversleeping. One of the clerks in the office was a baker's son, who had been a 'pye crier' in his youth; for him, £24 was a step up but, for anyone contending with Edinburgh rents, it was meagre. Not put off by this, Melville copied out a paper of 100 pages for this employer who offered him a position which he declined when it was insisted he must engage for a full year.

ALLEGED MALPRACTICE

The close relationship between lawyers and clerks in the various offices led to friction, and the WS Society was prepared to complain when there was malpractice. In 1774, for example, it sought to remedy the poor writing by the 'young lads', employed as amanuenses by the substitutes under the clerks of session, who were in charge of the register of deeds.[66] The Society made several proposals. One was that new candidates for recruitment should send a sample of their handwriting to the Signet Office so that WS Society commissioners might approve or reject them. Another was that, in future, no WS be made substitute keeper of the register of deeds because the substitutes should devote all their time to the important task of registration which involved securing custody of the original document, copying it and comparing the copy to the original. They also wanted the comparer (who might be the substitute or an amanuensis) to initial an extract once it had been checked for accuracy and, if errors were missed, to be liable to a fine as well as being obliged to produce a corrected extract free of charge. The production of fictitious minutes of debate by the depute clerks' servants was a more serious matter than poor handwriting. It was a practice which the judges specifically condemned in 1741 when they became aware of it.[67]

The Bill Chamber was a particular target for complaint. In 1757 the WS Society alleged that the clerks there were breaching their own regulations by allowing the presenters of bills to see written answers, thus allowing them immediately to produce a written duply.[68] This led to extra expense for litigants because a duply might lead to a triply and then a quadruply, all before the lord ordinary had even seen the answers to the original bill. The business of the Bill Chamber was by no means restricted to bills of advocation and suspension. Bills were supposed to be instantly verified, however; that is, the facts alleged within them should be obvious from documentary proof supplied with the bill or by reference to the other party's oath of verity.[69] No written response to answers to a bill was supposed to take place. Even worse, the clerks were allegedly allowing representations against bills which had been refused, prolonging the litigation further and increasing expense (as well as their own income).

Irregular procedure of this kind was a matter of importance to writers to the signet because drafting such bills fell within the privileged business that was exclusive to them. If the efficacy of such bills was being watered down by the practices of the clerks, then this would have a negative impact on their business. That is why the WS Society produced in 1773 proposals for reform of Bill Chamber procedure to correct abuses.[70] For example, they wanted the clerk to the bills, rather than tallying the number of bills on loose sheets of paper, to keep a regular book in which he recorded the dates of presentment and other judicial stages taken in all bills presented to the chamber.

COLLECTORS OF FEES

According to correspondence in 1806 the collectors of the clerks' fees settled monthly with the extractors, requiring them to confirm their own fees which the collector, with each extractor, personally compared with the clerks' record in their responde book. The collector then made up a summary of what was owing to the clerks and compared this to the responde book in the presence of one of the depute clerks before the joint fees of all three offices were totalled. The fees were then divided proportionately among the clerks and paid from the funds collected.[71] In each office the funds were physically collected by a depute who was allowed to retain sufficient funds for the payment of his own salary and that of the principal collector.

The office of collector of the clerks' dues was in the gift of the lords of session. There was no bar preventing an advocate or, at least in later practice, a PCS, from holding it. Thus, while the writer Walter Pringle was appointed collector in 1726 to replace Thomas Gibson WS when the latter was promoted to PCS, fifty years later there was no difficulty in appointing Alexander Tait as collector despite him already being a PCS.[72] Gibson had replaced James Hamilton as collector in 1719 with his father, Alexander Gibson of Durie PCS, standing as cautioner.[73] Thomas had been a DCS since 1715 although the collector, as was the case with Pringle in 1726, did not need to be appointed from the ranks of the clerks themselves.

In 1781 the advocate Robert Craigie demitted office as collector of the clerks' fees and was replaced by James Newbigging whose cautioner was another advocate, Robert Dundas.[74] Like his predecessors, Newbigging appointed deputes in each of the three offices with the consent of the relevant principal clerks.[75] In 1787 he commissioned the extractor Gilbert Mair as his depute in the office of Home and Sinclair, with power to collect and grant receipts for the dues of

> all decreets, acts, dues of depositions of parties and witnesses, inrollings, callings, summonses and others in the said office … and also the dues arising from Petitions and Answers to be given in to the said Lords.[76]

Mair was entitled to receive the neat dues, that is, the exact amount owed in pounds, shillings and pence. He became entangled in 1788 in a bitter dispute with the extractor Thomas McLeay partly because McLeay habitually sent his servant with banknotes, rather than with the precise dues, expecting Mair to provide change. There seems to have been a number of other petty disputes between them leading to threats and the hint of violence. For instance, McLeay is alleged to have deliberately taken away the stool from under one of the young servants, causing him to fall and hit his head on the ground, because, as an 'officer of court', he felt entitled to use any mere servant's stool. McLeay was alleged to have written papers in processes that properly belonged to another extractor. This reveals an element of appropriation: once a document had been extracted in a process, the same extractor was apparently entitled to extract all documents in that process until it came to an end. McLeay had allegedly written out a 118-page absolvitor in a case in which Mair's predecessor had written an incidental diligence; therefore Mair demanded he hand over all his income from the absolvitor. The dispute was submitted to the clerks.

This episode confirms that particular agents tended to employ particular extractors to work for them. The prerogative of selecting the extractor generally lay with the agent of the party raising the summons.[77] In the 1740s, for instance, the writer John Mair records debts owed to him by the extractor Hugh Finlayson which hint at a regular working relationship.[78] Extractors were certainly not obscure figures to the College's lawyers. In Durie's office in 1719, Alexander Keith had orders to extract a decreet of adjudication on behalf of the Duke of Montrose from both Andrew Graham, one of the duke's agents, and James Graham, his advocate. He also spoke to George Robertson about it and asked him for payment.[79] This suggests a long-standing relationship with the duke's lawyers. Agents had similar relationships with those working in the Bill Chamber. If a bill of suspension against a decreet was expected, for example, it was perfectly natural for a lawyer to leave word in the chamber to let him know when it arrived so that he might see it and draft an answer.[80]

THE CHANCERY AND THE PRIVY SEAL

The director of chancery, his deputy, and two clerks were members of the College; as were two clerks who were appointed by the lord clerk register to keep the records.[81] The latter appointments reflect separate offices, one private and one public, and the personnel carried out different tasks, as was evident in 1746 when searches were ordered in the records preparatory to the enactment of the Heritable Jurisdictions Act.[82]

The director of chancery had an annual salary of £25 in 1761 though the fees were estimated at about £500 'one year with another'.[83] An office under the Crown, the director appointed the deputy (who would take about £100 in fees) and the clerks. The fees were taken from those who had writs which had to pass through the chancery, the general role of which was 'to make out all deeds passing the Great Seal in Scotland and all Brieves issuing furth of the Chancery and to record the retours made to such of them as are Retourable Brieves'.[84]

Like the keeper of the privy seal, whose office will be discussed below, the director of chancery was a member of the College because his traditional functions related intimately to legal practice. Royal signatures (documents authorising the making of a royal grant) were prepared by writers to the signet and approved, from 1708, by the barons of exchequer.[85] They were the essential precondition to the granting of rights under the privy seal or the great seal. By the eighteenth century, little had fundamentally altered in procedures that had been followed since 1603 apart from changes brought about through the creation of the Court of Exchequer in 1708 and the introduction of a new seal after the Union in place of the great seal that was formerly used.[86]

The detailed administrative procedure whereby commissions, precepts, gifts and confirmations came under the great seal, privy seal and sign manual is beyond the scope of this work. It was something in which, to engage in practice, all lawyers about the court needed to be well versed. To gain validity, certain documents, depending on their purpose, had to pass under the privy seal or the great seal or, sometimes, both. Gifts of moveable property (such as a pension) passed under the privy seal, for instance, provided they did not involve any element of heritable property; where landed estates were included in the grant, then the great seal was used.[87] The purpose of passing under the seal was to authenticate (that is, give authority to) the grant. A signature itself did not do this, and a signature could be stopped in its progress through the seals if it had been granted inappropriately to the person who applied for it, or for a variety of other reasons, such as the sudden revocation of the original grant which inspired it.[88]

As well as being responsible for the production of documents, the director of chancery was charged with maintaining them. This included the great seal register and the records of retours.[89] Prior to 1718, according to the chief clerk in the chancery, William Smith, the retours lay 'in a great heap of confusion', the writs having been tied in bundles and kept in a room too small for the purpose. In the 1740s, Smith claimed, it took him nine years to put them in order and to produce an alphabetical index.[90]

This mattered because litigants sometimes relied on the ability of chancery staff to retrieve evidence. Thomas Fraser of Struie, for instance, set his lawyers the unenviable task of searching chancery records to locate the royal pardon granted to the Jacobite, Lord Lovat, in 1700.[91] He was trying to enforce a bond granted to him by Lovat after he had supposedly been pardoned. Lovat's defence must have been infuriating: the pardon, he claimed, was neither solicited nor properly enacted, therefore the bonds he granted to his kinsmen, after his return to Scotland in 1702, were granted by him as a declared traitor trying to raise funds to overthrow the government. Because they were granted *ob turpem causam*, they could not possibly be enforced against him. If a valid pardon could be found, Lovat's opportunistic defence would have been elided.

CUSTODY OF THE RECORDS

The question of who should have custody of the records was not free from doubt. By legislation in 1685, parliament required all clerks who kept registers – which were normally delivered to the lord clerk register for preservation in the register house – to deliver all books and registers dated before 1675.[92] Thereafter they were only to retain ten years' worth of records, delivering anything older to the clerk register.[93] The legislation was used in 1714 in a bid to recover the register of forfeitures. This had been removed from the register house in 1690 to discover the proper procedural forms for making forfeitures; thereafter, it had been retained in the custody of Alexander Gibson of Durie, PCS and king's clerk, and then of his son and successor.[94] Fortunately, it had survived a fire that destroyed Durie's office (that is, his house) in Parliament Close and, in 1701, it had been delivered to Sir James Dalrymple and retained in his office.[95] In effect, what occurred in 1714 was an *actio popularis* which attempted to oblige the clerk register to have this register removed from a private office (that is, the office of Durie and Dalrymple, clerks of session) to the register house. Stress was laid upon the relative security of a public office, rather than a private one, where there was greater potential for accidents caused by careless servants and other inconveniences.

A further case arose in 1731 when the clerk register (Alexander, Earl of Marchmont) petitioned the lords seeking warrant to acquire records of the charters in the clerks' custody which were more than ten years old.[96] After debate, these letters were suspended in 1732. The suspension lasted almost forty years (the prescriptive period) until Lord Frederick Campbell, the then clerk register, successfully reopened the matter and had chancery records dating between 1646 and 1764 delivered into his custody.[97] Key to his argument was the fact that he already had custody of the great seal records prior to 1646. On the other hand, the director of chancery argued that the 1685 Act required only those documents which were 'in use' to be sent to the lord clerk register to be handed over and, because this meant by those nominated by the clerk register, it could not apply to him. Because the minute books in chancery lay open for free public inspection, whereas the register office charged a fee for inspecting any minute books, it was also argued that it would also have an impact on the public.[98] It was 'well known amongst the practitioners in the court' that the chancery clerks saved them from blunders because they were able to compare any suspicious retour submitted to them with the register of charters, in their custody, to ascertain whether the retour was based on incorrect information. Also, they charged less for searching and copying than did those who held the general registers. As Robert McQueen argued for the director, separating the charters and the retours would create problems for 'the gentlemen of business', because 'it would be troublesome to them, and expensive to their clients, to be running from one office to another'.[99] Despite these arguments, from 1774, the lord clerk register became *de facto*, as well as *de jure*, custodian of all the king's records and rolls that passed before the Court of Session.

In terms of personnel, the directorship of chancery was in the hands of Lord Charles Kerr (from 1694) and then in 1722 granted to him and his son, Robert, and the longer liver, jointly, with Robert sole director from 1724.[100] It was held for life. The 'office' was a private house, unlike the clerk register who maintained all the Crown's records in the Laigh Parliament House. Until the Union the director received an annual salary of £300.[101] Thereafter, he and his deputy relied purely on fees. The deputy director, who signed all charters, brieves, retours and other writs passing though the office in the absence of the director, was paid £40 per annum by the latter.[102] Three clerks, all writers, were employed to work in the office from 9 a.m. until 1 p.m. and then 2 p.m. to 7 p.m. They worked throughout the year, regardless of the vacations of the court. The first clerk in the office who, until the Union, was also salaried, drafted the writs and the responde book and sent a copy of the latter to the exchequer each year. It was up to him to compare writs drafted by the other writers with the warrants and also to maintain the minute book which was open to the public free of charge.

RECORD PRESERVATION

The history of attempts to preserve legal and historical records in eighteenth-century Scotland owes much to the role of lawyers.[103] The town clerks of Edinburgh, the Faculty of Advocates and the writers to the signet all played a part in preserving a large part of Scotland's written heritage. In 1753, when hogsheads of documents, returned from London after Cromwell's time, were discovered in a decaying condition in the Laigh Parliament House, the dean of the Faculty reported this to the lords. Three experienced writers to the signet were given permission to examine them and they duly reported back.[104] In 1764 a committee of judges, advocates and writers to the signet inspected the public records and the lords of session had clearly assumed a responsibility towards their care.[105]

The Laigh Parliament House ('the rooms below the inner session house') was designated in 1662 as the place where the public records were to be kept.[106] A wide range of material, from the register of sasines of Stirlingshire to the registers of admissions of notaries public, was kept there, and the removal of any documents, even to oblige a WS confined to his room through ill health, was strictly forbidden.[107] The staff working there are fairly obscure, at least up to the 1740s. In 1712 Walter Riddell swore on oath before Lord Polton that he had discharged his trust in keeping the registers in the Laigh Parliament Hall, and that no person to his knowledge had abstracted, embezzled or put away any of the writs or warrants kept there.[108] Riddell was an interim custodian of the records appointed by the lords themselves.[109] The oath he took was identical to that taken in 1702, before a committee of the lords, by James Hamilton PCS and the writer Alexander Baillie who was keeper of the registers under him. Hamilton further deponed that he had put into the house the records and warrants of the parliaments held from 1696 to 1702, together with registers and warrants surrendered by the clerks to the registers of sasines in the various shires, by the clerks of session and by others. He also delivered the keys to Lord Philiphaugh as the new clerk register (he had presented his patent three days before). Hamilton and Baillie were then exonerated by the lords.[110] The former clerk register had appointed Hamilton, Hamilton had appointed Baillie, and both appointments had lapsed when a new clerk register gained office.

In 1771 the town council received a petition from James Kerr and Alexander Robertson as keepers of the records in the Laigh Parliament House.[111] They asked that shelves and presses be built for holding the increasing number of records kept there. Although a number of records were apparently lying on the ground and in danger of perishing, the council were reluctant to spend money on this work, having already given some ground for the building of a new register office. They referred the matter to the clerk register and other trustees appointed for that project.

A memorandum preserved among the Saltoun papers records the difficulties with the incommodious, damp and ill-lit laigh Parliament Hall.[112] This was a single room, and what was needed and eventually built was a single building to house the public records. Until the General Register House, designed by Robert Adam, was opened in 1789 as the first purpose-built record repository in the United Kingdom, a number of offices, such as the teind office, the sasine office and the horning chamber, were maintained in single but separate rooms.[113] The clerks of session, in particular, had their three offices in three different buildings, each of which had private dwellings above and below and one was made of timber.[114] Each office consisted of six rooms, one each for the two principal clerks, one for each of their two deputes, one for the extractors and one for the clerks dealing with the register of deeds.

THE PRIVY SEAL OFFICE

The keeper of the privy seal had the direction of two officers, the writer to the privy seal and the depute writer. It was these men, not the keeper, who were College members. Henry Dundas, appointed keeper in 1800, was a College member only because of his status as an advocate; the previous keepers were generally noblemen and non-lawyers. The longest-serving keeper, James Stuart-Mackenzie, was the brother of the Earl of Bute but not titled himself. He felt awkward about being known in Scotland by the name of his office (just as the lord advocate and clerk register were always called by the name of their office, not their personal name) and uncertain about how to describe himself south of the border.[115]

It was in the writer to the privy seal's office that all writs passing the privy seal were drafted and warrants recorded. The writer to the privy seal was more than once described as being 'the same thing with respect to that seall, as the Chancery with respect to the Great Seall'.[116] The office, which was for life, had no salary but the average fee income was reckoned at £200 per annum.[117] The writer nominated his own depute whose income was estimated at about £60 yearly. Because the depute writer's office contained public records that had to be open to inspection, it was manned throughout the year by him or by a servant.

The offices of the privy seal and the great seal were central to the working lives of lawyers, whether ordinary writers or writers to the signet. George Robertson, for instance, knew his way around them very well. In 1717 he was able to report on the progress he had made with the warrant for the Duke of Montrose's salary (as keeper of the great seal) which the duke had sent him.[118] He had shown it to the barons, it had gone past the privy seal and it was to be registered in their office the following day. Similarly, in May 1721, he informed correspondents that the Duke of Queensberry's commission to be stewart of Kirkcudbright had not yet been presented at the great seal but that the Earl of Ilay's commission to be lord privy seal had passed the seals.[119]

Little is known of the personnel of these offices even though they had a hand in the appointment of a number of College members as well as a working relationship with agents and others. Letters patent under the privy seal, for example, were presented by macers prior to their appointment in the court. Regius professors of law were also appointed under privy seal letters.[120] On the other hand, clerks of session, keepers of registers, the keeper of the minute book, Crown law officers and others were appointed under the great seal. Francis Gibson's privy seal letter, bearing his appointment as a macer by the king with the advice and consent of the barons of exchequer in Scotland, was dated at St James's, as given under the privy seal, and then subscribed by Archibald Stuart and sealed in Edinburgh by Thomas Goldie WS. Stuart was deputy keeper of the privy seal, and Goldie was writer to the privy seal (an office which he gained in June 1733).[121]

The appointment of Goldie is an interesting example of the coincidence of circumstances which so often dictated the professional life of young legal apprentices. He had trained as a WS under William Alves who himself had been appointed writer to the privy seal in 1699.[122] Alves died in 1722 and Goldie (adm. WS in 1723) was one of the trustees of his estate.[123] A further indication of continuity with Alves's office is the fact that, later, Goldie employed Alexander Syme. Syme had acted as servant to Alves in 1717 and, some time before his admission as a notary at the end of 1733, he had become depute writer to the privy seal.[124] When Goldie died in 1741, Syme had custody of the records in the office. To deal with warrants requiring immediate attention, Goldie's son, Alexander, was appointed interim writer to the privy seal by the lords of session until a new commission was received.[125] Further continuity can be seen from the fact that Alexander Syme was followed in the privy seal office, after his death in 1752, by his son, John, who was a WS and depute writer to the privy seal under Goldie's successor, David Kinloch.[126]

The appointment of Archibald Stuart as deputy keeper by 1733 is also readily explainable. As a WS, in addition to being receiver general in Scotland, he was heavily involved with the Buccleuch estates and was also legal agent for the dukes of Atholl and Douglas.[127] His relationship to James, second Duke of Atholl, explains his connection to the privy seal because Atholl was its keeper for thirty years from 1733.

The keeper of the privy seal appointed his own depute.[128] As with other lesser offices of immediate concern within the College, the lords were prepared to make interim appointments to keep business moving. In 1765, for instance, they reappointed Archibald Campbell WS as depute, on a temporary basis, after his appointment to that office had lapsed when Lord Frederick Campbell was replaced by the Earl of Breadalbane who had yet to appoint a new depute. [129]

CONCLUSION

The personal relationships between clerks and writers to the signet provide a strong sense of community and were fundamental to all legal practitioners in the College. If the writing chambers failed to work efficiently or if an office was vacant, delay and substantive injustice might result, particularly when records could not be retrieved to establish and defend litigants' rights. It is clear, from a representation made at the time of a royal commission in 1733 enquiring into the offices of state, that the two clerks in the Signet Office (Archibald and Alexander Campbell) were well aware of the practices concerning income in other offices, both customary and set out periodically in the fee regulations.[130] Their own fees, which they claimed to be £30 per annum, were paltry; it was a common complaint that fees in all of these offices had not kept pace with the rising cost of living. In the Signet Office, the clerks were 'very often in the office every hour of the Day att the call of every writer that has diligences to Dispatch'.[131]

The offices relied heavily on men of integrity to exercise effective over-sight of their activities. The harsh experience of Charles Melville's friend was not universal, and sympathetic office managers can be found. As an act of charity, for example, in 1726 a writer in chancery named Bell, who had dislocated his thumb and was unable to write chancery hand, was permitted to retain his place and employ another clerk to do the writing for him.[132] A measure of discipline was necessary in every office because, without it, there might be chaos.

As director of chancery Robert Kerr was accused in 1740 of being too familiar with his staff, leading to laxness and neglect of duty. He was much criticised in a petition which sought better management of the office, the petitioner alleging that Kerr's deputy had 'prostrated its honour'.[133] Citing a Digest text in which Roman governors were warned that familiarity bred contempt, it was suggested that office-holders who appointed deputes should ensure they retained the power to remove them and should also demand that deputes have guarantors who would stand liable should loss be suffered through negligence or ignorance.[134]

Questions of responsibility for deputes were linked to an issue that, in the eighteenth century, was heavily litigated across a spectrum of offices in and out of the College. This was whether office-holders (including inferior judges, such as the judge admiral, and town councillors) had power to appoint a clerk or deputy for the subordinate's lifetime or whether such appointments expired when the commissioning officer or authority left office. Arguments in these cases typically centred on practice within the College of Justice itself. Comparisons were drawn with the lords of session, who admitted advocates for life, and the principal clerks of session, whose deputes were also appointed for life. A balance had to be struck in the question of venal office-holding. On the one hand, a clear vulnerability was felt by a successor in office when faced with having to accept potential liability for the actions of a clerk who was not his own choice and in whom he might place little trust. On the other hand, there were the interests of the clerk – who may have paid substantially for a life-rent interest that could become worthless overnight – and of the public who would generally be better served by an experienced office-holder than a succession of inexperienced ones.

The most complicated of these cases related to the office of principal clerk of the Bill Chamber in the College.[135] In 1684 the lords had decided that Harry Oliphant, one of the depute clerks, was entitled to remain in office until the death of Sir William Bruce, the principal clerk who had appointed him.[136] This was a unique decision, suggesting that a commission 'for life', could mean the lifetime of the commissioner and not the man he commissioned. By the 1760s, the judges took the more sensible view that an office granted for life meant the life of the grantee. After all, no man would invest a large sum to purchase a subordinate office which he might lose on something as uncertain as the death or resignation of the seller.[137] In the various cases that occurred concerning office-holding, advocates naturally raised the comparison of what happened in the various offices in the College itself, and there is a sense in which everything came to conform to the standard that was most familiar to the judges in their professional lives.

This type of litigation is but one illustration of the tensions which existed within writing chambers and between competing College members. Another is the petition brought in 1736 by the advocate John Crawford, clerk to the admission of notaries public. He asked the judges to prohibit the clerks of session from receiving requests from aspiring notaries to undergo their trial for admission, unless he had subscribed their representation.[138] In the Teind Court, matters became heated after the principal clerk, Joseph Williamson, appointed his son-in-law, Thomas Alves, as underclerk. Ill feeling prompted litigation with Hugh Buchan, sole extractor in the office and brother of the former underclerk, over the territorial boundaries of their respective roles. Buchan, allegedly 'too sharp' for his easy-going late brother, had been given and was keen to retain, the run of the teind office. He particularly demanded custody of the keys to the two presses, kept in the Advocates Library, where the warrants of the records were deposited.[139] No less than twenty-four writers and writers to the signet gave evidence as to how the office was run, some of whom had been using the office since they were apprentices in their early teens.

As with Robert Kerr as directory of chancery, if the principal office-holder fell into financial or other difficulties, this could affect the business of the office and even engulf individuals who did not work there. The most spectacular example is James Justice PCS. One of his cautioners, John Hay WS, was driven to contemplate leaving the country to escape creditors when he wrote in desperation to Lord Milton in 1734.[140] Hay suspected that Justice, and his father (and predecessor) Sir James, were engaged in underhand dealings to protect the family's interests at the expense of both creditors and cautioners. The domestic troubles of James Justice were legion: not only was he an alleged womaniser who deserted his wife and children (leading eventually to her divorcing him) but he attempted to persuade Thomas Bruce, collector of the clerks' dues, to redirect that income to cut off his wife's aliment.[141] Justice admitted his own extravagance and poor management but alleged that his wife, Margaret Murray, pulled the strings, claiming he scarcely had 'a Mouthful of Bread independent of his wife's pleasure'.[142] His domestic strife, which at one stage pulled in the advocates Henry Home and Archibald Murray as potential arbiters, was ultimately caused by his family debt for which the family estate at Crichton had to be sold by his father, Sir James, to the latter's brother-in-law, George Livingstone DCS, under reversion.[143] When Sir James died in 1735, Livingstone was appointed one of the two trustees of his estate. According to James Justice, Livingstone owed everything to Sir James, who had put him in office and 'had keeped him from starving', yet he intended, rather ungratefully, to ruin his son.[144]

Justice's debts increased after his father's death particularly in 1741 when Sir James Home WS (George Livingstone's son-in-law) failed in business and left the country. Justice had guaranteed £300 worth of Home's debts. His suspect judgement was confirmed when, in 1743, along with his accomplice the writer David Home, he was fined £500 sterling for his part in the attempted murder of John Simpson, a local tenant in Berwickshire, whom he had tried to shoot with a pistol.[145] To escape his creditors, Justice had to reside in the sanctuary of Holyrood. How disruptive this was is clear from an appeal for help he made in 1750 to Lord Milton in which he said he was afraid to attend the court 'from the malice of the President, & the unworthy behaviour of my Brethren clerks to me'.[146] In July 1748, he had appeared in court only to be 'nabb'd' for £12 by one of his creditors on the way out.[147] The following year he had been temporarily suspended from office by the lords for authorising the writer, Hugh Robertson, to break into his office, a matter that was investigated by his fellow clerks.[148] A plan in 1751 to sell his office fell through though he had hoped to realise £900 sterling for it (his father having paid £500 in 1727). He was never able to sell, however, because his creditors prohibited it; the fee income (estimated in 1761 as being about £370) was their only security that his debts might be paid, despite £80 of it each year going to his wife.[149]

Throughout his travails, Justice relied on friends about the court, including Lord Milton with whom there was a long-standing family connection, and a network of supporters in the Borders (he was originally from Lauder) where he claimed some electoral interest.[150] Unsurprisingly, when he died in 1763, he left his widow, Elizabeth Gilmour, destitute and lamenting that their son was the last representative of a family 'of once considerable fortune'.[151] Justice had his failings but he was also a victim of his indebted father's machinations.[152] A manipulative man (the writer John Fraser, in seeking a job as an extractor, was disinclined to seek his help lest he owe him any favours), Justice was not without pity.[153] When Alexander Tytler proved reluctant to give financial assistance to the widow and children of his predecessor as keeper of the register of bonds, it seems to have been Justice who shamed him into doing so.[154]

As well as revealing the web of debt that linked many College members to one another, the stories of individuals such as James Justice, demonstrate that their activities often had consequences beyond a narrow circle of colleagues, friends and creditors. The communities of clerks and keepers who did not operate in fixed offices, the subjects of the next chapter, had an equally wide influence in the workings of the College, and it is to them that we now turn.

NOTES

1. NRS, Hugh Forbes PCS, papers, RH15/38/118. Patrick Baillie to Hugh Forbes PCS, 26 June 1754.
2. In 1632 Alexander Gibson of Durie had resigned the office to obtain a joint commission of it, from the lord clerk register, for him and his brother, John. In 1649 the office had been granted for life jointly to William and David Hay and the survivor: ibid, CS1/9/, fo 43r; CS1/8, fo. 29r; 1/5, fos 56v–57v, 177v, 180r. By 1691 the office had become directly in the gift of the Crown, rather than the lord clerk register.
3. *RPS*, 1685/4/71.

4. The Bill Chamber had been reorganised so that there were two conjunct clerks, 'as the custom is in the other clarkships of the Session' in 1685: *Acts of Sederunt*, p. 164.
5. NRS, CS 1/9, fo. 44r; CS1/10, fos 148r, 152r; Pinkerton, *Min. Bk, 1713–1750*, p. 10. Moir's date of death is unknown. He was probably in his early fifties in 1691.
6. NRS, CS1/5, fos 29v–30r.
7. Ibid., fo. 30r. The lords directed that Alexander Gibson should continue in the chamber he shared with his father; Thomas Hay should continue in the chamber he served in with Robert Hamilton, and John Hay should take over the chamber he shared with Alexander Monro. Hamilton and Monro received 7,000 merks compensation; Gibson, and his father Sir John, were allowed to adhere to their own private agreement.
8. NRS, CS1/7, fos 120v, 121r.
9. AL, FR 339r/24
10. NLS, MS 17538, fo. 86r; J. Nicol, *A Diary of Public Transactions and other Occurrences, chiefly in Scotland* (Bannatyne Club, 1836), pp. 95, 357.
11. *Acts of Sederunt*, pp. 209–16.
12. Alexander Mackenzie of Delvine WS had only four years' experience on appointment in 1718, as had Alexander Tait WS in 1760; Archibald Campbell had been a WS for forty-two years before appointment in 1770. A similar diversity, within a smaller range, is found among the advocates.
13. NRS, CS1/10, fo. 144v. Robertoun replaced James Hamilton (Lord Pencaitland) who was promoted to the bench.
14. Ibid., CS1/10, fo. 217v. Alexander Mackenzie was admitted WS on 15 Dec. 1714.
15. Ibid., CS 1/16, fo. 55v.
16. ALSP, *The Claim of the Honourable Francis Charteris*, 14 Dec. 1748, Pitfour collection, vol. 5, no. 4.
17. ALSP, *Minutes, Robert Gray against James Paxton*, 12 Dec. 1772, Arniston collection, vol. 107, no. 15.
18. NRS, GD220/5/1711/20. 'Mr Alexander' refers to Robert Alexander of Floriat (adm. PCS, 16 Dec. 1693).
19. NRS, CS1/10, fos 85v–86v.
20. NRS, Hugh Forbes PCS, papers, RH15/38/102. Forbes had been fiscal in the High Court of Admiralty.
21. NLS, Yester, MS 7055, fo. 117r.
22. Dun, *Friendly and Familiar Advices*, p. 40.
23. For example, NLS, Yester, MS 7055, fo. 39v.
24. NRS, CS 1/12, fos 86v, 92r. The protest is scored out.
25. TCM, SL1/1/37/191–2. No subsequent reference to such payments appears.
26. Forbes, MS Gen 48, fo. 1808; NLS, MS 1505, fo. 184r.
27. For reform proposals, see NLS, Delvine, MS 1505, fos 189r, 192r.
28. NRS, CS1/12, fos 95r–v.

29. That is, 'To be seen & answered, or Refused, or to see in part and Refused in part'.
30. NLS, Saltoun, MS 17538, fo. 109v.
31. NRS, RH10/228. Peter replaced Robert Low (presumably his father). For Gibson's salary as king's clerk, see NLS, MS 17538, fo. 109v. He was commissioned in July 1743: NRS, CS1/13, fo. 5v, replacing the recently deceased Sir John Dalrymple.
32. NLS, Saltoun, MS 17538, fo. 86r.
33. NRS, CS1/10, fo. 106r.
34. ALSP, *Daniel Cunningham v. Major James Dalrymple of Nunraw*, Proof, 15 April 1766, Arniston vol. 83, no. 30.
35. NRS, CS1/10, fo. 179r. Punctuation added.
36. Ibid., CS1/17, fo. 178r.
37. Ibid., CS1/19 (unpaginated), for example, 9 July 1803.
38. ALSP, *Information for Elisabeth Luckley widow of Mr John Cameron*, 2 Feb. 1737, Kilkerran collection, vol. 4, no. 17.
39. NRS, CS1/7, fos 113v, 115v.
40. Ibid., CS1/8, fo. 32r.
41. NLS, Saltoun, MS 17538, fo. 86v. They made similar complaint in 1748: NRS, CS1/13, fo. 92r.
42. NRS, John Mair, memorandum book, RH15/134, fo. 56.
43. Ibid., fo. 36r.
44. NLS, Saltoun, MS 16557, fo. 84.
45. NRS, CS1/11, fo. 211r. Alexander Anstruther became a clerk to the bills on 27 Dec. 1694: NLS, Spottiswoode, MS 660, fo. 3.
46. NRS, CS1/13, fo. 183v.
47. Ibid, CS1/13, fo. 92r–92v.
48. 20 Geo. II. c.41.
49. Tytler was grandfather of Lord Woodhouselee. In 1728 he was seeking the office of sole keeper of the registration of bonds from James Justice: NLS, Delvine, MS 1110, fo. 117. Mackenzie and Justice voted at the 1727 meeting; Thomas Gibson was absent.
50. At the time the principal clerks were entitled to £3 Scots per full sheet of an extract, 8d. for each repeated sheet and only 14d. for each bill or answer, regardless of how many sheets it contained. Each extractor was due 14d. per sheet of any kind of document.
51. Being a civilian court, the lords permitted reclaiming bills, almost without limit, against their interlocutors. Attempts were made to bring this under control by restricting the number of reclaiming bills and the period for presenting them. See Finlay, 'Delay', pp. 145–7. This reduced clerks' incomes because, instead of being short and numerous, bills grew longer but fewer in number.
52. ALSP, *The Petition and Answers of Mr Alexander Mackenzie, and Mr James Justice, two of the Principal Clerks of Session, and Alexander Tytler*

writer in Edinburgh, one of the extractors in their office, 20 Feb. 1733, Craigie collection, vol. 6, no. 3.

53. I am grateful to Dr Athol Murray for this point.

54. *Principal Clerks of Session contra Extracters*, in H. Home. ed., *Remarkable Decisions of the Court of Session from the year 1730 to the year 1752* (Edinburgh, 1766), no. 20. The decision was cited in 1769 in a case concerning the teind office: ALSP, *Hugh Buchan writer in Edinburgh* (*supra* p. 71, n. 108), p. 8.

55. NRS, Samuel Shaw, memorandum book, RH15/135.

56. AL FR339r/12.

57. NRS, GD3/14/2/87. Baillie worked in the office of James Hamilton PCS where he kept the registers: NRS, CS1/9, fos 215r–v; Dr Murray regards Baillie as the first 'professional' keeper of the registers, 'Lord Clerk Register', p. 146.

58. NLS, Saltoun, MS17537, fo. 135.

59. NRS, Hugh Forbes PCS, papers, RH15/38/118. Also, *supra*, n. 1.

60. NRS, CS 1/14, fo. 1796. Home was John Murray's successor. Leslie contravened an act of sederunt from 1751: *Acts of Sederunt*, p. 457.

61. Ibid., CS1/17, fo. 131r.

62. Ibid., fo. 133v.

63. NRS, Lord Advocate's Department, correspondence, AD58/7.

64. General standards of Latinity among clerks were criticised: Murray, 'Lord Clerk Register', p. 152.

65. PKCA, B59/39/2/63

66. Ibid., 1505, fos 184r–192r.

67. NRS, CS1/12, fo. 154r; *Acts of Sederunt*, p. 369.

68. NLS, Delvine, MS 1505, fo. 73.

69. Stair, *Inst.* IV.52.iv.

70. NLS, Delvine, MS 1505, fo. 178r.

71. Ibid., Lord Advocate's Department, correspondence, AD58/7.

72. Ibid., CS1/11, fos 152v–154v; CS1/16, fo. 10v. Tait succeeded Robert Pringle of Lochtoun.

73. Ibid., CS1/11, fos 3v–5r. Walter Pringle's cautioner had been his father, Lord Newhall.

74. Ibid., CS1/16, fos 126r–129r. This reinforced Newbigging's Dundas connection, having formerly been Lord President Arniston's clerk.

75. For example, in 1754 Pringle of Lochtoun appointed John Stewart of Dalguise as his depute in the office of Murray and Forbes: NRS, Blair Oliphant papers, GD38/1/921.

76. NRS, John Mair, memorandum book, RH15/135/1/2.

77. NRS, Letter from George Murray to Home and Sinclair, 8 March 1791, RH15/134.

78. NRS, Samuel Shaw, memorandum book, RH15/134, fos. 11, 22.

79. NRS, GD220/5/1723/21.

80. For example, NLS, Delvine, MS 1263, fo. 94v.

81. On the late medieval chancery, see A. L. Murray, 'The Scottish chancery in the fourteenth and fifteenth centuries' in K. Fianu and D .G. Guth, eds, *Écrit et pouvoir dans les chancelleries médiévales: Espace français, espace anglais* (Louvain-law-Neuve, 1997), pp. 133–51.

82. NRS, CS1/13, fo. 43r.

83. NLS, Saltoun, MS 17538, fo. 103. The phrase 'one year with another' suggests an average figure.

84. NLS, Saltoun, MS 17532, fo. 21r.

85. A signature meant the royal superscription or the actual writing presented to the king, or to his commissioners, seeking the grant of some right or office. Before 1708, signatures were approved by the lords of exchequer acting with the lord treasurer (or lords of treasury) and treasurer-depute. I am grateful to Dr A. L. Murray for this point.

86. On earlier practices, see in general J. Goodare, *The Government of Scotland 1560–1625* (Oxford, 2004), esp. chapters 6 and 7.

87. Erskine, *Inst.*, II.5.83–4. According to Erskine, anything assignable was competent to the privy seal.

88. Ibid., II.5.86. See also ALSP, *The Answers for Mr Charles Hope to the Petition and Complaint of Dr William Nisbet of Drumcross,* 21 Jan. 1790, Arniston collection, vol. 182, no. 11, pp. 4–5.

89. For retours, see *Guide to the National Archives*, pp. 89–91.

90. NLS, Delvine, MS 1505, fo. 29r. An earlier great seal charter index, by John Corse, remained his private property and was never acquired for official use; see Murray, 'Lord Clerk Register', pp. 146–7. Smith may have exaggerated the significance of his work, given the existence of the register of retours begun in the 1630s by Scott of Scotstarvet: *Guide to the National Archives*, p. 91. On Smith, see Murray, 'Post-Union Court of Exchequer', pp. 113–16.

91. ALSP, *The Petition of Lord Lovat*, 6 Feb. 1745, Kilkerran collection, vol. 10, no. 128 (see also no. 127).

92. On this, see Murray, 'Lord Clerk Register', pp. 147–8. He notes that the 1685 Act had, in fact, been repealed.

93. *RPS*, 1685/4/63.

94. ALSP, *Information for Gordon of Buckie, and others*, 3 Feb. 1714, Forbes collection, vol. 1, p. 345.

95. The case was connected to the forfeiture of the Marquis of Argyll in 1661 (reversed in 1701). One argument was that the clerks of session were given custody by warrant of the Scots parliament and that they could give it up only in the context of a new warrant from the British parliament and only if a petition were brought there. The Duke of Argyll entered an interesting paper on his own behalf.

96. NRS, Lord Clerk Register against the keepers, SRO 1/77.

97. ALSP, *The Petition of David Scot, Esq. of Scotstarvet, Director of His Majesty's Chancery,* 11 Jan. 1774, Miscellany collection, series vii

(1773–74), vol. 3. Lord Kames was lord ordinary. The attempt to overturn his interlocutor, arguing that the decision on the bill of suspension in 1732 meant that *res judicata* operated, was rejected. Reported as *Lord Frederick Campbell* v. *David Scot*, 8 Dec. 1773, F.C., p. 233, no. 93.

98. ALSP, *Answers for Lord Frederick Campbell Lord Clerk Register of Scotland*, 27 Jan. 1774, p. 9.

99. ALSP, *Information for David Scot*, 24 June 1773, Miscellaneous collection, box 1, p. 10.

100. NRS, Great seal register, C3/14, fo. 79; C3/16, fo. 300; C3/17, fo. 39.

101. Ibid., fos 18r–v.

102. Ibid., fo. 18v.

103. Murray, 'Lord Clerk Register', esp. pp. 146–7, 150–1.

104. NRS, CS1/13, fos 180v, 182v.

105. Ibid., CS1/14, fo. 194v; also fo. 162r.

106. *RPS*, 1662/5/52.

107. The last reference is to Alexander Mackenzie WS in 1770: NRS, GD1/616/93; also, NRS, GD220/5/1736; NP2/22, 'Act in favours of The Clerk to the Admission of Nottars 1738'.

108. NRS, CS1/10, fo. 138v.

109. Ibid., CS1/10, fo. 138v.

110. Ibid., CS1/9, fos 215r–v

111. TCM, SL1/1/88, fos 219–20; Murray, 'Lord Clerk Register', p. 151; on Kerr and Robertson, see *Correspondence of Sir Robert Kerr, First Earl of Ancram and his son, William, Third Earl of Lothian* (Edinburgh, 1875), pp. cxxvii–cxviii.

112. Ibid., MS 17537, fo. 178. The Laigh Parliament Hall is in the basement of Parliament House. Use of it was acquired by the Faculty of Advocates (briefly referred to in 1789: TCM, SL1/1/113, fo. 217). The Faculty built a loft there in 1702 and a vent was added in 1777: ibid., SL1/1/37, fo. 48, SL1/1/95, fo. 290.

113. M. H. B. Sanderson, *A Proper Repository* (Edinburgh, 1992).

114. NLS, Saltoun, MS 17537, fo. 178r; Murray, 'Lord Clerk Register', 149–50.

115. N. S. Jucker, ed., *The Jenkinson Papers 1760–1766* (London, 1949), pp. 186–7.

116. NLS, Minto, MS 11033, fos 19r–19v; ALSP, *Duplies for Mr Charles Hope Advocate*, p. 4.

117. NLS, Saltoun, MS 17358, fo. 110r.

118. NRS, GD220/5/1935/1. The warrant was addressed to the treasury commissioners and the barons of exchequer: ibid, GD220/1/J/2/2/4.

119. Ibid., GD220/5/1728/6a.

120. For example, TCM, SL1/1/56, fo. 209, privy seal commission to George Abercromby, advocate, to be 'Royal professor of publick Law, Law of Nature and Nations' at Edinburgh, 17 Dec. 1735. Professorial appointments were generally made under the privy seal.

121. NLS, Minto, MS 11033, fo. 19r; NRS, Great seal register, C3/17, fos 332–3.

122. The *History of the WS Society* has him as depute keeper of the signet. He wrote to the privy seal from 1699: NRS, great seal register, CS3/5, fo. 278; ibid., CS1/10, fo. 38r.

123. NRS, *Register House charters*, 3rd series, RH8/1409.

124. NRS, Glencairn papers, GD39/4/6; *ARNP*, no. 960.

125. NRS, CS1/12, fo. 158v.

126. NRS, privy seal register, PS8/1, fo. 1r; PS3/8, fo. 491; NLS, Saltoun, MS 17538, fo. 110r. John became NP on 28 July 1748: *ARNP*, no. 1310. He had been an apprentice WS under Thomas Goldie. Kinloch, writer to the privy seal, was a relative and long-time correspondent of Lord Milton.

127. NLS, Yester, MS 7045, fo. 86r.

128. Clearly implied in William Bryce's petition: NRS, privy seal register, PS8/1, fo. 166.

129. NRS, CS1/15, fo. 17r.

130. Ibid., Clerk of Penicuik, GD18/2764. For the commission, ibid., great seal register, CS3/17, fos 348–51.

131. NRS, Clerk of Penicuik, GD18/2764.

132. NLS, Saltoun, MS 16749, fo. 4r. Bell has not been definitely identified.

133. NLS, Saltoun, MS 17730, fo. 136.

134. D.1.18.19.; Saltoun, MS 17730, fo. 182.

135. ALSP, *Answers for Charles Inglis, Depute clerk to the Bills,* 28 June 1764, ALSP, Dreghorn collection vol. 1, no. 19; *Information for Robert Waddell, one of the conjunct principal Clerks of the Bills,* 14 June 1768, Dreghorn collection, vol. 30, no. 47. This case reveals the complex development of this office.

136. Reported by Fountainhall, *Decisions,* 12 Feb. 1684, i, pp. 269–70; see also pp. 247, 256–7.

137. ALSP, *Answers for Aeneas McLeod Town Clerk of Edinburgh,* n.d., Forbes collection, vol. 3, fo. 2321.

138. ALSP, *Report to the Lords of Council by Lords Royston and Elchies … upon the Petition of the Clerk to the Admission of Notars,* 7 Feb. 1738, Kilkerran collection, vol. 1, no. 181.

139. ALSP, *Hugh Buchan writer in Edinburgh* (*supra,* p. 71, n. 108), pp. 4–5, 12. For Alves appointment, see ibid., p. 16.

140. NLS, Saltoun, MS 16557, fo. 22. For the clerk to the admission of notaries public, see J. Finlay, 'The History of the Notary in Scotland' in M. Schmoeckel and W. Schubert, eds, *Handbuch zur Geschichte des Notariats der europäischen Traditionem* (Baden-Baden, 2009) pp. 402–4.

141. NRS, Murray of Cringeltie papers, GD436/2/5/1.

142. ALSP, *Information for James Justice,* 13 July 1737, miscellaneous collection, box 1, p. 2.

143. Ibid. Sir James (who died in 1736) attempted to entail the land; Justice

litigated against his children to have the entail declared null in 1737. Livingstone was appointed DCS before June 1708: NRS, CS 1/10, fo. 67r.

144. NLS, Saltoun, MS 17730, fo. 21v.
145. ALSP, miscellaneous collection, vol. 15.
146. NLS, Saltoun, MS 16671, fo. 90.
147. Ibid., MS 16660, fo. 96.
148. NLS, Delvine, MS 1263, fo. 132v.
149. NLS, Saltoun, MS 17538, fo. 103.
150. Ibid., Saltoun, MS 16675, fo. 132.
151. NLS, Saltoun, MS 17730, fos 24r–v.
152. See, generally, *Information for James Justice* (*supra*, n. 1129).
153. NLS, Erskine Murray, MS 5076, fo. 33r.
154. NLS, Delvine, MS 1110, fos 73–4.

8

Subordinate and Minor Office-holders
in the College

It may be true, that those duties, however important, do not necessarily require a very great degree of genius, or capacity for their execution; but still, attention, diligence, and assiduity are required; and the attendance very considerable.[1]

Like any court, the College of Justice contained minor office-holders who were essential to the orderly conduct of its business. Many of them would have been better known in Parliament House than most of the advocates. Nor should 'minor' be taken pejoratively; they were minor only compared with those considered in the previous chapters. The range of these offices, from agents and clerks to keepers, was considerable and they encompassed a number of administrative tasks, some of which involved considerable application and practical skills. Those who filled them often enjoyed lengthy careers and sometimes flitted from one office to another. Whether they filled wholly subordinate positions, or enjoyed a measure of independence, all worked under the ultimate authority of the lords of session.

ADVOCATES' CLERKS

According to John Spotiswood, advocates typically had two clerks, a first clerk (who dealt with clients' business) and a personal servant who waited on the advocate himself.[2] The second clerk might function as an amanuensis. This was the case with Robert Craigie's second clerk who earned a bonus of six shillings for legal writings of extraordinary length in 1742, and also Alexander Lockhart's second clerk who received a similar type of payment in 1752.[3] It was certainly true of the Edinburgh writer and notary, Archibald Govan, who was second clerk to the advocate Hugh Murray-Kynnynmond.[4] Govan sued his late master's executors for the price of mourning clothes which he had purchased only to be given another set paid for out of the estate. The tradition of clerks and servants being provided with mourning clothes as part of the funeral costs (therefore constituting a preferential debt on the estate) was widely acknowledged and accepted, for example, by William Hall PCS, one of the creditors of Lord Kimmerghame.[5]

Although advocates appointed their own clerks independently, the Faculty of Advocates regulated the appointees to ensure that they were properly qualified to act as agents in the College of Justice. A 1772 Faculty report required them to undergo examination, and its terms suggest that an advocate's clerk might himself be an advocate though, in fact, there is no known eighteenth-century example.[6] Like advocates themselves, however, clerks were drawn to Edinburgh from across the country.

In January 1777, the seven clerks nominated as examinators of advocates' first clerks were probably all notaries.[7] It is likely that Thomas Buchanan, servant to the lord advocate David Dalrymple in 1716, was a notary as probably was John Blair, clerk to Robert Craigie (then HMA) in 1743.[8] Advocates clearly prized the notarial arts: of the sixty-one clerks mentioned in Williamson's *Directory* in 1773, no less than forty-nine may have been notaries. A high proportion of later clerks were notaries though the proportion was probably smaller than that of WS Society members. A small number of first clerks also became writers to the signet.[9] Others developed family links to the bar. Ludovick Grant, clerk to James Montgomery when he was lord advocate, was the son of an Edinburgh writer and the father of an advocate (both called William).[10] James Keay, clerk to John Mackenzie, was also father of an advocate.[11]

The backgrounds of first clerks varied enormously, and their ranks included the sons of church ministers, merchants, shipmasters, wrights, wig-makers, farmers and writers from Inverness to Selkirkshire. They were not necessarily young men. John Craigie's clerk in 1773, Edward Rutherford, had become a notary as early as 1729; Alexander Lockhart's clerk the same year, Lachlan Grant, had been a notary for forty years. Indeed, of the forty-nine notaries identified as advocates' clerks in 1773, ten had become notaries prior to 1750.

The first clerks' admission register (maintained by the Faculty) is preserved in the Advocates Library along with a number of individual letters of appointment, dating from the nineteenth century, that were lodged with the Faculty clerk.[12] The earliest entries in the register were made in 1775. Because only four of those in Williamson's *Directory* appear, the register clearly operated prospectively from that date. It records the examination and admission of first clerks but also reveals when clerks, having once been admitted, were reappointed by another advocate. When he was appointed clerk by John Macfarlane in January 1796, for example, Lewis Gordon had considerable prior experience. The 1773 *Directory* shows that at that time he was clerk to another advocate, Cosmo Gordon (d.1800), who became a baron of exchequer in 1777. For his part, Macfarlane went through at least four first clerks, including Lewis Gordon. The first, Thomas Walker Baird, became his clerk in February 1790 before his own admission to the bar on 26 February 1793. He was almost immediately replaced, on 9 March, by John Weir who himself was replaced the following December by John Craw.

Macfarlane had been at the bar just for over a year before appointing a clerk. In this he was followed by another serial employer, John Bushby Maitland, who was admitted in 1788 and changed his first clerk in 1789, 1792, 1799 and 1803. Although it is not unusual to find advocates making several appointments over a number of years, most waited longer than a year to employ a clerk for the first time; indeed, it was common to wait three or four years. It took this long to generate sufficient business to make the role worthwhile. The few advocates who had been writers in private practice before coming to the bar, on the other hand, tended to develop a good practice from the start. While Thomas Walker Baird (having been one himself) did not register a clerk, Stuart Moodie did. In January 1797 he employed Alexander Mackenzie and then, in November of that year, Graham Leny. Moodie had himself been a WS before going to the bar in 1793, and Leny was training to become a WS in the chamber of Moodie's former fellow apprentice, William Anderson. The other notable writer who transitioned to the bar at the end of the eighteenth century was John Pattison. Like Baird, Pattison rose quickly at the bar and he is one of a minority of new advocates who appointed a clerk soon after admission. In his case, after only a month in practice, he appointed James Spence.

These appointments are interesting because they illustrate two practices. First, perhaps like Moodie's short-lived clerk, Alexander Mackenzie, some men were appointed on a temporary or trial basis. Another example is James Dundas, appointed clerk by Thomas Wilson in May 1791, only to be replaced the following December by William Wilson. Because both Wilsons were from Renfrewshire, they may have been related. Secondly, James Spence, clerk to Baird but also to John Swinton, is one of a number of clerks who acted simultaneously for more than one advocate. There was no pattern to this. The Edinburgh writer Alexander Hart, for instance, was clerk to two advocates from Perthshire though he himself was originally from Dunfermline; likewise, two advocates from Fife shared a clerk who was originally from Aberdeen.[13]

The number and pattern of clerks' admissions demonstrate that, like Baird, not every advocate registered a clerk with the Faculty. Of the 194 advocates admitted in the period 1775–1800, only eighty-eight had done so by the beginning of 1800. While this does not necessarily mean that the remainder had no clerks, it does mean they had no clerks authorised to act as agents in College processes which, given the modest size of the working bar, is not surprising. On the other hand, clerks having once been appointed might regularly change employer from advocate to advocate. Burnet Bruce (d.1813) employed a new first clerk in 1793, 1797 and 1808. The last of these, the notary Alexander Hutchison, was appointed first clerk by Alexander Thomson (admitted 1820) in July 1823 and then by two other advocates in 1829 and 1847 respectively. It was not uncommon for clerks to outlast their masters and demonstrate considerable longevity.

The main methods of recruiting a clerk made use of provincial, family or Edinburgh connections. It is no coincidence that some advocates had first clerks who came from their own locality. John Munro's clerk, William McKillop, was a Stirling writer and Munro himself was from Auchinbowie in Stirlingshire. Advocates from Glasgow, including John Connell, John Orr, Thomas Muir and John Millar jr, tended to recruit Glasgow writers as their clerks. Claud Boswell's clerk, Thomas Lister, was the son of a farmer in Boswell's native Fife; Robert Dalziel from Glenae in Ayrshire employed William Johnstone, an Edinburgh-trained writer and the son of an Ayrshire excise man. Advocates from the Borders also tended to use local connections. Thomas Tod, second son of Thomas Tod WS, whose family came from Melrose, had as clerk the son of a burgess from Lauder. One of John Bushby Maitland's clerks was the son of a Dumfries accountant; Maitland himself came from Eccles in Dumfriesshire. As clerks migrated from one advocate to another, such local connections might be retained. John Forman, for example, the son of a Stirling magistrate, was appointed clerk by Burnet Bruce in 1797 and by James Erskine in 1808. Both Bruce and Erskine were from Clackmannanshire.

Recruitment within the family also took place. William Boswell, admitted advocate in 1800, recruited his brother Alexander as his clerk in 1804. Alexander, as their father, Robert, had done, went on to be admitted a WS. This also demonstrates a Borders connection because Robert, who was from St Boswells, had trained with Thomas Tod. Alexander Boswell, incidentally, was not the only clerk to qualify as a WS. Of the 253 writers to the signet admitted between 1790 and 1809, twenty-one are known to have served as advocates' first clerks prior to admission. Further examples of family connection include Alexander MacLachlan, a writer in Fort William, who was clerk to Donald MacLachlan from Loch Awe; Alexander Irving whose clerk was John Irving, and Robert Corbet who employed William Corbet in 1786.

The third, and most common mode of recruiting a clerk, was simply to find one among the writers of Edinburgh. Some advocates probably had little alternative. Archibald Macdonald of Sanda, off Kintyre, employed as clerk the writer David Barclay, son of an Edinburgh tailor. Two of his later clerks were also Edinburgh writers, though one was the son of a brewer in Crail (Perthshire) and the other the son of a merchant in Falkland (Fife).[14]

Many clerks were notaries and many notaries trained in Edinburgh even if they came from distant parts to do so. Alexander Hay's clerk, William Ross, is probably the same man as the writer of that name from Dornoch in Sutherland who became a notary in 1717.[15] He was mentioned by Lord Milton as a potential successor to his father as commissary of Ross-shire, a post for which Hay recommended him.[16]

Perhaps the most remarkable thing about advocates' first clerks is how invisible they were as an interest group until the nineteenth century. The regulation of educational standards, established in 1772, was repeated in 1836 in which year a 'Society of Advocates First Clerks' was sanctioned by the Faculty of Advocates.[17] Application for membership was through petition to the dean who would remit candidates to examinators appointed by the Society itself. This differed little from earlier practice. The examinators, appointed annually by the dean (five constituting a quorum), were normally drawn from the most recently admitted advocates' clerks, and their names appear in the Faculty's minute book. Their remit was 'to take Trial of the Qualifications of Advocates First Clerks for acting as Agents or Solicitors before the Court of Session'. The necessary qualifications prescribed in 1836 were more demanding than those in 1772, and included university attendance, but the essential procedure was the same. The clerk of Faculty was made responsible for maintaining the accuracy of the roll of first clerks and intimating changes to the clerks of session and the clerks to the bills.[18]

By the late eighteenth century, advocates' first clerks tended to be classified along with writers to the signet. Both groups were College members whose status entitled them to act as agents but members of neither group were directly appointed by the lords of session.[19] In 1647 the lords had ordered the clerks of session to mark nothing on any court papers unless the papers were presented by advocates or their principal servants.[20] This act was aimed at ensuring the payment of appropriate fees to macers and to the writer of the minute book but it also made it clear that macers were not to admit agents to Parliament House (and that they were only to admit such expectant advocates as were specifically privileged by the lords). Acting as law agents had always been the first clerks' primary function, and the Faculty was consistently prepared to defend their role in dealing with processes. This is clear from a memorial presented in 1699.[21] The following year the first clerks themselves, in a memorial to the dean and Faculty, stressed the position of trust and confidence that they enjoyed which was the fruit of their knowledge and practical experience.[22] It may be significant that, in a petition to the lords in 1800 regarding fees in the Bill Chamber, advocates' second clerks were associated as a group not with writers to the signet but with apprentices, agents and solicitors.[23]

The position of first clerk was therefore one of some status. William

Forbes, who was appointed one of the principal clerks of Edinburgh in January 1743, had, until then, been clerk to the advocate James Graham of Airth.[24] One of his three competitors for the post, Andrew Chalmers, had been clerk to the late Hugh Murray-Kynnynmond and was then one of his executors.[25] In fact, in 1742, Forbes had paid money to Chalmers to pay off an earlier debt he had incurred to Murray-Kynnynmond.[26] Of the candidates, Forbes was evidently in funds to make the best financial offer for the council clerkship and, despite having earned the low opinion of Thomas Hay, he could no doubt have relied on the support of Graham, one of the assessors of Edinburgh and also dean of the Faculty of Advocates, who had influence with the council.[27] His competitor Chalmers, son of an Edinburgh writer and himself a writer, notary and accountant, did become involved with the College when he participated in the lucrative task of examining claims for compensation for the loss of heritable jurisdictions in 1748.[28] Another competitor was the highly regarded George Chalmers WS (later father-in-law to the advocate and judge, William Miller).[29]

The attachment of clerks to particular advocates, however it came about, was well known to College practitioners and also to the librarians. In 1764, the Faculty determined that an advocate might send his clerk to the Advocates Library to borrow a book or a bound collection of session papers for him, provided he had nominated the clerk in advance to the library's curators.[30] This system, in which the clerk signed the receipt, was abandoned in 1778 when advocates themselves were required to sign receipts. Because the assistant librarian, William Gibb, began to subscribe the admissions register of first clerks from 1796, in token of having received applications for registration, the clerks continued to be well known in the Advocates Library.[31]

Whether advocates in private practice took their clerks to House of Lords appeals is unclear though London was not short of Scots solicitors to assist them. The lord advocate, heading to London on appellate and political business, would take his law clerk with him. A letter in 1745 from an Edinburgh agent to the London attorney Alexander Baillie, asked him to remind John Blair, the lord advocate's clerk, that his master had been retained some time before to act in an upcoming appeal and that this had been noted in Blair's book.[32]

JUDGES' CLERKS

Upon promotion to the bench, an advocate either caused his clerk to cease acting as an agent or simply obtained a new one. Judges' clerks, however, constitute the most obscure category of College member. Their basic task was to act as secretaries, helping to prepare for each court day. They had to receive, collate and arrange the judge's printed papers and ensure the appropriate material was laid before him the day before the relevant cases were to be advised in court. In addition, these clerks maintained contact with the clerks of session and, if necessary, with agents and counsel in Parliament House.

Normally little attention is drawn to judges' clerks in the records, apart from the regulation of their activities in several acts of sederunt. A table of fees was set down in 1789 to inform the public what the clerks of the lords ordinary had a right to extract from them.[33] At each of the following stages, three shillings were payable to the ordinary's clerk: 1 when a cause was pled and taken to avisandum; 2 when a cause was inrolled in the judge's hand roll; 3 when a paper (such as a memorial or answers) was given in; 4 when the lord ordinary advised objections to witnesses or to questions to be put to witnesses; and 5 when a cause was reported to the lords, or when avisandum was made after a prepared state of the cause had been made. The same fee was also paid for every bill of suspension or advocation that was passed or refused. Other circumstances were set out where larger fees might be charged though the table was exclusive: no additional or greater fees were to be charged than those specified. In 1798, the lords prohibited any agents in the court from submitting papers for their attention except through the clerks of session or their assistants; at the same time, they prohibited clerks to the lords ordinary from receiving such papers directly from agents.[34]

The role of clerk was a confidential one, requiring constant attendance during the session provided, of course, the judge was present: each clerk's livelihood depended entirely on the health of the judge who employed him.[35] There was agitation in 1806 to increase fees but nothing was done prior to the remodelling of the court into two divisions in 1808. A committee set up in 1810 to look at this issue was obliged to order research to be carried out to discover what the clerks' average income then was.[36] As a result, the question of fees was put off again.

Individual clerks are rarely conspicuous. Lord Henderland's clerk, the Edinburgh writer James Cunningham, stands out because he complained in 1790 that he had been assaulted and defamed by Archibald Milne WS who was fined and briefly imprisoned as a result.[37] In 1760 James Allison, another Edinburgh writer, was clerk to Lord Coalston.[38] Duncan Forbes referred to George Ross as his former clerk, and had reason to correspond with him when he became lord president, but Ross had by then established a career for himself as an agent in London.[39] Judges' clerks seem generally to have been writers but neither Cunningham nor Allison was a notary and little else is known of them. John Stobie, who identified himself in a deposition in 1769 as clerk to Lord Auchinleck, had been a notary since 1745 and spent many years in practice as an Edinburgh writer.[40] Walter Wordie, a writer who was Lord Milton's clerk, features strongly in his correspondence and regularly made logistical arrangements when Milton was away from Edinburgh. For example, he was instructed on one occasion to ensure that Milton's session papers were kept and dated.[41] At Milton's death, his then clerk, John Robertson, was charged with putting his papers in order and making an inventory.[42] He was then appointed clerk to the trustees of his estate.

The clerks of Scottish judges had more in common with the workmanlike *greffier* of contemporary France or the Low Countries than the *adjutors*, often themselves jurists of ability, who assisted each judge in the Roman Rota.[43] Yet their obscurity should not diminish their importance. When a judge was sitting as lord ordinary, for example, his clerk would enter in the Outer House roll all the ordinary actions that week. Each week the judge sitting as lord ordinary in the Outer House, or in the Bill Chamber, subscribed the relevant roll and stated the total number of cases where the parties had entered appearance. For example, Gilbert Elliot (the first Lord Minto) subscribed the following typical entry: 'The total number of Ordinarie actiones taken up on Saturday the 7th of June 1712 extends to twenty two causes.'[44] For every cause that was enrolled, the judge's clerk obtained a fee. If the cause was called in the absence of the party's lawyer, then it would have to be enrolled again and a new fee would be payable. This led to the practice which Lord Cockburn called 'riding the clerk'.[45] A cunning clerk could make money by calling causes at inopportune times. According to Cockburn, some judges (he names Eskgrove particularly) shared these fees and might deliberately take their seats unexpectedly in order to have cases called, without reply, so that the fees would multiply.

It was natural for judges to act as patrons for their clerks and to seek offices for them. According to Gilbert Elliot (grandson of the first Lord Minto) who, as keeper of the signet, controlled the appointment of sheriff-clerks, two judges' clerks had their eye on the sheriff-clerkship of Clackmannanshire in 1767.[46] This office, valued at about £30 annually, could be exercised by a depute as the incumbent, Robert Rollo, had done. Having been clerk since at least 1712, he was now over eighty and blind, and his office was ripe for speculation.[47] Robert Auld, clerk to Lord Barjarg, competed with the (unnamed) clerk of Lord Kennet.[48] In the end, the successful candidate was the Montrose writer, John Jamieson, whose connections to the Erskine family (he was later factor on the Mar estate) make it plausible to suggest that he was the man referred to as Kennet's clerk.[49]

That judges felt responsibility towards their clerks is indicated by a provision they made in 1803.[50] The clerks had already established a private fund to support their families in certain circumstances, and the judges, recognising their importance as officers of the court, acknowledged how vulnerable individuals might be should a judge be absent from the court or excused attendance through indisposition. In those circumstances, his clerk would have no fees and would receive no papers. Therefore, the judges directed that additional fees were to be paid whenever a cause was enrolled in the Outer House or a bill presented in the Bill Chamber, to be collected as appropriate by the keeper of the Outer House rolls or the depute keeper of the bills, and paid over to those in charge of the clerks' common fund. A committee of judges (Balmuto, Hermand and Woodhouselee) was set up to oversee the arrangement.

KEEPERS OF PARLIAMENT HOUSE

The College had two distinct kinds of keeper: the doorkeepers and those who kept various books and registers. Under a contract made between the lords of session and the town council from 1694, the appointment of the two doorkeepers of Parliament House was a two-stage process.[51] First, a leet (or shortlist) was drawn up by the town council or the lords, each taking a turn, with the names of three candidates. Second, the successful candidate would be chosen by whichever party did not draw up the leet. The nominees, regardless of who put them forward, were normally merchants or tradesmen in Edinburgh. There seem, occasionally, to have been particularly favoured candidates. In 1785 the magistrates put forward a leet containing the name of George Murray, formerly servant to the late lord provost, Walter Hamilton.[52] The lords duly elected him and, in 1794, the magistrates elected John Whittit, servant to the lord president, Ilay Campbell, in preference to a wigmaker and a tailor whom the judges had also nominated.[53] The arrangement bears similarity to the method by which the University of Edinburgh chairs in Civil Law, Scots Law, and Universal History were filled. In that case, however, the Faculty of Advocates proposed two names and the town council selected the appropriate candidate.

The keepers had three principal functions. First, they reported the need for repairs to the fabric of the building to its owners the council (specifically the treasurer and dean of guild). Secondly, they provided necessary items such as coal, candles, pens and ink. Thirdly, they assisted the judges in the robing room and looked after advocates' gowns.[54] In 1703 the keepers petitioned either for payment of a salary from the Faculty or some effective means of making sure they received payment of the gratuities which custom dictated advocates should pay them.[55] The Faculty determined, eventually, rather than paying a salary, to recommend a minimum gratuity which advocates should pay annually and to discharge the keepers, in the case of non-payment, from 'keeping and putting on the Advocats gowns'.[56] Advocates, however, continued to be deficient in paying.[57]

The main duties were recounted by Hew McKaile in 1773 when he was subjected to an action to arrest his income.[58] McKaile, an Edinburgh writer, was appointed one of the keepers in November 1757 (at the age of about fifty-eight).[59] By then, the income of the office came in the form of fixed sums payable by the city of Edinburgh, the Faculty of Advocates, the commissaries of Edinburgh, the writers to the signet, and each individual practising advocate. The total from these sources amounted to almost £13 sterling annually for each keeper.[60] In addition, each keeper received half a guinea upon the admission of a new lord of session, five shillings on the admission of a new advocate, and sums payable at the service of a brieve and at each justiciary trial although a third of these latter two payments went to the underkeeper. The keepers also let certain shops and booths around Parliament House, drawing from this an income of £9 sterling annually. McKaile's litigation in 1773 concerned whether this rental income could be arrested by his creditors. One of his arguments was that his predecessor had also been in financial difficulties and that no such arrestment had taken place.[61]

Money was at the heart of Andrew Keay's demission from office as a keeper in 1736. Ostensibly, he resigned to provide some relief to whichever burgess the council elected to replace him who would then not require any financial relief from the council.[62] In return, the town council agreed to pay a pension of £10 sterling to his wife for the rest of her life. This private bargain, struck between Keay and the council, was the more easily obtained because his wife was Magdalene Fleming, daughter of a former lord provost. The main beneficiary was the new joint keeper, the goldsmith Kenneth Mackenzie. The appointment led, in September 1738, to an objection against Mackenzie's right to vote in the creation of a leet for the office of deacon of the goldsmiths.[63] Mackenzie denied that he was disqualified through holding a lucrative office from the town, explaining that he served the lords of session. Though he had been selected by the council, and worked in a building owned by the town, he was neither paid by the town nor directly subject to the council's orders. Though the majority of goldsmiths opposed Mackenzie having a vote, the council allowed it.[64]

Mackenzie had been nominated by the lords of session. When its turn came to nominate a leet for selection by the judges, the council seems to have chosen carefully. In 1743, for instance, it nominated a former council treasurer, a former dean of gild and a saddler (apparently a makeweight).[65] The merchant burgess and former treasurer, William Dundas, was the successful candidate.[66] In 1756, to replace the late William Wightman, the council selected three merchants. On that occasion, the lords of session were not unanimous in their choice. Objections were made to the council's leet, and it was suggested that leets be avoided in future. The judges finally elected William Hutchison, keeper of the mortality record.[67] That was not the end of the matter. The council disputed the choice because, in time of session, the 1694 contract required the judges to make their selection within ten days of the leet being presented and they had not done so; therefore, the choice reverted to the council and, in June 1757, the council elected Yaxley Davidson from the original leet.[68] Davidson, a former stabler and innkeeper, had in 1752 been appointed overseer of the rakers (that is, the municipal dung collectors).[69] The lords refused to accept his election and, in August, the magistrates approached the lord advocate for his opinion as to whether they should persist in their choice.[70] In the interests of cultivating 'a good harmony between the Bench and the Town Council' they agreed to waive their election of Davidson and to recognise Hutchison as one of the keepers, compensating Davidson with the office of keeper of the mortality record which Hutchison had vacated. Within months, however, Hutchison was dead and, in November 1757, the lords prepared their own leet and sent it to the magistrates who selected Hugh McKaile.[71]

As these appointments indicate, those who became keepers were not men of high status. Alexander Noble (elected by the lords in 1771) was a candlemaker.[72] His successor, elected by the council, was George Russell, a farmer's son.[73] Before being appointed in 1785, George Murray undertook to make a specified annual payment to support a merchant and his daughter, and to accept the risk of being deprived of his share of the income of any merchant booths removed as a result of alterations carried out to Parliament House.[74] This is another indication that the office was sought after despite its modest income.

BARKEEPERS

In addition to the keepers of the house, there was also a barkeeper in the Outer House, a servant of the Faculty of Advocates and not the College. It was his task to regulate entry to the bar, a square area opposite the bench in the Outer House to which there was one door which, dressed in his black gown and carrying a silver-tipped baton, he would guard.[75] Payments traditionally received from noblemen, gentlemen, writers to the signet and others who were allowed within the bar were stopped in 1678 when the lords apparently restricted entry to advocates alone (although this severe restriction did not last).[76] To compensate, the Faculty doubled the salary of the office to £200 Scots. In 1766, however, the salary was removed and the keeper had to rely purely on perquisites though these were substantial.[77] The incumbent in 1788, David Knox, presented his employers with a list of arrears which were owed to him by agents who had not paid his fees.[78] He did receive a salary of £100 Scots from the WS Society. He alleged, however, that while some three hundred men were obliged to pay, including agents, clerks and apprentices, less than fifty had done so, and complained that, because another was available, his entrance door was no longer used.

Like most of his predecessors, Knox, formerly an Edinburgh merchant, had been appointed in 1766 by a vote in the Faculty.[79] The barkeeper's commission, signed by the dean, subsisted during the Faculty's pleasure. Allan Livingstone, who retired aged seventy in 1764 on the grounds of old age, had missed only two days in thirty-two years.[80] Livingstone, a writer, was appointed barkeeper in 1748 having been depute to Robert Craig, advocate. Craig had become keeper in 1732 on the understanding that a depute would undertake the normal duties of the office.[81]

Apart from Craig, there is little obvious connection, beyond the nature of their employment, between the Faculty and its barkeepers, the role often been filled by former merchants or writers. In 1694, following a dispute with the macers over the role of the barkeeper, the Faculty had decided that in appointing barkeepers no preference be given to anyone who was dependent on the Faculty or its members.[82] This may have been a necessary concession because the suggestion had been raised that the judges should have the right to name the barkeepers, an idea Fountainhall regarded as unfair and akin to the Romans, having been called in to determine which of their neighbours owned a piece of land, deciding to claim it for themselves.[83]

The Faculty's nominee in 1694, James Dalrymple, who seems to have held the office permanently, was succeeded after his death in 1702 by Thomas Inglis, a writer and servant (perhaps clerk) to the lord president.[84] Hugh Inglis, who died holding the office in 1732, may have been related to Thomas, though several men of that surname practised law in Edinburgh, including two bailie court procurators and Charles Inglis, depute clerk of the bills in the 1720s.[85] Hugh's successor, John Hay, was (like David Knox) a former merchant.[86]

New barkeepers usually contracted to provide an annuity in favour of those retiring from office and their surviving dependants.[87] For example, Allan Livingstone, who replaced Inglis in 1732, agreed to demit in 1764 in favour of the merchant, John Hay, in return for an annual payment of £70 sterling for life from Hay, plus £200 to his children when Livingstone died.[88] The Faculty specifically agreed to this arrangement and the sum payable reflects the estimated level of fees for contemporary macers.

Latterly, the barkeepers struggled to maintain their income even though, in theory, College members who failed to meet their financial obligations to them might be deprived of office. They could petition the Faculty and WS Society to urge their members to pay what was due but they did have other sources of income.[89] These included the General Assembly, the commissioners of excise, the commissioners of the customs and the town council. On application in 1790, by the then keeper, James Stoddart, the council increased its annual payment to 2 guineas. This fully covered what was payable by the magistrates, councillors, clerks and others 'concerned in the Towns business when frequenting Parliament House'.[90]

KEEPERS OF REGISTERS

The category of those who kept books and registers is a varied one. Distinct offices belonged to the keeper of the minute book, the register of hornings, and the Outer House and Inner House rolls. Perhaps the most prestigious of these was the keeper of the Inner House rolls, who was always the lord president's clerk and continued only so long as the president remained in office. William Murray, clerk to Thomas Miller, enjoyed therefore a brief tenure in office because his master died only eighteen months after being sworn in as president in January 1788.[91] It was not necessary to be a notary to hold the office. While Murray may have been one, Patrick Hepburn, William Marshall and James Newbigging, were certainly not notaries at the time of their respective appointments in 1748, 1754 and 1760.[92]

James Newbigging later became keeper of the register of hornings (an office discussed further below) in November 1789, shortly after Walter Lockhart had replaced William Murray as keeper of the Inner House roll.[93] The son of a Lanarkshire merchant, Newbigging did well out of his connections to the Arniston family, being appointed to different offices in 1760, 1781 and 1789.[94] He was significant enough to be a freeholder in his native Lanarkshire in 1788 and, as collector of fees, his name sometimes appears in tables of expenses.[95] When, in 1809, it looked as though Newbigging would demit office owing to ill health, Walter Lockhart, hoping to gain for himself keepership of the register of hornings, wrote to inform the retired Ilay Campbell.[96]

The role of the keepers of the rolls is described at length in regulations issued in 1672.[97] The keeper of the Outer House rolls was to maintain two books, one containing all suspensions, advocations, removings, ejections and recent spuilzies to be heard before the lord ordinary, and the other containing all other types of action. Each Saturday afternoon, he was to note all these causes and the names of the parties and make a record whenever the process was outgiven and returned. The following Monday, he was to fix to the wall of Parliament House two rolls reflecting the contents of the two books. Advocations, suspensions and other matters in the first book were called on Tuesdays and Wednesdays, the other cases on the other days of the week. Anything not heard by the lord ordinary one week, with neither act nor decreet pronounced or protest made, would be heard the following week. The keeper of the Inner House roll was also to appear on Saturdays and insert in his book actions belonging to the Inner House, such as actions of proving the tenor of lost documents or actions for the reduction of heritable rights. The order of the various types of action, and circumstances in which they might go from the lord ordinary to the Inner House, were prescribed. This keeper also maintained a book of concluded causes containing evidence from the proof that was to be ranked by the lord ordinary on concluded causes before being presented to the Inner House. The keeper of the Inner House roll was entitled to higher fees for each action enrolled but this simply reflects the fact that there were many more actions in the Outer House than the Inner.

It would appear from the 1672 regulations that it was not anticipated that both rolls would be kept by the same person but, in fact, they were both later held by the same man, the writer James Craig. Described as 'servant to the lord president', Craig was appointed keeper of the Outer House roll in February 1705 and also received the Inner House roll in 1708.[98] When he resigned *in favorem* in December 1728, to be reappointed jointly with his son, he still held both offices. Such resignations were a common method of keeping offices in the family, and there are several examples of them in the history of the College. Craig and his eldest son, Hew, were appointed joint keepers of both offices on 1 January 1729 but they gave them up in 1738 in favour of George Ross.[99] Owing to the downturn in litigation, Ross probably paid significantly less for the offices than he would have done a generation earlier. In 1732, Craig had complained to Lord Milton that the 4 pence he and his son received for each cause enrolled in the Outer House roll, under the 1672 regulations, had never been increased and the number of causes inrolled were not a third of what they used to be.[100] When Ross demitted office as keeper of the Outer House roll, in January 1748, he was working in London and clearly carried on the work of the office by means of a substitute.[101] He retained the other keepership until Patrick Hepburn's appointment in November that year and, from then on, they were held separately though the income from these offices is not likely to have recovered very much until later in the century.

THE REGISTERS OF HORNINGS AND INHIBITIONS

The registration of hornings dates back to the sixteenth century.[102] Anyone denounced as an outlaw was traditionally 'put to the horn' typically by a messenger-at-arms or a macer. That officer then had to go to the local sheriff and intimate the denunciation to him, requiring him to compile an inventory of the outlaw's goods. The inventory was the basis of the escheat to the Crown for the contempt that had led to the horning, and its registration was a necessary preliminary to recovering property escheated to the Crown.[103] In 1731, when the lord clerk register tried to obtain custody of them, all the registers dating back to 1699 were being held (unlawfully) by the then keeper, William Douglas of Cavers.[104]

The keepership (or clerkship) of the general registers of hornings and inhibitions was an office held for life in the gift of the Crown.[105] Therefore it might be secured through an approach to patrons with influence in London, such as the Chief Baron of Exchequer or the lord advocate.[106] As with other Crown offices in the College, when a vacancy arose the lords of session assumed to themselves the power to appoint interim office-holders pending the presentation of a new commission. Thus, when the holder, the advocate John Mitchelson, died on 24 March 1728, his son was appointed interim keeper.[107] A similar appointment was made in December 1696 when the keeper, George Robertson, was ill but it was the lord clerk register who commissioned James Hamilton WS to act as interim keeper.[108] Hamilton was also appointed in 1697 keeper of the separate register of interruptions of prescription.[109] The register of hornings contained, inter alia, letters of horning, inhibition and interdiction.[110] Local registers of hornings were poorly kept by some sheriff-clerks. On receipt of such a local register in 1794, the clerk register brought it before the lords to obtain their authority for accepting custody of a volume his staff considered indecipherable and written contrary to the regulations.[111]

Mitchelson was not the only advocate to hold the office. It was also held, on an interim basis, by Ronald Dunbar WS, Edinburgh town council's solicitor, in 1748.[112] Clearly, it was not an insignificant position even if it was often exercised by deputies under the delightful title of underkeepers of the horning chamber. These were sometimes experienced writers and administrators, such as Hugh and George Buchan, who were appointed underkeepers in 1749 by the new keeper, the advocate, sinecurist, and disgraced former MP, Sir Archibald Grant.[113] In Grant's time, the fees were estimated to yield about £130 annually.[114] John Flockhart, an experienced writer, notary and procurator fiscal of Leith, who took over the keepership in 1778, viewed them as inadequate and initiated a number of changes.[115] In particular, he removed the anomaly of not charging full fees for copying half sheets into the register. Flockhart was status conscious enough to subscribe 10 guineas for raising the Royal Edinburgh Volunteers in 1780.[116] This was as much as some advocates contributed, though dwarfed by the contributions of a few prominent College members, particularly Lord Elliock and the advocate William Miller. Even so, it was an indication of the status of the office he was able to acquire.

THE KEEPER OF THE MINUTE BOOK

The keeper of the minute book was an officer distinct from, and less important than, the keeper of the rolls, although the same person might fill both offices simultaneously. Thus, Patrick Falconer had already been keeper of the minute book for almost five years when, in addition, he was made keeper of the 'bookes of enrolment for the utterhouse' in 1689.[117] The keeper of the minute book was positioned in the Outer House next to the depute clerks of session, 'within the innermost barre of the utterhouse'.[118] Maintaining the minute book was a continuous and immediate task. The office could not lie vacant for any length of time and the lords appointed interim keepers when the need arose.[119] Thus, when Thomas Butter died, his son, Charles, was made interim keeper until it came to attention, in February 1742, that he was still a minor.[120] The lords replaced him until a candidate with a regular commission (by this date from the Crown rather than from the clerk register whose patronage was diminishing) should present himself to the court.[121]

In fact, the next person to produce a great seal commission, John Murray, was also a minor. John's father, one of the Murrays of Cringeltie, had used his influence with Milton to arrange the appointment; his son's age, however (noticed by one of the lords of session) made him as yet incapable of holding the office. Unperturbed, the twenty-year-old would-be keeper presented a petition in his own favour, claiming to be better qualified than any previous keeper.[122] Not only had he completed an apprenticeship with Hew Crawford WS, he had attended lectures on Scots law at the university. He argued that no law expressly prevented a minor from occupying what was one of the easiest offices in the College. Perhaps unwisely, he referred to the fact that the lords had appointed Charles Butter interim keeper though Charles was younger than him (a fact the judges were quick to confirm).[123] The petition was unsuccessful. His uncle, the advocate Archibald Murray, wrote to Tweeddale asking him to block any further appointment until John, 'a very deserving young lad', was old enough to be admitted to it.[124] This was a wise precaution. The writer Andrew Raith had already written to Hew Dalrymple of North Berwick seeking his backing to secure the post which was for life and was worth, so Raith had been told, £70 or £80 sterling per year.[125] This was a reasonable estimate, although it was in 1761 said to be worth £100 per year.[126]

The duties of the office, as set out in Murray's petition, were primarily to transcribe into a single book the contents of several minute books of acts, decreets and protestations from the three offices of the principal clerks of session and to annotate them accordingly. In addition, the contents of the book were to be read out publicly at fixed times. From 1690, the lords also required the keeper to collect from the clerks of session his own dues, together with those payable to the macers, when extracts were made of decreets from the minute books. When any such extract was made, the keeper had to provide the extractor with a certificate stating the dues to be paid to the macers; he also had the right to inspect the clerks' responde books.

The minute book must be distinguished from the books of sederunt. The books of sederunt, maintained by the clerks of session, contain a note of which judges attended each day; they were the official record of the acts of sederunt and contained a range of documents recorded for preservation, as well as the record of admissions of office-holders in the College and further incidental information. The minute book, on the other hand, related narrowly to legal actions. It contained the names of the parties and their advocates, the nature of the action, and a note of any interlocutors made.

In 1771 the then keeper of the minute book, Alexander Gordon, sought an increase in fees and the WS Society was asked to report on the matter.[127] The Society estimated his income at just over £80 (this took into account both the cost of purchasing a minute book and the expense of having a boy write out a second copy and carry it around). The Society, not regarding the income as equal to the labour of the office, proposed increases. The fee on extracting a decreet was to go up from sixpence to a shilling; the same increase was to be imposed on entering a protestation in the minute book. Moreover a fee of one shilling for each judicial act extracted from the minute book was imposed. In total, these changes were thought to increase the fee income to about £150.[128]

Out of this examination by the WS Society came the proposal to provide printed copies of the minute book. The practice hitherto had been for the keeper to write the principal book and for his clerk, and a younger servant, each to write out a copy. About 128 agents, each week, had for about an hour the opportunity to read either the principal or the copy to inform themselves which actions were depending before the court and what interlocutors had been pronounced. The younger servant would take the principal book to agents' houses and, in return, they paid an annual fee; those who were given the chance to read the copy paid a lower fee (reflecting the fact that it was less accurate). The consequences of this system were described in 1776:

> If one happens to be indisposed or to be out of town or to be interrupted by people or pressing business at the fixed hour the Book is snatched away and the opportunity of reading it that week lost till the next without a great deal of trouble; or if one keeps it a little longer than his time which often happens all the subsequent hours for that day, if not for the whole week, are disarranged and many people disappointed.[129]

As well as mitigating the inevitable inaccuracy of the manuscript books, printing would allow the keeper to check the proofs and enable an annual index to be compiled and circulated. It was calculated that, because printed copies of the principal book might be obtained each week for little more than the collective cost in fees paid to the keeper, printing should be introduced. This was not done, however, without objection. The main fear was that publicity might be detrimental. What could be published in a printed minute book could be reprinted in the newspapers; and greater circulation of information about bills of suspension against decreets for debt, or acts of adjudication (in which debts were often paid at the last minute), might be prejudicial to the public credit of certain litigants. Those favouring publication argued that the dry material of the minute books was not the kind of thing for which the public had much appetite. Besides, it was said that the 'Office marks and whole Language of the Minute Book is unintelligible to all the world except Gentlemen of the Law'.[130]

MACERS

The College of Justice contained four macers who carried out varied duties which included attending the lords ordinary and calling summonses, seeing to the execution of incidental warrants and, occasionally, presiding over the service of heirs as sheriffs *in hac parte*. In the latter case, the rule after 1672 was that a WS must act as clerk whenever a macer presided.[131] Disputed succession cases might lead to litigation before the lords, as it did in 1759 when the advocate, William Baillie, competed with his half-sister, Agnes Tennent, to gain title to their grandfather's estate. Both parties initially obtained brieves which were to be heard before the macers, with Lords Auchinleck and Barjarg acting as their assessors, arrangements which demonstrate an interesting dimension to their working relationship with other College members.[132] Despite this occasional relationship, the macers were always under the discipline of the lords of session and subject to punishment by them.[133]

In terms of income, macers received a fee every time an advocate, WS or notary was admitted and they were entitled to modest dues whenever a decreet was pronounced, an act made or protestation presented, and when a party or witnesses gave evidence on oath. They also attended the royal commissioner to the General Assembly, occasionally escorted bankrupts from Holyrood Abbey to the court, and, in times of scarcity, summoned landed men to depone as to the price of grain in the country.[134] They might also be used by the lords as couriers, sending documents to lawyers or litigants.[135] Traditionally, a macer stood in front of the bar while advocates were pleading, a right which they shared only with the clerks of session, the lord advocate and the clerk of the bills and his deputes. Macers had authority to apprehend and detain any advocate or his servant inclined to 'keepe up processes' (that is, to retain unlawfully possession of process papers) when complained upon by the other party.[136]

At least twenty-seven men were appointed macers in the period 1700–99 (with six appointments in the period 1685–1700). It is difficult to analyse

their backgrounds. Because the town council had no role in their appointment, the council minutes have virtually nothing to say about them and they
seldom appear in the notaries' admission register. Some were certainly
writers. Andrew Grant, appointed as a macer in 1711, may have been the
former servant of George Turnbull WS.[137] Three macers, William Skene (in
1686), William Maxwell (in 1693) and Thomas Graeme (in 1720), became
notaries after gaining office but there is no presumption that any of them had
a legal background.[138] In 1724 there is mention of Humphrey Colquhoun,
an Edinburgh skinner, who was one of the macers of justiciary.[139] These
were probably not very distinct, in terms of social origins, from macers in
the Court of Session.

The macers consistently complained about their difficulties in earning a
living. Prior to 1707, they received fees for acting as macers to parliament
when it was in session; this included sums paid to them whenever patents
passed conferring honours, ranging from that of duke to knight bachelor.
Following the abolition of the Scots parliament, as they complained to Lord
Ilay in 1729, they were increasingly unable to provide for themselves and
their families 'in a Creditable manner'. Indeed, the 'decay of business' before
the court had diminished the profits of their office by a half.[140] In 1761 it was
estimated that, apart from their annual salary of £10, the macers earned
fees of about £70 per year.[141]

While messengers had their wands, and barkeepers carried batons, the
macers were named after their symbol of office, the mace. In 1760, a
committee of the lords, inquiring into the conduct of the macers, discovered
that the widows and children of deceased macers had been selling maces on
to their successors.[142] Thus, the mace of Charles Maitland (d.1728), was
sold for 16 guineas to his successor, John Grierson.[143] Grierson's widow sold
the mace to Francis Gibson for 15 guineas when he took office in 1736.[144]
When, in 1757, Gibson resigned, to be replaced by Walter Colville, they
disagreed about the price of the mace.[145] Falling ill and in need of money,
Gibson borrowed from the Edinburgh writer, Robert McMurray, handing
him the mace as security (which he retained until 1760 before lodging it with
the clerks of session). It was also discovered that another macer, Francis
Gibb, had succeeded Patrick Grant of Bonhard and purchased both his mace
and his gown. Alexander Mitchell's executors, on the other hand, found no
buyer for his mace and simply melted it down.[146] The lords determined that
the maces, as badges of office, were the property of the court and not to be
sold privately. They ordered Moncreiff of Reddie to have a new mace made
and given to Mitchell's successor, Francis Scott, while McMurray was to
hand over Gibson's mace to Colville.[147]

Apart from one heritable macer (an office, in the gift of the family of
Moncreiff of Reddie, traceable back to James III), the three other macers

were direct Crown appointments by letters patent under the privy seal.[148] Men did, however, obtain grants of the office jointly with their sons, with the office going to the survivor.[149]

Traditionally, the macers in the College were superior in status to those who acted in the criminal court or in other courts. The High Court of Justiciary had three macers whose main duties were to execute indictments, cite jurors and witnesses, and attend the judges and jurors during diets of the court.[150] This superiority was exemplified by the temporary appointment of macers drawn from the High Court, or the Teind Court during the criminal circuit, to replace College macers who were absent for prolonged periods.[151]

The difference in status between macers in various courts was not always reflected in income. The College macers complained of this to the WS Society in 1772, contrasting their fees with the higher ones charged in the Teind Court. Moreover, with increasing living costs, and changes in legal practice, they faced growing hardship. A particular issue was the fact that the judges acting as lords ordinary on oaths and witnesses, who heard witnesses between 3 p.m. and 5 p.m. on each court day, were now granting commissions to others (often advocates) to take depositions. Commissions had always been used when evidence had to be taken locally but now it was happening 'even within the verge of the Court'.[152] The fee to a macer when there was a deposition in presence of a lord ordinary was 2 shillings, double what it was for a deposition taken before a commissioner.

Collectively, College macers were visible in two principal ways. Socially, they had their own loft reserved in the New Kirk, placing them next to the magistrates in a way which identified them as an occupational grouping.[153] Professionally, they petitioned collectively in defence of their rights, not only to political managers, seeking fee increases, but also to the judges. In 1736, for example, they petitioned against the writer Gabriel Napier who had refused to pay their fee.[154] They also acted together in 1694 when objecting to the fact that the Faculty of Advocates had named a barkeeper to replace the late John Bannatyne.[155] Presumably, they hoped to acquire this role for themselves but, as was noted earlier, they were unsuccessful. Throughout the succeeding century, the macers were fighting a rearguard action. Walter Scott in *Guy Mannering* portrays them as ignorant men of low status.[156] By his time, the office had certainly declined significantly from the sixteenth century when it was held by men who enjoyed significant responsibilities as sheriffs *in hac parte* and as tax collectors.

CONCLUSION

The lesser offices provided opportunity for men to buy their way into the College without exhibiting any high level of skill. They represent the working of patronage at a low level. At the same time, they were an investment and brought, as a by-product, the privileges of College membership and the costs and benefits of involvement within a wider professional and social community.

David Knox, for example, was immediately initiated into his community responsibilities when, as part of the consideration for the office of bar-keeper, he agreed to pay his predecessor's widow £30 a year, a sum he kept paying until she died twelve years later. To add to his burdens, the dean of Faculty, Henry Dundas, ordered him to pay his own sisters £20 a year to save them from poverty. This pre-empted the Faculty being called upon to support them in the event he failed to do so. In return, Knox looked to the Faculty to deal firmly with the 'most incorrigible Delinquents' among its members who not only refused to pay his fee but dared to 'menace and abuse him for asking it'.[157]

In a real sense, the men who held the offices described in this chapter formed part of a working community, acting collectively with some, co-operating with others, and competing with rivals, in events that could be of great, or of absolutely no, significance to the nation. Yet mundane events demonstrate how functions interlinked. When the macers were sent to the abbey of Holyrood in 1750, for example, to retrieve the father of the late advocate, James Geddes, on a charge of having defrauded his creditors, James Pringle PCS was sent along with them to preserve the evidence and seal the unfortunate man's charter chest.[158]

While the macers and clerks rubbed shoulders every day, both groups looked to their collective interests more readily than advocates' clerks did. The clerks may have managed legal actions but they seem to have been singularly ineffective in protecting their monopoly against both the WS Society and unlicensed agents. Perhaps the downward adjustment in the status of clerk, a class which had produced advocates in its own right in the seventeenth century, inhibited their development. After all, their employers collectively made great gains in status as their Faculty, in terms of organisation and influence, went from strength to strength between 1660 and 1808. Even in 1836, the Society of Advocates' First Clerks lacked autonomy and had to report to the dean of Faculty, and it was the clerk of Faculty, not the President of the Society, who maintained the roll of first clerks. Whatever the gradations in status between College members, however, so long as minor office-holders maintained an independence of function, as by definition the keepers and first clerks had and which the macers fought to maintain, their place in the College was recognised and kept secure.

NOTES

1. ALSP, *Memorial for Hugh McKaile, Writer in Edinburgh*, 4 Feb. 1773, Arniston collection, vol. 107, no. 22, p.3.
2. J. Spotiswood,*The form of process, before the Lords of Council and Session* (Edinburgh, 1711), p. xliii.
3. NLS, *Agnes Murray Kynnynmond claim papers,* MS 13281, fo. 190v; ALSP, *Answers for Joseph Allan,* 14 Jun. 1757, Arniston collection, vol. 41, no. 3, p. 21.
4. ALSP, *The Petition of Mr. James Geddes of Rachan, Advocate*, 25 Feb. 1743, Elchies collection, vol. 14, no. 61; *ARNP*, no. 1669.
5. ALSP, *Information for Patrick Lindsay and Archibald McAuley merchants*, 18 Dec. 1732, Elchies collection, vol. 5, no. 29, p.5.
6. Stewart, ed., *Min. Bk 1751–1783*, p. 232. Thomas Walker Baird was, before joining the bar, first clerk to John MacFarlane. There are seventeenth-century examples.
7. Stewart, ed., *Min. Bk, 1751–1783*, p. 280.
8. NRS, CS 1/18, fo. 188r; two Thomas Buchanans appear in the notaries' admission register, in 1702 and 1707: *ARNP*, nos 91, 218. Blair is mentioned in NLS, Yester, MS 7055, fo. 15r. An Edinburgh writer called John Blair became NP in 1701: ibid., no. 23.
9. Between 1775 and 1805, 122 of the 236 registered AFCs were notaries and a further thirty-eight are likely to have been (giving a range of between 52 and 68 per cent). In the same period, 220 of 323 WSs were, or soon became, notaries (68 per cent). Of the sixty-one clerks mentioned in Williamson's *Directory*, three (who were also notaries) became WSs: George Cuming, Charles Sibbald and William Leslie. A fourth possibility is James Dallas.
10. Ludovick was adm. NP on 28 Jul 1748; his son was admitted advocate on 10 Aug. 1773: *ARNP*, no. 1311; NRS, CS1/15, fo. 148v.
11. His son, James, entered the Faculty on 25 June 1799: NRS, CS1/18, fo. 145r. James himself was admitted NP on 5 Aug. 1771. Roderick McLeod, clerk to John Swinton jr, may have had a son at the bar assuming he was the father of Robert McLeod of Cadboll (adm. advocate, 3 March 1789).
12. AL, FR 34B. Subsequent references to registration refer to this mansuscript.
13. Hart's background is given in *ARNP*, no. 1446. The Aberdeen clerk was Alexander Ferguson (see Williamson's *Directory*) whose background is found in ibid., no. 2342.
14. Ibid. For Barclay, see Williamson's *Directory*; other appointees are given in FR34B, fos 46, 76.
15. *ARNP*, no. 489.
16. NLS, Saltoun, MS 16749, fo. 24v.
17. AL FR34B, *Report of the committee appointed to consider The*

Regulations regarding the Qualifications and admission of advocates first clerks, etc. (March, 1836); ibid., FR339/1, 'Minute of a Meeting of the Society of Agents or Solicitors Supreme Courts in the capacity of Advocates First Clerks held within their Hall on Monday the 27th Jany 1845 at 2 o'clock'.

18. Stewart, ed., *Min. Bk, 1751–1783*, p. 232.
19. See chapter 6.
20. NRS, CS 1/5, fo. 169v.
21. Pinkerton, *Min. Bk, 1661–1712*, p. 205.
22. Ibid., pp. 210–11.
23. NRS, CS1/18, fo. 157v.
24. TCM, SL1/1/63, fo. 280.
25. Ibid., fo. 62r; ALSP, *Answers for George Gordon of Gordonbank, Writer in Edinburgh*, Hamilton-Gordon collection, 4 July 1743, vol. 41, no. 60; *Petition of Mr. James Geddes of Rachan, Advocate*, p. 2; NLS, *Agnes Murray Kynnynmond claim papers,* MS 13281, fo. 39v.
26. NRS, RH15/38/100, *William Forbes to Hugh Forbes,* 3 June 1742.
27. NLS, Yester, MS 7053, fo. 62r. The fourth competitor was George Turnbull (probably George Turnbull WS).
28. TCM, SL1/1/57, fo. 113r; SL1/1/70, fo. 165; ARNP, no. 742 (with the spelling Chalmer); NLS, Saltoun, MS 17538, fo. 87r; NRS, CS1/13, fo. 69r.
29. For example, NLS, Saltoun, MS 16641, fo. 196. George Chalmers was also employed in 1748 searching records anent heritable jurisdictions: NRS, GD220/5/1663/5, 13.
30. Stewart, ed., *Min. Bk, 1751–1783*, pp. 128, 292.
31. Gibb's involvement begins with the entry of James Anderson: AL, FR34B, fo. 92.
32. NRS, CS228/B/3/53, Alexander Baillie against Alexander Stevenson.
33. NRS, CS1/17, fos 99r–v.
34. Ibid., CS1/18, fo. 111v.
35. See CS1/120 (unpaginated), entry dated 4 July 1810.
36. Ibid.
37. Ibid., CS1/17, fo. 115r. Milne was depute keeper of the privy seal in 1810.
38. NRS, Exchequer, E746/140/1.
39. J. Finlay, 'Scots lawyers and House of Lords appeals in eighteenth-century Britain' 32 (2011) *JLH*, 249–77
40. Ibid., ed., *ARNP* no. 1263; ALSP, *Hugh Buchan writer in Edinburgh* (*supra*, p. 71, n. 108), p. 77.
41. NLS, Saltoun, MS 16551, fo. 234. For Wordie being described as clerk, see ALSP, *The Petition of James Hepburn younger of Humbie*, 18 Nov. 1736, Hamilton-Gordon 1st collection, vol. 28, no. 34.
42. NLS, Saltoun, MS 16755, fo. 25r.
43. On the *adjutor*, G. Dolezalek, 'Litigation at the Roman Rota' in A. Wijffels, ed., *Case Law in the Making* (Berlin, 1997), p. 344.

44. NRS, CS90/1/5. The clerk's name does not appear in the rolls either of ordinary causes or in that of suspensions and advocations.
45. Miller, *Cockburn's Millennium*, p. 308.
46. NLS, Minto, MS 11033, fos 110r, 117r, 118v.
47. *ARNP*, no. 383.
48. Auld was admitted NP in 1754: ibid., no. 1444.
49. For example, NRS, Mar and Kellie papers, GD124/17/364.
50. NRS, CS1/19 (unpaginated) 9 June 1803.
51. A copy of the contract is given in NLS, MS 17538, fos 15r–16r.
52. NRS, CS 1/17, fos 12r, 13r.
53. Ibid., CS 1/18, fos 19v, 20r.
54. Hence the allegation by Patrick Haldane in 1721 that he 'had not so much as a Pin put up for him by the Faculty's Gown Keepers so small was his attendance'. NRS, RH2/4/398, 90, cited by Scott, 'Politics and Administration', p. 249.
55. Pinkerton, *Min. Bk, 1661–1712*, pp. 198, 204, 232,236, 237, 239; for the petition, AL FR339r/9.
56. Pinkerton, ibid., p. 236, 264, 269, 270.
57. For example, Pinkerton, ed., *Min. Bk, 1712–1750*, pp. ii, 185.
58. ALSP, *Memorial for Simon Holiday, ship-builder in Greenock*, 6 Feb. 1773, Arniston collection, vol. 107, no. 22.
59. NRS, CS1/14, fo. 92v. McKaile (d.1785), was born in about 1699. His duties were probably latterly carried out by substitute.
60. Not including £9 from shop rents. A total of £18 sterling was taken from practising advocates at half a crown each (2s. 6d.) per session, suggesting seventy-seven practising advocates in 1773. My estimates for the minimum size of the practising bar are fifty-nine in 1771 and eighty-four in 1781 (see p. 139, Table 4). The absolute maximum number in 1771 is eighty-three. The estimate is based on known attenders who acted for five or more clients. It is possible (but unlikely) that the fee in 1773 was also paid by those engaging in chamber practice whose names would not appear in the Outer House rolls. In the period 1740–72, 184 advocates were admitted, of whom fourteen were certainly dead by February 1773 (in a further seven cases, the date of death is not known) and seven had become lords ordinary. On any measure, the majority of Faculty members did not practise.
61. ALSP, *Memorial for Hugh McKaile*, p. 4.
62. TCM, SL1/1/56, fos 254–6; see also SL1/1/64, fo. 347.
63. Ibid., SL1/1/59, fos 212–13.
64. Ibid., fos 219, 221.
65. Ibid., SL1/1/63, fo. 340.
66. NRS, CS1/13, fo. 3r.
67. TCM, SL1/1/74, fo. 2; NRS, CS1/14, fo. 86v.
68. Ibid., SL1/1/74, fo. 147. Davidson is mentioned as a stabler at SL1/1/55, fo. 69.

69. Ibid., SL1/1/70, fo. 361.

70. Ibid., SL1/1/74, fos 213–14. The lord advocate was Robert Dundas (the future fourth Lord Arniston).

71. NRS, CS1/14, fos 92v, 94v; TCM, SL1/1/74, fos 301–2.

72. NRS, CS1/15, fo. 109v; TCM, SL1/1/88, fos 145–6.

73. NRS, CS1/16, fo. 83v; TCM, SL1/1/98, fo. 260.

74. TCM, SL1/1/106, fos 264–5, 289–90. The connection to the merchant Robert Cleugh and his daughter Violet is not known.

75. Stewart, ed., *Min. Bk, 1751–1783*, p. 165, n. 207. Described by Forbes as 'a Brasil Baton mounted with silver Bars': GUL, 'Great Body', MS Gen. 1248, fo. 1742.

76. Pinkerton, *Min. Bk, 1661–1712*, p. 40; Lang, *Mackenzie*, p. 128. The restriction was later varied by the Faculty, ibid., pp. 72–3, 185, so that noblemen and WSs were still permitted entry. In 1702 two advocates were to exercise discretion over the question of entry and to direct the barkeeper accordingly: ibid., p. 231.

77. Stewart, ed., *Min. Bk, 1751–1783*, pp. 131 (n. 207), 165.

78. AL, FR339/1; summarised in Stewart and Parrat, ed., *Min. Bk, 1783–1798*, p. 94, n. 151.

79. Stewart, ed., *Min. Bk, 1751–1783*, p. 165.

80. Ibid, p. 131; ALSP, *The Petition of John Pattullo*, 26 Feb. 1766, Arniston vol. 80, no. 45.

81. Pinkerton, ed., *Min. Bk, 1713–1750*, p. 138.

82. Ibid, *Min. Bk, 1661–1712*, p. 134.

83. Fountainhall, *Decisions*, i, p. 621.

84. Pinkerton, ed., *Min. Bk, 1661–1712*, pp. 134, 230–1; TCM, SL1/1/35, fo. 295(2)r; SL1/1/41, fo. 394.

85. TCM, SL1/1/57, fo. 16; SL1/1/50, fo. 273; 1/1/52, fo. 29. For example, Robert Inglis became joint procurator fiscal in 1725: TCM, SL1/1/51, fos 575–6.

86. Stewart, ed., *Min. Bk, 1751–1783*, p. 131.

87. E.g. Stewart, ed., *Min. Bk, 1783–1798*, p. 140.

88. ALSP, *The Petition of John Pattullo*, p. 2.

89. For example, petition of the under-barkeeper Patrick Borthwick in 1766: Stewart, ed., *Min. Bk, 1751–1783*, p. 161.

90. TCM, SL1/1/116, fo. 23; ALSP, *The Petition of John Pattullo Writer in Edinburgh*, 26 Feb. 1766, Arniston collection, vol. 80, no. 45.

91. NRS, CS 1/17, fos 63r, 64r, 101v.

92. NRS, CS1/13, fo. 96v, CS 1/14 fos, 9r, 133r. A William Murray was admitted notary in 1762; James Craig, appointed keeper in 1705, was probably a notary: CS1/10, fo. 68r; NRS, NP2/17, fos. 56r, 143r. Newbigging became a notary in 1778: *ARNP*, no. 2142.

93. NRS, CS 1/17, fo. 105v.

94. Keeper of the Inner House roll (1760); collector of the fees of the clerks

of session (1781); and keeper of the register of hornings (1789). He would have been clerk to Robert Dundas as both advocate and lord president.

95. C. E. Adam, *A View of the Political State of Scotland in the Last Century* (Edinburgh, 1887); for expenses, e.g. NRS, Samuel Shaw, *Memorandum Book*, RH15/134, fo. 39, where he is noted as receiving in a fee of 7s. 6d. in Feb. 1787.

96. GCA, Campbell of Succoth papers, TD219/6/422.

97. *RPS*, 1672/6/50.

98. NRS, CS1/10, fos 27v, 68r. Craig was probably a notary: NRS, NP 2/17, fos 56r, 143r.

99. NRS, CS1/11, fos 185v, 187r; CS1/12, fos. 82v, 84r.

100. NLS, Saltoun, MS 16549, fo. 84r.

101. NRS, CS1/13, fo. 59r.

102. *RPS*, 1579/10/28.

103. This remained true until a procedural change in 1748 although the register continued in use thereafter. See generally, *Guide to the National Archives*, p. 213.

104. NRS, Records originally at Edinburgh castle, SRO1/77/1. Cavers held office during 1728–48.

105. Sources are not always precise. George Robertson, for instance, refers to 'the register of Inhibitions & adjudications': NRS GD220/5/1716/10. Hornings, inhibitions and abbreviates of adjudications were three distinct registers.

106. For example, NRS, RH15/134. Sir Archibald Grant, on appointment, was brother of the serving lord advocate.

107. Ibid., CS1/11, fos 177r–v. Mitchelson junior (b.*c*.1704) became an advocate on 1 Feb. 1729.

108. NRS, CS 1/9, fos 136r–v. It is not known whether this was the same George Robertson who later acted for the Duke of Montrose. As with the clerkship of session, the right to commission office-holders returned to the Crown during the eighteenth century.

109. NRS, CS1/9, fo. 141v. On this register, see *RPS*, 1696/9/137.

110. Horning referred to the practice of a debtor being 'put to the horn' i.e. outlawed for failing to meet his pecuniary obligations; an inhibition was an order preventing a party, at the instance of his creditor, from alienating heritable property. Interdiction was a process whereby a party agreed not to deal with his own (normally heritable) property without the consent of another; in effect, it was a voluntary guardianship undertaken by those with assets but reason to doubt their own judgement in administering them.

111. NRS, *Petition & Complaint Lord Clerk Register against John Bushby*, 10 July 1794, CS94/37.

112. *Acts of Sederunt*, p. 409; NRS, CS1/13, fo. 61r.

113. NRS, CS1/13, fo. 133r. Grant held office from 25 July 1749 until his death in Sept. 1787, and was succeeded by John Flockhart in Nov.: ibid., CS1/13,

fo. 131v; CS1/16, fo. 51v. Grant was expelled as an MP for his involvement in fraud: R. Sedgwick, *The House of Commons, 1715–1754* (London, 1970), pp. 77–8; NLS Saltoun, MS 16549, fo. 222r.

114. NLS, Saltoun, MS 17358, fos 103; 110. The estimate dates from 1761; Grant was appointed on 25 July 1749: CS1/13, fo. 131v.

115. ALSP, *Memorial for John Flockhart Writer in Edinburgh*, 16 Jan. 1779, Miscellaneous collection, ser. 3, vol. 14 (1774–78), no. 58.

116. TCM, SL1/1/99, fos 139–46.

117. NRS, CS1/8, fo. 66r; CS1/9, fo. 10v.

118. Ibid., CS1/9, fo. 24v.

119. For example, NRS, CS1/13, fo. 4r; CS1/15, fo. 22r ; CS1/18, fo. 154r. See also *Acts of Sederunt*, pp. 590–1.

120. NRS, CS1/12, fo. 163r. Thomas was appointed in 1711: CS1/10, fo. 125v. Note also, William Butter, clerk of 'the taxations' in the College in 1632: CS1/5, fo. 51v.

121. A. L. Murray, 'The Lord Clerk Register' 53 (1974) SHR, p. 145.

122. NRS, CS1/12, fos 161v–163r.

123. Ibid., CS1/12, fo. 163r. He was removed and replaced by John Dingwall as interim keeper.

124. NLS, Yester, MS 7045, fo. 33r. The wording of Murray's letter suggests he may have drafted his nephew's petition to the lords.

125. NRS, Hamilton-Dalrymple papers, GD110/917/3.

126. NLS, Saltoun, MS 17358, fo. 107v.

127. NLS, Delvine, MS 1505, fos 123r–124r. Gordon had been appointed in 1766: NRS, CS1/15, fo. 22r.

128. NLS, Delvine, MS 1505, fo. 124r; *Acts of Sederunt*, pp. 588–9, extended by further acts, ibid., pp. 615, 619.

129. NLS, Delvine, MS 1505, fo. 218r.

130. Ibid., fo. 219v.

131. *RPS*, 1672/6/50, r. 33; Finlay, 'Lower branch of the legal profession', pp. 45–6; the rule was later confirmed in the Court of Session Act 1821, s.12.

132. ALSP, *Information for Agnes Tennent, Spouse to Mr Andrew Chatto*, 25 April 1766, Arniston collection, vol. 82, no. 30, pp. 2–3; Walker, *Legal History of Scotland*, v, 402.

133. For example, *Acts of Sederunt*, p. 561.

134. NLS, Mackenzie of Delvine papers, MS 1505, fo. 153.

135. For example, ALSP, *The Petition of James Wilson of Gillies*, 22 Feb. 1744, Kilkerran collection, vol. 10, no. 171 (handwritten note 'what follows was wrote on the ordinarys own copy of it [the petition], q[uhil]ck he sent to me by a macer at advising pet[ition] & ans[we]r).

136. NRS, CS1/9, fo. 45r.

137. *ARNP*, no. 342.

138. NRS, NP2/15 (unpaginated, 3 Mar. 1686); NP2/16, fo. 231r; NP2/18, fo. 356r.

139. TCM, SL1/1/50, fo. 219.
140. NLS, Saltoun, MS17538, fo. 31.
141. Ibid., fo. 103. Complaints about fee levels arose periodically. For example, a committee of judges allowed additional fees in 1791: NRS, CS1/17, fo. 133v.
142. Ibid., CS1/15, fos 131r–132r.
143. Greirson (adm. 9 Nov. 1728): CS1/11, fo. 182v. Maitland (adm. 15 Nov. 1681): CS 1/8, fo. 13v.
144. Gibson (adm. 16 Jan. 1736): CS1/12, fo. 47v.
145. Colville (adm. 14 June 1757): CS1/14, fo. 84v.
146. Grant (adm. 29 Dec. 1705); Gibb (adm. 11 June 1721): NRS, CS 1/10, fo. 38r, CS 1/11, fo. 36v; Mitchell (adm. 26 Feb. 1735): CS1/12, fo. 34v.
147. Scott (adm. 27 Nov. 1754) had a commission from Major George Moncreiff: CS1/14, fo. 30v. Moncreiff and McMurray each reserved a right of relief against the previous holders of the mace.
148. NLS, Saltoun, MS 16720, fo. 20r; 1931 Scots Law Times (News), 123.
149. For example, Andrew and Thomas Graeme in 1717; David Hamilton and his son, David, in 1782: NRS, CS1/10/205r; CS1/16/138r.
150. NLS, Saltoun, MS 17539, fo. 68.
151. For example, NRS, CS1/14, fo. 7r; CS 1/15, fos 109r, 148r; Acts of Sederunt, p. 526.
152. NLS, Delvine, MS 1505, fo. 153.
153. Ibid., SL1/1/50, fo. 120.
154. NLS MS 17539, fo. 136.
155. Fountainhall, Decisions, i, p. 621; see also Walker, Legal History of Scotland, v, pp. 402–3.
156. I am grateful to Dr A. L. Murray for reminding me of this reference and for providing information on macers generally.
157. AL, FR339r/1/1.
158. NRS, CS 1/13, fo. 142r.

9

Conclusion

Dined at Ilay Campbell's with a company to take leave of Mr Macqueen before he went to the bench. Baron Maule kept us all merry with his forcible humour and variety of anecdotes. I drank largely. Then went to Moncrieffe's, played at whist, and lost.[1]

The easiest way to become immersed in the community of the College of Justice is to read James Boswell's journals. A constant round of breakfasting, dining, tea drinking, theatre-going and overindulgence in wine, punctuated a life at the bar marked by personal relationships with fellow advocates, judges, agents, and others about the court. Rich as it is, however, Boswell's personal record remains but one perspective from thousands.

The character of the College was shaped not only by its more distinguished lawyers but by the writers, notaries and clerks who came to train within its precincts. In the absence of institutions such as a circuit mess or large provincial courts, it was from here and here alone that Scotland's legal culture radiated. Such centrality was an advantage; lawyers in England, by comparison, sometimes felt the lack of a single edifice which formed the centre of their professional community.[2] Members of the four Inns of Court in London could only envy the ability of the Scottish bar, through the dean of the Faculty of Advocates, to speak with one voice.[3]

From this centre, the College provided an example to provincial legal societies throughout Scotland for whom its practices set the standard. Local writers, notaries, messengers and clerks fell under the supervisory jurisdiction of the lords of session. In their pleadings, advocates compared the nefarious practices reportedly occurring in the inferior courts to what happened, or was supposed to happen, in the College. It was in Edinburgh, therefore, under the gaze of the lords of session, that the principles of ethical legal practice, such as they were, were laid down for the whole country.

In some cases, experienced College lawyers literally dictated the rules that were exported to local jurisdictions up and down the country. When the Duke of Montrose removed the sitting bailie of the regality of Lennox in 1713, his advocate, James Graham of Airth, detailed precisely how the new bailie should run the court.[4] A generation later, the law agent acting for James Graham's own son, William, looked to Edinburgh, in the shape of John Mackenzie WS, for advice on many points of legal practice. Mackenzie was a source of practical information on matters ranging from conveyancing to how Edinburgh inhabitants dealt with the new window tax.[5] Although the contemporary lawyer–client relationship does not fall within the scope of this work, the interaction of Edinburgh lawyers with provincial lawyers was of the utmost relevance in reinforcing the importance of the College as an institution. Many clients needed both a local lawyer (in William Graham's case, this was Robert Leckie) and a College member, like Mackenzie, to deal with their litigation in Edinburgh or, if a further appeal were involved, London.

At the same time as being a national institution, the College was strongly integrated into the fabric of Scotland's capital city. Its members actively contributed not only to the law but also to the cultural growth of Edinburgh, its administration, and its urban and economic development. This went beyond influencing the social calendar, buying property or lending weight to the proceedings of important trusts, intellectual societies and institutions. A great deal of legal business, from the hiring of writers for various offices to the giving of consultations by advocates, was undertaken in Edinburgh's coffee houses and taverns which reaped rewards from the influx of litigants. The College's lawyers, with other professional groups, made a significant contribution to creating a distinct middle-class identity in Edinburgh.[6] By the end of the eighteenth century, many advocates, like English barristers, might have identified themselves as a kind of 'gentlemanly bourgeoisie' though the high status of their 'noble office', as confirmed by centuries of *jus commune* literature, was something in which they had long revelled.[7] For their part, the College's agents and writers to the signet were particularly connected to Scotland's commercial life, drafting and negotiating for merchants as well as assisting them in managing their capital. Not only might they find a place for an apprentice writer as a favour for such a client but they might use them as contacts, as James Dundas WS did when, as a favour, he placed a young man in his client's Glasgow trading office.[8] Lawyers often provided a vital channel of communication between clients who were sometimes of very different backgrounds.

Within the College itself, different communities of interest generally found a workable balance that tended to minimise conflict between them. The WS Society is a good example. Collectively they had their long-standing rivalry with unlicensed Edinburgh agents and writers even if, individually, these were the very men with whom they were sometimes obliged to conduct a client's business. On the other hand, the Society developed a relationship of general co-operation and mutual support with the Faculty of Advocates, particularly in defence of shared College privileges. This rapport even led, in the 1770s, to a proposal that both groups might come together 'as brothers' and share the same library.[9] These attitudes reflected the professional priorities of the Society's members in whose interest it was to maintain good relations with the bar, as well as with the keepers, clerks and more junior office-holders about the court, while acting aggressively against those who challenged their privileged status.

The most enduring legacy of the professional culture of the College can be seen in the literature which it produced and preserved. This did not only include an increasing body of collected decisions of the court but encompassed a distinctive literature which, remaining under the influence of the continental tradition, was increasingly drawn towards London and the common law world. Besides foreign works amassed in personal libraries, the original works which emerged from the competitive atmosphere of the College, particularly those written by men outside the universities, such as Sir George Mackenzie, William Forbes (before 1714), Andrew Macdouall, Henry Home, Alexander Wight and (early in his career) George Joseph Bell, did much to develop the breadth of legal literature, often in pursuit of comparisons between Scots law and the law of England. The possibility of transmitting knowledge of Scots law to the educated layman, and to the English lawyer, had never been higher. A case can also be made that the lawyers in the College played a vital role in preserving Scotland's public records for posterity. It can also be argued that the College, in its provision of legal aid to the poor, was an institution whose members demonstrated a strong social conscience even if this is sometimes overshadowed by their zeal to defend their own privileges.

THE WIDER SIGNIFICANCE OF COLLEGE MEMBERS

It has not been possible in this book to discuss in any depth the significance of the College as an arena within which Scottish politics took place. This is an important dimension of the communities within the College, not only because of the ubiquity of patronage but also because lawyers and judges had a very important role in the conduct of politics and the development of electoral law. Some of them, including most notably Alexander Wight, developed the latter as a particular specialism.

Evidence drawn from Charles Adam's *Political State of Scotland* (compiled about 1788) shows that 129 advocates controlled 221 electoral votes, representing 7.9 per cent of all votes in the country.[10] Samuel Mitchelson WS, by then appointed a clerk of session (in 1789), held superiorities entitling him to vote in Orkney, Caithness, Midlothian, Peeblesshire, Renfrewshire, Dumfriesshire and Lanarkshire.[11] In total, College members (past or present) held 381 direct votes, constituting 14.3 per cent of all the votes that could be cast across the country.[12] This does not include thirty-nine votes held by Edinburgh writers or sixty-six votes held by men described as writers in general, nor does it fully reflect the state of things, because many College members had considerable 'interest', that is, the ability to influence other freeholders who would look to them for guidance on political matters.[13] In short, as a grouping, College members collectively had substantial political weight even though, in party terms, they did not all travel in the same political direction.

Their importance did not stop at possessing votes. As landowners, they also created votes and played an important role in elections, the more controversial of which led to litigation.[14] Entire volumes of session papers from the later eighteenth century consist of nothing but election cases where the underlying legal issues routinely related to the question of voter qualification.[15] Meetings of freeholders, convened by the local sheriff-depute (who, from 1748, was always an advocate), were supposed to determine who enjoyed the right to vote but such meetings were not always conducted impartially.[16] Kenneth Mackenzie reported a heated parliamentary election in Edinburgh in 1728 where three men, including the lord president and his nephew, were rejected from the electoral roll. The decision seemed inconsistent with the treatment of others in similar circumstances, and Mackenzie commented drily that 'it was show me the man & I'll show you the Law'.[17] In the same letter, he noted that a great many gentlemen had left the College to go to the country to make their presence felt at the elections where, no doubt, in doing so they would generate further business for the bar.

Much more could be said about politics and patronage within the College. The key point is that there was no uniform political outlook among the membership despite the oaths many had to swear. It was an institution that could readily absorb Jacobite and Hanoverian, Whig and Tory. While its membership formed no political bloc, historians use appointments to the bench as an index of the political influence of the governing party.[18] The private rivalries and quarrels of College members rarely became public; the most famous instance probably occurred when, in 1796, Henry Erskine was ousted as dean of Faculty by his political rivals.[19] Appointment to any office in the College required the swearing of an oath of allegiance to the incumbent monarch, together with an oath to abjure allegiance to the Pretender and to do everything in one's power to support the Hanoverian succession.[20] Few seem to have baulked at this, in contrast to the political difficulties experienced at the bar in the 1670s.[21] In addition, judges, advocates and agents took the oath *de fideli administratione*. Judges swore 'to maintain the priviledges of the House'; others, like the advocate Philip Anstruther, on taking office as a PCS, swore the same oath as new advocates took 'to be obedient to the lords and to maintain the privileges of the College of Justice in his station'.[22] Promotion to the bench increasingly depended on service as a Crown law officer or on prior judicial experience as a commissary or sheriff-depute; and those with such experience were generally those whose loyalty to the state was least subject to question. Ultimately, however, self-interest dictated that all members, whenever necessary, would set aside competing loyalties to fulfil their oath to defend the privileges of the College.

THE COMMUNITY OF THE COLLEGE

Our theme has been that of the College as a community composed of lesser communities. Each community, and individuals across those communities, were tied together by familial, cultural, financial and professional bonds. An examination of any writer's account books, for example, demonstrates how much one individual relied on agents, advocates, clerks and keepers to continue in business. Thomas Tod WS carefully recorded debts he owed to writers for work they had done for him, and those who owed him for work he had done for them; payments to the keepers of Parliament House, and sums, such as that owed by the advocate William Wallace in 1778, which Tod later included among his 'desperate debts'.[23] The writer John Mair recorded making a loan of 5 shillings to the macer Francis Gibb in July 1758, which Gibb repaid in December; Mair was also lending money for John White DCS, on behalf of White's sisters, and paying ancillary accounts, such as that he held with the bookseller William Miller.[24] Another writer, William Leggat, kept many receipts and discharges. He even retained his invitation (from January 1704) to accompany the corpse of the advocate James Stewart, late town clerk of Edinburgh, from the Tron church, passing by the College to its final resting place in Greyfriars.[25]

Like any institution, the College ultimately relied on people and personal relationships, and the contexts within which those people lived are important in understanding how the institution operated. Those people did not leave their roots behind and maintained their local connections. Judges and lawyers, in particular, often held local office as justices of the peace, returning home regularly to their sphere of influence from where many of their clients were drawn. Simultaneously, as a result of their vocations, they had joined the 'artificial society' of the College, a society that allowed them to create new networks of personal contacts which themselves then spread out from Edinburgh in all directions.[26]

For advocates and writers to the signet who wished to progress, getting to know the College's social scene was a necessity. Even in retirement, men liked to keep up with developments. John Mackenzie PCS, having retired to his estate in Ross-shire, was kept informed (and supplied with the *Caledonian Mercury* and much else besides) by his former servant, Thomas Bruce.[27]

Bruce worked in the writing chamber of Mackenzie's son, Alexander, who had succeeded his father as a PCS in 1718. Bruce, at least when Alexander was absent, provided the retired Mackenzie with private news about engagements, elopements and the health or whereabouts of old friends. Others did the same. James Edgar, for instance, let Mackenzie know in October 1727 that Thomas Gibson WS, a recently appointed PCS, was 'throng in courting Collonel Dalzells only daughter', Jean.[28]

Humanity, and human frailty, are evident everywhere in the closely packed atmosphere of the College and the dirty tenements of the Old Town. Even advocates, on the way to their library in the late 1660s, had to suffer the indignity of trudging through 'a filthy Jack of nestiness' and piled-up rubbish.[29] This could lead, as we have seen, to heightened tensions, arguments and questionable conduct. For example, James Halyburton WS, as bailie-depute of the sanctuary of Holyrood abbey, was condemned in 1740 for his greed in charging an exorbitant 'booking fee' to those unfortunates, including fellow College members like James Justice PCS, forced to resort there seeking refuge from creditors.[30]

THE SOCIAL COMMUNITY

Contemporary judgements about a man's honesty or ability could be withering. The judge James Erskine of Grange SCJ was particularly scathing in private about some leading members of the bar who appeared before him.[31] As well as identifying the good and able lawyers, he pointed out the obstinate, shy, pedantic, stupid and untrustworthy as well as those whose fondness for drink had robbed them of all authority. For advocates, ability could compensate for some character flaws in ways that social prominence could not. Grange's view of Sir James Naysmith, for example, that he was 'tricky to the last degree', did not mean he lacked employment. Sir Patrick Home, though 'very dull & stupid', was one of those advocates who 'sticks at nothing'. This was a genre. Men of the stamp of Alexander Lockhart, at least early in his career, took up causes others might find distasteful – the actions, as Kames would have it, 'of rascals'. According to Lord Cockburn, John Haggart was in the same mould, gaining success only through 'degrading his profession by the ardent patronage of any villainy, against any worth'.[32] This 'ruined him for respectable practice' though he was another who was never short of clients. A man of apparently gross manners, Haggart was the most successful of the 'Itch Club', a group of 'unemployed middle-aged disreputables' within the Faculty who, when Cockburn was a young advocate, frequented their own recess on the west side of the Outer House. The nicknames, the subgroups, the everyday familiarities of practitioners, were all part of the living atmosphere of the College, recollected in part by the pens of Boswell, Scott and Cockburn. Forgotten aspects of the character and culture of the College are beyond reconstruction though hints of it appear in songs and poems and collections such as the *Court of Session Garland*.

In these and other sources, judges comprise another group that does not escape comment. Some faced the charge of stupidity even if it was brought from a safe distance by men with an axe to grind. To Cockburn's attack on Lord Polkemmet's lack of intellect (see p. 92), might be added Colin Mackenzie's view of him as being 'totally devoid of talents', a man promoted in 1793 only because of the influence of the Earl of Roslyn.[33] Polkemmet had been sheriff of Linlithgowshire though his practice at the bar was never extensive. On the other hand, both of these commentators regarded Lord Bannatyne positively, not for his abilities but for his good nature. According to Cockburn, he was the best sleeper in the court, habitually rising early in the morning the better to enable him to nap while on the bench.[34] A number of judges, like Duncan Forbes and George Fergusson, were renowned heavy drinkers. Some promising advocates, such as Andrew Crosbie and Otho Herman Wemyss, who might have reached the bench, eventually fell from business through alcoholism and ended their days in poverty. Physical changes wrought by alcoholism were obvious to contemporaries; some advocates are described as 'hungry' or 'mean' looking; some were indolent; for some, their legal knowledge did not compensate for their lack of oratory or presence. Robert Bennet, for some years dean of Faculty, was in Lord Grange's opinion 'of mean appearance', and a poor speaker, and both traits affected his standing. Thomas McGrugor, according to Cockburn, even had the look of a beggar.[35]

A COMMUNITY OF PATRONAGE

The propensity of men to make judgements about others is obviously relevant to the dispensing of patronage within the College. Space has not allowed a wider consideration of this subject, yet patronage was ubiquitous, drawing men closer to senior College members as well as influential men in Edinburgh, London and elsewhere, however tenuous their personal connection. The relationships which depended upon patronage, and those who relied on patrons, demonstrate another dimension of the College's social community, one that is worth briefly exploring by reference to the writer turned advocate, John Pattison.

In 1793 Pattison, with the support of Henry Dundas, had been elected assessor to Edinburgh town council, replacing John Swinton who had become sheriff-depute of Berwickshire. Since then, Pattison had sought to further his career through his connection to the council. His dedication was recognised in 1805 when he was twice awarded 30 guineas, first, on a motion by the lord provost, for his 'great attention ... to the occasional business in the council chamber', and subsequently for the 'extra trouble' to which he had been put in devoting 'a great portion of his time in advising causes before the magistrates'.[36] The committee which supported this second payment, which was made in October, also recommended that the magistrates use their interest with the government to procure him a commissaryship, sheriffship or any other office consistent with his honour. This latter payment appears to have been consolatory, for Pattison had been overlooked as a replacement for George Wallace, a commissary court judge, who had died in March 1805.[37]

Pattison had suffered other disappointments in his quest for a commissary-ship. Not only had he hoped to replace Archibald Campbell of Succoth (on what turned out to be a false rumour of him obtaining a sheriffship) but he had negotiated with another commissary, John Anstruther, on the chance that the latter might join the Court of Exchequer.[38] This also miscarried but Pattison, once again, had lobbied Dundas. His wife, Mary, was unable to discover whether Dundas had supported him and, on soliciting an associate of the Duke of Buccleuch to approach Dundas, she was told that the council had more say with him even than Buccleuch did. She thereupon wrote to the provost in 1807, reminding him that

> Mr Patison was bred an advocate, so that he can neither turn his hand to another business, nor can he obtain the smallest assistance, either from a clerk or partner & you must have access to know that suppose Mr Patison has possession of his intellects as well as ever, yet that owing to the severe disease with which he was many years ago afflicted, he yet speaks with the greatest difficulty, and of consequence must in a great measure be deprived of his business as a Barrister.[39]

Mrs Pattison, the daughter of an Edinburgh minister, was well informed. She had it on good authority that Archibald Campbell was to replace Lord Dunsinnan on the bench in the approaching winter session (November 1807). In fact, Dunsinnan's retirement was postponed though her information was correct because this succession took place in 1809. Her letter is tinged with desperation, being written on behalf of her large family and because her husband was 'very backward in speaking for himself'. Her personal acquain-tance with the provost gave her confidence that he and his colleagues would send their recommendation to Dundas. This they duly did, with a copy of her letter.

This episode demonstrates the importance of inside knowledge, gleaned from social contact within the College but relevant to a wider circle which included the great and the good within Edinburgh. Mary Pattison's inter-vention, though heartfelt, failed: the next vacant commissaryship went to Sir Thomas Kirkpatrick, twelve years Pattison's junior at the bar.[40] Pattison's professional disadvantages were highlighted in a broadside reproduced in *The Court of Session Garland*, and his failure to speak up for himself was damaging.[41] In a similar vein, Erskine of Grange regarded another advocate, Alexander McLeod, as being 'so excessively modest that he is even bashfull and that makes him too litle forward'.[42] This was simply not the kind of thing which a patron wanted to hear.

THE COLLEGE AS AN INSTITUTION

The College was a unique institution and bore only superficial similarities to other types of communities in the medieval and early modern world. Like universities, for example, it contained distinct groups (academics, faculties, students, printers) whose privileges and exemptions varied. A town council, composed of members of the different communities of tradesmen and merchants whom it represented, had a superficial similarity in appearance though not in function. Even by contemporary standards, the College was in no sense democratic. It did contain checks and balances, such as the arrangements that existed with the town council for creating leets in the appointment of the keepers of Parliament House and some of the university professors.

Comparison with the Royal College of Physicians, or Edinburgh's incorporation of surgeons, illustrates as many differences as similarities. The surgeons were not incorporated nationally, but locally. The Edinburgh barber-surgeons had been incorporated by a seal of cause ratified by James IV in 1506 and were taxed like any other incorporation.[43] The physicians, whose college was incorporated by royal charter in 1681, established a regulatory structure with similarities to that of the Faculty of Advocates. It even licensed provincial physicians who sought to practise outside Edinburgh, just as the judges in the College of Justice licensed notaries public. Like the College's lawyers, physicians and surgeons offered services to the poor for free. These organisations, however, did not share the same great diversity of membership as the College. No two professional groups had a greater rivalry than the physicians and surgeons and, while the difference in social status in both callings echoes the different social status of the advocate and the writer, the latter roles did not involve the same fundamental clash of interests. That is why no single college existed for both physicians and surgeons.

The College of Justice had even less similarity to any of the English Inns of Court, particularly because they were separate institutions from the courts of justice. Traditionally, once a man was promoted to the rank of serjeant (a requirement for promotion to the English common law courts) he was required to leave his inn and he would normally enter Serjeants' Inn.[44] Although inns had different ranks of inhabitants, they also had rules and social requirements, including compulsory attendance at dinners, which the

College did not have and, for attorneys, membership of an inn was unimportant after the 1729 Attorney Act.[45] Unlike the College of Advocates in England (known as Doctors' Commons), the College of Justice had no single treasurer and no single budget though both organisations did contain a mix of legal practitioners and non-practitioners.[46] Moreover, in England the ecclesiastical Court of Arches contained advocates who never became members of Doctors' Commons, while this was not true of the College of Justice in which all advocates had to be members of the Faculty. In the eighteenth century, the English institutions had largely become social clubs. The members of the College of Justice, however, did not participate in a communal social life; they socialised heavily but generally with men of similar rank. A macer would not appear at a judge's dinner table, though both were College members; an advocate or leading WS, on the other hand, might do so regularly.

For all the differences between English and Scottish legal practice, there were similarities, and Berlanstein's study of the eighteenth-century bar in Toulouse also reveals some startling parallels, particularly in regard to the functioning of the bar and the process of obtaining clients and gaining a foothold in legal practice.[47] Men appear to have achieved eminence in Toulouse at an earlier age than in Scotland but the overall pattern, the gaining of reputation primarily through printed pleadings, and the tendency of leaders at the bar to dominate for long periods, can be compared directly to Edinburgh even if the architecture of the French legal system itself was quite different.

The history of the *Parlement of Paris* is also well documented and raises some parallels. Lord Swinton regarded the foundation of the College in 1532, and aspects of its later history, as having been strongly influenced by the example of Paris. Given the history of relations with France in the later eighteenth century, it is hardly surprising that he regarded this as an aberration because, in his view, 'our sister kingdom' of England had a legal constitution 'much more similar to ours'.[48] Letters of *commitimus*, for example, allowed those who held them (including *avocats*, *procureurs* and *huissiers*, broadly equivalent to advocates, writers to the signet, licensed agents and macers) the right to have any actions concerning them removed from inferior courts and heard exclusively in the Parlement. An annual oath was sworn by the *avocats* and the *procureurs* in the *parlement* and there is evidence of a similar oath being taken by College members each year. The Parlement, however, had no direct equivalent to the Faculty of Advocates. The Order of Barristers was a larger and different kind of organisation with a different culture though it was the product of the desire of members of the bar to come together to defend their interests against the magistrates. This bears similarities to the struggles in seventeenth-century Scotland between the College and Edinburgh, on the one hand, and the Faculty and the bench on the other.[49] The political role of the barristers in the Parlement in the eighteenth century was even more fraught. While the contextual differences are such that it may prove impossible for political historians to find useful parallels between Jansenism and Jacobitism in the respective institutional histories of the Parlement and the College, the attempt would be interesting.

Swinton's remark about England's constitution raises one last reflection about the College. It is how much historians still have to learn about social and political attitudes, about life in general, from the legal pleadings of eighteenth-century Scotland. These monuments to generations of lawyers, sometimes beautifully written, often carefully researched, have been relatively untouched by historians.[50] Some have a freshness, humour and vibrancy that transmit the personality, wit and professional culture of the men who wrote them.

BEYOND 1808

In 1808 the Court of Session was reorganised in a way that led those most familiar with its practices 'to growl at the spirit of innovation'.[51] What was lost? The collegiate nature of the court was retained and has been to this day. Nor, until the 1850s, did the voluminous session papers diminish. The structural changes did mean, however, that the collective sitting of all the judges in the Inner House was no longer the norm. As we have seen, those judges who could not stand each other, such as Hermand and Meadowbank, could now largely be kept apart and prevented from haranguing or interrupting each other.

A key thing that was not lost, at least not immediately, was the privileged status of College members. In a case brought by William Jamieson WS in 1815, the court determined that a legislative provision, whereby cases worth less than £25 had to be heard in an inferior court, did not affect the privilege of College members of having any action concerning them heard before the lords.[52] This case, representing 'settled law', provided strong legal authority.[53] Specific privileges, however, were slowly removed by statute, while the rest appear simply to have fallen into desuetude.[54] This was something the editor of Erskine's *Institutes*, the advocate Alexander MacAllan, thought inevitable in 1837 because 'taxing the inhabitants of a place for the general interest unequally' was unjustifiable.[55] After the wider political reforms of 1832, this could not have seemed otherwise.

The main difficulty in preserving the sense of community within the College was the expansion of Edinburgh, once the extended royalty was built and those who worked in the College no longer lived within easy reach of the court precincts. This came in tandem with the continuing growth in size of a College membership that was, in numerical terms, to become increasingly dominated by writers and agents. The advocates, so long the largest single group in the College, yielded that position towards the end of the eighteenth century never to regain it. Nonetheless, the advocates preserved their corporate spirit and have continued to hold a position of national prominence within Scots law. Beside them stands (in Edinburgh, of course) the Law Society of Scotland, a creature of statute, and the local societies of procurators, advocates, and law agents that have grown organically over centuries. These local societies today have their own communities of lawyers, sheriff-clerks and other court officers. In these institutions, it is to be hoped, future generations will retain something of the uniqueness of Scottish legal practice that will always be associated with the community of the College of Justice.

NOTES

1. Milne, ed., *Boswell's Edinburgh Journals*, p. 277 (6 Dec. 1776).
2. J. Finlay, 'Lawyers in the British Isles', in B. Dölemeyer et al., eds, *Anwälte und ihre Geschichte* (Tübingen, 2011), pp. 1109–13.
3. For dissent recorded in the Faculty minutes, see Stewart, ed., *Min. Bk, 1751–1783*, p. xxxvi.
4. NRS, GD220/5/1711/21.
5. NLS, Airth papers, MS 10862, fo. 203r.
6. S. Nenadic, 'The rise of the urban middle class' in T. M. Devine and R. Mitchison, eds, *People and Society in Scotland* (3 vols, 1988–90), i, p. 111.
7. Cf. Lemmings, *Professors of the Law*, pp. 312–13.
8. GCA, Stirling of Keir papers, T–SK 18/9/28.
9. NLS, Delvine, MS 1493, fo. 9. Various schemes of co-operation were mooted during the century, e.g. Ballantyne, *Signet Library*, pp. 29, 69.
10. See, generally, Adam, *View of the Political State of Scotland*.
11. J. Fergusson, 'Making interest in Scottish County Elections', *SHR* 26 (1947), 119 at 122.
12. Twelve lords of session, between them, had twenty-four votes and to this may be added the 109 votes held by seventy-six writers to the signet. The six PCSs, of whom two were advocates and the remainder writers, shared nineteen votes (eight of which were held by Charles Gordon WS).
13. Six Edinburgh writers listed by Adam were College agents (not including David Ross who, though listed, was dead, or James Fogo who had two votes but was not admitted to the College until 1794). This includes James Bremner, whose qualification to vote in Perthshire, was questionable because he was deputy solicitor of stamps.
14. For example, the vote Lord Alva made for his son-in-law, Peter Tytler, in Stirling in 1793. This involved assigning a life-rent and purchasing land to

make up the nominal qualification of £400 annual rent: NLS, Erskine-Murray papers, MS 5085, fo. 35r.

15. Signet Library papers receive analysis in W. Ferguson, 'Electoral Law and procedure in eighteenth and early nineteenth century Scotland' (PhD Thesis, University of Glasgow, 1957).

16. For voter qualification, see W. Ferguson, *Scotland: 1689 to the Present* (Edinburgh, 1968), p. 134.

17. NLS, Delvine, MS 1209, fo. 190.

18. For example, Shaw, *Management of Scottish Society*, p. 53.

19. Omond, *Lord Advocates of Scotland*, ii, pp. 167–9. Party politics was normally thought irrelevant in such elections.

20. J. S. Shaw, The *Political History of Eighteenth-century Scotland* (Basingstoke, 1999), pp. 90–1.

21. Simpson, 'The advocates as trade union pioneers', p. 169.

22. NRS, CS1/15, fo. 24r; CS1/11, fo. 29r; GD1/337/40/2. The lords took their oath to preserve the College's privileges seriously, e.g. *Acts of Sederunt*, p. 268.

23. Ibid., Leith-Buchanan papers, GD47/1241/17, 18, 25, 46.

24. Ibid., John Mair, writer, memorandum book, RH15/134, fos 3, 6, 9, 11.

25. NRS, papers of William Leggat, RH15/136.

26. Cf. Ives, *The Common Lawyers of Pre-Reformation England*, p. 381.

27. NLS, Delvine, MS 1110, fos 11–28, 45–85. Bruce became a DCS in 1746.

28. Ibid., fo. 114. Gibson subsequently married her.

29. AL, FR339r/14, Representation of William Blackwood, 1719.

30. ALSP, *Information for George Hamilton of Redhouse*, 8 Dec. 1740, Elchies collection, vol. 14 (F–Y), no. 22. The bailie-depute employed a clerk to enter the names of new entrants to the sanctuary.

31. NRS, Rose of Kilravock papers, GD125/15/981.

32. Miller, *Cockburn's Millenium*, p. 311.

33. BL, Althorp, G/64.

34. Others fell asleep during pleadings, e.g. George Buchan, when principal clerk of the Teind Court, was described as 'drowsy at the clerk's table in the Inner House, at the course of a pleading', suddenly awakening when the pleading ended: ALSP, *Hugh Buchan writer in Edinburgh* (*supra*, p. 71, n. 108), p. 62.

35. Miller, *Cockburn's Millennium*, p. 314.

36. TCM, SL1/1/141, fo. 248; SL1/1/144, fo. 244. For his election as assessor, see SL1/1/122, fo. 156.

37. Wallace was replaced by John Gordon, advocate.

38. Anstruther became sheriff-depute of Fife on 7 March 1811: NRS, great seal register, CS3/23, no. 8.

39. TCM, SL1/1/150, fo. 34.

40. NRS, great seal register, C3/17, fo. 321. Kirkpatrick was later sheriff-depute of Dumfries: ibid., C3/23, no. 10.

41. *Court of Session Garland*, p. 50.
42. NRS, Mar and Kellie papers, GD124/15/981.
43. This paragraph relies on H. Dingwall, *Physicians, Surgeons and Apothecaries* (East Linton, 1995), esp. pp. 6–7, 34–7, 109–14,
44. Baker, *Order of Serjeants*, p. 84.
45. Brooks, *Lawyers, Litigation and English Society*, p. 133.
46. G. D. Squibb, *Doctors' Commons* (Oxford, 1977), pp. 16–24.
47. Berlanstein, *Barristers of Toulouse*, pp. 11–23.
48. J. Swinton, *Considerations concerning a Proposal for Dividing the Court of Session into Classes or Chambers* (Edinburgh, 1789), p. 13; for comment, see C. Kidd, *Subverting Scotland's Past*, p. 164.
49. See Lang, *Mackenzie*, chapter 9; Simpson, 'The advocates as Scottish trade union pioneers', pp. 169–76.
50. Cf. A. Stewart, 'The Session Papers in the Advocates Library' in H. L. MacQueen, ed., *Miscellany IV* (Stair Society, Edinburgh, 2002), pp. 199–224.
51. The phrase is Cockburn's, cited by Thomson, 'The old fifteen', p. 244.
52. *William Jamieson, WS, Petr,* 21 Feb. 1815, F.C., no. lx.
53. *Bruce* v. *Clyne* 5 (1833) *The Scottish Jurist*, p. 197, no. 144.
54. For example, exemption from paying assessments levied 'for the Relief of the Poor' was not given under 8 and 9 Vict. c. 83, s. 50, despite the WS Society's objections: *History of the WS Society*, pp. 440–1.
55. J. Erskine, *An Institute of the Law of Scotland*, ed., A. Macallan (Edinburgh, 1838), I.3.17, n. 1.

Appendix 1

Figure 1 *Officer-holders admitted as Edinburgh burgesses, 1700–99*[1]

Office-holders	*Number*[2]
Advocates	121
Barons of Exchequer	7
Depute clerk on the bills	1
Depute clerks of session	5
Depute keeper of the session house	1
Deputy king's remembrancer in Exchequer	1
Director of HM Chancery	2
Keeper of the Advocates Library	2
King's remembrancer in Exchequer	1
Lord Clerk Register	1
Macer to the Lord High Chancellor	2
Macers in the court of session	4
Macers in the High Court	2
Ordinary lords of session	16
Principal clerk of the bills	1
Principal clerks of session	5
Professors of Law	2
Servant to a baron of exchequer	1
Servant to Lord High Chancellor	1
Servants to advocates	21
Servants to lords of session	27
Servants to writers to the signet	1
Writers in Edinburgh	209
Writers to the signet	56
Total	**490**

Figure 2 *Officer-holders, admitted to office 1700–99 admitted burgesses[3]*

Office-holders	Number	Total (percentage)[4]
Advocates	96	722 (13.3)[5]
Depute clerk of session	1	22 (4.5)
Ordinary lords of session	5	54 (9.2)[6]
Principal clerk of session	2	26 (7.7)
Writers to the signet	45	556 (8.1)
Total	159	1385 (11.5)

Figure 3 *College members and writers as kirk session elders 1701–20*

1701–20	Advocate	WS	DCS	CoJ	Writer	Combined[7]
NW parish	4	1	0	5	17	22 (18.3%)
NK parish	4	11	0	15	5	20 (16.7%)
NE parish	0	5	0	6	8	14 (11.7%)
SE parish	6	7	0	13	7	20 (16.7%)
SSE parish	1	0	0	1	1	2 (1.7%)
SK parish	5	8	0	13	4	17 (14.25%)
SW parish	1	0	1	2	14	16 (13.3%)
NNK parish	8	6	0	14	12	26 (21.6%)
No. of individuals	17	10	1	28	21	49
Years of service[8]	29 (3%)	36 (4.1%)	3 (0.3%)	71 (7.4%)	68 (7.1%)	139 (14.5%)

Figure 4 *Members of selected intellectual clubs and societies in Edinburgh[9]*

Office-holders	RC	SS	PC	RSE	PS
Advocates	8	62	22	39	24
Ordinary lords of session	3	19	8	18	10
Barons of exchequer	0	4	3	4	1
Writers to the signet	0	1	2	3	2
Principal clerks of session	0	0	1	1	0
Writers	0	6	0	1	2
College of Justice members[10]	11	82	33	61	36
Total	11	92	36	66	39

KEY

RC: Rankenian Club (1717)
SS: Select Society (1754)
PC: Poker Club (1762)

RSE: Royal Society of Edinburgh (1783)
PS: Philosophical Society (1737)

NOTES

1. Data extracted from the published Rolls of Edinburgh Burgesses. Table 1 measures those made burgess between 1700 and 1799 regardless of when they gained office; Table 2 counts those who gained office in the period 1700–99 who were made burgess regardless of when admission as burgess took place.
2. This figure counts each individual once. Lords of session are counted only if they were on the bench when admitted burgesses, otherwise they count as advocates. Likewise are counted advocates any, like William Crosse and Hercules Lindsay, who became professors after admission as burgesses. The number of writers to the signet excludes those holding another office such as DCS or deputy remembrancer. The dates are inclusive. Barons and exchequer staff are added for comparison; they were not members of the College of Justice.
3. This table includes only key College office holders admitted within those dates. Some in this group were made burgesses after 1799. Lords of session are included by date of elevation (some were burgesses before elevation); clerks of session are included by date of admission to clerkship. The dates at which servants and others became employed are usually not known; likewise, there is no list of writers completing their apprenticeships.
4. The total number admitted to the particular office in the period 1700–99 with, in brackets, the percentage of that total admitted burgesses of Edinburgh.
5. 727 advocates were admitted but five became burgesses as lords of session.
6. Seventy-eight ordinary lords of session were elevated but twenty-four of those were admitted burgess while advocates and are counted as such here.
7. This column counts writers as well as College members. Each parish elected 120 elders during this period (although only 958 accepted office). Each elder selected a deacon but no College member or writer was a deacon in this sample.
8. The figure in brackets represents the percentage of total service as elders by the forty-nine elders of the combined eight parishes.
9. The lords of session column refers to advocates who at any time were elevated to the bench. The numbers in this row have not been deducted from the numbers in the advocates' row. Likewise, three of the barons were advocates and these have not been subtracted from the number in the advocates' row. Resident members of the Royal Society 1783–89 have been included only but no members of any group counted as non-resident or foreign members of that society. Although Emerson gives sixty-one advocates as members of the Select Society, there appear to be sixty-two.
10. Barons of Exchequer from 1708 had equivalent privileges to College members but were not themselves part of the College: 6 Ann. c.26, s.11.

Appendix 2

EDINBURGH TOWN CLERKS AND AGENTS, 1687–1808

Town clerks 1687–1808

Name	Admission	Remarks
Sir James Rocheid	–	Died in November 1692.
Aeneas McLeod (joint)	1687	
James Stewart, advocate	16 September 1696	Joint interim town clerk with John Murray.
John Murray, advocate	16 September 1696	Joint interim office-holder with James Stewart.
George Home	23 April 1699	Joint town clerk with Aeneas McLeod (following McLeod court case).
James Stewart, advocate	18 September 1699	Joint town Cler with George Home, following resignation of McLeod. Resigned 5 January 1704.
Adam Watt, advocate	7 January 1704	Adm. advocate 19 June 1696; Admitted NP, 15 February 1704. Died 21 November 1736.
George Irving WS	18 September 1728	Writer in Edinburgh. Admitted NP, 22 July 1708. Writer in town clerks' chamber, before March 1712. Nominated to succeed Watt on 2 November 1720. Elected clerk to the barony of Calton, 20 January 1725. Becomes conjoined in Watt's clerkship on 18 Septemberr 1728; succeeds him in 1736.
Matthew Brown, DCS	–	Nominated to succeed Home on 2 November 1720. Never did so. Mooted as agent for the University of Glasgow.

Name	Admission	Remarks
Joseph Williamson, advocate	25 June 1742	Replaced the late George Irving WS.
William Forbes WS	15 July 1742	Conjoined with Williamson. Demits office, reserving his fees for life, 4 May 1763.
George Lindsay	4 May 1763	Admitted NP, 25 February 1736. Appointed depute clerk of Edinburgh, 11 August 1736. Nominated to be conjunct principal clerk on next vacancy in 1760 but this was anulled, 4 August 1762. Elected principal clark of Edinburgh, 4 May 1763.
John Dundas WS	13 February 1771	Replaced the late George Lindsay as joint principal clerk.
John Gray WS	24 November 1784	Resigned 4 February 1807.
Charles Cunningham (later WS)	–	Nominated to succeed his uncle, John Gray WS, 4 February 1807, when Gray resigned in favour of both men and the survivor. Acted as assistant joint clerk prior to this, along with Adam Bruce.

Depute town clerks

Name	Admission	Remarks
James Naysmith	–	Appointed before 1696. Sole holder of office until 1736. Died *c.*1742.
George Lindsay, writer in Edinburgh	11 August 1736	Conjoined with Naysmith. Engrossed in the record 26 August 1737. Admitted NP, 5 February 1737. Clerk of the bailie court from 1755. Known to be married to Christine Tytler in 1757. Elected principal clerk in 1763.
James Tait, writer in Edinburgh	4 May 1763	Conjoint with Duncan. Son of James Tait, Edinburgh goldsmith. Admitted NP, 8 August 1763. Clerk of the Canongate, 23 August 1780. Resigned this post and reappointed jointly with John MacRitchie in July 1794. Died 5 February 1798.

Name	Admission	Remarks
Alexander Duncan WS	4 May 1763	Conjoint with Tait. Resigned in April 1782 but reappointed. Resigned in January 1807 but reappointed jointly with Alexander Callender.
James Laing, writer in Edinburgh	30 August 1780	Writer in the Canongate. Variously clerk of Canongate, one of the extractors in the bailie court, clerk of police. Resigned in April 1782 but reappointed. Died in office in 1806, son, James jr (solicitor at law, procurator in the bailie court), shortly thereafter applied unsuccessfully for an office in the gift of the city.

Town agents

Name	Admission	Remarks
James Hamilton WS	26 June 1689	Town clerk with James Rocheid, 1685.
John Campbell WS	1697	Died in office in April 1699.
Ronald Campbell WS	12 May 1699	Died in office on 30 August 1726; depute director of chancery, 1724.
George Irving WS	7 September 1726	See entry as town clerk.
Ronald Dunbar WS	25 June 1742	Writer in Edinburgh; admitted NP, 8 January 1726 and WS, 27 January 1729. Died 23 December 1753.
John Davidson WS	2 January 1754	Son of Edinburgh bookseller. Writer in Edinburgh; admitted NP, 23 February 1742 and WS, 3 April 1749. Died 29 December 1797.
John MacRitchie, writer in Edinburgh	6 December 1797	Enters partnership with James Little before 1806. Died 2 November 1838.

Appendix 3

LEADERS OF THE BAR[1]

1701		OH	Adm.	Bench
1	Cunningham, William	106	1694	
2	Grant, Francis	101	1691	SCJ, 1709
3	Ferguson, Alexander of Isle	70	1686	
4	Ferguson, John	68	1681	
5	Calderwood, William	67	1687	SCJ, 1711
6	Fraser, Robert	63	1686	
7	Bennet, Robert	61	1672	
8	Black, William	60	1692	
9	Alexander, Robert*	53	1690	
10	Carnegie, Mungo	50	1691	

Ave experience: 13 years

1711		OH	Adm.	Bench
1	Boswell, James	97	1698	
2	Graham, James of Airth	95	1698	
3	Stewart, Walter	95	1698	
4	Ferguson, Alexander of Isle	75	1686	
5	Calderwood, William	61	1687	SCJ, 1711
6	Ferguson, James of Barrifurrow (senior)	58	1697	
7	Fleming, John of Polcalk	58	1694	
8	Fraser, Robert	58	1686	
9	Horne, John	57	1691	
10	Black, William	53	1692	

Ave experience: 17.3 years

1721		OH	Adm.	Bench
1	Hay, Alexander	130	1697	
2	Boswell, James	128	1698	
3	Graham, James, of Airth	112	1698	
4	Horne, John	79	1691	
5	McDouall, Andrew	54	1708	SCJ, 1755
6	Areskine, Charles	63	1711	SCJ, 1744
7	Hamilton, Archibald, of Dalserf	50	1690	
8	Forbes, John	56	1713	
9	Fleming, John of Polcalk	67	1694	
10	Forbes, Duncan	62	1709	LP, 1737

Ave experience: 18.1 years

1731		OH	Adm.	Bench
1	Boswell James*	121	1698	
2	Mcdouall, Andrew	96	1708	SCJ, 1755
3	Grant, Patrick	94	1712	SCJ, 1732
4	Graham, James of Airth (senior)	79	1698	
5	Forbes, John	65	1713	
6	Dalrymple, Hugh (i.e. Hugh Murray Kynnynmond)	63	1718	
7	Garden, Alexander	58	1712	
8	Craigie, Robert	53	1710	LP, 1754
9	Hay, Alexander (senior)	50	1697	
10	Horne, John	44	1691	

Ave experience: 24.3 years

1741		OH	Adm.	Bench
1	Home, Henry	120	1723	SCJ, 1752
2	Lockhart, Alexander	107	1723	SCJ, 1775
3	McDouall, Andrew	105	1708	SCJ, 1755
4	Hay, Thomas	76	1726	SCJ, 1754
5	Grant, William	75	1722	SCJ, 1754
6	Forbes, Hew	60	1728	
7	Ferguson, James of Pitfour	58	1722	SCJ, 1764
8	Murray Kynnynmond, Hugh	58 (1)	1718	
9	McLeod, John	48 (1)	1710	
10	Graham, James jr	45	1723	SCJ, 1749

Ave experience: 19.7 years

1751		OH	Adm.	Bench
1	Lockhart, Alexander	91	1723	SCJ, 1775
2	Hay, Thomas, of Huntingdon	87	1726	SCJ, 1754
3	Home, Henry	79	1723	SCJ, 1752
4	Miller, Thomas	55	1742	LJC, 1766
5	Ferguson, James of Pitfour	55	1722	SCJ, 1764
6	Boswell, Alexander	48	1729	SCJ, 1754
7	Pringle, Andrew	48	1736	SCJ, 1759
8	Hamilton Gordon, Charles	45	1735	
9	McDouall, Andrew	44	1708	SCJ, 1755
10	Burnet, James	40	1737	SCJ, 1767

Ave experience: 20.9 years

1761		OH	Adm.	Bench
1	Lockhart, Alexander	69	1723	SCJ, 1775
2	Rae, David	60	1751	SCJ, 1782
3	McQueen, Robert	58	1744	SCJ, 1775
4	Montgomery, James	53	1743	BEx(S), 1775
5	Stewart, Walter	37	1749	
6	Hamilton Gordon, Charles	34	1735	
7	Graeme, David	29	1727	
8	Dalrymple, John*	28	1748	BEx(S) 1776
9	Burnett, James	24	1737	SCJ, 1767
10	Dalrymple, David	18	1743	SCJ, 1777

Ave experience: 19 years

1771		OH	Adm.	Bench
1	McLaurin, John	67	1756	SCJ, 1788
2	McQueen, Robert	65	1744	SCJ, 1775
3	Campbell, Ilay	52	1757	LP, 1789
4	Wight, Alexander	48	1754	
5	Rae, David	47	1763	SCJ, 1782
6	Lockhart, Alexander	44	1723	SCJ, 1775
7	Gordon, Alexander	38	1759	SCJ, 1784
8	Armstrong, David	36	1763	
9	Gordon, Cosmo	31	1758	BEx(S), 1777
10	Douglas, John*	29	1759	

Ave experience: 16.4 years

1781		OH	Adm.	Bench
1	Campbell, Ilay	71	1757	LP, 1789
2	Erskine, Henry*	50	1768	
3	Hay, Charles*	47	1769	SCJ, 1806
4	Armstrong, David	44	1763	
5	Crosbie, Andrew	43	1757	
6	McLaurin, John	42	1756	SCJ, 1788
7	Blair, Robert	40	1765	LP, 1808
8	Craig, William*	38	1768	SCJ, 1792
9	Rolland, Adam	37	1758	
10	Honyman, William	36	1777	SCJ, 1797

Ave experience 15.2 years

1791		OH	Adm.	Bench
1	Ross, Matthew*	103	1772	
2	Honyman, William	100	1777	SCJ, 1797
3	Pattison, John	98	1787	
4	Hay, Charles	97	1769	SCJ, 1806
5	Erskine, Henry (DoF)	86	1768	
6	Wight, Alexander	82	1754	
7	Fergusson, George	81	1765	SCJ, 1799
8	Cullen, Robert	77	1765	SCJ, 1796
9	Corbet, Robert	76	1777	
10	McCormick, Edward	67	1772	

Ave experience 19.4 years

1801		OH	Adm.	Bench
1	Baird, Thomas Walker	78	1793	
2	Clerk, John	67	1785	SCJ, 1823
3	Gillies, Adam	56	1787	SCJ, 1811
4	Cathcart, David*	48	1785	SCJ, 1813
5	Corbet, Robert	45	1777	
6	Scott, Walter*	37	1792	
7	Monypenny, David	33	1791	SCJ, 1813
8	Erskine, William	32	1790	SCJ, 1822
9	Inglis, Henry David	31	1794	
10	Montgomery, James jr	31	1787	

Ave experience: 11.9 years

*   Indicates the more or most likely alternative, e.g. in 1801 ambiguous references in the record to 'Scott' are ascribed to Walter rather than William given what is known about Walter's career.

NOTE

1. These tables are based on the Outer House (OH) rolls, with the number of appearances in each sample year recorded in the column headed 'OH', and the year of admission recorded in the column headed 'Adm.'. The final column indicated the year of elevation to the bench of those who became ordinary lords of session (SCJ, i.e. Senators of the Court of Justice) or lord president (LP).

Bibliography

Manuscript references and citation of session papers are not included here but are given as they arise in the notes to each chapter. Record depositories are noted in the Abbreviations.

The Acts of Sederunt of the Lords of Council and Session, from the 15th of January 1553, to the 11th of July 1790 (Edinburgh, 1790).

Adam, C. E., *A View of the Political State of Scotland in the Last Century* (Edinburgh, 1887).

Ahsmann, M., 'Teaching the *ius hodiernum*: Legal education of advocates in the Northern Netherlands (1575–1800)' 65 (1997) *Tijdschrift voor Rechtsgeschiedenis*, pp. 423–58.

Arnot, H., *History of Edinburgh* (Edinburgh, 1779).

Baker, J. H., *The Legal Profession and the Common Law* (London, 1985).

Ballantyne, G. H., *The Signet Library, Edinburgh and its Librarians, 1722–1972* (Glasgow, 1979).

Barclay, J., *The SSC Story: Two Hundred years of Service in the College of Justice* (Edinburgh, 1984).

Berlanstein, L. R., *The Barristers of Toulouse in the Eighteenth century* (Baltimore, 1975).

Bickley, F. ed., *The Diaries of Sylvester Douglas, Lord Glenbervie* (2 vols, London, 1928).

Birks, M., *Gentlemen of the Law* (London, 1960).

Bowie, K., *Scottish Public Opinion and the Anglo-Scottish Union, 1699–1707* (Woodbridge, 2007).

Bowsma, W., 'Lawyers and early modern culture' 78 (1973) *American Historical Review*, pp. 303–27.

Brady, F., *James Boswell: The Later Years* (New York, 1984).

Broadie, A., *The Cambridge Companion to the Scottish Enlightenment* (Cambridge, 2003).

Brooks, C. W., *Pettyfoggers and Vipers of the Commonwealth: The 'Lower Branch' of the Legal Profession in Early Modern England* (Cambridge, 1986).

—*Lawyers, Litigation and English Society since 1450* (London, 1988).

Brougham, H., *Memoir of the late Hon. Allan Maconochie of Meadowbank one of the Senators of the College of Justice* (Edinburgh, 1845).

—*Speeches on Social and Politics Subjects* (2 vols, London, 1857).

Brown, I. G., *Building for Books* (Aberdeen, 1989).

Brunton, G. and Haig, D., *A History of the Senators of the College of Justice* (Edinburgh, 1832).

Buddle Atkinson, R. H. and Jackson, G. A. eds, *Brougham and his Early Friends: Letters to James Loch, 1798–1809* (3 vols, London, 1908).

Cadell, P. and Matheson, A., *For the Encouragement of Learning, Scotland's National Library 1689–1989* (Edinburgh, 1989).

Cairns, J. W., 'Institutional Writings in Scotland Reconsidered' (1983) *Journal of Legal History*, pp. 76–117.

— 'The formation of the Scottish legal mind in the eighteenth century: themes of humanism and enlightenment in the admission of advocates' in *The Legal Mind: Essays for Tony Honoré*, ed. N. MacCormick and P. Birks (Oxford, 1986), pp. 253–77.

— 'John Millar's lectures on Scots criminal law' 8 (1988) *Oxford Journal of Legal Studies*, pp. 364–400.

—'Sir George Mackenzie, the Faculty of Advocates, and the Advocates Library' in G. Mackenzie, *Oratio Inauguralis*, ed., ibid. and A. M. Cain (Edinburgh, 1989), pp. 18–35.

—'Rhetoric, language, and Roman Law: legal education and improvement in Eighteenth-Century Scotland' (1991), *Law and History Review*, pp. 31–57

—'The origins of the Glasgow Law School: The professors of the Civil Law 1741–61, *The Life of the Law*, ed. P. Birks (London, 1991), pp. 151–94.

— 'John Spotswood, professor of Law: A preliminary sketch' in W. M. Gordon, ed., *Miscellany III* (Stair Society, 1992), pp. 131–59.

—'William Crosse, Regius Professor of Civil Law in the University of Glasgow, 1746–49: a failure of enlightened patronage' (1993) xii, *History of Universities*, pp. 159–96.

—'Adam Smith and the role of the courts in securing justice and liberty' in R. P. Malloy and J. Evensky, eds, *Adam Smith and the Philosophy of Law and Economics* (Kluwer, 1994), pp. 31–61.

—'From "speculative" to "practical" legal education: the decline of the Glasgow Law School, 1801–1830' (1994) *Tijdschrift voor Rechtsgeschiedenis*, pp. 331–56.

— 'The law, the advocates and the universities in late sixteenth-century Scotland' 73 (1994) *Scottish Historical Review*, pp. 171–90.

—'Lawyers, law professors, and localities: the Universities of Aberdeen, 1680–1750' 46 (1995) *Northern Ireland Legal Quarterly*, pp. 304–31.

—'"Famous as a school for Law, as Edinburgh … for medicine": Legal Education in Glasgow, 1761–1801' in A. Hook and R. B. Sher, eds, *The Glasgow Enlightenment* (1995), pp. 133–62.

—'Importing our Lawyers from Holland: Netherland's Influences on Scots Law and Lawyers in the Eighteenth Century', *Scotland and the Low Countries, 1124–1994* ed. G. G. Simpson (East Linton, 1996), pp. 136–53.

—'Advocates' Hats, Roman Law, and admission to the Scots Bar, 1580–1812' 20(2) (1999) *Journal of Legal History*, pp. 24–61.

—'Alfenus Varus and the Faculty of Advocates: Roman visions and the manners that were fit for admission to the Bar in the eighteenth century', 28 (2001) *Ius Commune*, 203–32.

—'Legal Theory', in A. Broadie, ed., *The Cambridge Companion to the Scottish Enlightenment* (Cambridge, 2003), pp. 222–42.

—'The Face that did not fit – race, appearance, and exclusion from the bar in Eighteenth-century Scotland' 9 (2003) *Fundamina*, pp. 11–43

— 'Revisiting the Foundation of the College of Justice' in H. L. MacQueen, ed., *Miscellany Five* (Stair Society, 2006), pp. 27–50.

—'Attitudes to Codification and the Scottish Science of Legislation, 1600–1830' 22 (2007) *Tulane European and Civil Law Forum*, pp. 1–78.

—'The Origins of the Edinburgh Law School: the Union of 1707 and the Regius Chair' 11 (2007) *Edinburgh Law Review*, pp. 300–48.

Camic, C., *Experience and Enlightenment: Socialization for Cultural Change in Eighteenth-century Scotland* (Chicago, 1983).

Campbell, N., et al., *The Royal Society of Edinburgh (1783–1983): the first two hundred years* (Edinburgh, 1983).

Campbell, R. H., and Skinner, A. S., *The Origins and Nature of the Scottish Enlightenment* (Edinburgh, 1982).

Carlyle, A., *The Autobiography of Doctor Alexander Carlyle of Inveresk*, ed. J. Hill Burton (Edinburgh, 1910).

Carter, *Letters from Europe, comprising the Journal of a Tour through in the Years 1825, '26, and '27* (2 vols, New York, 1827).

Chambers, W., *The Book of Scotland* (Edinburgh, 1830).

Cockburn, H., *Memorials of His Time* (Edinburgh, 1856).

—*Letters Chiefly Connected with the Affairs of Scotland* (London, 1874).

Cocks, R., *Foundations of the Modern Bar* (London, 1983).

Cosh, M., *Edinburgh: The Golden Age* (Edinburgh, 2003).

Coutts, W., *The Business of the College of Justice in 1600* (Edinburgh, 2003).

Davidson, P., 'Paper gardens: garden ideas and garden poems in Scotland and the Netherlands in the seventeenth century' in A. Adams and M. van der Weij, eds, *Emblems of the Low Countries* (Glasgow, 2003), pp. 171–83.

Dawson, J. P., *A History of Lay Judges* (Harvard, 1960).

Devine, T. M., and Mitchison, R., eds, *People and Society in Scotland* (3 vols, 1988–90).

Dickson, W. K., 'Sir Walter Scott and the Parliament House', xlii (1930) *Juridical Review* 1–11.

— ed., 'Letters to John Mackenzie of Delvine from Revd. Alexander Munro, 1690 to 1698' in *Miscellany of the Scottish History Society, Fifth volume* (Edinburgh, 1933), pp. 211–90.

Dingwall, H. *Late Seventeenth-Century Edinburgh: a Demographic Study* (Aldershot, 1994).

—*Physicians, Surgeons and Apothecaries* (East Linton, 1995)

Duman, D., *The English and Colonial Bars in the Nineteenth Century* (London, 1983).

Duncan, D., *Thomas Ruddiman* (Edinburgh, 1965).

Duff, H. R., ed., *Culloden Papers* (London, 1815).

Dwyer, J., and Murdoch, A., 'Paradigms and politics: manners, morals and the Rise of Henry Dundas, 1770–1784' in J. Dwyer et al., eds, *New Perspectives on the Politics and Culture of Early Modern Scotland* (Edinburgh, 1982), pp. 210–48.

Emerson, R. L., 'The social composition of enlightened Scotland: the select society of Edinburgh, 1754–64', 114 (1973) *Studies on Voltaire and the Eighteenth Century*, pp. 291–330.

—'The Philosophical Society of Edinburgh, 1737–1747' 12 (1979) *Journal of British Studies*, pp. 154–91.

—'The Philosophical Society of Edinburgh, 1748–1768' 14 (1981) *British Journal for the History of Science*, pp. 133–76.

—'The Scottish Enlightenment and the end of the Philosophical Society of Edinburgh' 21 (1988) *British Journal for the History of Science*, pp. 33–66.

—*Professors, Patronage and Politics: The Aberdeen Universities in the Eighteenth Century* (Aberdeen, 1992).

—*Academic Patronage in the Scottish Enlightenment* (Edinburgh, 2008)

[Erskine, D.], *Lord Dun's Friendly and Familiar Advices adapted to The various stations and Conditions of Life, and the mutual Relations to be observed amongst them* (Edinburgh, 1754).

Erskine, J., 'Letters of Lord Grange', in J. Stuart, ed., *The Miscellany of the Spalding Club, volume third* (Aberdeen, 1846).

Feenstra, R., 'Scottish–Dutch Legal Relations in the Seventeenth and Eighteenth Centuries', in T. C. Smout, ed., *Scotland and Europe, 1200–1850* (Edinburgh, 1986), pp. 128–42.

—'Teaching the civil law at Louvain as reported by Scottish students in the 1430s (MSS. Aberdeen 195–97) (1997) *Tijschrift voor Rechtsgeschiedenis*, pp. 245–80.

Feenstra, R. and Waal, C. J. D., *Seventeenth-century Leyden Law Professors and their influence on the development of the Civil Law* (Amsterdam and Oxford, 1975).

Ferguson, W., *Scotland: 1689 to the Present* (Edinburgh, 1968).

Fergusson, J., ed., *Letters of George Dempster to Sir Adam Fergusson 1756–1813* (London, 1934).

—'Lord Hermand – A biographical sketch' in F. P. Walton, ed., *Lord Hermand's Consistorial Decisions 1684–1777* (Edinburgh, 1940), pp. 1–40.

—'Making interest in Scottish County Elections', *Scottish Historical Review* 26 (1947), pp. 119–33.

Finlay, J., 'James Henryson and the origins of the office of king's advocate' 79 (2000) *Scottish Historical* Review, pp. 17–38.

—*Men of Law in Pre-Reformation Scotland* (East Linton, 2000).

—Ethics, etiquette and the early modern Scots advocate' (2006) *Juridical Review*, 147–78.

—'Advocacy, patronage and character at the eighteenth-century Scots bar' 74 (2006) *Tijdschrift voor Rechtsgeschiedenis*, pp. 95–119.

—'The lower branch of the legal profession in early modern Scotland' 11 (2007) *Edinburgh Law Review*, pp. 31–61.

—'Advocates unlimited: the *numerus clausus* and the college of justice in Scotland' 87 (2008) *Historical Research*, pp. 206–28.

—'Pettyfoggers, regulation and local courts in early modern Scotland' 87 (2008) *Scottish Historical Review*, pp. 42–67.

—'Advocates unlimited: the *numerus clausus* and the College of Justice in Scotland' 82 (2009) *Historical Research*, pp. 206–28.

—'The History of the Notary in Scotland' in M. Schmoeckel and W. Schubert, eds, *Handbuch zur Geschichte des Notariats der europäischen Traditionem* (Baden Baden, 2009), pp. 393–428.

—'Lawyers and the Early Modern State: Regulation, Exclusion, and *Numerus Clausus*', 44 (2009) *Canadian Journal of History*, pp. 383–410.

—'The History of delay in Civil Procedure: Scotland 1600–1808' in C. H. van Rhee, ed., *The History of Delay in Civil Procedure* (Berlin, 2010), pp. 121–52.

—'Lawyers in the British Isles' in B. Dölemeyer et al., eds, *Anwälte und ihre Geschichte* (Mohr Siebeck Verlag, Tübingen, 2011), pp. 1097–1126.

—'Arbitration in Eighteenth-century Scotland' (2011) *Juridical Review*, pp. 277–91.

—'Scots lawyers and House of Lords appeals in eighteenth-century Britain' 32 (2011) *Journal of Legal History*, pp. 249–77.

— ed., *Admissions Register of Notaries Public in Scotland, 1700–1799* (Scottish Record Society, forthcoming, 2012).

—'Corruption, regionalism and legal practice in eighteenth-century Scotland' 86 (2012) *Transactions of the Dumfries and Galloway Natural History and Antiquarian Society* (forthcoming).

Fitzsimmons, M. P., *The Parisian Order of Barristers and the French Revolution* (Harvard, 1987).

Fletcher, R. J., *Pension Book of Gray's Inn* (London, 1910).

Forbes, W., *The Journal of the Session* (Edinburgh, 1714).

Foster, J., ed., *Register of Admissions at Gray's Inn, 1521–1889* (London, 1889).

Fry, M., *Dundas Despotism* (Edinburgh 1992, repr. 2004).

Gibb, A. D., *Judicial Corruption in the United Kingdom* (Edinburgh, 1957).

Gilhooley, J. *A Directory of Edinburgh in 1752* (Edinburgh, 1988).

Goodare, J., *State and Society in Early Modern Scotland* (Oxford, 1999).

—*The Government of Scotland 1560–1625* (Oxford, 2004).

Grant, F., *The Faculty of Advocates* (Edinburgh, 1944).

Grant, J. *Cassell's Old and New Edinburgh* (3 vols, London, 1881–83).

Gray, J. M., ed., *Memoirs of the Life of Sir John Clerk of Penicuik, Baronet, Baron of the Exchequer, Extracted by himself from his own Journals 1676–1755* (Edinburgh, 1892).

Haakonsen, K., *The Science of a Legislator: The Natural Jurisprudence of David Hume and Adam Smith* (Cambridge, 1981).

Hannay, R. K., *The College of Justice* (reprinted, Edinburgh, 1990).

Harris, B., 'The Scots, the Westminster parliament, and the British state in the eighteenth century' in J. Hoppit, ed., *Parliaments, nations and identities in Britain and Ireland, 1660–1850* (Manchester, 2003), pp. 124–45.

Harris, B., and Whatley, C. A. 'To solemnize his Majesty's birthday: new perspectives on loyalism in George II's Britain' 83 (1998) *History*, p. 397.

Hill Burton, J., *The Lives of Simon Lord Lovat, and Duncan Forbes, of Culloden* (London, 1847).

Hogan, D., *Legal Profession in Ireland, 1789–1922* (Dublin, 1986).

Hook, A., and R. B. Sher, eds, *The Glasgow Enlightenment* (East Linton, 1995).

Horwitz, H. and Polden, P., 'Continuity or change in the court of Chancery in the seventeenth and eighteenth centuries?' 35 (1996) *Journal of British Studies*, pp. 24–57.

Houston, R. A., 'Mortality in early modern Scotland: the life expectancy of advocates' 7 (1992) *Continuity and Change*, pp. 47–69.

—'Fire and Filth: Edinburgh's environment, 1660–1760' 3 (1994) *Book of the Old Edinburgh Club*, pp. 25–36.

—*Social Change in the Age of Enlightenment, Edinburgh 1660–1760* (Oxford, 1994).

—'Writers to the Signet: estimates of adult mortality in Scotland from the sixteenth to the nineteenth century (1995) *Social History of Medicine*, pp. 37–53.

Houston, R. A. and Whyte, I. D., *Scottish Society, 1500–1800* (Cambridge, 1989)

Innes, J. (wrongly attr.), *Idea Juris Scotici* (London, 1733).

Innes, J., 'Legislating for three kingdoms: how the Westminster parliament legislated for England, Scotland and Ireland, 1707–1830' in Hoppit, J., ed., *Parliaments, nations and identities in Britain and Ireland, 1660–1850* (Manchester, 2003), pp. 15–47.

Kagan, R. L., 'Law students in Eighteenth-century France' (1975) *Past and Present*, pp. 38–72.

—*Lawyers and Litigants in Castile, 1500–1700* (Chapel Hill, 1981).

Kidd, C., *Subverting Scotland's Past* (Cambridge, 1993).

Kilday, A.-M., *Women and Violent Crime in Enlightenment Scotland* (Woodbridge, 2007).

Lang, A., *Sir George Mackenzie, His Life and Times* (London, 1909).

Lauder, Sir J. of Fountainhall, *The Decisions of the Lords of Council and Session from June 6th 1678, to July 30th, 1712* (2 vols, Edinburgh, 1759, 1761).

—*Historical Notices of Scotish [sic] Affairs* (2 vols, Edinburgh, 1848).

Lehmann, W. C., *Henry Home, Lord Kames, and the Scottish Enlightenment* (The Hague, 1971).

Lemmings, D., *Gentlemen and Barristers* (Oxford, 1990).

—*Professors of the Law: Barristers and English Legal Culture in the Eighteenth Century* (Oxford, 2000).

Lieberman, D., *The Province of Legislation Determined* (Cambridge, 1989).

Lucas, P. 'A collective biography of students and barristers at Lincoln's Inn, 1680–1804: a study in the "aristocratic resurgence" of the eighteenth century' (1974) *Journal of Modern History*, pp. 227–61.

Lynch, M., ed., *The Early Modern Town in Scotland* (London, 1987)

McDonald, T. P., 'Sir Walter Scott's fee book' lxii (1950) *Juridical Review*, pp. 288–316.

Macdouall, A. (Lord Bankton), *An Institute of the Law of Scotland* (3 vols, Edinburgh, 1751–53; reprinted, Stair Society, 1993–5).

McDougall, W. 'Gavin Hamilton, bookseller in Edinburgh' 1 (1978) *British Journal for Eighteenth-century Studies*, pp. 1–19.

Mackenzie, Sir G., *Works* (2 vols, Edinburgh, 1716, 1722).

Mackenzie, H., *Account of the Life of Lord Abercromby* (Edinburgh, 1796).

Maclaurin, J., *Arguments and Decisions in Remarkable Cases, before the High Court of Justiciary, and other Supreme Courts, in Scotland* (Edinburgh, 1774).

MacMillan, A., *A Complete System of Conveyances of, and Securities upon Lands; or, of heritable rights, according to the present practice of Scotland* (Edinburgh, 1787).

MacQueen, H. L., *Common Law and Feudal Society in Medieval Scotland* (Edinburgh, 1993).

—'Two visitors in the Session, 1629 and 1636' in ibid., ed., *Miscellany Four* (Stair Society, 2002), pp. 155–68.

Maidment, J., *Court of Session Garland* (Edinburgh, 1839).

Malcom, C. A. 'The lord justice clerk of Scotland, II' xxvii (1915) *Juridical Review*, pp. 375–89.

Manolescu, B. I., 'George Mackenzie on Scottish Judicial Rhetoric' 20 (2002) *Rhetorica*, pp. 375–89.

Melikan, R. A., *John Scott, Lord Eldon, 1751–1838* (Cambridge, 1999).

Menary, G., *The Life and Letters of Duncan Forbes of Culloden* (London, 1936).

Menzies, W., 'Alexander Bayne of Rires' 36 (1924) *Juridical Review*, pp. 60–70.

Miller, F., 'Andrew Crosbie, advocate, a reputed original of Paulus Pleydell in "Guy Mannering"', 7 (1921) *Transactions of the Dumfriesshire and Galloway Natural History & Antiquarian Society*, pp. 11–32.

Miller, K., *Cockburn's Millenium* (Harvard, 1976).

Milne, H. M., *Boswell's Edinburgh Journals, 1767–1786* (Edinburgh, 2003).

Mossner, E. C., *The Life of David Hume* (Oxford, 1980).

Munro, J., 'Clansmen and clients', 12 (1965) *Scottish Genealogist*, pp. 36–50.

—'A chief and his lawyer' 45 (1967–68) *Transactions of the Gaelic Society of Inverness*, pp. 257–83.

Murdoch, A., *The People Above* (Edinburgh, 1980)

—'The advocates, the law and the nation in early modern Scotland' in W. R. Prest, ed., *Lawyers in Early Modern Europe and America* (New York, 1981), pp. 147–63.

—'The importance of being Edinburgh' lxii (1983) *Scottish Historical Review*, pp. 1–16.

Murray, A. L., 'The Lord Clerk Register' 52 (1974) *Scottish Historical Review*, pp. 124–56.

—'The post-Union Court of Exchequer' in H. L. MacQueen, ed., *Miscellany Five* (Stair Society, 2006), pp. 103–31.

Murray, T., *Literary History of Galloway* (2nd edn, Edinburgh, 1832).

Nenadic, S., 'The rise of the urban middle class' in T. M. Devine and R. Mitchison, eds, *People and Society in Scotland* (3 vols, 1988–90).

— ed. *Scots in London in the Eighteenth Century* (Lewisburg, 2010).

Nève, P., 'Disputations of Scots Students Attending Universities in the Northern Netherlands', in W. M. Gordon and D. Fergus, eds, *Legal History in the Making* (London, 1991), pp. 95–108.

Norrie, W., *The Annuity Tax* (Earlston, 1912).

Omond, G. W. T., *The Lord Advocates of Scotland* (2 vols, Edinburgh, 1883).

—*The Arniston Memoirs* (Edinburgh, 1887).

Parratt, D. R., *The Development and Use of Written Pleadings in Scots Civil Procedure* (Edinburgh, 2006).

Phillipson, N. T., 'Lawyers, landowners, and the civic leadership of post-Union Scotland' 1976 *Juridical Review*, pp. 97–120.

—'The Social Structure of the Faculty of Advocates in Scotland 1661–1840' in *Law-Making and Law-Makers in British History*, ed. A. Harding (London, 1980), pp. 146–56.

—*The Scottish Whigs and the Reform of the Court of Session, 1785–1830* (Edinburgh, 1990).

Pinkerton, J. M., ed., *The Minute Book of the Faculty of Advocates, 1661–1712* (Edinburgh, 1976).

—'Cockburn and the Law' in A. Bell, ed., *Lord Cockburn: A Bicentenary Commemoration* (Edinburgh, 1979), pp. 104–23.

— ed., *The Minute Book of the Faculty of Advocates, 1713–1750* (Edinburgh, 1980).

Pottle, F. A., *James Boswell: The Earlier Years, 1740–1769* (London, 1966).

Prest, W. R., *The Inns of Court under Elizabeth I and the early Stuarts, 1590–1640* (Harlow, 1972).

— ed., *Lawyers in Early Modern Europe and America* (London, 1981).

—*The Rise of the Barristers: A Social History of the English Bar, 1590–1640* (Oxford, 1986).

Rae, T. I., 'The origins of the Advocates Library', in Cadell and Matheson, eds, *For the Encouragement of Learning* (Edinburgh, 1989), pp.1–22.

— ed., *The Union of 1707* (Glasgow, 1974).

Ramsay, J., of Ochtertyre, *Scotland and Scotsmen in the Eighteenth Century*, ed. A Allardyce, 2 vols (Edinburgh and London, 1888).

Riley, P. W. J., *King William and the Scottish Politicians* (Edinburgh, 1979)

Robertson, J., *The Scottish Enlightenment and the Militia Issue* (Edinburgh, 1985).

— ed., *A Union for Empire: Political Thought and the Union of 1707* (Cambridge, 1995).

Robinson, O. F., Fergus, D and Gordon, W., *European Legal History* (3rd edn, Edinburgh, 2000).

Robson, R., *The Attorney in Eighteenth-century England* (Cambridge, 1959).

Ross, I. S., *Lord Kames and the Scotland of his Day* (Oxford, 1972).

Ross, W., *Lectures on the Practice of the Law of Scotland* (2 vols, Edinburgh, 1792).

St Clair, J., and Craik, R., *The Advocates Library: 300 Years of a national Institution, 1689–1989* (Edinburgh, 1989).

Sanderson, E. C. *Women and Work in Eighteenth-century Scotland* (London, 1996).

Sanderson, M. H. B., *Mary Stewart's People* (Edinburgh, 1987).

Scott, G., and F. Pottle, eds, *The Private Papers of James Boswell* (18 vols, New York, 1928–34).

Shapin, S., 'Property, patronage and the politics of science: the founding of the Royal Society of Edinburgh', 7 (1974) *The British Journal for the History of Science*, pp. 1–41.

Sedgwick, R., *The House of Commons 1715–1754* (2 vols, London, 1970).

Shaw, J. S., *The Management of Scottish Society 1707–1764* (Edinburgh, 1983).

—The *Political History of Eighteenth-century Scotland* (Basingstoke, 1999).

Sher, R. B., 'Moderates, managers and popular politics in mid-eighteenth century Edinburgh: The Drysdale "Bustle" of the 1760s' in J. Dwyer et al., eds, *New Perspectives on the Politics and Culture of Early Modern Scotland* (Edinburgh, 1982).

—*Church and University in the Scottish Enlightenment: The Moderate Literati of Edinburgh* (Princeton, 1985).

Simpson, J. M., 'The advocates as trade union pioneers', in G. W. S. Barrow, ed., *The Scottish Tradition* (Edinburgh, 1974), pp. 165–77.

Somerville, T., *My Own Life and Times* (Edinburgh, 1861).

Spotiswood,*The form of process, before the Lords of Council and Session* (Edinburgh, 1711).

Squibb, G. D., *Doctors' Commons: A History of the College of Advocates and Doctors of Law* (Oxford, 1977).

Steuart, W. O. 'The Lockharts of Lee' xl (1928) *Juridical Review*, pp. 142–49.

Stewart, A. ed., *The Minute Book of the Faculty of Advocates, 1751–1783* (Edinburgh, 1999).

—'The Session Papers in the Advocates Library' in H. L. MacQueen, ed., *Miscellany IV* (Stair Society, Edinburgh, 2002), pp. 199–224.

Stewart, A., and Parratt, D. R, eds, *The Minute Book of the Faculty of Advocates, 1783–1798* (Edinburgh, 2008).

Stone, L., *The University in Society: Europe, Scotland, and the United States from the Sixteenth to the Twentieth Centuries* (Princeton, 1974).

Sunter, R. M., *Patronage and Politics in Scotland, 1707–1832* (Edinburgh, 1986).

Swinton, J., *Considerations concerning a Proposal for Dividing the Court of Session into Classes or Chambers* (Edinburgh, 1789).

Szechi, D., *George Lockhart of Carnwath, 1689–1727* (East Linton, 2002).

—*1715: The Great Jacobite Rebellion* (London, 2006).

Taylor, J., *A Journey to Edenborough* (Edinburgh, 1903).

Thomson, J., 'The old fifteen' (1921) *Juridical Review*, pp. 225–44.

Thomson, J. M., *The Public Records of Scotland* (Glasgow, 1922).

Tompson, R. S., *Islands of Law: A Legal History of the British Isles* (New York, 2000).

Topham, E., *Letters from Edinburgh, written in the years 1774 and 1775* (London, 1776).

Townley, M., *The Best and Fynest Lawers and Other Raire Bookes* (Edinburgh, 1990).

Tytler, A .F., *Memoirs of the Life and Writings of the Honourable Henry Home of Kames* (2 vols, Edinburgh, 1807, 1809).

Tytler, J. S. F., ed., *A History of the Society of Writers to Her Majesty's Signet* (Edinburgh, 1890).

Van Strien, K., and Ahsmann, M., 'Scottish law students in Leiden at the end of the seventeenth century: the correspondence of John Clerk 1694–1697' 19 (1992) *Lias.* pp. 271–330; 20 (1993) pp. 1–65.

Walker, D. M., *A Legal History of Scotland* (7 vols, Edinburgh, 1988–2004).

Walker, R. S., ed., *The Correspondence of Boswell and John Johnstone of Grange* (London, 1966).

Watson, C. B., *Roll of Edinburgh Burgesses and Gild-Brethren 1701–1760* (Edinburgh, 1930).

—*Roll of Edinburgh Burgesses and Gild-Brethren 1761–1841* (Edinburgh, 1933).

Watt, J. C., *John Inglis: A Memoir* (Edinburgh, 1893).

Whatley, C. A., 'Royal day, People's day, the monarch's birthday in Scotland', in R. Mason and N. Macdougall, eds, *People and Power in Scotland: Essays in Honour of T. C. Smout* (Edinburgh, 1992), pp. 170–88.

—*The Scots and the Union* (Edinburgh, 2006).

Whetstone, A. E., *Scottish County Government in the Eighteenth and Nineteenth Centuries* (Edinburgh, 1981).

Willock, I. D., *The Origins and Development of the Jury in Scotland* (Edinburgh, 1966).

Wodrow, R., *Analecta, or Materials for a History of Remarkable Providences* (4 vols, Edinburgh, 1842–43).

Wollschläger, C., 'Civil litigation and modernization: the work of the municipal courts of Bremen, Germany, in five centuries, 1549–1984' 24 (1990) *Law and Society Review*, pp. 261–82.

Wood, M., ed., *The Edinburgh Poll Tax Returns for 1694* (Edinburgh, 1951).

Wood, P., *The Scottish Enlightenment: Essays in Reinterpretation* (New York, 2000).

Youngson, A. J., *The Making of Classical Edinburgh* (Edinburgh, 1966).

PHD THESES

Alexander, J. M. B., 'The Economic and Social Structure of the City of London, *c.*1700' (London School of Economics, 1989).

Brown, D. J., 'Henry Dundas and the Government of Scotland' (University of Edinburgh, 1989).

Desbrisay, G., 'Authority and discipline in Aberdeen, 1650–1700' (University of Aberdeen, 1989),

Dingwall, H., 'The social and economic structure of Edinburgh in the late seventeenth century' (2 vols, University of Edinburgh, 1989).

Ferguson, W., 'Electoral law and procedure in eighteenth and early nineteenth century Scotland' (unpublished, University of Glasgow, 1957).

Scott, R., 'The politics and administration of Scotland 1725–1748' (University of Edinburgh, 1981).

Watt, D., 'Chiefs, lawyers and debt: a study of the relationship between Highland elites and the legal profession in Scotland *c.*1550 to 1700' (University of Edinburgh, 1998).

Index of Subjects

Index of Persons

Dates in brackets indicate date of admission to office